Electric Boats and Ships

Electric Boats and Ships

A History

Kevin Desmond

Foreword by Christoph Ballin

McFarland & Company, Inc., Publishers

Jefferson, North Carolina

LIBRARY OF CONGRESS CATALOGUING-IN-PUBLICATION DATA

Names: Desmond, Kevin, 1950– author.
Title: Electric boats and ships : a history / Kevin Desmond ;
Foreword by Christoph Ballin.
Description: Jefferson, North Carolina : McFarland & Company, Inc.,
Publishers, 2017. | Includes bibliographical references and index.
Identifiers: LCCN 2017038172 | ISBN 9781476665153
(softcover : acid free paper) ∞
Subjects: LCSH: Electric boats—History. | Electric boats.
Classification: LCC VM345 .D47 2017 | DDC 623.82/04—dc23
LC record available at https://lccn.loc.gov/2017038172

BRITISH LIBRARY CATALOGUING DATA ARE AVAILABLE

ISBN 978-1-4766-6515-3 (print)
ISBN 978-1-4766-2768-7 (ebook)

On the cover *clockwise from top*: The solar-powered hydrofoil of (TU Delft);
the *Eoseas*, a 305-meter five-hulled pentamaran cruise ship concept
(Stirling Design International); Gustav Trouvé tests *Le Téléphone*
(from Georges Barral, *L'Histoire d'un inventeur*, 1891)

Printed in the United States of America

McFarland & Company, Inc., Publishers
Box 611, Jefferson, North Carolina 28640
www.mcfarlandpub.com

To
Ἠλέκτρα (Elektra),
to Ἥλιος (Hēlios)
and to Ποσειδῶν (Poseidon)

Acknowledgments

The author would like to thank the following for their kind help in this book:

Jean-Louis Aucouturier; Hans Asijee; Christoph Ballin; Pamela Bromley, Archivist, Warwick Castle; Lorne Campbell; Roy Cooper; Jérome Croyère; Laurent Roblin, Le Musée da la Batellerie (Conflans-Sainte-Honorine); Julian Delmar-Morgan; Alexandra Desmond; Claude Didier; Arthur Dobley; Raphaël Domjan; Patrick Droulers; Marshall Duffield, Duffy Boats; Jack Edwards; The Electric Boat Association; Alan T. Freeman; Rear Admiral Philip Gick; Monty Gisborne; Guy Gorius; Gideon Goudsmit; Edward Hawthorne; Colin Henwood; Hertfordshire Archives and Local Studies; Jean-Michel Horvat; Charles Houghton; Tom Hesselink; Pete Jager; Damien Kuntz, EDF Electropolis; Rupert Latham; Roger Martire; Xavier de Montrgros (Association Français du Bateau Electrique); Malcolm Moss; Julie Curran, The Motorboat Museum; Irene Overtoom (TU Delft); Jacques Pichavant; Diplom-Ingenieur Hermann Preinerstorfer; Jitze Prinsen; Ian and Sylvia Rutter; Anton Schiere (Platform Elektrisch Varen); Theo Schmidt; Bob Slatyer; William C. Swanson; Nikolai Vaguin; Verkehrshaus der Schweiz (Martina Kappeler); Paul Wagstaffe; Guy Wolfensberger; New Zealand Maritime Museum.

Thanks also to Alexandra Desmond (my long-supporting wife) and Kathryn Cooper (my indexer).

Table of Contents

Foreword
by Christoph Ballin

This is the first international history of the birth and rebirth of the electric boat and ship from 1835 to the present day. It celebrates the Golden Era of electric launches, 1880–1910. It narrates how, despite the arrival of the internal combustion engine, electric propulsion continued its progress with the turbo-electric ship. It shows how sustainable and hybrid technologies, pioneered in small river craft towards the end of the 20th century, have recently been scaled up to oceangoing ships. The threads running through have always been fourfold: how silent in running, how far, how fast, and how long to replenish the energy. Kevin Desmond is neither an electrical engineer nor a boat builder, but rather a journalist with a passion for historical research. Understanding the key role of history for the future, he appreciates the importance of chronicling the present so that history can repeat itself, but better than before.

Kevin Desmond's chronicle of electric boats and ships provides the background of an important development of our time. In November 2016, the Paris Climate Agreement was ratified by over 100 countries at the COP22 in Marrakech; also at this meeting, the Climate Vulnerable Forum announced that the 47 member countries, the poorest nations in the world, including Bangladesh, Ethiopia and Yemen, were moving towards 100 percent green energy between 2030 and 2050. As part of this goal, it is obvious that electric boats will be playing a key part.

Driven by such political and technological developments in environmental protection and among others in battery technology, we are about to enter a new golden era in electric mobility. Electric mobility on the water is likely to capture a larger share than ever before. At the dawn of this development, Kevin Desmond's book comes at exactly the right moment.

Christoph Ballin is cofounder of Torqeedo GmbH, marine electric motor manufacturers. Since 2006, Torqeedo has made and sold more than 75,000 units.

Preface

In 1977, I was researching for a book about the history of motorboating in the library of the Science Museum, South Kensington, London: a somewhat challenging task. But the Scottish librarian was proving very helpful.

"Would motorboating history include electric boats?" he asked.

"Yes," I replied. "But I don't exactly know what electric boats are."

"Then you'd better take a look at this," he suggested. It was a slim beige folder, marked "electric boats." Turning through its pages, fragile old news cuttings, I learned about battery-powered launches in the early 1900s—on the River Thames, on the Austrian lakes, in the USA, and in France. Two of the articles mentioned a French engineer called Trouvé. It was the beginning of a long-term quest which would not only lead me to my recent biographies of Gustave Trouvé, but also into joining a crusade to revive silently running electric boats, which is, as you read through these pages, still ongoing some forty years later. The extraordinary thing is that nearly everything we have been doing since the 1980s had already been achieved almost one hundred years before.

In writing this book, I have found myself with three roles, that of an historian, then a biographer, and then a news reporter. As I completed writing this book in 2016, the penultimate chapter is devoted to the most recent developments in electric boating for inland and coastal waterways over the past twenty or so months, which may also point the way to the next decade … 2027, for which, apart from accidents, I as a historian hope to be around, if not longer!

ONE

Origins (1837–1889)

The origins of electric boating are found in the early part of the 19th century.

At the time, a small fleet of steam-engined paddleboats were braving the oceans, although cautiously still rigged with masts and sails. The only way for narrowboats to travel around the growing network of Britain's canals was to be towed by shire horses. There was only one inter-city steam locomotive route in operation, the Liverpool and Manchester Railway. All those who had visited London's Royal Institute to marvel at the late Sir Humphry Davy's unique electrical Great Battery had arrived by foot or horse-drawn carriages. The teenage Princess Victoria was yet to inherit the throne from her uncle King George III. Andrew Jackson was President of the USA.

In 1825 William Sturgeon, 42-year-old lecturer in science and philosophy at the East India Company's Military Seminary at Addiscombe, Surrey, exhibited his first electro-magnet on a wooden stand. This was a horseshoe-shaped piece of iron that was wrapped with about 18 turns of bare copper wire. The iron was varnished to insulate it from the windings. When a current was passed through the coil, the iron became magnetized and attracted other pieces of iron; when the current was stopped, the iron lost magnetization.

Eleven years later, Sturgeon was working at the experimental laboratory of the Royal Victoria Gallery for the Encouragement of Practical Science in Manchester, England, when he started up a journal, *The Annals of Electricity, Magnetism and Chemistry*.[1] In its April 1837 edition, on page 250, in the column "Miscellaneous Articles," Sturgeon reports: "In the first number of these 'Annals' I have described an Electro-magnetic Engine, by means of which, pieces of machinery are put in motion. I have now to announce that I have *succeeded in propelling a boat*, and also a locomotive carriage, by the power of Electro-magnetism. The particulars of their construction will be communicated as soon as their present rude state is sufficiently corrected for their appearance in public. W.S." Unfortunately, no further information about Sturgeon's electric boat has come to light, although it is likely that the boat trial was on the local Manchester Ship Canal. His personal papers were destroyed in a bombing raid during the Second World War.

A more important (even if unsuccessful) trial took place in St. Petersburg, Russia. It was just before midday on September 13, 1838. From the Peter and Paul Fortress (Petropavlovsk), a paddleboat was rowed out into the midstream of the River Neva. At the given signal, the oars were shipped, the paddles began to turn and the boat started to move up against the current. Above the water, unlike what would be expected of a steamboat, there was no smoke, nor was there any puffing or clattering engine noise, the paddle turning noiselessly, moved by the "magnetic engine." The boat reached a speed of 1.5 knots. She was the *Elektrokhod*, the world's first ever passenger-carrying electro-magnetic boat.[2]

Four years before, in April 1834, in the town of Königsburg (present-day Kalinsgrad), a German engineer called Moritz Hermann Jacobi had presented a model of "a magnetic apparatus," as he called it. Its horizontal motion was provoked by the layout of magnets

and a disc covered with annealed copper wire. The force of the apparatus reached 0.002 hp.

Jacobi wrote about this apparatus to the Academies of Science in Paris and St. Petersburg. On December 3, his work was published by the Academy of Sciences in Paris. Jacobi's "magnetic apparatus" was based on work on electromagnetic induction, carried out several years before by an English blacksmith's son called Michael Faraday.

It was in 1831 that as thirty-year-old Fullerian Professor of Chemistry at the Royal Institution, London, Faraday had published an article in *Philosophical Transactions* titled "Induced Electricity," backing this up by successfully demonstrating a model. Jacobi was among those who read the article.

In 1835 Jacobi was invited to Russia by Count Kankrine, finance minister at the time. He would spend the rest of his life there. In 1842 he was elected a member of the Academy of Sciences of St. Petersburg. He married and they had four children. Acquiring Russian citizenship, he would become known as Boris Semonovitch Iakobi.

In 1837 Iakobi wrote to the president of the St. Petersburg Academy and to Culture Minister Count Ouvapov, explaining his invention to them. He was keen that "his new homeland" take full advantage of electric motors.

Claims to be the first are always open to question. Unknown to Iakobi and his Russian colleagues, in Paris in 1832, Hippolyte Pixii, a 24-year-old scientific instrument maker, had already operated a small electric motor with power drawn from batteries, while three years later in 1835, Thomas Davenport, a Vermont blacksmith, had already exhibited a model electric railway.

Top: In 1837, William Sturgeon of Manchester, England, succeeded in propelling a boat on the Manchester Ship Canal by the power of electro-magnetism (courtesy Institution of Engineering and Technology Archives). *Bottom:* Boris Semonovitch Iakobi (1801–1847), Russian pioneer of electric boats (Musée EDF Electropolis, Mulhouse).

At this time, with the goal of modernizing Russia, Tsar Nikolas I decided to organize the transport system. Having created the first railway line from St. Petersburg to Pavlovsk, he summoned Iakobi, who had just installed an electric telegraph around the capital.

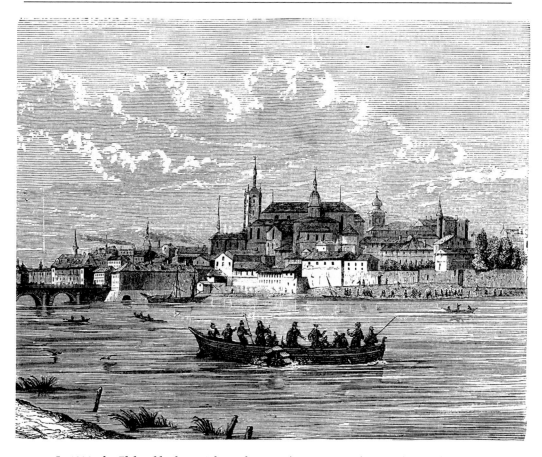

In 1838, the *Elektrokhod* on trials on the Neva (Musée EDF Electropolis, Mulhouse).

The Tsar became particularly interested in Iakobi's machine and envisaged it replacing steam engines. Iakobi's salary was increased from 2,500 rubles per year to 12,000 rubles. He settled in St. Petersburg and began working on a considerably larger scale. He wrote: "The invention of a new way of locomotion must not be seen as a curiosity but as a world event."[3]

During 1838, Iakobi assembled a motor intended for paddleboat propulsion with transformation of the rotary motion into horizontal motion. It was installed in a standard eight-oar naval sloop dispatched from the Baltic Fleet. It measured 7.5 meters (24 feet) long, 2.3 meters (7 feet) in beam, and with a draft of 0.65 meters (2 feet). Energy came from a cell developed by London chemist John Daniell. This was battery of 320 couples, containing plates of zinc and copper, 36 square inches each, and excited by a charge of sulfuric acid and sulfate of copper.

On September 13, 1838, trials of the *Elektrokhod* took place on the Neva, both against and with the current. But the battery gave out nitrous fumes in as big a quantity as smoke from a steam locomotive. Iakobi and his volunteer passengers, choked and asphyxiated by these sickening and suffocating fumes, were obliged to temporarily halt their observations.

But as Iakobi wrote to Faraday: "Although we journeyed during entire days, and usually with ten or twelve persons on board, I was not well satisfied with this first trial; for there were so many faults of construction and want of insulation for machines and batteries, which could not be repaired on the spot, that I was terribly annoyed. All these repairs and important changes being accomplished, the experiments will shortly be recommenced. If Heaven preserve my health, which is a little affected by continual labors, I hope that within a year from this time I shall have equipped an electro-magnetic vessel of from forty to fifty horse power."[4]

These new experiments were carried out with slightly larger boat in 1839. It measured 8 meters (26 feet) in length, 3 meters (10 feet) in beam, with a 75 cm (3 feet) draft. It was equipped with a battery of sixty-four cells on the system recently developed by 28-year-old Welsh scientist William Grove of Swansea. The Russian minister of finance supplied 16 kg of platinum made up into 64 pairs of plates, measuring 230 cm² (36 inches²) each. This battery was one-fifth the size of the one used the previous year and was charged with concentrated nitric and sulfuric acids. But the power of this motor reached only 0.75 hp and the boat, with fourteen passengers on board, reached a disappointing speed of 3 mph (4.8 kph).

Studying these experiments, Admiral Adam von Krusenstern estimated that these were laboratory studies and one could not hope that the *Elektrokhod* could arrive at results on a par with those regularly achieved by steam-engined boats. In 1841, an even more powerful battery was installed in the boat, but the experiments only gave disappointing results.

In 1840, chemistry professor Sibrandus Stratingh of Gröningen in the Netherlands built a model electric boat which he launched on the canal near his farm.[5]

In August 1848, an electric boat was demonstrated on the private lake of John Dillwyn Llewelyn's Penllergaer estate near Swansea, Wales. Its electric galvanic motor was designed and built by an eccentric, long-haired inventor called Benjamin Hill of Clydach, and its energy came from a cell developed by "local boy" William Grove. Grove later invented the gas battery, forerunner of the fuel cell.

John Llewelyn's father kept a diary in which he wrote: "January 9, 1841. Drove in the afternoon to meet John at Lewis's laboratory to try a small electric galvanic apparatus, as invented by Mr. Hill, for propelling boats instead of steam. It worked beautifully and John is constructing a larger machine for an experiment with his boat on the lake at Penllergaer."[6] A report about this Welsh electric boat appeared in the *Cambrian Supplement* of August 18, 1848. It was titled "The Nautical Application of the Grove Cell":

> [T]he boat, which was impelled by electric current, was, however, the principal object of attraction. It was constructed for the purpose, but the boat was ordinarily used for pleasure purposes, capable of conveying about six persons.... [B]y the action of the rotating magnet on a screw propeller, by means of a cog wheel attaching to the axle of the rotating magnet and another wheel on the axle of the screw propeller, the boat was put into motion. This is capable of carrying seven persons, but on this occasion not more than five were in it, at one time. With the cargo the speed at which it was propelled was 3½ miles an hour—a speed some of our readers think not too great, but it must be recollected that the boat was not constructed for fast sailing. The large body of visitors who witnessed this ingenious contrivance expressed the greatest satisfaction at the result of this trial of electro-motive power.[7]

In the year 1848, at a meeting of the British Association at Swansea, Hill was asked by some gentlemen connected with the copper trade to make some experiments on the electrical propulsion of vessels. They stated that, although electricity might cost thirty times as much as the power obtained from coal, it would nevertheless be sufficiently economical to induce its employment for the auxiliary screw ships employed in the copper trade with South America. Mr. Robert Hunt, in the discussion of his paper on electromagnetism before the Institution of Civil Engineers in 1858, mentioned that he had carried on an extended series of experiments at Falmouth, and at the instigation of Benkhausen, Russian Consul-General, he communicated with Jacobi upon the subject.[8]

In a letter sent to the author in November 1990, Professor R.M. Barker commented:

"The demonstration was successful enough to impress Faraday, Wheatstone and Grove but there must surely have been trouble with the fumes from the Grove cells. Also, Hill's motor had a wooden frame, so there was no magnetic circuit, its efficiency would be poor."

In 1856 an electric boat was constructed by Searle & Sons of Stangate, Lambeth on the Thames, London, for eccentric electricity enthusiast George Edward Dering of Lockleys Manor in Hertfordshire. It was worked by a motor in which rotation was effected by magnets arranged within coils, like galvanometer needles, and acted on successively by currents from a battery.[9]

William Grove, inventor of the battery which powered Llewelyn's boat in 1848 (author's collection).

In France, in 1855, while electric devices abounded at the Palace of Industry, scarcely any were to be found at the Champs de Mars Exhibition in 1857.

Then in 1858, Gaston Planté, a 24-year-old French physicist working at the Conservatoire des Arts et Métiers in Paris, invented the lead-acid battery. His first model contained two sheets of lead, separated by rubber strips, rolled into a spiral, and immersed in a solution containing about 10 percent sulfuric acid. A year later, Planté developed a battery consisting of nine of the elements, housed in a protective box with the terminal connected in parallel.

Although from a Venetian patrician family, in his youth, Count Antoine de Molin had fought valiantly for the French Emperor Napoleon I. He had then become interested in astronomy, physics, agriculture and oceanography, but above all he was passionate about developing an efficient electric motor. Ignorant of Planté's battery, de Molin chose to use the galvanic battery developed some years before by Robert Bunsen, professor of chemistry at Marburg University, even though he knew that when in operation Bunsen cells emitted noxious fumes of nitrogen dioxide. With energy from the Bunsen cells, de Molin installed his "electro moteur" in a boat. The vessel chosen was an iron-hulled flat-bottomed keelless electric paddleboat, and the water space selected was the Lac Inférieur, one of the two lakes in the Bois de Boulogne, Paris. Weighed down by several thousand kilograms of battery and 14 passengers, with its chain-driven bronze paddles doing their best, the de Molin prototype slowly started to head out from the chalet and down the lake against the wind, disappearing behind the island that forms the center of the lake—but did not reappear. Had its battery fumes, like those of Iakobi's boat, asphyxiated its passengers? We shall never know. The aged Comte de Molin dying in August of that year, and the experiments were not resumed.[10]

But the word "electricity" was certainly in the air. Although not powered by electricity, the steamboat christened *l'Elettrico* was part of the Ignazio & Vincenzo Florio Steam Navigation Company (Società in Accomandita Piroscafi Postali-Ignazio & Vicenzo Florio). Following the *Indipendente, Corriere Siciliano, Etna*, and *Archimede*, *l'Elettrico* went into service in 1859 between the Sicilian ports of Palermo, Messina and Naples; with Capitano Andrea de Bartolo at the helm, she showed an exceptional turn speed for the time of 13 knots.[11]

Twenty Thousand Leagues Under the Sea is a classic science fiction novel by French writer Jules Verne, published in 1870. It tells the story of Captain Nemo and his electric submarine *Nautilus*; the submarine's electricity was provided by sodium/mercury batteries (with the sodium provided by extraction from sea water). But it was a fiction.[12]

The successful realization of the battery-powered electric boat was made by a modest but brilliant electrical engineer, with his workshop in downtown Paris, by the name of Trouvé.

Until recently, the name Gustave Trouvé, Chevalier de la Légion d'Honneur, prolific Parisian electrical instrument inventor, was absent from any popular French encyclopedia. Yet, when at the end of the 19th century, Alexander Graham Bell, the world-famous inventor of the telephone, visited Paris, before leaving, he insisted on visiting Trouvé's workshops. He told Trouvé: "I wanted to surprise you amongst your works that I so much admire. In addition, I want to take away to America, a complete collection of all your inventions, because for me they make up the highest expression of the perfection and the ingenuity of the electric science in France."[13]

Gustave Pierre Trouvé was born on January 2, 1839, at La Haye-Descartes, northeast of Poitiers. His father Jacques Trouvé was a gentleman-farmer who, with Gustave's mother Clarissa, brought up five children.

From his earliest years, although Gustave did not show the greatest passion for math, he was very keen on mechanical objects. He never played with children of his age. From morning to night, armed with a knife, a hammer and several nails, he amused himself by fashioning little chariots, telegraphs, rabbits and automatons fitted with wings moved by the wind. In 1846, the seven-year-old boy built a little fire pump from a sardine tin. Then, with nothing more than hairpins and bits of lead, this prodigy made a miniature working steam engine, using an old tinderbox for the generator.

Four years later, between October and December 1850, Trouvé began his studies alongside his brother Jules at Chinon College. But as he wanted to specialize in math and mechanics, Gustave left his large family and his region to study at the Imperial School of Industrial Arts and Crafts at Angers. The marks obtained by the teenager (Control N°264) for the first term of the 1854 school year are surprisingly lower than average, his strongest point being drawing.

By 1859, aged only 20, young Trouvé had obtained a job at one of the principal Paris clockmakers in France. During his spare time, he studied architecture, math and precision work. Seven years later, he set up his own establishment for the creation and manufacture of precision and scientific instruments, of which he would conceive and construct some 75 in all, particularly in the field of electricity.

Among these were instruments for use in transportation, both ashore and afloat. Recently Werner Siemens and Johann Halske of Berlin-Kreuzberg in Germany had developed an electric motor to power both the world's first elevator and streetcar. Trouvé improved the efficiency of this motor and built one weighing only 5 kg, which he patented

(Patent N° 136,560—dated May 8, 1880). Having used it to power a converted English tricycle, he began to consider his little engine for the propulsion of boats. At first he envisaged two such motors, each directly driving a paddle wheel on either side of the hull. After this, he progressed to a multi-bladed propeller. Modifications to this master patent date from August 1880, then March, July, November and December 1881. To quote: "It is the rudder containing the propeller and its motor, the whole of which is removable and easily lifted off the boat...."

On August 1, 1881, Trouvé made his benchmark report to the French Academy of Sciences:

I have the honor to submit to this Academy, in the session of 7th July 1880, a new electric motor based on the eccentricity of the Siemens coil flange. By successive studies, which have allowed me to reduce the weight of all the components of the motor, I have succeeded in obtaining an output which to me appears quite remarkable.

A motor of 5kg [11 lb.] powered by six Planté secondary elements, producing an effective work of 7 kg per second, was placed, on 8 April, in a tricycle whose weight, including the rider and the batteries, amounted to 160 kg [352lb.], and took it at a speed

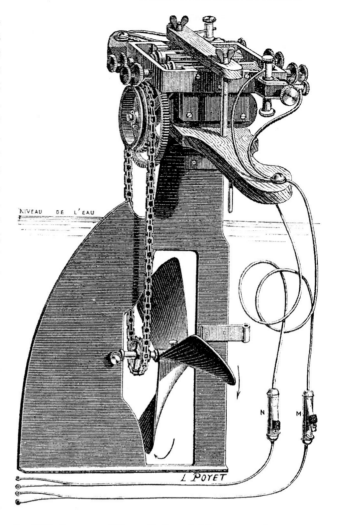

An 1881 close-up of Trouvé's detachable marine electric motor as published in his patent—the world's first outboard engine (from Georges Barral, *L'histoire d'un inventeur*, 1891).

of 12 km/h [7.4 mph]. The same motor, installed on the 26 May on a boat of 5.50 m [18.5 feet]long and 1.20 m [4 feet] wide, containing three people, recorded a speed of 2.50 m/sec on going down the Seine to the Pont-Royal [bridge] and 1.50 m/sec on going back upstream. The motor was powered by two pile batteries of dichromate de potassium each of six elements, and the propellant was a three-bladed propeller.

On the 26 June 1881, I repeated this experiment on the calm waters of the upper lake of the Bois de Boulogne, with a four-bladed propeller 28 cm in Diameter and 12 électrique of Ruhmkorff-type Bunsen plates, charged with one part hydrochloric acid, one part nitric acid and two parts water in the porous vase so as to lessen the emission of nitrous fumes.

The speed at the start, measured by an ordinary log, reached 150 meters [164 yards] in 48 seconds—or little more than 3 meters [3 yards] per second; but after three hours of functioning, this had fallen to 150 meters [164 yards] in 55 seconds and after five hours, this had further fallen to 150 meters [164yards] in 65 seconds. One bichromate battery, enclosed in a 50 cm [20 inch] long case, will give a constant current of 7 to 8 hours; this is a great saving of fuel and cleanliness.[14]

Dressed for the occasion, Trouvé tests his boat along the Seine. He named it *Le Téléphone* in homage to Alexander Graham Bell (from Georges Barral, *L'histoire d'un inventeur*, 1891).

The journalist Georges Dary was one of the observers:

> Crowds of passers-by stop on the bridges to gaze with astonishment, for among the many bateaux-mouches and hirondelles [passenger ferries] which are running up and down the Seine in Paris, a lightweight vessel is heading up river without any visible engine, nor steam machinery, nor telltale funnel. It stops, continues or slows down without any movement from its "patron" who without moving steers from the stern. This boat at such a strange pace, seems alive, as intelligent as a horse which obeys the slightest sign, under the simple pressure from the knees of its horseman. It did not take long to learn that here was a new advance in electricity realized by the friendly constructor whom all Paris already knows: Gustave Trouvé, who is always on the trail of innovations considered impossible.[15]

In the autumn of 1881, Paris decided to organize an International Electrical Exhibition to display the advances in electrical technology since the small electrical display at the Universal Exposition only three years before. George Berger was the commissioner general. Aside from the provision of the building by the French government, the Palais de l'Industrie in the Champs Elysées, the exhibition was privately financed. Organizers would donate profits to scientific works in the public interest. A total of 1,786 exhibitors came from the United Kingdom, the United States of America, Germany, Italy and Holland, as well as from France. It caused a great stir.

Many of the 880,000 visitors had their first ever experience of an electric tram to take them from the Place de la Concorde to the galleries of the Palais de l'Industrie (Industry Palace), where they were able to discover and marvel at a new branch of science—electrical engineering.

The first thing that they came across in the center of the nave of the Palais was "The Lighthouse of Progress," a full-scale electric lighthouse of the Ministry of Public Works, which projected alternating beams of red and white light in every direction. At its foot was an artificial clover leaf–shaped pond. Circulating around the pond was Trouvé's electric skiff, enabling visitors to enjoy seeing "its little evolutions on the clement waters of this tranquil ocean of Lilliput."

It was at this benchmark exhibition that electrical engineers and scientists standardized the terminology to encourage easy and exact communication. The units agreed on—

In 1881, the International Electricity Exhibition was held at the Industry Palace, Paris. At the foot of the electric Progress Lighthouse is Trouvé's electric launch. Among those who rode on this boat was Antony Reckenzaun, an Austrian-born engineer over from London (Musée EDF Electropolis, Mulhouse).

volt, amp, ohm, watt, farad, etc.—were named in honor of the electrical pioneers. Thus was born the "absolute practical system of electrical units."[16]

Trouvé's electric outboard motorboat and his electric motor–powered model dirigible—both world firsts—were admired by thousands of visitors. Most important of all, they inspired a handful of inventors each to play a key part in the birth of the battery-electric transport industry.

Other exhibition visitors were Messieurs Reynier and Camille Alphonse Faure of Paris, who then developed a twenty-one cell battery; the substantially improved performance of Faure's battery came from coating its lead plates with a layer of red lead oxide. Although it would be further improved, Faure's invention was to make electrical storage a commercial proposition. The innovation of storage cells (called "secondary") was made possible by the reversible chemical reactions of its elements, permitting the cell to be recharged and used again and again.[17]

The way seemed clear. One of those who were to make a major contribution to marine electric propulsion was Antony Reckenzaun, chief engineer of the London-based Electric Power Storage Company. Reckenzaun was born in Graz, Austria. He served his apprenticeship at his father's ironworks whose main client was the Hungarian Railways. In 1872, Reckenzaun, aged only 22, moved to England and obtained work at the marine engineering firm of Ravenhill & Miller, where he became involved in steam engine design and construction. After his first visit to the Paris Exhibition of 1879, he resolved to devote himself to the study of electrical engineering. In 1881, again at the Electrical Exhibition in Paris, Reckenzaun spent nearly every day for three months walking from stand to stand in the Palais d'Industrie, including a very careful examination of Trouvé's boat. One wonders whether Reckenzaun met Trouvé and conversed. The Austrian returned to England with a unique knowledge.[18]

The EPS Co. became the first concern to manufacture real batteries on a commercial scale, and with the acquired Faure rights, it held a monopoly until later manufacturers made a success of the Planté plates.[19] The EPS works at Lollar Wharf, in the East London suburb of Millwall, began serious business from 1882 by supplying lighting plants for businesses and private residences. Batteries were offered in 1, 2 and 5 electrical horsepower sizes, later known as L15, L31, and L59 types. With the EPS works at Millwall on the Isle of Dogs beside the River Thames, and given Reckenzaun's earlier training as a marine engineer, the company soon acquired a 26-ft (8 m.) steam-engined tugboat built at the Yarrow shipyard. They stripped out the engine and boiler and replaced it with two Siemens D3 dynamo motors with regulators and reverse gear putting out 3–4 hp. Energy came from 45 Planté accumulators, weighing 2,700 lb. (1,225 kg), modified by Messrs. Selon and Volckmar to total 96 volts and supply power for six hours. Either or both motors could be switched into circuit at will. A Collis-Browne propeller of 20 inches (50 cm) diameter and 3 feet pitch was employed. While the

Antony Reckenzaun, who pioneered electric boating in England and America (courtesy Institution of Engineering and Technology Archives).

motors revolved at 950 revolutions per minute, the speed of the screw was reduced to 350 revolutions.

On September 28, 1882, the boat, suitably named *Electricity*, made a pioneering trip on the River Thames to London Bridge and back. One of those on board wrote of his experience to *The Times*:

> Sir, having been one of a privileged party of four, the first ever propelled on the waters of the river Thames by the motive power of electricity. I think some details of this may be of interest.... [A]fter a few minutes' run down the river, and a trial of the powers of the boat to go forward, slack, or go astern at will, her head was turned Citywards, and we sped—I cannot say steamed—silently along the southern shore, running about eight knots an hour against the tide. At 37 minutes past 4, London Bridge was reached, where the head of the launch was put about, while a long line of onlookers from the parapets surveyed the strange craft that without steam or visible power, with even a visible steersman—made its way against wind and tide. Slipping down the ebb, the wharf at Millwall was gained at 1 minute past 5, thus in 24 minutes terminating the trial trip of Electricity.[20]

The journal *Engineering* published its report on October 6, 1882:

> ...The batteries are charged while the boat is at anchor by wires which come across the wharf from the factory, bringing currents generated by dynamos fixed in the works. The electric engines are arranged so that either or both of them may be furnished with the current, there being a switch to each lead. There is also a commutator to switch into circuit any number of cells from forty upwards. The motors are connected by belts to pulleys on a countershaft, from which a belt passes down to a pulley on the propeller axis, whose speed is thus reduced in the proportion of 950 to 350 rpm. The steering is managed by the same person who operates the switches, seat in the central cabin. A whistle being impossible in the absence of steam, this necessary feature is replaced by a large electric bell, also worked by the accumulators. The calculated average speed is 9 mph. This speed was actually attained on the trial trip from Millwall to London Bridge and back; the design and construction of the boat are chiefly due to a Mr. Reckenzaun, mechanical engineer to the EPS Co.

In March 1883, *Electricity* was taken out for her first official trial on the Thames. With respected electrical engineer Professor Sylvanus P. Thompson, head of the Department of Physics at the Finsbury Technical College, on board, she put up a speed of 7 mph (11 kph) and proved capable of returning to Millwall jetty under her own power.[21] It was Professor Thompson who had recently speculated that "before the Electric Age is over, our knives will be polished, our coffee roasted, our shoes shined, our vehicles driven … by the self-same agency that will bring light into our dwellings."

Commenting on *Electricity*, Georges Dary, Paris technical journalist and Trouvé enthusiast, wrote to the London journal, *Nature*:

> The Thames reclaims its electric boat; the science of motors must progress from day to day and one must carefully welcome the smallest ideas which can serve as a point of departure for important discoveries. But has there really been progress? The accumulators of the boat *Electricity* weigh 1,270 kg and give 90 volts of motive force. The weight of the Trouvé machine (8 batteries) is only 120 kg and gives the same motive force. But these figures are not enough, they must be applied to experience; the result is therefore convincing. Any of Trouvé's electric dinghies always reach 6 knots, obviously a maximum speed for a little vessel, because one knows that speed is proportional to tonnage. As for the distance travelled, dichromate batteries enable them to make voyages which one can almost qualify as long distance. The distance which separates Rouen from Le Havre cannot be covered in 24 minutes, and many boat builders and owners of electric boats come and go on the Seine to points some 12 to 14 miles away. Two batteries are enough to operate this miracle each and every day.[22]

Electricity also created considerable interest and speculation and provoked much guesswork about her power source when she appeared on the river among the smoking

(A. A. A. A. in the Diagram, show the positions of the Electric Accumulators.)

THE ELECTRIC BOAT ON THE THAMES.

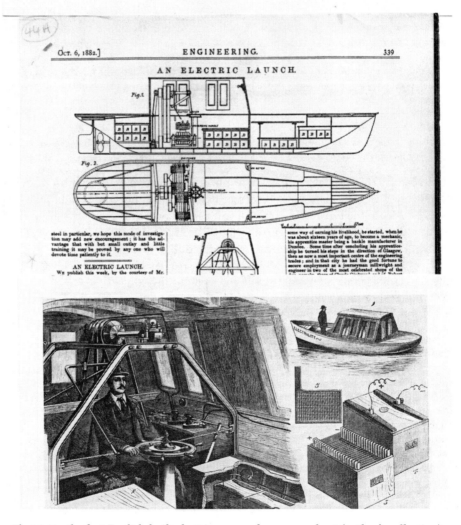

AN ELECTRIC LAUNCH.

Fig. 1.

Fig. 2.

Fig. 3.

steel in particular, we hope this mode of investigation may add new encouragement ; it has the advantage that with but small outlay and little training it may be proved by any one who will devote time patiently to it.

AN ELECTRIC LAUNCH.

We publish this week, by the courtesy of Mr.

some way of earning his livelihood, he started, when he was about sixteen years of age, to become a mechanic, his apprentice master being a hackle manufacturer in Dundee. Some time after concluding his apprenticeship he turned his steps in the direction of Glasgow, then as now a most important centre of the engineering trades ; and in that city he had the good fortune to secure employment as a journeyman millwright and engineer in two of the most celebrated shops of the

Electricity, the first English-built electric-powered passenger boat (author's collection).

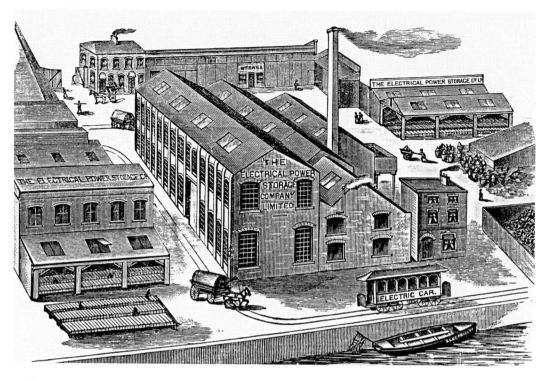

Electric Power Storage Company's plant at Millwall on Thames, showing an electric boat and electric streetcar (Woburn Abbey Collection).

steam launches during the Oxford-Cambridge Boat Race in April 1883. In the same year, the *Beni*, a 12-meter (40 ft) steel launch built by Alfred Yarrow of Poplar, East London, and designed to carry 45 passengers and equipped with a special galvanized steel propeller, was shipped for use on the Ornamental Lake at the Vienna Exhibition in Austria. As prepared by the EPS of Millwall, her accumulators were stowed away under the floor; so was the motor, but owing to the lines of the boat, the floor just above the motor was raised a few inches. This motor was a Siemens D2 unit, capable of working up to seven horsepower with eighty accumulators. *Beni* was first steered by the ill-fated Crown Prince Rudolph,[23] and her reliability in respect to range was afterwards demonstrated to foreign journalists and other interested parties by an 80 km (50 mile) cruise down the Danube from Vienna to Bratislava. During one trial the speed of the boat, which was over 8 mph (12 kph), could be varied by a commutator, which threw more or fewer cells in operation.

News of electric boats soon arrived in the USA. From August 12 to October 21, 1882, those regular readers of the science fiction periodical *Frank Reade Weekly Magazine; Containing Stories of Adventures on Land, Sea and In the Air* would have read the latest adventure "Frank Reade and His Electric Boat." This was written by "Noname," aka Dr. Harry Enton.[24]

Meanwhile, Gustave Trouvé was not the only one experimenting with electric boats. Cloris Baudet, another Paris inventor, had come up with an "impolarizable" fuel cell for multiple uses, including boats. Basically the operator could refuel the cell through a siphon as their boat cruised along. Little is known of Baudet. His workshop was at 14, rue Saint Victoire, close to Monge Square. He was a member of the National Agricultural

Academy; a member of the Central Society for Beekeeping, Silkfarming and Insectology; a member of the French Association for Scientific Progress; and a founder and member of the International Society of Electricians.

His impolarizable cell was refueled as follows: The porous pot was divided into three; the central part usually contained zinc and acidulated water. On either side were two smaller porous vessels, one of which was filled with sulfuric acid and the other potassium dichromate. All were immersed in a stoneware vase containing carbon and dichromate solution. The depolarizing substance could then be renewed constantly, and the item would last longer than an ordinary dichromate cell. In addition, it was odorless.

In Baudet's own words:

> For electric boats, we recommend flat Bunsen cells or electric generating accumulators. The rectangular Bunsen elements give the best results. One can install these elements with the vases and accessories of our n°4 cells by putting a carbon in place of the zinc in the porous vase that one fills with nitric acid, and two zincs linked by a wire in the exterior vase, which one fills with acidulated water. Mounted in this way, these batteries have the advantage of taking up very little space in the boat and of developing, weight for weight, an energy and an autonomy much better than any other system. If one has a long voyage to make, one can take along a supply of the acids necessary to recharge the batteries en route, which is impossible with accumulators. If one uses accumulators one must recharge them with land machines.

Presumably the refueling would be carried out on calm waters.

In a catalogue Baudet published,[25] there is the following testimonial, written as early as 1883:

> To Cloris Baudet—Yesterday and today I carried out some canoeing experiments with your two double motors on my boat which measures 7m50 long × 1m10 beam. To a battery made up of 8 cells weighing 6 kilos, I harnessed the two motors: With the propeller and two motors I covered 5 km 500 meters in one hour. With the paddles and two motors, I covered 7km 200 in one hour. With one prop and motor I covered 4 km. You will observe that the paddles are better than the propeller for the type of skiff that I have, while the propeller and its chain only slow down the cruising. But this is not the only advantage. With the propeller, each time one passes through weeds, one is obliged to lift up the shaft to clear them off the blades, not so easy with the narrow stern. This inconvenience disappears entirely with the paddles. The facts that I am communicating to you are somewhat feeble than strong. Perhaps one should add an additional cell and so obtain a speed of 8 kmh. Yours sincerely, Jules Simon. Vouziers, 10 July 1883.[26]

In the same city, when Charles Renard and Arthur Krebs were testing the flow batteries to use in their electric airship, *La France*, they gave them a trial along the Seine in a boat they called the *Ampère*.[27] Trouvé had also been applying his genius to a whole range of electric boats. There was, for example, the *Sirène*, specially designed for a Monsieur de Nabat, so that its owner could change at will from propulsion by propeller to paddles. *Sirène* measured 9 m (30 feet) long by 1m80 (5 feet 10) beam, and its owner used this boat three times a week during long periods, and cruised regularly at between 14 and 15 kilometers an hour (9 and 10 mph), its propeller turning at between 1,200 and 1,800 rpm. Trouvé considered that for electric propulsion, the Dupassieux paddles were more efficient than a propeller. It was called the *Sirène* because it was equipped with an electric horn Trouvé had adapted from a special effect he had created for a theater performance.

Madame Louise de Nabat took her husband's boat and had it temporarily converted into a Japanese junk, complete with a Chinese pagoda decorated with luminous electric flowers. This won Madame Nabat first prize in a benevolent regatta given on the Marne

River in 1887. Another boat, belonging to Monsieur de Dampierre, traveled on the River Eure. It could carry six passengers, and its two paddle wheels enabled it to travel on rivers where water weed was abundant and could foul up a propeller.[28]

To show the speed with which an electric boat could move in a race situation, on October 8, 1882, a Trouvé motor and battery was taken to Troyes, about 150 km (93 mi) southeast of Paris to feature in a rowing regatta organized by that town's Nautical and Gymnastic Society. G. Riousse, the society's secretary, reported on the event in a letter to the journal *l'Electricité*:

> ...Two points particularly attracted the attention of the amazed crowd of spectators who came—the whole of Troyes was there. On the one hand, it is the great simplicity with which the machine adapted itself as well as the facility of maneuvering which enable it to turn absolutely on the spot, and on the other hand the speed with which Monsieur Trouvé's boat led the race. The boat obtained by us for Monsieur Trouvé, a boat which he had never seen, arrived in the race area only five minutes before the Start; nevertheless, this Start took place on time, without any delay, at gunfire. As one of those who were on this boat, I wanted to take an exact account of the speed and was able to observe, not without astonishment, that we covered more than 3,200 meters in 17 minutes while slowing down to make four turns around the buoys. This works out at speed of 11 km/h (6.8 mph)....[29]

The Trouvé motor and dichromate batteries were also fitted onto the back of another boat and demonstrated on the Seine at Rouen. In the years that followed, it is not known how many Trouvé electric motors came to be installed in pleasure-launches, but it amounted to a small fleet. Some of these were fitted with his pioneering electric headlights and electric klaxons.

The first seagoing electric launch was a 29 ft (8.8 m) cutter into which the French Admiralty installed accumulators and an electric motor for trials in Le Havre harbor in 1887. Built by the Société des Forges et Chantiers de la Mediterranée, it was equipped with a Krebs motor that drew its energy from the Commelin-Dezmazure batteries. The total weight of electric machinery was 45 kg (100 lb), still heavier than the equivalent steam machinery necessary, so it was not long before they abandoned their trials.[30]

That year, Trouvé delivered a visionary speech to the Cercle de la Voile de Paris (Paris Sailing Club) at their clubhouse in Argenteuil. He had come up with a revolutionary

The French Navy tests its electric boat offshore in 1888 (Musée EDF Electropolis, Mulhouse).

new approach which would enable electric boats to make extended sea voyages by converting the sea salt into the required energy. His generator was made up of a series of swift discharge batteries for winching; the number of these batteries would be greater or smaller depending on the power required. Each of these batteries would be contained in an oak trough equipped with ebony vats and topped by a ratchet and latching winch of six elements of zinc and carbon, their voltage created by mobile contacts, of the exciter fluid, sulfuric acid and dichromate of potash in predetermined proportions. According to his calculations, an electric ship 100 meters (330 feet) long, trawling a battery raft using large zinc and copper plates which were regularly plunged 4 meters (13 feet) into the seawater as the exciter liquid, could develop 5,120 horsepower and cruise for thousands of sea miles!

Another electrical engineer, Henri De Parville, criticized Trouvé's proposed system, noting that the zinc and copper would wear out very quickly, and questioning whether such a battery would continue to work as it became covered with algae and crustaceans. Nor did he see this system set up along the riverbanks to produce electricity for local inhabitants.

Back in England, whether for publicity purposes or to test the relative merits of hull material, a widely advertised electric boat race took place on September 30, 1884: the iron-hulled *Electricity* versus the mahogany *Australia*, built by Forrest of Millwall and also fitted with EPS accumulators. *Australia* was ultimately destined to go out to the firm of Stephen Smith & Co. based by Kaipara Harbour, on the northwestern side of the North Island of New Zealand (then part of the British colony of New South Wales). But before being shipped to the other side of the world, *Australia* raced *Electricity* on a course from Millwall to Charing Cross Bridge and back. Two stoppages were made, one to cool and slacken the stern gland of *Australia*, the other to bail out *Electricity* after shipping water when passing a large steamer. Allowing for stoppages, total traveling time was 70 minutes. After reaching Greenwich, both boats cruised around for another couple of hours. There is no record of which boat won, but apparently *Australia* was very slightly ahead at Charing Cross on the way upstream.[31]

That same year a 62 grt steam-engined paddle tug called *Electric* went into service in Sunderland, northern England; during 1917 she would be requisitioned by the Royal Navy for harbor and dockyard service and normally flew the Red Ensign. Despite the ship's name, there is no evidence of an electric propulsion system.[32]

Over in Germany, Siemens und Halske, now with their premises along the banks of the western Spree River in the Berlin suburb of Charlottenburg, tested the *Elektra*, its first electric boat, on local waters. The wooden hull and two 40 cm diameter propellers were supplied by the Reinhold F. Holtz shipyard in Harburg to Berlin. The *Elektra*, carrying up to 25 passengers, was demonstrated during the Berlin Trade Fair at a speed of up to 14 kph (9 mph).[33]

Perhaps the most detailed documentation about any electric boat during this early period was discovered by the author in the archives of the Bedford Estates at Woburn Abbey, England. It concerns *Electra*, the world's first electric launch tender. In 1883, Hastings, the sixty-two-year-old 9th Duke of Bedford, sold his yacht *Claymore* and purchased the Registered Steam Ship *Northumbria*. Robert F. Collins (paid £4 per week) was her sailing master, while James Birkett (paid £3 5 shillings and sixpence per week) was her engineer.

His Grace the Duke, with estates in Eaton Square, London, and Woburn Abbey, Bedfordshire, was a man keen on technical innovation. *Northumbria* was therefore well

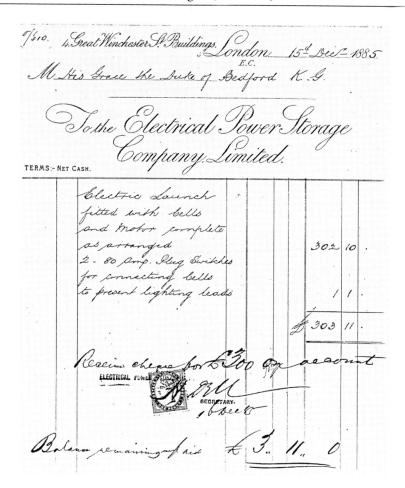

This is perhaps the first invoice for an electric boat (Woburn Abbey Collection).

fitted out. A steam whistle was supplied by Maudslay, Sons & Field and electric ship-steering indicating lights from Sir William Thomson (later Lord Kelvin). But perhaps most innovative of all, *Northumbria* was fitted with electric lighting from incandescent lamps, as supplied by the Anglo-American Brush Electric Lighting Corporation for £661. Given this approach, it was perhaps natural that the Duke should choose a slightly different yacht's tender. On December 15, 1885, Bernard Drake, managing engineer of the EPS Company, sent His Grace an invoice for an "Electric Launch fitted with bells and motor complete as arranged—£302. 10/-." "As arranged" included the motor by Reckenzaun and hull dimensions of 25 ft (7m60) LOA × 5ft (1m50) beam.

During *Electra*'s shakedown trials, EPS manager Drake was giving her a trial cruise on the Thames below Millwall, when a smart sailing yacht overtook them on one or two tacks, and when jibbing into a further tack, its helmsman shouted "Good-bye!" But to the utter amazement of its crew, Drake switched on, turned directly into the wind, and with his sails idly flapping shouted an equally sarcastic "Good-bye to you!" and forged well ahead.

The Bedford archives conserve a letter dated March 12, 1886, from *Northumbria*'s Captain Collins to G.H. Smith Esq.:

Dear Sir. Will you kindly obtain, and forward to me the exact weight of the electric launch, as it is important to know the exact weight for calculating the size of the davits to carry her. The weight given to me last year was about 2 tons. But I think it is possible that this weight may be exceeded. Sincerely, Robert F. Collins.

Almost two months later, His Grace the Duke received an invoice from EPS Ltd. dated May 18, 1886, for: "Painting launch and writing on each side of the prow the word *Electra*—£25." Then for June 22: "Expenses in connection with three trips of launch *Electra* 17th–27 ult and 5th inst—£7." Next:

August 23: Voltmeter to measure up to 6 volts	- £2 2/-
1 Pocket Voltmeter	12/6d
1 Hydrometer	1/3d
2 gallons sulphuric acid Type 1170	9d

Then finally at the end of the season: "August 30, 1886: Overhauling, washing and cleaning launch, painting outside and varnishing inside; making numerous alterations and additions to fittings and gear, including mast, yard and lug sail, additional oars, boathooks, horsehair cushions etc.: £37 17s 11d." These additions might imply that the electric propulsion system was not always reliable!

When 1887 arrived, the Duke decided to have his beloved *Northumbria* fitted with an electric windlass, as designed by the Anglo-American Brush Electric Light Corporation of Lambeth, SE London: "Arranged to raise both anchors at once, and either separately—£244."

The administrative problems of keeping an electric launch are also in evidence. This letter sent to the Duke on July 20, 1887, by none other than Thames Conservancy:

My Lord Duke,

I am directed by the Conservators of the River Thames to state that it has been reported to them that the launch *Electra* owned by you has been navigated on the river above Kew Bridge without your having taken out the necessary certificate of registration as required by the Thames Act 1883.

The Conservators understand that you have some doubt on the subject of your vessel being classed as a steam launch on account of its being driven by electricity, but I am to point out to you that in the interpretation of the terms in the Act referred to, the term "steam launch" is made to include any vessel propelled by steam or other mechanical power, and your vessel is consequently liable to the various requirements of the said Act....

Although the certificate of registration cost some 20 shillings, the Duke was a man known for his penny-pinching attitude, especially when people were attempting to extract money from him which he didn't think they deserved. On August 10, 1887, Thames Conservancy received the following terse reply: "...I am informed that as His Grace did not intend to take the launch up the River again—there is nothing to pay..."

More than that, the launch *Electra* had been taken far further afield than the Upper Thames. The Duke's friend, Charles Douglas Richard Hanbury-Tracy the 4th Lord Sudeley, a keen electrical engineer, next demonstrated the *Electra* in foreign waters. This is evidenced from the following letter, written in longhand on small notepaper and dated July 4, 1887:

My dear Duke!

A most delightful cruise—the finest weather and the smoothest sea I have ever seen, and with the yacht and *Electra* all that could be desired.... July 3: 4 p.m. Started in *Electra*—taking Birkett, pilot guide called Mr. Muller and two men for a cruise up the Amstel; As we went through the canals and under the bridges, the astonishment and amusement of the natives were very great. In no place is it possible to conceive a better opportunity for testing an electric boat. The complete power you have

The 9th Duke of Bedford's yacht, *Northumbria,* **with** *Electra* **in her davits (Woburn Abbey Collection).**

over her enables you to go at a considerable speed without the slightest danger and to glide between the barges with perfect ease and safety. It is difficult to imagine a better way to see Amsterdam and I never enjoyed a trip so much. We went up the Amstel River about 4 miles and stopped at a café at about 5.30 for coffee. In the splendid weather with a cloudless sky, nothing could be more glorious and I sincerely wish you had been with us. The speed was well maintained but owing to the shaft being a little tight in the tube, a good deal of heat was generated and we had to stop a little to allow the motor to cool. There was no danger from this heat but it means waste of power and must be prevented. If allowed also to go beyond a certain point, it would damage the copper wires.... I will give directions that this be attended to by the Storage Company when the *Electra* goes there tomorrow.... As we came down, I took *Electra* close to the Dutch training ship and turned her in a very short space to the astonishment of the officers on board.... I think you had better take into Your Grace's serious consideration taking a cruise into the Mediterranean this winter starting in September and of course your humble servant to go with you!.... Please forgive a long yarn and only read as it seems fit to you. Yours most gratefully, Sudeley.

Instead of cruising south, with Bedford's permission, during the next two years, Charles Sudeley took *Northumbria*—and *Electra*—to the Channel Islands, to Belgium, and on a more extended cruise to Stockholm and the Baltic. He wrote up this cruise in a journal:

Cruise of the *R.Y.S. Northumbria* when lent by the Duke of Bedford to Lord Sudeley. June 1889
   When the *Northumbria* docked in Stockholm:
   ...In the afternoon, we took a cruise in the Electra round the Training Ships. The Electra was the object of much curiosity by the officers of the training squadron; and also as we cruised about by the inhabitants of Stockholm, who crowded the quays wondering where the power of the little boat came from. Owing to the town being on islands, beside the numerous excursions on the adjoining lake, there is no place we have yet been to here Electra was so useful, also so much admired...

They next visited Karlskrona, the principal naval station of Sweden, where they were welcomed by the port vice-admiral, Baron Fredrik von Otter:

...at 5.30 we landed in the electric launch which created a great deal of interest and found the Admiral's carriage waiting. The following day, Sunday 30th, we took the electric launch on shore for the Admiral and his family and after taking them amongst the Swedish vessels for a cruise and to show off the powers of the launch, we brought them all on board [*Northumbria*] and gave them luncheon as they were anxious to see the accommodation of the yacht....

Returning to England on July 5, 1889, Lord Sudeley concluded, "It might also save a great deal of trouble and expense in charging the electric launch if a new dynamo were obtained with a greater electric motive force."

It was all very well for steam yacht to carry an electric launch in its davits, but could an electric launch go to sea?

Since 1885, Antony Reckenzaun had been in business on his own account for the purpose of innovating boats, cars and electric motors for various purposes. In 1889, to improve secondary batteries, he arrived at the production of active material upon the surfaces of plates by means of the electric spark or arc. The surfaces of metals become oxidized and physically changed under the influence of electric sparks. He patented this process in six countries (Patent No. 18,755).

One of his first creations was called the *Volta*. Designed by Alfred Yarrow and built by Stephens, Smith & Co. of Milwall, her Siemens-steel hull measured 37 ft (11 m) LOA × 6 ft 10 in (2 m) beam. She could accommodate 16 passengers, her draft being 3 ft (90 cm) with a displacement of 3 tons, while the 70-cell battery powered a 4 hp motor for a speed of 8 mph (13 kmh). The 20-inch (50 cm) diameter, three-bladed prop turned up to a maximum of 1000 rpm.

Following the usual christening ceremony, *Volta* cruised from Milwall to Westminster, where demonstration trips were given to members of both houses of Parliament. On one of these demonstration runs, Reckenzaun set out to prove that electric boats could be used very advantageously for both police and customs work. On the night of May 28, 1885, he took the *Volta* along the Thames to Westminster Bridge alongside the Houses of Parliament. With observers on board, a crowd leaning over the bridge and politicians looking out of windows from both the Houses of Commons and Lords, he switched a very powerful searchlight (3,000 candlepower) on and off. Reckenzaun pointed out that by adding this accessory to the silence and low waterline of an electric boat, remarkable service could be rendered to the pursuit of criminals both ashore with guarding wharves and afloat.[34]

In 1885 he took out English Patent No. 5,376 for a brush reverser for electric motors: "The object of my present invention is to provide means whereby the direction of rotation of an electric motor or motors can be reversed, and at the same time to effect such reversal only at the moment when no current is passing through the armature or armatures of the propelling apparatus."

But he did not stop there. Next stop, Calais! On September 8, 1886, *Volta* quietly *sailed* from the West India Docks down to Dover to make preparations for her offshore cruise. While her precautionary masts and sails were taken down for the trip, they were kept on board, as well as oars, in case of mishap. Frank Clark, a builder of Northampton Quay, Dover, had undertaken to recharge her batteries using the steam-engined dynamo at his works. George Toms, landlord of the Shakespeare Inn, a pilot previously engaged by Captains Webb and Cavill to accompany them on their Channel swim, was engaged to take charge of *Volta*'s navigation.

At 10:35 a.m. on September 13, 1886, with George Toms, General Frederick Brine

R.E., Antony Reckenzaun, John Stephens and enough courageous scientific gentlemen to make up a total of 10 (and so increase her weight) on board, *Volta* was rowed out of Dover Docks:

> As she reached the pier head, at 10.41 am to be precise, imagine the fascination of the large crowd watching from the pier when—with oars shipped—she continued to cruise on, in the direction of La France!
>
> The sea was flat calm and the sun shining. *Volta*'s cells had a capacity of 240 ampere/hours which at a normal rate of discharge was about 28 amps which at 120 volts was equivalent to 4½ hp. Dividing 240 by 28 we get 8½ hours maximum period of discharge. Pilot Toms was actually able to cruise almost to the limit of that charge. On the outward trip, the tide carried *Volta* some considerable distance out of her straight course, so that before she turned about, she had clocked 50 miles (80 km). Having made Calais pier head at 2.32 p.m., it would be interesting to see if she could reach Dover before sunset. Her passage was so smooth and noiseless that in mid–Channel Pilot Toms observed a gannet, a seabird large as a goose, floating fast asleep on the water. Whilst he skillfully brought *Volta* alongside, someone else seized the poor bird by hand before it knew what was happening. Gannet was brought ashore alive and unhurt.
>
> Because *Volta* kept her speed to slow the return journey which took 4 hours 14 minutes—giving her a total running time of 8 hours 14 minutes. Her current draw remained constant at 28 amperes up to 5 p.m., but at 6 p.m. dropped to 25, and again down to 24 before Dover. Then to prove how excellent a margin of power remained—the last half mile was run at 1,000 rpm![35]

Other electric launches were soon being supplied to crowned heads of state such as Umberto I, king of Italy. Abdul Hamid II, the sultan of the Ottoman Empire, had commanded the construction of an artificial lake, surrounded by a multitude of artificial cascades, at an enormous cost which necessitated embankment works 24 ft high. Before the construction of the shore roads on both sides of the Bosphorus, the only way to access palaces and mansions along the Bosphorus shores was by boat. Along the banks there were small landing places like those of the many country seats along the river, and in the center was an islet, near which rocked lazily a flotilla of sailing boats and steam and electric launches.[36] Mulam Thirunal Rama Varma Maharajah of Travancore, southwest India, commissioned a deluxe model with elaborate electric fan fitments.

The Royal Gunpowder Factory at Waltham Abbey appreciated the safety of electric launches. The Royal Gunpowder Mills were set in 170 acres of Alder woodland, and this part of the site was referred to as the island due to the network of canals; much of the water network is man-made, feeding off the River Lea. Water was crucial both to the manufacturing process and the transport of explosives. Soon after his appointment as superintendent of the factory, in 1886 William Henry Noble replaced the steam pinnace on the local River Lea with an electric vessel he called *The Spark* for his internal communications around the factory. The bank of 30 EPS lead acid accumulators was charged up by the dynamo at the steam generator house. The boat then proceeded under the power of a small electric motor to a powder house, where it was connected to electric lights in safety housings. It was a major improvement over previous lighting methods. *The Spark* was only allowed precisely because there was no spark.[37]

About this time, Chaimsonovitz P. Elieson, former works superintendent of the EPS Co., attempted to set up the Elieson Electric Co. to supply and operate tramcars involving a separate accumulator car, the passenger car being a trailer. Elieson also tried to improve the battery plate design. In the first flush of successful tramway experiments, Elieson ordered Lester and Perkins of the Royal Albert Dock to build them a boat to use these new cells. Her motor was designed by Rookes Crompton.

A practical two-fold demonstration of the application of electric motive power has been made by the running of electrically propelled tramcars at Stratford (London) and a trial trip of the electric launch, the *Countess*, in the Albert Dock…. In the electric launch, which has been built by Messrs. Lester and Perkins, the motor and gearing are the same as those employed upon the tramway, but on a larger scale. The boat is 90ft (27 m.) long, and it is intended that her engines shall work up to 60-horsepower, imparting 200 revolutions a minute to a screw propeller 3ft. 6in (1 m.) in diameter, with a pitch of 5ft 6 in (1m7). Mr. Elieson started that the power at work yesterday was not more than 17-horse, and with this *The Countess* ran in the still water of the Albert Dock between eight and nine miles an hour (14 kph). The working of the machinery was nearly noiseless there was little vibration and of course no smoke. A vessel of this description would necessarily depend upon her accumulators as a steamboat upon her coal; but as many war ships and large commercial steamers possess dynamic machinery with which to charge the cells, it would often be a great convenience to have a launch ready at a moment's notice for any emergency.[38]

The builders of *The Countess* challenged Messrs. Stephens, Smith & Co., owners of the *Volta*, to a cross–Channel race, the loser to pay £25 to the poor box at Poplar Police Court. After *The Countess* had reportedly given an impressive demonstration of 15 knots (17 mph) to the representatives of several European embassies, the challenge was accepted. But then Elieson met with serious financial problems and the race never took place.

Perhaps most ambitious was the idea of building a seagoing electric pinnace, already unsuccessfully attempted by the French Admiralty (see above). *The Pilot* was built by William Sargent of Kingston Bridge for the famous soap manufacturer, Francis Pears. Carvel-built in mahogany, she measured 26 ft 6" (8 m) long by 5 ft 4" (1m6) beam, and accommodated 16 passengers. The 40 EPS cells powered the 3 hp motor to give *The Pilot* a running speed of 8 mph. We do not know how she fared in tidal waters.[39]

By the end of 1887 some 15 launches, with EPS batteries, had been supplied, including one launch which must have brought a decisive touch of modernity. Thanks to the Franco-Venetian "Società Veneta Lagunare," it first made its appearance amongst the gondolas on the ancient canals of that north Italian city, which had just been equipped with electric street lighting in October.[40]

In 1888 came the construction of the world's largest electric vehicle, a boat. That year, financed by the Viscount Bury, German-born electrical engine builder Moritz Immisch formed the Electric Launch Company at Platt's Eyot, Hampton on Thames. Immisch worked with W.S. Sargeant of Chiswick on the design of the hull, measuring 65½ ft (20 m) overall length by 10 ft (3m) beam with an average draft of 22 inches (55 cm). She had been constructed to unusually high standards: the hull was triple-skinned, two inner skins being diagonally planked teak, and the outer of narrow horizontal planks of bright mahogany. The keel, which ran from stem to taffrail, was in one single piece of American rock elm.

The electrification was carried out by Magnus Volk and F. Crawter. A total of 200 EPS cells of 145 Ah capacity were installed for use sufficient to propel the vessel for ten hours at 6 mph (10 kph) as regulated by the Thames Conservancy By-Laws. Two 7-inch (18 cm) Immisch motors converted the electrical energy into power, 7½ bhp at 1,000 rpm geared down to twin three-bladed contra-rotating steel propellers turning at 600 rpm, built by torpedo manufacturers Thornycroft & Co. of Chiswick. The engine switches were worked by the electrician in answer to bell signals from the man at the wheel. Each propeller could thus be worked independently and so greatly assist the steering in sharp bends of the river. In place of a steam whistle there was an electric bell for warning boats and signaling lockkeepers. All lights for port, starboard, masthead and cabin, lavatories, etc., would be incandescent electric lamps supplied by the accumulators. The rudder was encased in a gun-metal trunk to avoid being caught up by riverweeds. The steering wheel was placed forward on the deck to give the helmsman full view of any oncoming boat traffic.

The complement was 80 passengers, and 24 people would be able to dine in the 10-ft (3 m) saloon at the same time. The upholstering was of crimson-embossed velvet; the paneling was of molded teak, bright varnished throughout, the ceiling being molded and picked out in gold and white. The windows were of engraved plate glass, and those of the ventilator amber in color.[41]

It is interesting to know how such a sumptuous vessel came to have the name *Viscountess Bury*, together with the carved figurehead complete in Victorian dress and coronet. In the late 1870s, William Coutts Keppel, 7th Earl of Albemarle KCMG, PC styled Viscount Bury, went to Canada, being interested in certain railway projects in that colony. While there he met the inventor Thomas Alva Edison and discussed with him the possibilities of railway vehicles powered by the type of electric storage batteries that Edison was investigating. These were the days of London's first underground railway—the Metropolitan Railway had been opened in 1863—and the early Alpine railway tunnels. In both cases, the trains were steam-operated and ventilation problems were severe. The sulfurous fumes from the steam locomotives in the tunnels of the Metropolitan Railway were notorious.

It occurred to both Edison and Viscount Bury that if railway vehicles could be operated by electric power from storage batteries, the ventilation problems would be solved. Certainly there would be a ready-made market for such vehicles. On his return to England, Viscount Bury formed the Westminster Electric Traction Company to explore this idea. He employed Moritz Immisch to work out the engineering details. Although the railway company proved unsuccessful, Immisch felt that battery-powered pleasure boats might present fewer problems.

Financed by Viscount Bury, Immisch formed the Immisch Electric Launch Company. It seemed only natural that the boat be named the *Viscountess Bury* after Bury's wife Sophia, daughter of the Hon. Sir Allan McNab, Prime Minister of Canada. The figurehead was carved by Mr. David Gibb of Limehouse.

On its inauguration run from Kingston Bridge to Sunbury, during Christmas week, the party on board included the His Royal Highness Edward, the Prince of Wales.

Following the first season, it was realized that some modifications were desirable: the saloon must be lengthened to carry the 70 passengers more comfortably; the motor changed to a single kW unit driving a single 19-inch (48 cm) propeller; batteries reduced to 164 cells; and steering moved from the bow position to the forward end of the upper deck. The *Viscountess Bury* appeared up river during the summer of 1889, and at Marlow Regatta in July it was noted that "Immisch's *Viscountess Bury* and Mr. Bowen's *Ray Mead*, both electric launches, attracted no little attention, each being well decorated."[42] For the next four years, this elegant Thames cruiser was stationed at Windsor, on charter to His Royal Highness. The Viscountess Bury's sister ship was called the *Omicron*, named after the 15th letter of the Greek alphabet.[43]

Progress continued in America. Anthony Reckenzaun and his brother Frederick had crossed the Atlantic. In 1888, at a yard in Newark, New Jersey, the brothers built the *Magnet*. She was 28 ft (8m50) long, 6 feet (1m80) beam, and 3 feet (91 cm) deep amidships, with one Reckenzaun motor revolving a 2-bladed screw 18 inches (46 cm) in diameter, and with 56 storage cells made by the Electrical Accumulator Company. She had also a headlight with a 100-candlepower lamp and seven 16-candlepower incandescent lamps for interior lighting. Trials were made on the Passaic River, Newark Bay, Arthur Kill and Kill van Hull, and even up to New York: "She did service in New York waters until sent to California. In 1888 the present writer made a trip from New York to Newark and back in her, across New York Bay and the path of the ocean liners, the trip representing about 60 miles. As a result of this work, the Grand Duke Alexander of Russia when here ordered a similar launch sent to him at home, while one was obtained by the U.S. Navy Department and supplied by the Electric Launch Company for the U.S. Cruiser New York, to be used as a captain's barge."[44]

Over in Pittsburgh, Pennsylvania, Louis Semple Clarke, or "LS," the 22-year-old innovative photographer and member of the three-year-old South Fork Dam Fishing and Hunting Club on Conemaugh Lake, had come up with an ingenious idea for fishing. Onto a twin-hulled catamaran he mounted a homebuilt electric motor and a battery to drive a 10-inch (25 cm) screw at 460 rpm. Admired by club members and friends Andrew Carnegie, Andrew Mellon and Henry Clay Frick, wearing a sailor's suit, "LS" silently cruised out into the middle of the lake where he would cast his line. He recharged his electric catamaran's battery from the 8-light dynamo on his father's steam launch. He even fitted it with a searchlight on the front. As the craft was powered by electricity, it quickly attained the nickname *Sparky* or *Old Sparky*. Clarke never had the chance to pursue his innovation as the South Fork Dam failed during an unprecedented period of heavy rains, resulting in the disastrous Johnstown Flood on May 31, 1889, in which over 2,000 people lost their lives.[45]

On the other side of the world, customs officers of the Chinese Empire realized the silent superiority of an electric motor over a 30 hp clattering steam engine, during the tricky process of catching an opium smuggler unawares at night on his junk. The mission was to find a boat that could aid the fight against opium smuggling in the China Sea. The boat commissioned was a 30-horsepower Trouvé electric launch. It was steel-hulled, weighed 8 tons, and measured 15 meters (50 feet) long, with a bronze propeller of about 50 cm (20 inches). It was capable of a speed of 18 kph (11 mph). It also had an electric spotlight capable of projecting a beam of light with a range of 6 kilometers (3 sea miles). The Emperor Guangxu of the then ruling Qing Dynasty, who since his childhood had been fascinated by clocks and gadgetry, was so impressed that he commanded a scale model for exhibition at his Palace Museum in the Forbidden City in Peking.[46]

Not that all electric boats in France were French-built. Early in 1889, Messrs. Immisch of England supplied four launches with EPS batteries for use on the Seine near Paris. Although Gustave Trouvé had by now turned his restless and ingenious mind to other inventions such as a working model electric helicopter (tethered), an electric auxanoscope (image projector), and luminous electric fountains, electric boats were still in evidence at the 1889 Universal Exhibition in Paris. One of those thousands who visited the exhibition was the 60-year-old writer Lucien Biart, who wrote up his experiences in a 100-page book *Mes Promenades à Travers l'Exposition*. On page 77, he writes:

> We have stayed on the banks of the Seine, and I now propose to take us even closer. So I go back towards the gate of the Avenue de Suffren, I go down to the riverbank to find myself at the Fluvial and Maritime Exhibition. I arrive just in time to see a small boat running around, a real toy, from which neither steam or smoke is escaping, although from the bank, there is the noise of both a machine and that of a propeller. This toy, I suppose, is driven electrically, about which I've already made the

remark that it is tending to replace all other forces, to supplant them. It moves around with unparalleled grace, this small boat; it comes and it goes, slides, runs along and tacks with such perfect precision, almost as if one were observing a large swallow, swift and capricious, whose wings caress and skim the water. Suddenly its pilot is directing it towards the quay wall, which worries us. Is this man blind, crazy, or distracted, does he want to destroy this boat? Forecasting a disaster, you're about to cry: park! You move closer as quickly as possible so as to be able to rescue the unwary pilot, whose boat is about to smash against the wall from which he is only twenty paces away. Anxiously, your heart stops beating; you have to close your eyes to not see this inevitable catastrophe. Only ten paces, only five.... Phew! That's it. But no, the little boat bends over, and does an about-turn, just like the bird with which I have compared it, and then flying away along the shoreline, he triumphantly returns to the open waters, leaving you emotionally overwhelmed ... by the third circuit, you have understood that this is a only a game, a demo, but one so daring as to excite you again. For my part, still perturbed, I am wondering if the boat is not enchanted, if its driver is not some sorcerer?

Back on the Thames, Messrs. Immisch also created a six-strong hire fleet for the Upper Thames, named after the Greek alphabet (*Alpha, Beta, Gamma, Delta*), while siting five charging stations—at Maidenhead, Henley, Wallingford, and Oxford, with one at his workshops on the lower part of Platt's Eyott Island. The *Eta* was transported north to a boating firm on Lake Windermere.[47]

Although difficult to verify, Immisch's designer-builder, W.S. Sargeant, took the 30.5 ft (9 m) *Malden* 56 miles downstream at an average 10 mph (16 kmh), prior to this launch going into service on the Blackwater, for police patrol on the River Dee. (Elsewhere it is "reported" that a Monsieur Flaurin constructed a 52-ft (16 m) electric launch with a 60 hp electric motor, capable of traveling 30 nautical miles at 10 knots (18.5 kph) top speed, and 200 nautical miles at 5 knots (9 kph). This boat is erroneously reported to have weighed only 3 cwt (!))[48]

Interest in electricity and electric vehicles went as far as North Africa. Despite his people living a daily life on camels, horses and mules, since 1873 the Sultan Moulay-Hassan of Morocco and his son Abel-El-Aziz were passionate about European technology, but they played on European rivalries to maintain their independence.

In 1888, Moritz Immisch and his colleague Magnus Volk of England had sent out a four-wheel, four-seater electric dogcart, two in front and two behind. Its energy was supplied by 24 accumulators, weighing 358 kg protected inside a box placed between the seats. With an overall weight of 550 kg (1212 lb), the dogcart was capable of running for 5 hours at 16 kph (10 mph). The sultan and his son derived great pleasure from driving it around the courtyards of Ksar el Batha, their large palace at Fez. They also had an electrical laboratory, powered by a steam generator.

In spring 1889, Jules Patenôtre, the new French minister in Tangiers, decided on the diplomatic gesture of taking some fine gifts for the Sultan Moulay-Hassan. Concerning this, on February 27, he wrote to the Minister of Foreign Affairs, Paris:

Diplomatic gifts to offer to the Sultan

Dear Minister,

If the rainy season does not upset my projects, I am proposing to set off for Fez towards 29 March. I would be desirable that the four mares that the Government of the Republic must send to Moulay-Hassan must be shipped in sufficient time for them to arrive in Tangiers before our departure. I have already received one part of the other presents destined for the Sultan and I would like the complement to be sent to me as soon as possible.

Where *the electric-engined launch* is especially concerned, there will be room to get it accompanied by a foreman from the Trouvé firm who can assemble it on the spot and indicate its running to the Sultan's mechanics. The costs required to transport the foreman will not be very high. We will obtain, without doubt, from the Paquet Company, his free transportation from Marseilles to Tangiers: he will, during our voyage, have his expenses paid and I can, once he will have completed the assembly of the launch, send him back to France. So it only concerns paying him, beside the cost of his voyage, return ticket, 2nd class, from Paris to Marseilles.

A daily salary to negotiate with M Trouvé and which will be, if your Excellency authorises me carried by the general expenses of the extraordinary Embassy. I would be grateful if you would let me know the decision that you take concerning this.... Patenôtre. Legation of the French Republic in Morocco [emphasis added].

The mares mentioned, each four-year-old, white-socked bays, demi-thoroughbreds, came from the internationally renowned National Haras of Saint-Lô in Normandy, where no fewer than 300 breeding studs were looked after by some eighty blacksmiths. Their names were Mercedes, Heroïne, Hermosa and Hermine. They were purchased by Froidereaux, inspector-general of the Haras, who made the necessary arrangements for them to be sent, first to the Port Vendre in Paris, then to Marseilles by March 16, shipped to Tangiers, and then taken to Fez accompanied by the Haras blacksmiths. While they were considered as the finest horses France could provide, the Trouvé launch, built of mahogany, represented the finest technology.

On March 12, Paternôtre reported:

> I am at present without news of the horses and the electric launch intended for the Sultan. I hope they are already en route so as to arrive here before the end of the month.... Has Monsieur Trouvé decided to supply you with a foreman to steer his boat? I have learned that the Italian Mission at Fez is at present busy servicing the electric machinery of the Sultan. It would be most regrettable should we be obliged to depend on them for the boat in question. They tell me that you have asked Monsieur de la Martineau, just about to return to Morocco, to study under the direction of M. Trouvé the reassembly and the functioning of his boat. I do not suppose that he would wish to assume responsibility....
>
> Patenôtre.

On March 14, the following telegraph was sent from the port of Marseilles to the Minister of Foreign Affairs, Paris: "We will be able to embark the packages making up the electric boat for Tangiers, but warn that the ship of the 22nd will be several days late."

In his *Memoirs*, Patenôtre later recalled, "We took an electric boat in mahogany, intended for taking the harem of His Cherifian Majesty around the artificial lakes in the imperial gardens. This boat which was not less than 20 meters long and could not be dismantled had to be a big element of complication for the progress of our caravan. Having tried all ways of transporting it, we had to end up with a procedure renewed from Pharaonic times and forty blacks were charged with carrying for twelve days, on their heads or on their shoulders, this gigantic package which, by its shape, evoked the idea of some monstrous monolith."[49]

Paternôtre's eighteen-strong delegation included a young naval officer called Julien Viaud, later a famous novelist called "Pierre Loti." In his book *In Morocco*, Loti would recall the event: "An extraordinary object, which has followed us from Tangiers and which we are also used to looking for, sometimes ahead of us, sometimes behind, in the far distance, is the electric launch (!!?), six meters long, that we are carrying as a present for His Majesty the Sultan; it is enclosed in a greyish case which gives is the aspect of a block of granite, and it progresses with difficulty, via the ravines, the mountains, carrying on the shoulders of about forty Arabs. In the Egyptian bas-reliefs, one has already seen these enormous things moving past, carried, like this one, by throngs of men in white robes, with naked legs."[50] The caravan arrived in sight of the crenelated walls of Fez on the afternoon of April 15. The following day, the French made an entry into the holy city, welcomed by a crowd of 20,000 people who marveled at the strange packing case, still on the shoulders of the Arab porters.

Ironically, no mention was made, either by Patenôtre or by Loti, of the Sultan's reaction to the boat and of its ultimate use by his veiled harem!

TWO

Electric Boats Become
Popular (1889–1914)

On the afternoon of Wednesday March 26, 1890, the annual varsity boat race between the universities of Oxford and Cambridge took place on the River Thames from Putney to Mortlake in west London. Until that year, press coverage had been from the riverside. But the *London Daily Graphic* came up with the ingenious idea of hiring the electric launch *Alpha* from the Immisch Company. As the oarsmen raced down the river, the *Alpha* pursued them. Artists on board made sketches which were then dispatched to the newspaper offices using carrier pigeons. One report read in part: "Electric launches are now an indispensable feature of any nautical gathering on the Thames, and at the Oxford and Cambridge boat race on Wednesday the electric boats were, after the race itself, one of the most noticeable features. Messrs. Immisch had several large launches, among which the 'Alpha,' of the Daily Graphic, was conspicuous. One of Messrs. Immisch's charging stations was moored along the reaches. Mr. Sargent had several small electric pleasure-boats which flitted silently about among the throng, or rang the warning electric bell as they turned."[1] It was a good race, Oxford winning by one boat length!

At the Edinburgh International Exhibition, held between May 31 and October 11, 1890, for a fare of one halfpenny, no fewer than 71,075 paying passengers enjoyed rides up and down the Union Canal to Slateford and back. The four steel-hulled electric launches, designed by Morton & Williamson, were built by T.B. Seath, both of Glasgow. The 3½ hp 800 rpm Immisch motors were supplied by 48 Electric Construction Corporation accumulators, and the four boats were recharged simultaneously by a steam-powered generator driving an Immisch dynamo. On the busiest day 2,560 passengers were carried in balmy sunny weather. After the exhibition, the four launches were transported down to the English Lake District and went into operation on Lake Windermere.[2]

Immisch continued to do a stylish business. Eastern princes and rajahs provided a number of orders for the launches, while King Oscar II of Sweden and his wife Sophia journeyed from Richmond to Hampton Court in one of Immisch's boats.[3]

Some did not believe in *rechargeable secondary* batteries. John Vaughan-Sherrin of Codrington Road, Ramsgate, England, considered that the future of electric cars and boats still lay in a primary battery which each time it was discharged should be replaced. To promote his zinc-carbon primary battery, in 1889, Vaughan-Sherrin formed the Electric Tricycle, Carriage, Boat, and Machinery Syndicate, Ltd., and invited *"The Electrical Engineer"* to visit the premises:

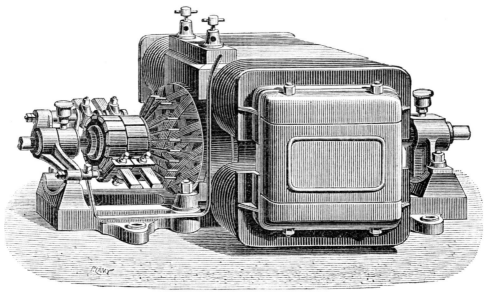

Top: One of the boats at the 1890 Edinburgh Exposition (author's collection). *Bottom:* The electric motor designed and built by Moritz Immisch was used in a whole fleet of boats (Musée EDF Electropolis, Mulhouse).

We have been up this week to 48, Eagle-wharf-road, Hoxton, the offices of the Henry Rifled Arms Company, to inspect an electric tricycle and an electric launch driven by a new primary battery and motor devised by Mr. Vaughan-Sherrin, electrical engineer, of Ramsgate.... We were afterwards treated to a ride in the primary battery electric boat. The two boxes of cells used in the tricycle were lifted out, and a third added and placed in the boat. This electric boat, which was shown at Henley last regatta, has a small propeller geared by chain gearing to a small ½ h.p. motor, and ran at a very fair pace, quite as quick as boats on the Thames want to progress. We had a trip up the canal and back on this boat. The cost for this is given at 3d. an hour, the weight of battery being 120 1b., lasting nine hours. Afterwards we inspected the large launch which he has also fitted up, and has used at Ramsgate. Mr.Vaughan-Sherrin promises to take a run with his large launch across from Dover to Calais with primary batteries, and some big social and electrical men are, he says, to be invited. He states that at need material for a 600-mile run can be stowed on board.[4]

In 1891, U.S. inventor Thomas Alva Edison equipped a boat, the *Reliant*, with an electric motor to test his revolutionary nickel-iron-alkaline battery.[5] After thousands of trials, Edison had developed a battery having nickel hydroxide as a positive plate separated by an alkaline electrolyte from an iron oxide negative. He had already tested this battery in a car two years before. For testing and for pleasure, the "Wizard of Menlo Park" went for cruises up and down the Caloosahatchee River at Fort Myers, Florida, where his winter home was fronted. Soon after, William K. Vanderbilt ordered an electric launch, the *Alva*, from Charles L. Seabury's yard. At 30 ft (9 m) long with a draft of 2 ft (61 cm), the *Alva* was capable of seating between 25 to 30 people.

The same year, the International Electrotechnical Exhibition was held between May 16 and October 19, 1891, on the disused site of the three former "Westbahnhöfe" (Western Railway Stations) in Frankfurt am Main. To ply the River Main to serve as aid in the traffic between the interior of the city and the eastern part, where the exhibition was situated, a sophisticated electric boat was built in the workshops of Oerlikon and the boatyard of Escher Wyss. It measured 16 meters (53 ft) long, 3 m (10 ft) beam, and with a very shallow draft. With a maximum speed of 12 kph (8 mph), the exhibition launch could carry up to one hundred people.

By this time the British government had seen the importance of marine electric propulsion. At the Naval Exhibition, held in London's Camperdown Gallery in 1891, visitors to the stand of Kerbey Bowen, Ray Mead Works, Maidenhead-on-Thames, could inspect an electric pinnace. The 50 accumulators of this mahogany and teak 36-footer (11 m), designed in the lines of the British Admiralty steam pinnaces, were located in teak boxes below the seating, They could be charged either while the pinnace was slung in the davits of—or moored alongside—one of Her Majesty's ships. The motor was much more powerful than those usually supplied by the company for use in the launches on the Thames and at Windermere, giving an increased sprint speed of 11 mph (18 kph). Since pinnaces were principally used for ship-to-shore purposes, speed and power had been considered of more importance than duration of run. During the Exhibition, a Bowen pinnace, 40 feet (12 m) long, 7 feet 9 inches (2m40) beam, and 2 feet (60 cm) draft, with a handsome teak cabin, was ordered by the Naval Department of the Russian Imperial Government.[6]

Another military application for electric propulsion was the jollyboat or troop transporter. The 48-ft (14m60) open boat, *The Electric*, with a seating capacity for 40 fully-equipped soldiers, was built in mahogany and teak at Woodhouse and Rawson United Ltd.'s Strand Electric Launch Works of Chiswick, London. The *Daily News* reported:

On the afternoon of March 10th the first electrical launch ever built for the British Government was sent off the stocks into the Thames at Messrs. Woodhouse and Rawson's yard, near Newbridge station.... She is to be used for the conveyance of troops between the dockyards of Chatham and Sheerness on the River Medway. With her 40 fully equipped soldiers, she can run at a speed of eight knots, or about 10 miles an hour. She is always ready to start at an instant's notice. *The Electric* can run for 10 hours with a single charge of electricity. That single charge will be far more than enough for her requirements when she leaves Chiswick for her station on the Chatham-Sheerness line. For emergency the boat was fitted with two masts and two balance lug sails. For the use of this first pinnace of the national service, and for the use of her successors, an electric "installation"—in other words, charging station—is to be put up at Chatham. As the demand for boats of this type is expected to be large, the company has just opened a second building yard, and a third is in course of preparation.[7]

Frederick L. Rawson teamed up with American-born Otway E. Woodhouse, a champion tennis player whose inventiveness ranged from a tennis racket grip to electric lighting. After a long illness, Woodhouse died in 1887 aged only 32. But the business of Woodhouse and Rawson United Ltd. continued as electrical equipment managers. In 1890, the company took over W. Sargeant's boatbuilding business at Strand Works, Chiswick, keeping him on as manager and appointing William R. Edwards as their assistant manager.

A number of electric boats went into operation in the British colonies. On the other side of the world, at the coastal Port Macquarie, New South Wales, Australia, an electric motor had been shipped out from London for installation in a sleek-looking 16-ft (5 m) hull, built of a variety of timbers including honeysuckle wood and Australian beech. The boat went into silent operation up and down the local Hastings River.[8] A Mr. Paterson from Invercargill was running an electric launch on Lake Te Anau in Fiordland, a geographic region of New Zealand in the southwestern corner of the South Island.[9]

Back on the upper Thames, the General Electric Power & Traction Co. built a deluxe touring launch *Flosshilde* (one of the Rhine maidens in Richard Wagner's opera cycle, *Der Ring des Nibelungen*) for the partially sighted William John Manners Tollemache, 9th Earl of Dysart. She was even longer than the *Viscountess Bury*, and also accommodated a 400-volt EPS battery: "His Lordship was present with a party of friends for the launching. The christening was carried out in the approved way by Mrs. Dixon, one of the party. The '*Flosshilde*' is a very handsomely appointed boat, on finer lines than those previously built."[10]

For more popular enjoyment, the Strand Electric Launch Works had delivered the 38-ft (12 m) 40-seater *The Bonnie Southport* to Southport Corporation for use on their Botanic Gardens artificial lake. With her Woodhouse and Rawson motor purring in its Sargeant hull, *Bonnie* proved very successful with the local "Sandgrounders" during the Easter holidays of 1892.[11]

Woodhouse & Rawson United Ltd. even looked across the English Channel to France. By this time, Gustave Trouvé had replaced his interest in electric boat innovations with building and testing multicolored fountains, domestic acetylene lighting, and even a model ornithopter, or mechanical bird. On August 9, 1892, the British yard's 11m20 pax boat, named *L'Eclair* (= *Lightning*) was launched into the Seine at Asnières. With energy from a battery of 40 Epstein accumulators, it was capable of a top speed of 12 kph for up to 5 hours, and at slower speeds a distance of 70 km. What was particularly interesting was that *L'Eclair* could be recharged from a bankside generating station, whose power was mostly used by an electrical metalworking plant at Saint-Ouen-les-Docks, where there was already an electric streetcar line; recharging of the boat at 50 Ah lasted 3 to 4 hours. If the operation was successful, Woodson & Rawson planned to export over other electric boats from the Upper Thames.[12]

One of those Parisians who *may* have been inspired by *L'Eclair* was the science-fiction writer, Jules Verne. One day Verne and his friend Jean Macé stood on the Pont des Arts in downtown Paris and watched a "bateau-mouche" (ferry boat) passing underneath.[13] It gave him the idea of writing a short story about an electrically powered pleasure island. *L'Île à hélice* (=*Propeller Island*) was first published in 1895 as part of his *Voyages Extraordinaires*. It relates the adventures of a French string quartet in Milliard City, a city on a massive ship in the Pacific Ocean, inhabited entirely by millionaires, whose pleasures are entirely produced by electricity. The island, made of steel, measures 7.2 km (4.5 miles) long × 5 km (3 miles) wide and a circumference of 17 km (11 miles). Enormous dynamos give it continuous electrical current at a moderate power of 20 kW. The dynamos drive a powerful system by screws—each engine develops 5 million horsepower using hundreds of boilers fed with petroleum briquettes. The maximum speed of the island underway is 8 knots and the most powerful storm waves have no influence on it.

By this time, the still popular *Frank Reade Weekly Magazine; Containing Stories of Adventures on Land, Sea and In the Air* contained Indiana Jones–style adventures such as *Franke Reade Junior's Electric Air Canoe or the Search for the Valley of Diamonds*. From the engraving on the front cover, the boat in question, called the *Flying Fish*, was a cross between a helicopter and a stern paddle wheeler. Also there was *Frank Reade, Jr., and His Electric Cruiser of the Lakes or a Journey through Africa by Water*. N°71 published in 1894. The fictional boat in question was the 150-ft-long, flat-bottomed gunboat *Spark*, with its guns pointing fore and aft and a powerful searchlight. Its mission: to suppress smuggling on the rivers and lakes of Africa! The writer of these two, with the nom de plume "Noname," was Luis Philip Senarens, a Cuban-American living in Brooklyn, and was often compared to Jules Verne.[14]

In 1891, Charles Jacquin, writing in the journal *La Lumière*, waxed poetic about electric boating:

> In addition, the electric motor lacks all the unpleasantness of a steam engine and its boiler. We no longer suffer dirtying coal dust, the stench of oil which goes with the engines, that unpleasant black smoke which obscures the view, that disagreeable noise produced by the rods and pistons. The electric boat whose propeller receives its rotation directly through the motor shaft, glides silently across the water surface, clean and gracious as a swan, with nothing to pick out the mysterious force which guides its progress. If one adds to all these amenities that of the countryside, which on the banks of the Thames is far from ugly, one can understand why the public has acquired a taste for this distraction.[15]

In 1892, William Main, an electrical engineer working for the Union Electric Company of New York, came up with the concept that if a slow-running motor were connected directly to the propeller shaft, this would eliminate all speed-reducing devices, which are noisy and wasteful of power. With its 77 batteries providing an autonomy of 9 to 10 hours per run placed below decks and in the stern of the hull, a 30-ft (9 m) passenger boat was built by Charles L. Seabury & Co., Nyack-on-the-Hudson, and christened the *Vashti*. That October, with journalists and electricians on board, *Vashti* made a very successful trip on the Hudson River, running from Nyack to Sing Sing and returning, sustaining a speed of 8 to 10 mph (12 to 16 kph):

> The whole operation of the boat is under control of one person, and simple in the extreme. The starting, stopping, and reversing is regulated by a single wheel, and any speed, from the maximum to zero, can be obtained by turning the wheel, as when moved to the right the propeller starts ahead, and the farther it is moved to the right the faster the propeller goes; on turning this wheel back to the starting point the motor comes to a standstill, and on turning it to the left the motion of the propeller

wheel is reversed. This starting wheel and the steering wheel are located together at the forward part of the cockpit and both can be operated by any one, though he be unfamiliar with boats and electricity.[16]

Hot on the heels of the Frankfurt Exhibition, an impressive exhibition was now planned for 1893: the World's Fair at Chicago. In February 1892 a small notice appeared in Thomas Fleming Day's monthly magazine *Rudder, Sail, and Paddle* (later to become *Rudder* magazine): "Launch and boat builders are requested to send to Chief Burnham, Marine Division, Transportation Exhibits Department, World's Fair, Chicago, bids for supplying fifty 34-foot boats to be propelled by power of any description, and to be able to carry thirty people. Lieut. A.C. Baker, U.S. Navy, has been placed in charge of the marine division of the transportation exhibits department." Chief Burnham and Lieutenant Baker scheduled demonstrations for four companies in July of 1892. Willard & Co. and Meeker & Co. each brought a steam launch, while the Columbian Launch Company and the new Electric Launch & Navigation Company demonstrated electric-drive launches. According to *Scientific American* (then a weekly magazine), Columbian's *Volta* was thought to be superior to the others, including Electric Launch's *Electra*.

The impetus for the effort to recruit electric launch builders came from world-famous landscape architect Frederick Law Olmstead, who had traveled to a world's fair in Edinburgh, Scotland, and seen several reputable electric launches there. After the tryouts, the Electric Launch & Navigation Company (Elco) won a contract to supply 55 electric launches, each 36 ft (11 m) long, to the Chicago exposition. As *Rudder* noted, these launches were designed by Charles Mosher, partner of William Gardner, and apparently were constructed under Mosher's supervision by Charles Seabury & Co. of Nyack-on-Hudson, New York, as well as 25 by the Racine Hardware Mfg. Co. of Racine, Wisconsin. Inspired by the fringed canopy top often fitted to the four-wheeled Surrey horse-drawn carriage, the boats also had a fringe on top.

The story behind the Electric Launch Navigation Company had begun eight years before when a prolific Philadelphian inventor named William Woodnut Griscom obtained a patent for a small electric motor intended for sewing machines (rather like Trouvé). Griscom then created the Electric Dynamic Corporation to manufacture those motors, which he supplied to the fledgling electric boat company. The Electric Storage Battery Company, which was supplying the batteries, was run by a Bavarian-born lawyer called Isaac Leopold Rice, who had acquired the patent rights to French immigrant Clément Payen's *chloride accumulator* battery. The hulls were designed by Charles Mosher and built by Seabury and Racine's yard.[17]

On May 1, 1893, President Grover Cleveland pushed a button to inaugurate the World's Columbian Exposition celebrating Christopher Columbus's first voyage. For the first time on a large scale, 11,000 kilowatts of electricity illuminated 250,000 electric light bulbs, instantaneously igniting wonder in everyone. Scores of electric motors also silently sparked life into fair exhibits, enkindling the imaginations of industrialists and entrepreneurs. Among them the electric launches which were a resounding success, and established the company's reputation. Visitors were greeted with 633 total acres (256 ha) of fairgrounds, 65,000 exhibits, and restaurant seating for 7,000. They were amazed by the clean and safe elevated railway and the electric launches plying the canals and lagoons. Managed by General C.H. Barney, the fleet of launches made 66,975 trips during the six and a half months of the exposition, carrying 1,026,346 passengers 200,925 miles (323,357 km) and earning $314,000 for the World's Fair organizers. Their greatest test came on

Chicago Day when 622 trips, each trip of three miles, were made by fifty boats. Six of these boats averaged over 40 miles (65 km), carrying on each trip about 40 people. *There were no fewer than 25,000 passengers carried that day alone.* Not bad for a company that had incorporated a month after the first bids were requested, and which had no plant, no equipment, no staff of boat builders or designers, and no track record.[18]

> The exhibition launches are of a very graceful model, about thirty-six feet long and six feet breadth of beam. They are designed to carry thirty passengers, and have motors capable of exerting four horse-power. The batteries are placed beneath the seats and flooring, and as the motor is also beneath the flooring the cockpit is clear of any obstruction. Each launch carries seventy-eight battery cells, which, by appropriate connections, may be grouped in various combinations. For the regular operation of the boats the cells are grouped in three divisions containing twenty-six cells each, arranged in series. The batteries are charged for a run of ten to twelve hours, and are then recharged at the power station of the fleet in from five to seven hours. The launches run over a course of about three miles, at a speed of six miles an hour, and make landings at the principal buildings, all of which front upon the water-ways.

A report "Electricity at the World's Fair," published in *Popular Science Monthly* in October 1893, describes how: "The machinery used for the fountains is also used for charging the electric launches. There are fifty of these beautiful little boats, averaging forty feet long and having a carrying capacity of thirty people. After five or six hours charging each little launch will have stored away in its hold about forty horse-power hours of effective electrical energy, sufficient for ten or twelve hours continuous run. This charging station, located south and east of the Agricultural Building, is the most extensive ever put in in the United States, and probably in the world. It housed a 2,500 hp generator."[19]

The report continues:

> One of the most delightful experiences which one may have during a visit to the Fair is a voyage around the waters of the lagoons in one of the dainty electric launches. Without smoke, noise or odor, they plow their way rapidly along through the South Canal, the Basin, the North Canal, the Lagoon, and the North Pond. The Wooded Island is encircled, and a delightful view is had of every building.
> The architects of the Fair paid great attention to the landscape effect of the whole, as it would appear from the water, and no one should miss the opportunity to see the display from this point of vantage. A fleet of more than fifty of these is constantly passing and repassing on the lagoons and canals during all the hours that the Fair is open to the public. The course over which they run measures about three miles for the round trip, and there are landings at all the large buildings and principal points of interest. The boats thus furnish the best communication between different parts of the ground and at the same time an excellent means of refreshing one's self when tired of sight-seeing in the exhibit buildings.[20]
> The electric launches each have a motor man, who guides the craft, and a deck hand. The uniforms of all the officials connected with water transportation at the Fair are navy blue in single and double-breasted coat patterns. The rank of the official is on his cap and the company to which he belongs on his coat collar. Every species of craft under World's Fair control flies two flags, the American and the Columbian maritime flag. The latter is of white bunting with an orange-colored wreath of oak leaves in the center surrounding a blue anchor.[21]

After the World's Fair had closed, the fleet was dispersed. When the site grounds reverted to Jackson Park, several electric boats continued to go back and forth from the Wooded Island at 10 cents for a round trip. A syndicate of Italians purchased another one for $2,000 and sent it directly to Venice to serve as a nucleus of a fleet on the historic canals. Slightly modifying her hull to look like a gondola, and copper-sheathing her hull to protect her from the weeds and canal water, they renamed her *Venezia.*[22] She would not be the last "barca elettrica" to be seen on the Grand Canal.

Still in Italy, Aldo Taroni and his son, Giorgio, at their boatyard in Stresa, a popular retreat for European aristocrats beside Lake Maggiore in northern Italy, may have heard

During the 1893 Chicago World's Fair, more than one million passengers were taken on cruises by a fleet of fifty electric launches built by the Electric Launch Company (courtesy Tom Hesselink).

about *Venezia* because they soon followed the fashion and built elegant electric launches whose lines and varnished wood glass cabins resembled those being made in England and the USA.

Another purchaser of a World's Fair boat may have been William K. Bixby, who had made his fortune by founding the American Car and Foundry Company in St. Louis, Missouri, which had a near monopoly on the manufacture of railroad cars. He owned a summer home at Bolton Landing on Lake George. According to Bixby's great-grandson Charles G. Houghton:

It is my understanding that my great-grandfather, as a key member of the 1904 St. Louis World's Fair Committee, had gone to the 1893 Chicago World's Fair with my Great Grandmother and they took a ride on one of the Electric Launch Company's 36' boats for an individual fare of $0.25. My Grandfather, W.H. Bixby, would tell the story that there was a company salesman on the dock when his father and mother got off the launch. The salesman asked them if they might be interested in buying a boat. My great-grandfather did buy a boat for $1,736.00 but we are not sure if it was a World's Fair boat or a new boat. It certainly had the tugboat look of the World's Fair boats.

Our boat was shipped to Lake George for the next summer season in 1894. Sometime in June of 1894, when my Great Grandparents arrived by private rail car and then steamer at around 10:00 a.m. at the property at Bolton Landing called "Mohican Point," my great grandfather was excited about going out for a ride on his "new" or "used" (we will never know) electric launch. However, when my Great Grandmother saw all the electrical wires on poles running over her lawns and gardens, she said "Father, I feel sure that you will not want to use your electric boat until those ugly wires are removed from our lawns." By 1:00 p.m. 50 men were digging trenches and burying wires from the waterfall to the boathouse, so that my great-grandfather could use his electric boat. As both my grandparents

Why Electric Launches
are the Ideal Form of Marine Navigation

SAFE.
Nothing to explode.
Nothing to take fire.
Cannot sink (air chambers under decks prevent).
Will not tip over (all machinery, etc., below water-line.)

SIMPLE.
No government inspection.
No licensed engineer.
No engineer at all.
Can run your own boat.
Wife can do likewise.

COMFORTABLE.
No heat.
No odor.
No smoke.
No noise.
No dirt.

RELIABLE.
Always ready.
Always certain.
Always steady.
Always under complete control.

ECONOMICAL.
Runs 50 to 75 miles on a single charge. Costs 2½ cents per mile.
No waste of power.
No waste of room.

All machinery beneath the flooring.
Portable charging outfits furnished.

Search-lights if wanted.

——Illustrated Catalogue mailed on request.——

THE ELECTRIC LAUNCH COMPANY, Bayonne, N. J.

Formerly Morris Heights, N. Y. City.   *21 minutes from New York City via Liberty St. Ferry.*

79

Elco was well marketed as is shown by this advertisement (courtesy Tom Hesselink).

made clear, my Great Grandfather always believed that his success in life and business was due to meeting my great grandmother, so he made sure to do what she wanted at all times. The boat was named the *St. Louis*, because it was in St. Louis, Missouri that my great grandfather made his fortune. When in 1901, the *St. Louis* began to ware [*sic*] out, he bought a new 36ft Elco, which is the one the family still uses today, a century later from Memorial Day until Christmas.[23]

A year and a half after the World's Fair closed, the General Electric Launch Company—whose role in the exposition is still unknown—filed papers to change its name to the "World's Fair Electric Launch Company." Henry Weston, attorney for the Electric Launch and Navigation Co., and a founding partner of the General Electric/World's Fair Launch Co., signed the papers, as did several other executives who had a leg in each camp. Five months later, the World's Fair Electric Launch company changed its name back to General Electric Launch Company. Two months later, on January 25, 1895, the firm solved its identity crisis by changing its name, one last time, to the Electric Launch Company. Simultaneously, the stockholders of the initial firm—the Electric Launch & Navigation Company—voted to dissolve their corporation. At last there existed a single corporate entity, and it existed under the name it kept for the next half century: better known as Elco.[24]

In 1892 the Altoona & Logan Valley Electric Railway Company in Pennsylvania had been developed with 18 electric cars. The advent of electric cars allowed for the development of suburban property. Passengers no longer needed to live within walking distance of their jobs. During this period, the company began a pattern of sustained growth that would continue for approximately 40 years. In 1893, the service was expanded to Hollidaysburg, then to Bellwood, expanding the total line to nearly 20 miles. The electric railway company developed Lakemont Park and began its operation in 1894. At Lakemont there was a 13-acre artificial boating lake with rowboats and a 36-ft Elco launch for hire.[25]

Another two ex–Expo Elco launches would be purchased in 1897 for use on the 18.3-acre (7.4 ha) reservoir created by the Mechanicville Hydroelectric Dam across the Mohawk River north of Albany, New York. A well-protected harbor had been built for them at the north end of Quack Island and the launches were available for hire.[26]

In 1895, Austrian theater impresario, Gabor Steiner, created arguably one of the world's first theme parks in Vienna's Prater Park. He called it Venedig in Wien (Venice in Vienna). This replica of Venice included its canals and an artificially recreated lagoon around which both gondolas and electric launches transported not only Viennese high society but also Bohemian servants and the soldiers of the Austrian-Hungarian multi-ethnic state.[27]

Germany must have been impressed by the fleet at the Chicago World's Fair because in 1896, 10 electric sightseeing boats with Siemens electric engines were used during the Great Industrial Exposition of Berlin. They gave rides on the "New Lake" ("Neuer See"), an artificial water basin occupying 10,000 square meters (2 acres).[28]

Four years later, in 1901, a fleet of twenty-five 30-footers (9 m), some built by Elco and others by the Truscott Boat and Engine Company, St. Joseph, Michigan, each with its uniformed pilot, went into operation alongside Venetian gondolas with singing gondoliers on board, as managed by the Abergo Baroni Catering Company's "Venice in America" concern. They gave rides to 85,700 visitors to the Pan-American Exposition in Buffalo. Thomas Edison used one of these launches to film a cruise around the canal system:

It is called the Grand Canal, is over a mile in length and extends around the central group of large buildings. Winding lagoons connecting with the canal branch off in all directions. The Mirror Lakes in the Southern portion of the canal form a picturesque feature and add tenfold interest to this picture. The electric launches and gondolas which make the trip around the exposition, and which are controlled by the Venice in America Co., represent the climax of comfort and elegance. The ride is a refreshing one with charming views at every turn. Romantic bridges span the waterway at convenient points, statuary placed everywhere contribute to the picturesque effect. The above named picture was secured by special permission of Mr. Burgee, of the Venice in America Co., and our picture was made from the bow of an especially chartered electric launch which made the trip for us at a high rate of speed.[29]

In 1904, Truscott also supplied several 30-footers, with tilting sun awnings, for the Louisiana Purchase Exposition (also known as the St. Louis World's Fair) for crossing the lagoons. Seats in electric launches could be secured at the various landings for 25 cents per person: "The Grand Basin is a part of the lagoon system, the lagoon to the right encircling the Palace of Electricity, and the one to the left surrounding the Palace of Education. Upon these lagoons is a great variety of craft including gondolas brought from Venice, peacock boats, swan boats, dragon boats and handsome electric launches."[30]

But electric boats were not only used for exhibition water taxis. An ingenious application was made in 1889 by Harrison P. Eddy, a 28-year-old civil engineering graduate, during works being carried out on a large sewer in Worcester, Massachusetts. The sewer was 18 feet (5m50) wide by 13 feet (4 m) high, and in order to divide the storm water from the sewage it was decided to construct a small sewer 6 feet (1m80) wide along some 4,000 feet (1 km) of larger sewer to take the normal flow. The work was carried out by means of cofferdams. The electrical equipment consisted of a dynamo and engine placed near a main shaft at about the center of the sewer. From this dynamo two overhead trolley wires, supported on insulators from the arch of the sewer, were supplied. These wires served as the lead and return conductors respectively, and were also employed to light the sewer. All the materials required for the constructional work were taken down the shaft and placed into scows.

The electrical boat was of the catamaran design, 22 feet (6m70) long and 5 feet (1m50) wide. It had a small paddle-box constructed in the middle in such a way as to prevent the paddle splashing up the sewage. The paddle wheel was driven by a 2½-horsepower motor, and this was found to be quite sufficient for hauling six of the loaded scows. A normal day's work of this electric tugboat was the conveyance of 12,000 bricks, 50 barrels of cement and 100 barrels of sand. It also was equipped with a 14-horsepower motor, coupled to a pump, which was used for emptying the cofferdam of water. Harrison P. Eddy went on to found the internationally recognized engineering firm Metcalf & Eddy.[31]

Some vessels were named *Electric* simply because the word was in vogue at the time. In northern England, the iron-side ketch-rigged trawler *Electric* was built by Earles Co. of Hull (Yard no. 332) and fitted with a 55-hp T 3-cylinder coal-fired *steam engine*. She was purchased by the Grimsby Steam Fishing Co. as a crabber, registered GY236. She was later requisitioned into the Royal Naval Fishery Service in 1917, flew the white ensign, continued commercial shipping under naval contract, and was then returned to her owners in 1919.[32]

By 1891, following the amalgamation of Woodhouse & Rawson United with Messrs. Immisch of Platts Eyott, Hampton, and using Mr. Sargeant's charging station at Eel Pie Island, a hired fleet of twenty launches were now in operation. Eight of these included EPS batteries with one Epstein launch and one Elieson Lamina. In addition, they

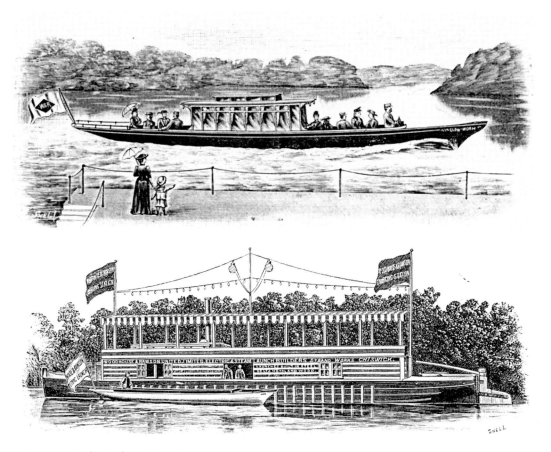

Top: In 1891 the 53-foot *Glow Worm*, built by Sargeant of Chiswick, could carry forty passengers at a speed of nine mph (Musée EDF Electropolis, Mulhouse). *Bottom:* This barge on the Upper Thames enabled launches to plug in overnight and recharge their batteries (Musée EDF Electropolis, Mulhouse).

employed two mobile floating charging stations, named *The Ohm* and *The Watt*, on regular Thames service.[33] The initial success and popularity of these launches influenced the national newspaper *Daily Mail* to suggest in a leading article that a municipally owned electric accumulator boat service should be adopted for river transport throughout London.

The innovative idea of an auxiliary electric motor for sailing boats was even conceived and patented in 1893 by Kerbey Bowen, at his successful Maidenhead yard on the Thames. In his patent application, Bowen states:

> In steam launches it is not possible to arrange the vessel so that it can be conveniently propelled by sails or by oars when the occasion may render it desirable to use such means of propulsion. The object of my invention is to provide a launch or vessel which can be used either as a launch propelled by power within itself or when the need occasionally arises by means of sails…. the driving mechanism and battery, being below the waterline, act as ballast for the launch or vessel and leave also space to accommodate a seat or seats for an oarsman or for oarsmen and also to accommodate a mast or masts for a sail or for sails and further leave sufficient space for the oarsman or for the manipulation of sails.[34]

Interestingly, an almost identical system was presented by two Frenchmen, Séguin and Jacquet, for "un bateau de chasse à propulsion par voiles ou par hélice" (= a hunting boat for propulsion by sails or screw).

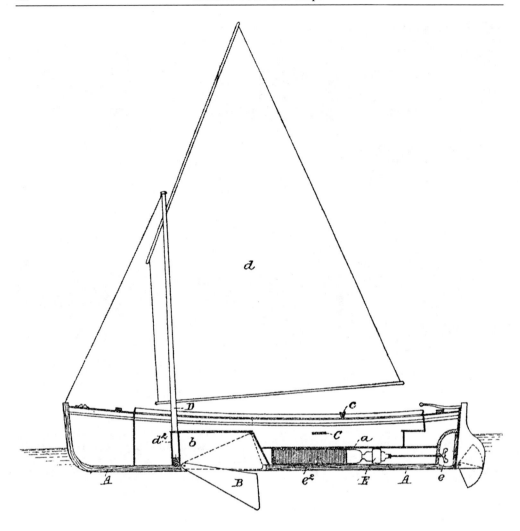

In 1893, Kerbey Bowen of Ray Mead Works in Maidenhead-on-Thames took out this innovative patent for an electric motor acting as an auxiliary to a rowboat with sails: the original motor-sailor (Patents Office).

It was on November 16, 1893, that the death occurred of Antony Reckenzaun, the visionary engineering genius behind many of the above-mentioned electric boats. He had been suffering from consumption. He was only 43 years old. He lies buried at Tower Hamlets Cemetery, Bow, East London. Ever untiring in his efforts to popularize electric traction, Reckenzaun had addressed a large number of scientific meetings and associations and wrote extensively for the technical journals on the subject he had made exclusively his own. Although he met with failures and disappointments, his successes and experiments considerably advanced battery design.

By now electric boats merited a publication of their own: *Electrical Boats and Navigation*, by Thomas Commerford Martin and Joseph Sachs, New York, 1894. This is the first American book on the subject. Its dedication: "To the memory of Anthony Reckenzaun, A pioneer whose work in electrical navigation is herein set forth, this volume on the art he strove so earnestly to perfect, is dedicated."

In June 1894, the Wörthersee Lake in Austria saw its first electrically driven motor-boat. She was called *Auguste* and was built in Great Britain by Stephens, Smith & Co. Her owner, Viennese businessman Moritz Mayer, used to spend his summers in a large lakeside residence in Pörtschach. In order to light up his residence, and also recharge *Auguste*, Herr Mayer had a steam-powered generator installed. Any surplus electricity was used to power the street lamps in Pörtschach village, so making it one of the very first electrically lit villages in the surrounding Carinthia province. *Auguste* could cruise at a speed of 7 mph (12 kph) and her batteries consisted of 40 single elements producing 240 Ah.[35]

A detailed example of how an electric launch arrived at a British stately home is found at Warwick Castle. Beside the River Avon, the castle is the family seat of Francis, the 5th Earl of Warwick, and his wife Frances Evelyn "Daisy," the longtime mistress of Albert Edward, Prince of Wales, who later became King Edward VII.[36] In 1894, the innovative Warwicks decided to have the 600-year-old grain mill on their estate converted to generate electricity for the castle. It became known as the mill and engine room. Banks of accumulators were delivered and stored across the floor of the mill room. By December 1894 the work was complete, and on the evening of December 10, no fewer than 475 Swan light bulbs were lit, to the delight of the Countess Daisy, as it coincided with her 33rd birthday. Three months later, for £8.8s., the Birmingham Telegraph Factory supplied and fitted a telephone between the castle and the engine room.

Thereafter, day after day, year after year, the mill engineer, William Bissell, a former whitesmith, reliably tended the system and kept it running. For this task he received the important salary of £1–5s a week, making him the second-highest-paid worker on the estate. He must ensure that accumulators were charged during the day, normally the morning and evening. He would have to manually control the output of the dynamos so that the electrical current remained at safe levels, and also switch between the direct output from generators to the castle. On special occasions, such as a ball or dinner party, he would be on called to ensure against any mishaps.

For centuries, pleasure craft from the castle had cruised on the River Avon and the pools that once existed downstream. "Daisy Warwick" now decided that she would like to have an electric launch, similar to the ones which she and her former lover, His Royal Highness Prince Edward, had already enjoyed on the River Thames.

A new thatched boathouse was built on River Island. It was connected by cables to the generators at the mill, enabling batteries to be recharged at electric points in the boathouse. A down payment of £207 for the launch was made to the busy yard of Kerbey Bowen Ltd. at Maidenhead on June 5, 1895. It was to be a 26-footer (8 m), with a mahogany hull sheathed in copper, a brass propeller, and its batteries housed in ebonite beneath wooden planks. It would be provided with carpets, blinds and cushions, their patterns chosen by the Countess. Wherever craftsmanship is concerned, there is always a waiting list.

The Castle Accounts Book for July 26, 1895, records a payment of £117.10s. to Fowler, Lancaster & Co., who had exhibited at the 1892 Crystal Palace Electrical Exhibition. They were employed as the castle's consulting engineers "For advice and report on Electric Lighting of the castle, supervision of installation, and fee for eventual inspection and Report on Electric launch." Three months later, Fowler, Lancaster & Co. provided special switches for launch and rewiring a boat throughout. They then installed a switchboard for changing the turbine dynamo to and from the launch battery to the castle lighting battery. The boat's batteries were delivered by rail in February 1896 so that Bissell could learn this operation in advance. The next task was to build a boathouse; a local team of laborers began by digging out the foundations and hauling timber, but it was not until October that the boathouse was ready, complete with its metal tube fencing, brick steps and thatched roof traditionally made of Ling heather.

Daisy wanted to have her boat by Queen Victoria's Diamond Jubilee Celebrations, but it was not yet ready, so she was obliged to hire a pleasure boat from Leamington. Finally, on July 1, 1898, her electric launch was loaded on a car behind a steam locomotive of the Great Western Railway Co. at Weybridge Station. Following a 100-mile journey north, it was delivered to Warwick Station for the price of £3.6s.6d. It then completed the mile from the station to the castle and the waiting river. All that was needed was a launch awning supplied by the Leyland and Birmingham Rubber Co. Ltd., an electric light for the launch, and a flexible silk cable provided by the Edison & Swan Electric Light Co.

Daisy was delighted with her boat. Its batteries were recharged almost every day through the summer months and then regularly through autumn until Christmas. On board, the Warwicks and their friends would cruise at a leisurely five miles per hour simply for pleasure or for a wildfowling trip up from Spiers Lodge in Castle Park along the local River Avon. According to the castle guestbook, those among them may have been the Duke and Duchess of Devonshire, Lady Randolph Churchill, the Duke of Marlborough, the Duke of York, Lord and Lady Curzon and Lord Roberts.[37] The boat was in operation until a flood in May 1932, when it was washed away and is supposed to have lodged in trees near the dogs' graves. It was put in the stable yard and remained there until at least 1945.[38]

During his commission as the governor general of Canada, from 1893 to 1898, John Campbell Hamilton-Gordon, 1st Marquees of Aberdeen and Temair, the Earl of Aberdeen, enjoyed electric boating on the Ottawa River. To recharge his launch, the current was taken from a 250-volt motor owned by the Standard Electric Co., a rheostat being used to reduce the current input.[39]

In Bergen, northwest Norway, an electric ferryboat fleet was about to go into operation. From the 1850s, increased industrial trade had led to a growing population in Bergen. In 1894, an engineer called Jacob Trumpy saw the need for a ferry across the harbor. Inspired by the idea of an electric ferry during his stay in Westphalia, Germany, he introduced idea of electric propulsion to the Bergen government. On May 15, 1894, Bergens Elektrische Faergeselskab (Bergen Electric Ferry Company) was formed.[40]

Despite protest from politicians that the e-ferries would take away the livelihood from ferrymen, two ferries started operation in August 1894. By the end of that year an additional six ferries were employed on different routes linking the six different districts that surrounded the port. The ferries were not given names, simply numbers such as "BEF 1" and "BEF 2." This was unlike Kristiania's (today Oslo's) first electric boat, fitted out by Norsk Elektrisk and named *Glimt* (= *Spark*).

By 1895, 1,600 passengers were commuting across Bergen Harbor on the new ferries. Each BEF measured 8 meters (26 feet) long by 2 meters (6 feet) wide, with a draft of 0.8m (2 feet). They had a displacement of 5.9 tons and could transport 18 passengers (including crew). They were open at the front and aft with only a canvas roof. This gave passengers little protection against the rainy Bergen weather.

In the Norwegian tradition of double-ender hulls, they were constructed symmetrically, with a propeller at each end, so that when leaving a station they did not have to turn about. The two propellers were mounted on a common shaft, which was coupled directly to a 3-horsepower electric motor with a weight of 300 kg placed in the center under the planking. The Hagen batteries were distributed under the seats and weighed 1400 kg (3087 lb). Their capacity was of 20,000 watts-hours and the speed obtained with an output of 2300 watts was 10 kph, a speed sufficient in a crowded fishing port like that of Bergen. One of these eight boats left every 5 minutes from 7 o'clock in the morning until 9:30 in the evening, carrying out a daily course of 40 sea miles and transporting an average of 1800 passengers.

During the night, placed in a special station at Bradbenken in Vagen, the BEFs did their main battery recharge with the aid of a 30-horsepower dynamo. They could also receive a 4-minute "topping up" between trips. During 1896, the BEF fleet transported a total of 486,000 passengers, or 40,500 per month.[41]

Following Trouvé's initial invention of an outboard or detachable electric motor in 1881, several Americans had each tried out their version. American William Woodnut Griscom was first in 1882. Two years later another Philadelphian, F.A. LaRoche, developed an aluminum battery-powered electric motor that was never produced beyond the construction of the model. Samuel H. Jones, Newark, New Jersey, in 1885, designed one that was never was built. In 1892, F.G. Curtis of New York City designed an electric outboard motor that never reached the production stage.[42]

The first outboard motor, electric or gasoline powered, to be made on a production basis was Frank Allen's "Electric Oar" in 1895. Allen's New York City–based firm made enough of a splash to plant the seed for America's lucrative outboard motor industry. In this they were helped by the recently launched magazine *Field & Stream*. Their product featured an electric power plant that drove a propeller via a flexible bronze shaft through a long, angled tube. It weighed 35 pounds (15 kg). Adapting a patent by the late Anthony Reckenzaun, it could be thrown from forward into reverse and back (U.S. Patent No. 432,561). Associated batteries could add more than 250 pounds (113 kg) and increase the range. Allen motors were marketed through 1899. As the catalogue reads: "Among the advantages presented by electricity as an engine for small craft, one of those which will certainly be most appreciated when the sources of electricity will be sufficiently available to popularize its use, will be the ease of fixing and taking off devices which can be made completely independent of the boat which they are driving along."

During this time, the increase of the electric boating business in England had been progressing well, with several Thameside yards in regular production: the Immisch Electric Launch Co.; the Thames Valley Launch Company; the Upper Thames Electric Launch Co; Woodhouse & Rawson United Ltd; Saunders Patent Launch Building Syndicate; Bonds of Maidenhead; and Kerbey Bowen & Co. During 1897 alone, the Thames Valley Launch Company supplied sixteen launches at prices ranging from £500 to £2,000, in all cases equipped with EPS batteries. Two of these—*Water Nymph* and *Venus*—were sent out to Ceylon (today's Sri Lanka) to serve as ferries in Colombo between Pettah Station and Slave Island.[43]

In 1897, the Clayton Foundry Company was commissioned by Lever Brothers of Port Sunlight, soap makers, to supply two 40-hp electric motors to power a barge that would ferry people from Wirral across the River Mersey. In Leeds, Northern England, at Roundhay Park, from 1899, a 70-ft (21 m) electric teak and oak passenger boat, named the *Mary Gordon* after the Lady Mayoress of Leeds who launched her, began to give rides

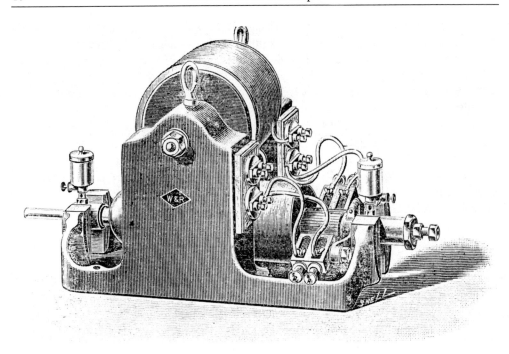

The Woodhouse and Rawson engine was also exported (Musée EDF Electropolis, Mulhouse).

to 75 adults or 120 children up and down Waterloo Lake.[44] She was built by Sargeant of Eel Pie Island then transported up to Roundhay Park on the back of a steam lorry.[45]

The English Lake District had a number of electric launches for hire, such as the Lodore and Derwentwater Hotels' two electric launches, *Iris* and *May Queen*, carrying 50 and 84 passengers, respectively. They were built in Burmese teak by T.W. Hayton of Bowness-on-Windermere and were hauled the 20 miles to Derwentwater, including the 780-ft-high (238 m) Dunmail Rise, by teams of horses. The Irish and Scottish lochs followed suit.[46] Along the coast of the English Channel coast, another 6 charging stations were set up between Southampton and Torquay.

The Imperial Russian Navy's electric seagoing launch, constructed by the Vril Launch company, was powered by two 3.7 kW motors and 42 Fauré-King accumulators. This guaranteed it a speed of 7 knots for four hours, or 4.5 knots for ten hours.[47]

In June 1899, races for autoboats were organized by the Hélice Club de France (French Propeller Club) at Argenteuil on the Seine, with twenty-three participants (14 gasoline, 7 steam, 1 naphtha, but only 1 electric). The 6m50 (21 ft) *Riquiqui* of Monsieur Oudin, built by Luce of Argenteuil, was propelled by a 5-hp electric motor and batteries from the Société Anonyme des Voitures Electriques and batteries système BGS.[48]

This was the golden age of silent battery-boating, largely thanks to the managerial genius of people like Henry R. Sutphen, a minister's son from Morristown, New Jersey, and an electrician by trade. Sutphen arranged for Elco's first public showroom to be located next to Grand Central Palace in New York, and to have a removable wall that allowed visitors to the Motorboat Show to walk into the discretion of the Elco showroom. He advertised heavily in the boating magazines: "*Electric Launches—Safe, Reliable, Noiseless. 65 to 100 miles on one charge. The Ideal Launch.*" But he knew that his company's reputation for service and discretion was spread by word of mouth among the very

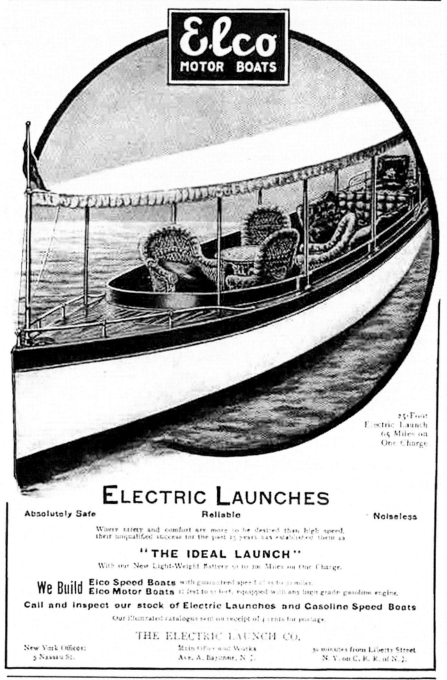

Elco was well marketed as is shown by this advertisement (courtesy Tom Hesselink).

wealthy. Well-heeled customers asked for custom work, and they got it. Many Elco customers put their prized possessions in winter storage at the Elco yard in Bayonne, New Jersey, where full winterizing and other services were available.[49]

In December 1900, the magazine *The Rudder* published a report about *Lutuhizi*, a 36-ft electric launch owned by wealthy banker Walther Luttgen Esq. of New York. The boat had been used chiefly about the Columbia Yacht Club, of which her owner was then commodore. He used this launch for club events including electric launch racing, while occasionally making runs to Linden on the Raritan. It had enough battery capacity to cruise all day at 6 knots (7 mph) and could be customized to sleep two or four persons: "The difficulties of re-charging, which have formerly been the greatest drawback to the general use of these boats, are now reduced to a minimum by the portable charging outfits, which can be obtained at a nominal expense. Of course, where the base of operation is near some power house or electric light station it is a simple matter to have a line extended to some dock, where the boat may lie while recharging. As a motive power it is almost perfect, as the machinery is all concealed under the boat's floor, and is noiseless and without vibration. This boat was built by the Electric Launch Company of Bayonne City, New Jersey."[50]

In 1902 Elco issued a catalog of "Launches and Yachts," with a choice of fifteen models ranging from an 18-ft electric fishing boat (price $775) to a 65-ft (19 m) electric cabin yacht (price $13,000), including dayboats, cabin launches, passenger launches, and yacht tenders. By 1903, over 250 electric launches had been built by the yard.[51]

They became were popular at summer resorts such New York's Thousand Islands, where many business magnates owned summer homes. Customers included Mrs. Marguerite Westinghouse, Baron Nathaniel de Rothschild and John Jacob "Jack Ass" Astor IV. Astor, a millionaire, had made electricity a study and spent hundreds of thousands of dollars to prefect his experiments in replacing steam with electricity. During 1893, Astor put into commission an electric launch called the *Corcyra* (named after the Ionian island), built in accordance with his designs, and those of Edison-trained Jacob Chester Chamberlain, whom he consulted. This cost him $3,000. She was so immediately successful that her lines and general plan were adopted by the American and Russian naval authorities.[52]

From the 36-ft (11 m) *Corcrya*, Astor progressed to the 47-ft (14 m) *Progresso*, Elco Hull n°63, capable of 8 to 12 mph (13 to 20 kmh), and the 72-ft (22 m) *Utopia*. The latter, a tender to his steam yacht *Nourmahal*, was designed from the owner's plans by Charles D. Mosher, and built by Ayers at Nyack. She was described as "the largest privately-owned electric launch in the world" with two masts and two centerboards. Her two motors each developed around 25 hp, supplied by 480 cells of battery to give her a projected 14 hours' autonomy. The Samuel batteries were experimental in that no grids were used, nor was any lead nucleus present. *Utopia* was luxuriously fitted out like a miniature *Titanic*. Built in the best mahogany, teak and oak, with 46 windows, she had 5 staterooms, 2 bathrooms, an enclosed galley and an entrance lobby on the port side.[53] She cost Astor a staggering $350,000 (unadjusted).

Then there was also an Elco 55-ft (16m80) twin-screw cabin yacht capable of running 125 miles on one charge of its storage batteries![54]

Other American clients included Admiral of the U.S. Navy George Dewey, who named his 25-footer *Rambler*.[55] Industrialist William H. Dunwoody of New Brighton, Minnesota, whose wealth came from the flour mills of Minneapolis ("Mill City"), called his Elco *Pennhurst* after his Elizabethan-style brick mansion. George R. Bidwell, a U.S. Customs inspector for the port of New York, owned the 42-ft *Varick,* named after the town in Seneca County.

Isaac Seligman, the son of German-American banking giant Joseph Seligman, was attending Columbia College when his crew won the university eight-oar college race on Saratoga Lake in 1874. Three years later, his family was excluded from one of Saratoga's most prestigious hotels, the Grand Union. The ensuing national scandal led to Seligman's desire (and that of many of Jews) to own his own holiday resort. Sekon Lodge and Fish Rock Camp on Upper Saranac Lake, New York, was built in 1893 for the Seligman family. Isaac also acquired one of the Columbia Exposition fleet to enjoy cruising along Lake Saratoga. For the rest of his life, "Izzy" Seligman continued to campaign against anti–Semitism in New York City, a trustee of the Temple Emanu-El, the Hebrew Orphan Asylum, and the United Hebrew Charities.

Abraham G. Mills, president of the Association for the Protection of the Adirondacks, acquired an Elco for the Adirondack League Club's estate around Honnedaga Lake, New York. Called *Honnedaga,* this club launch was used to take members from one lodge to the other 25 miles down Lake Honnedaga. Members having camps around the lake who desired the club launch to deliver mail or stop for any purpose at their respective camp sites had to provide a permanent or floating dock, so located with respect to navigation that landings could be made without necessitating any change in the general direction of the club launch course. Any other type of powered launch was strictly forbidden.

M.C.D. Borden of Fall River, Massachusetts, headed the American Printing Company, the largest cloth-printing company in the world, earning him the nickname "the Calico King." It seemed fitting that Borden, a member of the Seawanhaka Corinthian Yacht Club with a deluxe steam yacht called *Sovereign,* should enjoy his 36-ft Elco.

In 1903, the 32-ft (9 m) Elco *Wenona* was purchased second-hand by Pastor Ernest M. Stires, who, owning a Christian camp at picturesque Shelving Rock Falls, used her to preach the Word of God. Stires later became third bishop of the Episcopal Diocese of Long Island.

This rare photograph shows an electric launch in the process of installation—each member, wearing a protective apron, shows a separate component (courtesy Tom Hesselink).

One 36-footer was shipped out for use by Eduardo Ribeiro, rubber baron and governor of Manaus, Brazil, in the middle of the Amazon rain forest. Ribeiro was transforming his town in to the "Paris of the Tropics" by installing electricity, street lighting, a telephone exchange, streetcars, and even an opera house, the latter constructed with bricks brought from Europe, French glass and Italian marble.

Not all were happy stories. Hugh Tevis, a young San Francisco millionaire, had acquired a 42-ft (12m80) Elco for his hacienda, Casa de Las Olas, on a single estate that stretched 1,000 feet along Monterey Bay. He had built the ranch in 1901 as a wedding present for his bride, Cornelia Baxter. The property had a pier and ship launch. Sadly, before he could fully enjoy the estate and the launch, Tevis died at Yokohama, Japan, of appendicitis while on his honeymoon.[56]

The batteries of most of these launches had hitherto been recharged by an independent steam-powered generator, but with the setting up of electricity-generating power stations for domestic lighting such as the one at Newport, Rhode Island, things began to change.

Grand Duke Alexander of Russia, attending a naval review in New York in 1893, wanted an Elco so badly he insisted on buying the one already ordered by the captain of the newly launched armored cruiser USS *New York*, who then had to wait for a new one. When the Grand Duke's cousin, Tsar Nicholas II, saw Alexander's Elco, he liked it so much he bought one too and ended up commanding three electric launches in succession. His Imperial Highness's American Elco-built launch had been originally ordered in 1898 by the Naval Attaché of the Russian Embassy, and subsequent battery plate renewal orders to the EPS Company indicate use over a considerable period. His last was a 37-ft (11 m) electric launch, destined for use aboard his Imperial yacht *Polar Star*. Imperial orders required that its oak hull be sheathed in brass. Velvet carpets in the cockpit were required to soothe Romanov feet, and no royal buttock could sit in a wicker chair that wasn't first upholstered in Russian leather cushions. It was unthinkable for a peasant to share the Tsar's cockpit, so two small circular wells were installed fore and aft for the two crewmen aboard the gig.

In 1902, the brilliant Hungarian-born stage manager Imre Kiralfy presented the exhibition "Paris in London" at Earls Court, London. In the official guide and catalogue he writes:

> Facing us in wide extent are the rippling waters of the lake, cool, translucent and refreshing. Little wonder that the luxurious *motor launches*, which skim hither and thither, are a source of delight to thousands of passengers, young and old. Every visitor to Paris is impressed with the beauty, as well as utility, of the little boats on the Seine, which, usually crowded with passengers, glide to and fro past the quays in constant succession. The antiquated and clumsy craft which at times do duty on our own great water-way, the Thames, emerge badly from a comparison. As M. Zola would say, they are "hors concours," not in the complimentary sense.
>
>   Large as it is, the Lake at Earl's Court would hardly accommodate boats of the dimensions of the "Bateaux Parisiens." But in point of comfort, speed and elegance, the vessels which the Exhibition authorities have put into commission may fairly claim to vie, on a small scale, with their exemplars on the Seine. Hence, no doubt, the increasing popularity of the little pleasure voyages round the lake. In this way may the numerous nooks and fairy-like recesses of the charming stretch of water be explored, the delights of boating and sightseeing being sufficiently combined.[57]

Kiralfy was referring to "Les Libellules," the fleet of partially enclosed electric passenger boats operated on the Seine since 1897 by La Compagnie Générale des Bateaux Parisiens of 125 Avenue de Versailles, Paris. During the 1900 Paris Universal Exhibition, these boats are reported to have ferried 40,000 passengers.

In 1904, the title of "the largest electric passenger boat in the world" was taken with Will Sargeant's design and building of the 93-ft (28.4 m) *Victory*; she was licensed to carry 350 passengers above Westminster Bridge.[58]

Electric cruising was often enjoyed by the Royal Family. The 45-ft (14 m) teak-hulled *The Angler* was the flagship of Ned Andrew's electric hirefleet. In June 1904, His Majesty King Edward VII and Queen Alexandra boarded *The Angler* from the king's boathouse at Windsor and visited the Grenfells, sportsman William Henry Grenfell and his wife Ettie, at Taplow Court for afternoon tea. In 1905, Grenfell was raised to the peerage as Baron Desborough, of Taplow in the County of Buckinghamshire.[59]

An electric pinnace was also used by their Royal Highnesses for the royal yacht, HMY *Victoria and Albert*.[60]

Top: This elegant poster advertising an electric passenger launch service named Les Libellules électriques (the electric dragonflies) was designed by F. Hugo d'Alési for the Compagnie Générale des Bateaux Parisiens (© Bibliothèque Forney/Roger-Viollet). *Bottom:* His Majesty King Edward VII, Queen Alexandra and the Royal circle enjoyed many electric cruises from Windsor Castle (author's collection).

Sometimes the Americans came to Great Britain. In 1907, George A. Kessler, the American millionaire, spent £30,000 on remodeling "Riverside House" at Bourne End on the Thames, renaming it "New York Lodge." He installed electric lighting with 3,000 lamps, not only in the house, but among the trees and shrubs along the riverside, the whole being powered by a dynamo driven by a 65 hp engine. Carr's electric cabin launch complemented the house. Built by Bond of Maidenhead, she was named *Charlotte* after Kessler's attractive wife. At one Cookham Regatta, with the Maharajah and Prince Gackwar of Baroda as the Kesslers' guest, *Charlotte* was illuminated all over and decorated with colored electric lights in the form of the Star of India.[61]

For lesser mortals, the Submerged Electric Motor of Menomonie, Wisconsin, was a less expensive option. Its inventor, Tracey B. Hatch of Chicago, had organized a small group of investors to series produce his "electrical propelling mechanism" (U.S. Patent 650558) in a converted barn.[62] By 1900 the plant was producing its "electric portable propellers," advertised as "auxiliary power for sailboats and houseboats." Two 100-amp, six-volt batteries powered the unit, which featured a motor housed in a sealed capsule that also served as the rudder and supported the nine-inch, two-blade propeller. The advantage of positioning the motor beneath the water was that the cooling water prevented overheating.

Since the motor, rudder, and propeller were all submerged, the company pointed out that it "saves room in the boat...." What the advertisement failed to mention was that there was quite a need to save "room in the boat," since an operator needed the space to store the batteries. There was enough power in the motor to "propel a small boat with two men aboard at three mph for four hours." If one wished to stay out on the water longer than that, it meant more batteries. Boats, awnings, batteries, and rechargers were all sold by Submerged Electric. In 1907, Thomas Thorsen, the company engineer, patented a modification to the motor to include a tiller arm (U.S. Patent 871459):

> Mr. McLachlan, in England, has patented a similar device and which appears extremely practical. The firm Cadiot et Cié has become the French dealer for this patent and offers to make a series of boats powered by this engine available to the public, during the Universal Exposition of 1900, as much on the Seine as on Lake Daumesnil at Vincennes. Above all, for the test, where one will be able to renew the electricity of the accumulators these boats will be usable.
>
> This rudder-motor weighs only 15 kg (33 lb.), and develops more than 1 horsepower. It is wound for a tension of 40 volts and a current of 12 amps, and drives a propeller at 600 rpm.
>
> Through the help of the rudder, supple conductors link the motor to the little box of accumulators which is placed in the boat: a switch placed on the tiller enables establishing at will the connections and to go ahead or astern, slowly or at a great speed. Transmission is by toothed gearwheel (preferably by chain) and to avoid the problem of weeds and mud, etc., the entire movement is encased in an envelope that shelters the engine, transmission and gears.
>
> The battery of accumulators includes 15 to 20 elements, depending on the size of the boat and these are in enclosed in three or four wooden boxes of teak fitted with leather handles for ease of handling. Each of these boxes measures 38cm by 18cm and the weight of the three boxes containing 15 elements is less than 68 kg (150 lb.). This battery enables autonomy of five hours at full speed, that is 10 kph. (6 mph), or a total of 50 km (30 miles), sufficient in most cases. On the Thames, where this type of boat has obtained a great success, one finds enough electricity stations for recharging the battery at will and so extending the cruise. We hope that soon the same will be said for the Seine and for our main waterways.
>
> The trials of M. McLachlan carried out at Cowes have proved that this engine is capable of pushing a boat 4m85 (15 ft.) long by 1m55 (5 ft.) beam, with a displacement of 91 cm (36 in.) at the stern and carrying six people at a speed of (10 kph) 6 mph.[63]

From 1874, the lake and the land surrounding Silver Lake became a popular amusement park in the Akron area in Ohio. In the 1890s the 36-ft 25 pax *Magnolia* regularly took visitors on a tour of the lake. In 1902, it was decided to landscape Silver Lake with an island. Several times the *Magnolia* had narrowly avoided running aground on a sand bar, about 70 feet by 100 feet and just two feet under water and near the center of the lake. To convert the sand bar into the island, when pilings were dug for the construction of the island, it was discovered that the sand bar was chiefly solid blue clay. Oxen were used during that winter to haul old wooden railroad ties to the edge of the lake. These were then loaded onto *Magnolia* and taken out to the sand bar. The logs were then arranged in an irregular pattern and covered with topsoil and plants, again taken out on the *Magnolia*, so the island would look as if it were a part of nature and not something man-made.[64] One wonders whether among the islet's plants were some magnolia bushes!

Johann Albert Tribelhorn, an electric automobile and truck manufacturer, was based at Feldbach, a village near Rapperswil, Switzerland, located on the north bank of the lake of Zurich. It was perhaps inevitable that he also adapted the technology to boats. Working with lakeside boatyards such as Johann Faul of Wollishofen and Treichler in Kilchberg, in 1902, Elektromobilfirma Tribelhorn sold the *Schwan*, an electric cabin boat, to Frau Kommerzienrath Eduard Oehler. It was the first of 26 boats fitted out by Tribelhorn for clients such as G. Dust Syz from Zollikon, J. Mark Walder from Küsnacht, engineer Herrmann from Rapperswil, Councillor Glättli from Küsnacht, and Arthur Wiskemann from Zurich. The cabin of one 20 pax 10 meter boat was even fitted with stained glass windows.[65]

In 1906, French journalist Georges Dary wrote:

> There are now a good number of electric yachts with suitable names: the *Volta*, the *Eclair*. The French Navy also has its electric boat since 1891.[66] Also the Spanish Navy. Let us mention the *Planté*—the speedboat of the Sultan of Koetei (Borneo). Built at the boatyard of L. Smit & Zoon, at Kinderdijk, Rotterdam, Holland and with sister ships in varying types already in service somewhat everywhere such as the *Koningin Wilhelmina*, the *Electronaus*, the *Triphasé*, the *Nelly*, and the *Politic* (used by the Rotterdam Police).
>
> Smit and Zoon's boat is 16 meters (53 feet) long, equipped with 80 Tudor batteries in two groups with a capacity of 350 amps. There is a manipulator which can take six positions and inverter switch enabling grouping the batteries in parallel or in series. But successively placed the manipulator in its various notches, one can group the coils in different ways thus obtaining a variety in speed and in current consumption. Maximum speed of the *Planté* is 10 knots/normal speed 8 knots, average speed can be maintained for 3 to 4 hours.[67]

L. Smit & Zoon of Kinderdijk produced a catalogue of their range of electric launches which ran to 23 pages as it was in in four languages, in French, English, German and Dutch. Ten versions were offered, ranging in overall length from 8 to 17 meters (26 to 56 feet), with a top speed of between 12 and 19 kph (7 to 11 mph) and a cruising range of 100 km (60 miles). The catalogue reads: "The voltage of our launches is the same as the voltage of electric light plants viz 150 or 75 volts. This is done in order to make it easier to get the battery loaded."[68]

The Franco-British Exhibition of 1908 attracted 8 million visitors and celebrated the *Entente Cordiale* signed in 1904 by the United Kingdom and France. Visiting "The White City," Shepherds Bush, London, visitors could ride on the swan boats or electric launches on the artificial lagoon for 6d, from the Court of Honor and around the lagoons seeing many of the fine buildings including the "Senegalese village."

The luxury yacht *Germania*, built for the Krupp family in Kiel, was equipped with Siemens engines and batteries by the Akkumulatorenfabrik AG in Berlin. The same company had fitted out an electric barge the *Tre Kronor* (Swedish *Three Crowns*).

L. Smit & Zoon at Kinderdijk, Rotterdam, Holland, built a range of electric launches, including the *Koningin Wilhelmina,* **the** *Electronaus,* **the** *Triphasé,* **the** *Nelly,* **and the** *Politic* **(used by the Rotterdam police). They had a speed of 12 to 19 km/h (7 to 11 mph) and a cruising range of 100 km (60 miles) (from Georges Dary,** *A travers l'éléctricité).*

On the Königsee lake, in Bavaria, near the Austrian border, electric boats first appeared due to the railroad, which was completed in 1909. Siemens had not only supplied the trains, it also supplied the technology for the Gartenau power plant near Berchtesgaden. In 1909 the decision to equip the boats with electric drives was not prompted by environmental considerations. Instead, Prince-Regent Leopold, who ruled Bavaria at the time, feared that the noise created by combustion engines would scare off wildlife in his hunting grounds alongside the lake. Therefore he was very much in favor of procuring electric boats that would travel noiselessly on the lake. The first of the fleet was called *Akkumulator,* a 38-passenger mahogany-hulled electric boat supplied by the Siemens-Schuckert plants. Its 12 batteries gave it an operating range of 100 km (60 miles). It was followed by the electric ferry boat *Godesberg.*[69]

Electric boats did not only benefit the wealthy. From 1908 to 1912, the Parks and Cemeteries Committee of the Northern English city of Manchester gave work to some 2,333 unemployed men using only shovels and hand-pulled trucks to excavate, line and fill an 11¼ acre boating lake at Heaton Park. From its official opening in March 1913, one hundred boats were hired out while two electric launches took people around the lake for 2d each.[70]

Could an electric boat be remote-controlled? In 1898, watched by thousands of spectators, Croatian inventor Nikola Tesla had demonstrated the application of Herzian waves when he radio-controlled his 4-ft (1m20) "teleautomaton" model electric boat up and down a pond at the recently completed Madison Square Garden, New York, during an electrical exhibition. Tesla was able to control the boat's motor, sending it zipping around the pond seemingly under its own control. He even installed lights on it he could blink at a distance from his control box. Many observers, unfamiliar with radio waves, thought that the device must have a brain of its own or that somehow Tesla was controlling it with his mind. When it was first shown "it created a sensation such as no other invention of mine has ever produced," Tesla would later write. He had taken out U.S. and UK patents for it.[71]

Siemens and Halske's test boat *Akkumulator* on the Spree River, near Berlin (Siemens Archives).

Twelve years later, in 1910, an experiment was carried out with a full-scale boat on Dutzendteich Lake near Nuremberg, Germany. Christoph Wirth, an electro physicist, having patented a wireless-controlled current distributor, decided to test it out in a boat. Together with the manufacturer Beck and a merchant named Knauss, Wirth set up the demonstration of a 33-ft (10 m) boat called the *Prinz Ludwig* with a 3 kW motor and an accumulator battery of 80 volts and 300 ampere-hours. The experiment began with the pilotless boat positioned out in the center of the lake in front of the clubhouse of the Kaiserliche Marine (=Imperial German Admiralty). At the given signal, a gunshot, the *Prinz Ludwig* silently accelerated to a speed of 10 mph (16 kmh). It was then made to turn right or left or to stop completely and start again by the controlling operator in obedience to the requests from members of the club. Each order was executed within from one to five seconds, and signal lights flashed back the receipt of the impulses. The maneuvers were continued for several hours. In the weeks that followed, "das Geisterschiff" (= "The Phantom Ship") attracted many spectators—military, scientific, and the simply curious—who paid a small sum for admission to the immediate neighborhood of the operator on the bank.

In 1912 a boat 50 feet (15 m) in length was later exhibited in Berlin, again at the invitation of the Kaiserliche Marine Club. An antenna of four wires was stretched between the cupola of the Kaiser Pavilion and the restaurant on the shore of the Wannsee. The transmitting apparatus that was installed at the restaurant was of the induction coil type, and was of about 100 watts capacity. The various operations performed on the boat were accomplished by sending impulses by means of a Morse key. The boat was equipped with an antenna of four wires about 15 feet (4m50) high, a radio receiver capable of adjustment to different wavelengths from the transmitter, a distributor or selector, electric steering apparatus, signal guns, lights, and fireworks apparatus. The tuning of the apparatus could be altered by sending a long signal; this was for the purpose of evading interference. The implications of such a device for controlling the direction of a torpedo were not to be ignored.[72]

Meanwhile on the backwaters of the Upper Thames, one British engineer had come up with an ingenious "hybrid" solution of combining *several* power sources into one hull. His name was John Delmar-Morgan.[73]

Returning from the Boer War in South Africa, Delmar-Morgan had specialized as an engineer in electric DC traction systems. Having trained at the City and Guilds in London, he served a three-year apprenticeship with J.H. Holmes & Co. Ltd., electrical motor manufacturers at Hebburn, Newcastle-on-Tyne. Here he learned about armature and magnet winding, instrument-making and switchboard work. He also gained experience "in the erection of engines and dynamos, switchboards, lamps, cables and various details of electric light installations both on board steamships and in buildings such as factories, mills, shops and private houses." In 1904, he was working with Drake & Gorham Ltd., noted electrical engineers of Glasgow.

By this time Delmar-Morgan was courting Miss Dorothy Locker-Lampson, whose family seat since 1848 had been Rowfant House, Crawley, West Sussex, while they also had a property at Newhaven Court, Cromer. And during this courtship which led to their marriage, Jack met up with two other gentlemen: Colonel Greville Duff, and Dorothy's 25-year-old barrister brother by name of Oliver Stillingfleet Locker-Lampson.

Motor vehicles were just coming into fashion and the three of them decided to set up "Duff, Morgan & Vermont Ltd., Motor Car Agents & Electrical Engineers and Exporters." Locker-Lampson preferred to use the U.S. State of Vermont, where the Lampson branch of his family had estates. The company was based at the Victoria Garage, Saint Stephen's Street, Norwich, although it would also have offices at Premier House, N°48 Dover Street, in London's fashionable Piccadilly (phone 401, 2 lines).

Of course Jack Delmar-Morgan's electric engineering experience proved invaluable to such an enterprise. Indeed, by April 1909 in the classified advertisements index of *The Autocar*, the company was offering "Cars for Hire. Repairs. All tyres stocked Gaulois, Continental, Michelin. Open always."

One of the first things Jack did when he had married Dorothy was to acquire one of the newfangled motor launches, a beaver-tailed, white-hulled 30-footer (9 m). Dorothy was a keen horse-rider and in 1901 had ridden a fine Arab mare by name of "Mansura." The new motor launch was also christened *Mansura,* and in 1911 they shipped her to Holland for an extended, but somewhat Spartan cruise on the canals of Northern Europe.

Duff, Morgan & Vermont, with Jack as managing director, had built up a successful trade in the fledgling motor business. That year, the company had "for immediate delivery, the following new 1911 cars: Alldays, Peugeot, Hupmobile, Swift, Leon Boller, Opel and Adler." Jack's partner and brother-in-law Oliver had become MP for North Huntingdonshire. Continuing his interest in motorboating, Jack decided to have a second *Mansura* built. The lines of this 33-ft lugger were drawn out by Linton Chorley Hope & Co., "Specialists in Motorboats." She was to be built at the yard run by James C. Taylor and William

B. Bates on the River Thames at Chertsey Wharf in Surrey. Her hull was mahogany-planked with white Kauri-pine decking. Her roomy watertight cockpit and cabin were externally painted in a "raven blue" livery.

But perhaps most fascinating and unique of all was the fact that *Mansura* was designed to run: under gasoline power alone; electric power alone; sail alone (ketch rigged); gasoline and sail; electric and sail. The highly innovative design of this "auxiliary" was worked out by none other than Jack, using what was available at the time.

The gasoline unit was a V8 aero-unit built by ENV. This was designed by a Mr. Rath in England and built at Courbevoie in France, and the name came from the fact that it was "en V," French for its configuration. It had been used by the legendary Louis Blériot, the first man to cross the English Channel in a monoplane. It was one of the best engines available and among its innovations were the electro-deposited copper water-jackets on cast-iron cylinders, two valves per cylinder driven from a camshaft. To this Jack added a Zenith carburetor. For the unit developing 60 hp at 1200 rpm but geared down, Jack would have paid £450. A dynamo that charged the 2 tons of lead-acid batteries was chain-driven from the propshaft (a Thornycroft prop). Should the main engine be temporarily put out of action, the clutch was thrown out of gear and the dynamo could be used as a reversible electric motor, obtaining its current from the batteries. The accumulators replaced the lead normally used to ballast such a boat.

With this configuration, the electric engine running in either direction made a mechanical reverse gear unnecessary. At a time when nearly all gasoline-engined transport was started using a crank handle, the engine could be started electrically.

As if this were not enough, Jack Delmar-Morgan equipped *Mansura* not only with electric lighting, electric fans and bilge pumps, but in her cabin could be found constant hot water, an electric cooking stove and electric kettle, electric frying pan and saucepan. No other cabin cruiser in 1912 had such luxuries!

The hybrid cruising adventures of *Mansura* were later collated into a book by Jack's son Edward. A very limited edition of this book for family and friends was printed in 1935 by the Jimbo Printing Service of Yokohama in Japan.[74] The book's introduction is enchanting, as if recounted by the boat's carved tiller head: "The Skipper's wife conceived the idea, one of her trained carvers carried it out, and so out of a piece of oak my head and mane appeared. I took my place in the ship to steer her on many voyages, and now with wooden brain I will recount what I have seen and done."

Following her launch in May 1912, *Mansura* showed what she could do: "Speed under petrol power: 9 knots. Speed under electric power 5 knots for six to seven hours, 8 knots for 3 hours. Top speed obtained by running electric and petrol together was 11 knots. Cruising electric—easy to control, complete silence and wonderful maneuverability. Weak points: considerable weight and bulk of machinery, great initial expense and keeping electric apparatus functioning properly in salt-laden air."[75]

In 1913, flying the burgee of the Royal Thames Yacht Club, *Mansura* crossed to Boulogne and on to Dieppe, running her gasoline engine offshore and cruising in and out of harbors "silently."

War declared, Winston Churchill, then First Lord of the Admiralty and a frequent visitor to the Locker-Lampson family home of Newhaven Court in Cromer, was secretly encouraged by "Vermont" to develop both tanks and armored cars for offensive work. When a Royal Naval Air Service Armored Car Division was formed, its HQ was none other than 48 Dover Street, the same address as Duff, Morgan and "Vermont"! And while

Top: Jack Delmar-Morgan pilots his hybrid-electric cabin cruiser *Mansura* on the Thames at Putney in 1911. *Mansura* was designed to run under petrol power alone; electric power alone; sail alone (ketch rigged); petrol and sail; or electric and sail (courtesy Julian Delmar-Morgan). *Bottom:* *Mansura* moored, 1911 (courtesy Julian Delmar-Morgan).

much of the basic design work for these cars was undertaken by Royal Naval Air Service staff, probably at their depot in Barlby Road near Wormwood Scrubs (also the location of the Talbot car works), it was the staff at D, M & V who were primarily engaged in converting the designs into working drawings and providing draftsmen. Among those marques converted—Austin, Rolls-Royce, Pierce-Arrow, Ford and Springfield.

Mansura became part of the Motor Boat Reserve. As ML 41 she was painted gray, given a White Ensign flag, and a searchlight, and with a light rifle as her sole armament was sent to HMS *Thames* at Harwich, where she was used by "Major Jack" for carrying dispatches and code books for the Harwich Force. HMS *Thames* acted as the depot ship for the 5th Submarine Flotilla, made up of C class submarines fitted with a 16-cylinder Wolseley gasoline engine made by Vickers and called the Vickers engine, developing 600 bhp at 400rev/min. As Jack wrote to a friend, "I examined the engines and electrical gear of a submarine the other day. It is exactly like Mansura's arrangement on a large scale."

So far *Mansura's* machinery remained unaltered and must have driven the boat many thousands of miles. "On one occasion she made a passage of 25 miles (40 km) on battery power alone. The battery was only half discharged on arrival and the speed averaged 6 knots. It was not unusual for her to do a 15-hour day in any weather and at any time; her ease of control and silence were frequently commented on by admirals and dockyard hands."

Following the Armistice, Jack decided to gut his unique lugger of her original equipment and to make new designs for a lighter, more compact installation. These incorporated a 6 hp two-cylinder two-stroke Watermota inboard engine and dynamo as auxiliary, and a set of Edison batteries.

Neither the Watermota nor the Edison units proved up to the task. So from September 1924 to August 1925, working in London's Grosvenor Canal, Jack again gutted the machinery, replacing the old ENV with an American-built 4-cylinder Redwing 18–24 hp "Thorobred" and with a 10 hp Aster coupled to a suitable dynamo as auxiliary. He also built a new wheelhouse. The electric control system was identical to that used on a London tram. *Mansura's* skipper was determined to prove that the gasoline-electric hybrid was viable, but at times it seemed as if he were a prophet crying in the wilderness. The new approach seemed to work. During the late 1920s and 1930s, *Mansura* not only cruised around the British coast, she crossed over to the Scilly Isles, the Channel Islands, and even across to Holland. To quote from a letter written from Yarmouth, Isle of Wight, on August 9, 1937: "It was necessary to change Mansura's berth, so I got underway electrically and came up to the other side of Mr Rynd's Sea Horse."

In 1948, *Mansura* left the Delmar-Morgan family, sold to a Dutchman called Hausmann, who took out her electric machinery and had her made into a conventional internal combustion–engined cruiser. Of course, the horse's head tiller had been removed by the family. In his book *Small Craft Engines and Equipment*, published by Adlard Coles in 1963, Jack's son Edward writes: "So for the next generation of yachtsmen I put forward the hope that they too will have this type of propulsion but naturally without as in the case of Mansura's 2 tons of lead accumulators!" Indeed, *Mansura's* hybrid arrangement had already been scaled up to an oceanic scale, in the form of the turbo-electric ship.[76]

THREE

The Turboelectric Ship
(1920–1960)

The most important cause behind the decline of the quiet battery-electric launch was the development and ease of maintenance of the marine oil engine. Gottlieb Daimler's engine of 1888 was soon being applied to almost every type of "autoboat," from lifeboats, fishing trawlers and drifters, to tugs, runabouts, cabin cruisers and canal boats. This in turn led to the popular adoption of Dr. Rudolf Diesel's rational heat engine, once it had been improved to run at greater speeds, and of Ole Evinrude's lightweight rowboat gasoline motor, which was bolted onto the transom of countless small craft. Such internal combustion units had the advantage that they could be refueled swiftly and gave a greater autonomy, so their users were prepared to put up with the noise and fumes. Pure lead-acid battery technology was simply unable to provide the compact energy density required for comparable speed and long range.[1]

Those who had formerly applied their innovative minds to electric propulsion had soon converted to automobile engineering ashore and afloat. Even Gustave Trouvé tried his hand at a constant and variable level carburetor for internal combustion engines, although this was soon surpassed by simpler and more efficient carburetors (Patent N° 295,103). Louis Semple Clarke and his brothers, who had built a prototype electric catamaran, set up the Autocar Company, and in 1901 produced what is considered to be the USA's first multi-cylinder, shaft-driven car. One wonders whether innovators such as Moritz Immisch or Antony Reckenzaun, had they lived, would have converted over to internal combustion.

There were, however, some electrical engineers, on a larger scale than Jack Delmar-Morgan's *Mansura*, who ingeniously combined the best of internal combustion with the best of electric propulsion and came up with ever more promising results.

Perhaps the first use of the diesel-electric hybrid appeared in Russia in 1903 and 1904 for two 800-ton Volga River tankers, the *Vandal* and the *Sarmat*, belonging to the Brannobel Company of St. Petersburg. Designer Karl Hagelin thought of using single gasoline engines, but the difficulty was in gear-changing. Hagelin then conceived that reversing the engine and regulating its speed could be done with an electrical transmission, and contracted the Swedish ASEA to test the electrical drive system. He then recruited naval architect Johnny Johnson of Gothenburg to design the ship. Johnson placed the diesel engine and electric generator in the middle, and the electric motors in the stern, driving the propellers directly. The ship's power plant (3 × 120 horsepower) was built by Swedish Diesel (Aktiebolaget Diesels Motorer) and ASEA. Each engine had three cylinders with a bore of 290 mm and stroke of 430 mm. They ran at a constant 240 rpm and the electrical transmission, controlled by the helmsman using a streetcar-like lever, varied the propeller speed from 30 to 300 rpm. *Vandal* was accidentally damaged on its maiden voyage, repaired and served on the Volga route for ten years. Her sister ship, the larger *Sarmat*, with four 180 hp engines, was launched the next summer. Unlike *Vandal*, *Sarmat*'s engines could be coupled to the propellers directly, bypassing the electrical drive and saving up to 15 percent of engine power that would be otherwise lost in the electric transmission.[2]

On the outbreak of World War I, a very limited number of E-Class submarines were built. They measured 181 feet (55.17 meters) long and displaced 660 tons. When surfaced, these submarines operated twin 8-cylinder diesels, 1,600 hp (1,200 kW), for both propulsion and to charge the main storage battery. When submerged, this battery provided the sole source of energy for the two 630 kW electric motors, for the operating of all equipment, lighting, and the living needs of the crew. Hence it was the battery that allowed the submarine to operate as a submarine: that is, underwater. The limited battery energy of the time meant that they generally remained on the sea surface until they needed to submerge to either attack or evade an enemy. Typically, an E-Class sub operated at a very slow speed of about 2 knots (4 kph) and could remain submerged for about 48 hours. At higher speeds of 6–8 kph, submerged autonomy was reduced to about 1 hour. Each submarine had four 18-inch torpedo tubes, and carried eight torpedoes.

One of two such E-class submarines was the fledgling Royal Australian Navy's HMAS *AE2* also known as the "Silent ANZAC." *AE2* was built by the British engineering company Armstrong Whitworth, based in Tyneside, and was commissioned in 1914. Together with her sister submarine, HMAS *AE1*, the boat then sailed to Australia in what was, at the time, the longest voyage ever undertaken by a submarine.

The Gallipoli Campaign of 1915–16 is most commonly associated with the invasion of the Gallipoli Peninsula by Allied forces, including the Australian and New Zealand Army Corps (ANZAC), in an effort to weaken the Central Powers and take control of the Ottoman Empire. The invasion was the beginning of seven months of costly land battles, ending with the evacuation of Allied forces. However, another campaign was fought beneath the waters surrounding the Gallipoli Peninsula, one in which honors for both sides were even, with victories and disasters for both Allied and Ottoman forces.

AE2 became the first Allied submarine to silently penetrate the Dardanelles Strait in 1915 as part of the Gallipoli Campaign, on the very morning the ANZAC soldiers landed at Anzac Cove. *AE2* became the first Royal Australian Navy (RAN) warship to conduct a torpedo attack against an enemy warship. But after five days she finally fell to Ottoman gunfire and was scuttled, or sunk. Her commander, H.G. "Dacre" Stoker, and crew were captured and spent the rest of the war as prisoners of the Ottoman Empire.[3]

But it was in the USA, in Schenectady to be precise, that the successful adoption of the turboelectric ship took place. This was largely due to the genius of one man: William LeRoy Emmet.

Emmet was a great-grandson of Thomas Addis Emmet, an Irish revolutionary exiled in the 19th century, who came to America and became attorney general of New York. William LeRoy Emmet was born on July 10, 1858, at New Rochelle, New York. Raised in a family left in financial ruins by the aftershocks of the Civil War, he was educated at schools in Canada and New York. Emmet graduated from the United States Naval Academy in

1881 and for two years served as a cadet midshipman on the USS *Essex*. Leaving the Navy, Emmet became a $7 per week laborer on the night shift of the United States Illuminating Company. Applying knowledge of electricity learned in college "to some problems that cropped up at the factory," the 25-year-old gained the self-confidence that he had up to that point lacked.[4]

Emmet left to join the Sprague Electric Railway and Motor Company in 1888, where he worked as a troubleshooter for the installation of electric streetcar systems in several cities, including Cleveland, St. Louis, Wichita, and Harrisburg, Pennsylvania. He organized a group of Italians into mechanics to assist him in the overhaul of 120 electric motors for the company in Allegheny City. From there he worked for the Westinghouse Electric and Manufacturing Company and for the Buffalo Railway Company, before joining the Edison General Electric Company as engineer in the Chicago district in 1891. The following year Edison merged with Thomson-Houston to form the General Electric Company, and Emmet's services were retained. His career was interrupted in 1898 by the Spanish-American War when he served as a navigational officer on the steam-engined collier, USS *Justin*.

Returning to GE, in 1901, Emmet collaborated with Charles G. Curtis on the improvement of steam turbine engines. Working with his assistants, Swedish-born engineers Eskil Berg and Oscar Junggren, in 1903 Emmet directed the construction and installation of a 5,000 kW turbo alternator at the Fisk Street power plant of the Chicago Edison Company. For a former naval officer who had served on steamships, the natural progression was to use electric turbines for ship propulsion. As early as 1909 he attempted to point out that electric ship propulsion was more feasible, economical and practical than the Parsons steam turbines then in popular demand. For the all-important electrical coupling between the steam turbine and the propeller, in order to reverse the propeller and in order to regulate the speed between cruising speed and full speed, he used the patent taken out by another Swedish inventor, Ernst Alexanderson.

In 1908, according to historian William McBride, Canadian inventor Reginald Fessenden submitted a proposal to the Navy for a turboelectric drive that was rejected. Fessenden, however, was allowed to contact other companies that might be interested in the idea. Emmet at General Electric proved enthusiastic about the possibility of turboelectric drive and formulated detailed drawings from Fessenden's proposal. Emmet outlined his ambitious plans in a lengthy paper in the *Transactions of the Society of Naval Architects and Marine Engineers* in 1909. Describing two systems—the first being a hybrid electric/ steam turbine combination, the other a pure turboelectric drive—Emmet advocated for the installation of electric drives in the Navy's battleships, even though he admitted in practice they had never been tested on anything larger than firefighting boats in Lake Michigan: the *Joseph Medill* and *Graeme Stewart*, each with a modest 400 hp DC turboelectric drive, had been built in Manitowoc and both saw service in Chicago, Illinois.

At first the U.S. Navy was not convinced. Emmet met resistance and cynicism from officials such as the assistant secretary of the Navy, a certain Franklin Delano Roosevelt, who told him to stop bothering them. But others were on his side, such as George von Lengerke Meyer. Leveraging an endorsement of turboelectric drive from the Navy's General Board, Meyer authorized the installation of electric propulsion in one of three new colliers that began construction in 1910.

Cyclops, *Neptune* and *Jupiter* all had the same hull design and could thus be considered sister ships. But the difference was in their propulsion system. On April 4, 1911, the

Bureau of Steam Engineering proposed that electric propulsion be installed in the 542-ft (165 m) *Jupiter*. On April 13, the General Board replied that the successful performance of the proposed method of propulsion would result in military advantages sufficient to warrant its trial and recommended its installation in the collier. The propulsion plant of *Jupiter* consisted of a single 5,000-kilowatt turbine generating unit which provided power to two AC induction motors, one on each of the ship's two propeller shafts. William L. Emmet and his GE team personally supervised the installation.[5]

According to a report by chief engineer S.M. Robinson, *Jupiter* exceeded General Electric's economy predictions over the rival engines by 18 percent. Emmet also triumphantly declared in his own report on the trials, "If my first design for a warship made over four years ago [in 1909] had been accepted by the Navy Department, the vessel produced would have been very greatly superior in respect to economy, reliability, weight, simplicity, and cruising radius to any ship now afloat."

While *Jupiter* was proving herself in 1912, a merchant ship, the *Tynemount*, using 500 hp AC Diesel-electric drive, went into operation on the Canadian Great Lakes.

Won over by the successful performance of the fleet collier *Jupiter*, in 1915 Secretary of the Navy Josephus Daniels put his official O.K. on an order to outfit the 624-ft (190 m) *New Mexico* (BB-40) with four General Electric turboelectric AC motors totaling 31,000 hp. They would operate the *New Mexico*'s four propellers and enable her to make her accredited 21 knots on sea trials in 1917.

General Electric ran an advertisement titled "The 'Constitution' of To-day— Electronically Propelled" with a drawing of the *New Mexico* next to USS *Constitution*. The ad touted the battleship as "'the first of any nation to be electrically propelled.' GE called it one of the most important achievements of the scientific age and related it to consumer products noting that 'so general are the applications of electricity to the needs of mankind that scarcely a home or individual today need be without the benefits of General Electric products and service.'" An illustrated booklet titled *The Electric Ship* was offered free of charge upon request.[6]

The secrecy imposed by warfare lifted, in 1919 Emmet obtained U.S. Patent 1,313,078 titled "Electric Ship Propulsion"; it was one of 122 patents to his name.

Peacetime soon saw the application of turboelectric to commercial vessels. In 1920 the New Electra Line Company's *Cuba* (ex *Powhatan*, built 1894) was retrofitted with GE machinery. From January 1923, *Cuba,* a luxury ship, began operations between Portland and San Francisco, and was publicized as the first turboelectric-driven vessel on Pacific coastwise routes. Gradually the turboelectric fleet grew.

Emmet was recognized for his contribution: he was awarded the Gold Medal for vertical shaft turbines at the St. Louis Exposition, the Gold Medal for electric ship propulsion at the San Francisco Exposition, the Edison Medal for 1919, and the Elliott Cresson Medal in 1920. Although approached with several attractive offers to leave General Motors at Schenectady, Emmet was never tempted and even turned down offers of promotion. He was content to carry out R&D in his lab and let others shoulder the responsibility of management.

In 1926, Thomas Edison wrote to Emmet: "I want to thank you for your enclosure, and at the same time extend my congratulations to you on the successful outcome of your ideas. The worst is to come, for its takes about seven years to convert the average man to the acceptance of a solved problem. With all good wishes to you, I remain yours very truly, Thomas Alva Edison."[7]

The U.S. Coast Guard followed in 1921. Captain Quincy B. Newman, chief of engineering, designed and installed an innovative turbine-electric-drive power plant, which developed 3,350 shp, with alternating current, and a synchronous motor for propulsion, in his 250-ft (76 m)-class cutters *Tampa*, *Haida*, *Mojave*, *Modoc* and *Chelan*. Then there were diesel-electric fireboats such as the *Port Houston* (1926); the USN's aircraft carriers *Saratoga* and *Lexington* followed in 1927. Before very long it was the turn of turboelectric ocean liners, starting in 1928 with the Panama Pacific Line's 20,000-ton *California*, then her sister ships the *Virginia* and *Pennsylvania*.[8]

The first generation of electric drives, however, never proved in practice to be as radically more efficient than their mechanical rivals as their proponents had theorized, and these were the last major ships to receive electric systems. USS *Lexington* proved the versatility of the electric drive, however, when in late 1929 and early 1930 it provided power for the city of Tacoma,

William LeRoy Emmet, an electrical engineer working for the General Electric Company, campaigned for and then became the brains behind the introduction and development of the turbo-electric ship (U.S. Department of the Interior, National Park Service, Thomas Edison National Historical Park).

Washington, during a drought that had depleted the town's power-generating reservoir.[9]

The technology went across the Pond. A British subsidiary of the General Electric Company (GE) of Schenectady was Thomson-Houston (BT-H) of Rugby, Warwickshire, who built turbo-generators. In 1927, P&O Line ordered a new ship from Alexander Stephen and Sons of Glasgow, to be fitted with BT-H turboelectric propulsion. She had six water-tube boilers with a combined heating surface of 32,500 square feet (3,019 m²) that supplied steam at 400 lbf/in² to two turbo generators. These supplied current to electric motors with a combined rating of 3,565 NHP that drove twin screw propellers. She was originally to be called *Taj Mahal*, after the 17th-century mausoleum of Mumtaz Mahal in New Delhi. But when, at a cost of £1,090,987, she was completed in March 1929, she was named *Viceroy of India* and gave faster service to the long run from Tilbury, England, to Bombay, India, and on to Australia.

The same year, to increase the speed of another P&O ocean liner RMS *Mooltan*, her engines were supplemented with British Thomson-Houston exhaust-driven turbo generators powering electric propulsion motors. The addition of turboelectric power alongside her original quadruple-expansion engines increased *Mooltan*'s total installed power to 2,878 NHP and raised her top speed to an impressive 17 knots (31 kph).

A whole fleet of turboelectric ocean liners followed: the *Morro Castle*, the *Oriente*, the *President Coolidge* and *President Hoover*, the *Strathnavar* and the *Strathhaird,* and finally the *Monarch of Bermuda* and the *Queen of Bermuda*. By 1933 the electric ship total output had climbed to a staggering 1,200,000 horsepower.

During this rise of the steam turbine-electric, the diesel-electric had been making slow progress. Two Finnish Navy coastal defense ships, *Ilmarinen* and *Väinämöinen*, laid down in 1928–1929, were among the first surface ships to use diesel-electric transmission. Each had a four-engined Krupp diesel power train totaling 3,500 kW.

In 1933, the Star Ferry Company in the British protectorate of Hong Kong built the first diesel-electric passenger ferry. The Crossley-Premier engine generators and propelling motors of *Electric Star* were installed by the South China Motor Shipbuilding and Repairing Works in Tokwawan. *Electric Star* served from 1933 to 1968, and was retrofitted with a conventional diesel engine in 1948.[10]

In Switzerland, the 63-meter paddle steamer *Genève* on Lake Geneva had her aging steam unit replaced for the 1934 season with geared Sulzer *diesel-electric* drives. The system proved so successful that the Compagnie Générale de Navigation sur le lac Léman (CGN) applied the hybrid system to half of their lake fleet.[11]

During the 1930s, diesel-electric tugs began to appear on the River Thames. The 92-ft *Lectro*, built by Henry Robb Ltd. at Leith, was delivered to the Union Lighterage Company; two 360 bhp 4SCSA 6-cyl 12.5" × 19" Mirrlees-Bickerton-Day diesels drove a BTH 580hp electric motor. The Thames Steam Tug and Lighterage Co. Ltd. ran three innovative diesel-electric tugs on the traffic-dense Port of London: the *Framfield*, the *Wortha* and the *Irande*, built by J.I. Thornycroft & Co. Ltd. at Woolston. Two 6-cyl English Electric type built around 1936 by the Smith Dockyard Company for the Erith & Dartford Lighterage Co., Ltd.[12]

The world's first diesel-electric icebreaker was the 4,330-ton Swedish *Ymer* in 1933. With 9,000 hp divided between two propellers in the stern and one propeller in the bow, she remained the most powerful Swedish icebreaker until the commissioning of *Oden* in 1957. *Ymer* was followed in 1939 by the Finnish *Sisu*, the first diesel-electric icebreaker in Finland. Both vessels were decommissioned in the 1970s and replaced by much larger icebreakers in both countries, the 1976-built *Sisu* in Finland and the 1977-built *Ymer* in Sweden.

Marine diesel-electric propulsion was also tried out in Scotland. In 1935, when Clydeside shipyard A. & J. Inglis built a new 215-ft (65 m) paddle steamer ferry for the London and North Eastern Railway, she too was equipped with diesel-electric propulsion. The 1,300 hp shunt-wound e-motor was manufactured by the English Electric Company of Stafford, while to supply current to the motor there were four diesel engines, each having a normal output of 400 bhp at 600 rpm. Capable of 17 knots and of carrying over one thousand passengers, the *Talisman* was based at Craigendoran, sailing to Dunoon, Rothesay and the Kyles of Bute.[13]

But for the bigger ships, steam held sway. In 1935, Harold K. Hales (1868–1942), a member of Parliament and owner of a shipping company, commissioned a Sheffield goldsmith to produce a large trophy to be presented to the fastest ship crossing the Atlantic. During the next five years, two superliners would compete with each other for the Hales Trophy: the 1,019.4-ft (310.7 m) *Queen Mary* and the 1,029-ft (313.6 m) SS *Normandie*. The latter was built at Saint-Nazaire for the French Line, Compagnie Générale Transatlantique (CGT). Her 160,000 hp turboelectric transmission was supplied by the company Alstom of Belfort. Alstom had been founded in 1928 from a merger between none other than the Thomson-Houston Electric Company (still part of General Electric) and the Société Alsacienne de Constructions Mécaniques. One can almost sense William Emmet in the wings.

At the foot of 42nd Street, New York, 1939, are the turbo-electric greyhounds of the sea: Cunard's latest liner *Queen Elizabeth* (bottom) and *Queen Mary* (second from bottom) laid up on pier 90, with the French liners the *Normandie* and *Mauretania* at top (University of Liverpool Library, Special Collections and Archives).

CGT chose turboelectric transmission for the ability to use full power in reverse, and because, according to CGT officials, it was quieter and more easily controlled and maintained. The engine installation was heavier than conventional turbines and slightly less efficient at high speed but allowed all propellers to operate even if one engine was not running. Around this power plant was a revolutionary hull, designed by Vladimir Yourkevitch, a former naval architect for the Imperial Russian Navy, who had emigrated to France after the Revolution. His ideas included a slanting clipper-like bow and a bulbous forefoot beneath the waterline, in combination with a slim hydrodynamic hull.

The combination proved a success. In May 1935 SS *Normandie*, with Capitaine René Pugnetout at the helm, went on her first trials and reached a top speed of 32.125 knots (36.96 mph; 59.496 kph); she also performed an emergency stop from that speed in 1,700 meters (1859 yd). She entered service as the largest and fastest passenger ship afloat.

RMS *Queen Mary*, Cunard White Star Line's superliner, then took it in turns with the SS *Normandie* to win the Hales Trophy. In 1937, SS *Normandie* made her fastest crossing, averaging 30.58 knots (56.63 kph). William LeRoy Emmet, a confirmed bachelor, died on September 26, 1941, at age 82.

By this time World War II was underway and very soon both steam turboelectric and diesel-electric were put into operation with destroyer escorts. The 102 Buckley-Class escorts and the 50 Rudderow escorts were fitted with General Electric steam turboelectric propulsion. The Evarts and the Cannon Class escorts were also known as the GMT, or General Motors Tandem diesel drive.[14]

It was, however, to be another 50 years before the tandem diesel-electric drive was found to give greater range than its battery equivalent.

FOUR

Wartime Interlude

Despite the devastation of the First World War, an electric boat survived here and there as is seen by this remarkable testimony, made November 2006 by Dave de Kiesby as a guestbook entry in the website titled *The Ruhleben Story: The Prisoners of Ruhleben Civilian Internment Camp 1914–1918*. Ruhleben Camp was 10 km to the west of Berlin.

My great grandfather George Backhouse, a trawlerman from Grimsby, took his son Charlie, 15, to sea for the first time. Unfortunately they happened to be on one of the first boats to be captured by the Germans at the outbreak of the First World War. Both father and son were interned in Ruhleben. Due to their ages both were to be repatriated but before they were out of German hands Charlie turned 16 so the Germans turned him around and sent him back to Ruhleben. His father returned to England without his son, who remained in Germany for the rest of the war. I have been told that he became the camp boxing champion at some stage.

Maybe someone can clarify this for me? He made a model boat, which is still in the family possession. The *Blanche* is a cabin cruiser style boat *with an electric motor*. Interestingly the wiring for the windings came from the race track which was next door to the camp. Charlie, as he was only 16 was a "Trustie" who was allowed out of the camp for various reasons. It was whilst on one or more of these outings that grandad stole the wiring. The nails were from boots and the propeller is made from beaten pennies. The keel is made from a hockey stick given to him by the camp Commandant. The Germans took an interest in the boat and would supply bits and pieces for the construction of her.

Getting the "Blanch" home proved difficult with Queen Wilamena of Holland getting involved. Only problem was that the Queen didn't want to part with it! Eventually it made it to England in one piece, where, as I said earlier it still is.

Examples of the use of electric boats for war, such as the following, are few and far between:

The Secretary of State for War has received the following Despatch from General Sir George F. Milne, K.C.B., D.S.O., Commander-in-chief, British Salonika Force: General Headquarters, British Salonika Force. 1st December 1918.

My Lord—I have the honour to submit the following report on the operations of the British Army in Macedonia from 1st October 1917, to the present date.... On the Doiran front, where the enemy held strongly entrenched and continuous positions in mountainous and rocky country, operations were necessarily restricted to small raids and artillery bombardment. In all these, casualties were inflicted on the enemy at slight loss to ourselves. One raid, novel in its plan and bold in its execution, is worthy of special notice. Shortly after midnight on the 15th–16th April, in bright moonlight, a mixed naval and military party left the shore of the lake by Doiran Station *in four boats, silently driven by electric motors*, which had been brought up from Salonika and assembled under the eyes of the enemy. From Doiran Station to Doiran Town by water is two miles, but the party landed well within the enemy lines unchallenged. Sentries were left to guard the boats, the town was searched and the lakeside road patrolled. Not a Bulgar was seen, and so, as the main purpose of the raid, the capture of prisoners, could not be achieved, the party embarked, re-crossed the lake in safety and apparently unobserved, and landed again on our shore at four o'clock. This daring operation stands out as a striking testimony to the enterprise of the troops, and its skilful execution was undoubtedly due to the energy and care displayed by Captain R.S. Olivier, R.N., Senior Naval Officer at Salonika, and the officers and men of HMS *St. George* (below—Photo Ships), who not only trained the detachment on this occasion, but have at all times cordially assisted the Army....[1]

In 1918, the Italian Navy planned a secret attack on the fleet of dreadnought battleships moored at the Austro-Hungarian Naval Base at Pula, Istria. What was required was a small fleet of electric assault boats, whose silence would enable them to sneak into Pula under cover of night, and then to launch two destructive torpedoes. Designed by Attilio Bitio of the SVAN (Venice Naval Yard), the 16-meter (50 ft) flat-bottomed wooden boats were equipped with twin 10 hp electric motors supplied by Rognini & Balbo (Elettromobili) of Milano, already known for their electric streetcars. The coupling of both motors to a single shaft would enable them to cruise at 4 knots for 30 miles. Each boat was armed with twin 450mm (17.7 inch) torpedoes. They were also equipped with four pulleys (two aft and two forward) on which ran two Galles-type caterpillar chains with crampons for cutting through harbor barrages. Each had a four-man crew and was named after a jumping insect: *Cavalletta, Grillo, Locusta* and *Pulce* (= *Grasshopper, Cricket, Locust* and *Flea*).

On the night of March 13–14, 1918, *Grillo*, manned by Commander Mario Pellegrini and three other crew, was towed from Venice across the Gulf of Trieste by a MAS torpedo boat. After she had been released from her tow near Pula Harbour, the *Grillo* proceeded on her own electric power towards the port. To reach the battleships, she must get past nine barrages, one after the other, each made up of large poles driven into the sea bottom, protruding on the surface and connected by heavy chains and steel cables crosslinked. For each barrage, the crew first had cut the cables too high on the water with the wire cutters provided. After only two minutes of feverish work, a searchlight beam flashed. *Grillo's* crew, taken by surprise, interrupted their work: Pellegrini understood that the surprise factor had now faded, and although reason and the circumstances suggested their retreating, he decided to risk advancing. He ordered the marines to resume work, and use the Galles chain to cut the last cable. *Grillo* then accelerated to the second barrier, but, during the operations to climb over, the little assault craft was picked out by more searchlights and fired at by machine guns and cannon. *Grillo* accelerated to the third barrier despite enemy fire, cutting through it and then the fourth. She was approaching the fifth barrier when one of the engines was hit by shrapnel and stopped. An Austrian gunboat approached and used the overhead flares to fire at the little craft which, riddled with bullets, was now sinking. Pellegrini ordered his crew to abandon ship, while he opened the engine valves to accelerate scuppering and adjusted the explosive charges to enable self-destruction. While the Italian commander and his crew were being hauled onto the Austrian gunboat, the dull roar of an explosion underwater was heard. The crew was taken prisoner and spent the rest of the war in captivity. The wreck of the *Grillo* was later raised by the Austrian Navy, who tried to copy her. The first assault by a miniature electric boat had failed. The vessel, although ingenious, proved slow and noisy because of its cumbersome and not concealable clanking chains. It was considered that the experience gained with *Grillo* might serve later in designing the next assault craft. But following the signing of the Armistice between Austria and Italy in November 1918, the other boats in the fleet ended up in a breaker's yard.[2]

Postwar: Inland Inactivity 1920–1960

During the rise of the turboelectric ship, fleets of smaller electric boats continued to give reliable service on the backwaters of the world's lakes and rivers. Electric boating cruised silently on.

On the 8 km Königsee in Germany, a growing fleet of electric passenger boats was in regular use taking tourist pilgrims across this lake to the chapel of St. Bartholemae. The queen of this fleet was the 38-passenger *Akkumulator*, ordered in 1909 by the Prince of Bavaria.

In 1922 the German company Gelap (Gesellschaft für elektrische Apparate = Company for Electrical Appliances) in Berlin-Marienfelt, brought out an electric outboard fed by batteries in wooden storage boxes. This Gelap outboard was manufactured until 1933, when Gelap merged with the Siemens & Halske aero-engine works.[3]

In 1919, the Bedford Steamboat Company on the River Ouse in England changed from steam to electric tripping boats: the *Lady Lena* and the *Lorna Doone* were brought from Maidenhead on Thames; then the steam launch *Lodore*, which had started operations in 1898, was converted to electric.[4]

In 1924, Messrs. John I. Thornycroft Ltd. built thirty 25-ft (7.5 m) electric launches for the British Empire Exhibition at Wembley, North London, a huge spectacle that ran for two summer seasons and attracted millions of visitors: "It was a wonderland of flowers, gardens and trees, a great lake on which electric launches purred between the trim pavil-

The Gelap submerged electric outboard was built in Berlin and used during the 1920s (author's collection).

Dodgem boats were as almost as popular as dodgem cars. Illustration published in *Le Pélérin* in 1933 (Musée EDF Electropolis, Mulhouse).

ion of New Zealand at the one end, past the gigantic 'Palaces of Industry and Engineering' and the great colonnaded pavilions of Canada and Australia."[5]

In 1922, Kensington Gardens, Lowestoft, eastern England, had been opened as a pleasant retreat from the bustling activity to be found on the nearby beach. Among the attractions, the Electric Boating Lake, designed by River Board Chief Engineer S.W. Mobbs, was a small canal along which children could drive a 15-strong fleet of small well-padded electric "scootaboats," or dodgem motor boats. They became immensely popular with long queues of eager children stretching around the lake from the landing stage, waiting their turn. They operated on a tram-type power system, with a pole at the back of each boat connected with an overhead electrified network driven by a DC generator. At night the lake was lit by hundreds of fairy lamps. A similar attraction was used at the Dreamland Amusement Park, Margate, Kent. By the 1970s Lowestoft boats were leaking and the electricity faulty. In 1974 they were replaced by battery-electric boats which were not as popular; they were later replaced by canoes, and the central islands were removed.[6]

Ten miles north of Lowestoft, the town of Great Yarmouth had also created a new attraction in the form of the Venetian Waterways, public water gardens on the seafront with man-made winding watercourses designed for electric boating. The construction of the Waterways was started on January 2, 1928, and completed on June 30. With the exception of a few key men, the Waterways were laid out as a "relief scheme" by the unemployed, who received one shilling per hour for their labors. They dug out the channels by hand, using just shovels and wheelbarrows. Over 6,000 tons of soil were brought over from Caister to construct the ornamental gardens. It was hoped to open the attraction to the public in July, but owing to difficulties obtaining the charging apparatus for the boats, this had to be delayed until August 2. There were five boats specially built by the local yard of J.W. Brooke & Co. of Lowestoft and each was named after a Broadland River: the *Yare, Ant, Bure, Waveney* and *Thurne*. Each boat had its own designated boatman who was supplied with a jersey pullover bearing the name of the boat. The boatmen earned £3 per week and the money-taker (Mr. S.L. Gough of York Road) earned 30 shillings. The man in overall charge when the Waterways first opened was Mr. E. Harlock of Alderson Road. This service survived the war, and in the 1950s there were a series of nursery rhyme tableaux around the sides of the Waterways, which were illuminated at night, and provided much fun and entertainment for both young and old alike. "As a child it was a treat to be taken on a trip around the waterways at dusk (or later) either by foot, or preferably by boat, as amongst the flower beds were neon figures/tableaux of famous fairy story characters."[7]

From 1925, an electrical engineer called Captain J.M. Donaldson MC (formerly of the King's Royal Rifles) enjoyed weekend cruising on England's Norfolk Broads in *Kenmure*, his traditional 28-ft (8m50) river cruiser, built by C&G Press at Belaugh of Norwich. Donaldson was assistant engineer to the North Metropolitan Electric Power Supply Co., and almost uniquely, *Kenmure* not only had electric lighting but an electric inboard motor and batteries, personally installed by Donaldson.[8]

In the English Lake District, on Windermere, local builder G.H. Pattinson dammed a local tarn and laid a pipe to a boathouse he had equipped with a hydroelectric generator. Three beautiful electrically driven launches were built: *Rose, Thistle* and *Shamrock*, which proved a huge success. The problem of spilling sulfuric acid battery fluid and rotting the wooden hulls eventually caused Pattinson to stop the operation.[9]

Meanwhile on the Upper Thames, the Ray Motor Co. and Bonds at Maidenhead, Meakes of Marlow and Hobbs of Henley all supplied electric canoes on the Thames. Mr. Carr at Ray built his first 25-ft (7.5 m) canoe in 1920, fitting it out with a 2½ hp and chloride exide AXE8 batteries. It was acquired for £460 by a Mr. Anagnos, who named her *Aris*. Horsham Ltd. built two more canoes, the *Gena* and the *Genetta*, for Carr's own hire fleet of five canoes. At the same time, the aeronautical firm of Short Brothers of Rochester had also entered the electric canoe market. Their advert describes them as "Luxuriously fitted—handsomely upholstered with corded velveteen in rose, green or blue. The decks are covered with Wilton Pile carpets and they are the acme of river luxury and comfort." From 1945 to 1955, officers of the Grenadier Guards Club at Maidenhead, with clubhouse on Bucks Ait, an island in the River Thames at Maidenhead, regularly hired electric canoes.[10]

In 1930, millionaire automobile manufacturer, 53-year-old Louis Renault, ordered a 14.15 m (47 ft) Marconi-rig motor sailor yacht from the British Camper & Nicholson yard in Portsmouth, England. It was to be built with Burmese teak on riveted oak frames, with a teak deck. Instead of the conventional gasoline or diesel drive, he drew on the technical expertise from the Renault Car Company's Paris-based engineers at that time producing cars in their "Stella" and "Quatre" range. A 55 hp Renault-Couach marine motor, built in Arcachon, was adapted to charge up 30 batteries which supplied energy to an electric motor. Renault called his yacht *Briseïs* (= sailfish) and cruised it from his beloved Chausey Isle around the other islands of the English Channel.[11]

Roaring Gap Lake in North Carolina, USA, had been formed in 1926 when the dam was built. The 70-acre spring-fed lake that formed actually flooded over a small town, and at one time, the church steeple could still be seen. The main attraction to the club was the private golf course and riding stables. During 1930–35 a large community boathouse was built on one side of the lake and most residents ordered an electric boat from a Syracuse, New York, company called Electri-Craft, who declared themselves "The Largest Manufacturers of Electric Boats in the World."

The brain behind this firm was Julian S. Brown, son of inventor Alexander T. Brown. In 1925 Julian Brown put together the innovative Julian Sport Coupé automobile, aka Julian Six. The one-off prototype was a revolutionary air-cooled, rear-engined automobile, whose platform and tubular backbone frame anticipated Ferdinand Porsche's Volkswagen Käfer by over a decade. In 1930 Julian presented his version of the electric outboard motor, marketing it with a 15-ft pleasure boat. The engine cost $75 while the boat cost $200. It was supplied with two cushioned seats, each holding two adults and covered with a canvas shelter top; steering was by means of ropes passing along the sides of the boat to the motor in back. Two years later Brown had engineered a battery-powered electric boat motor equipped with a DC rotary switch that stepped up the voltage from 6 volts to 12 and 24 volts, thus giving the craft a choice of three speeds. "Syracuse will soon have a new industry in which it is planned to provide employment for between 350 and 400 workers. Julian S. Brown, Syracuse inventor, will start manufacturing within a few weeks a new type electric motor for small boats designed by him after several years of study. Manufacturing operations will be carried on at the now idle plant of the Julian Motor Car Company in Eastwood."[12] Brown decided to call his firm Electri-Craft.

One of the most interesting features of the Detroit Regatta week was the display, in the Hotel Whittier lobby, of the new Electri-Craft. This was the first public showing of this all-electric boat, which is being built by the Electri-Craft Corporation, of Syracuse, N.Y., and is being distributed nationally by the Electri-Craft Boat Company of Detroit. The Electri-Craft is particularly adaptable for use by women and children. It is also an ideal boat for the man who enjoys trolling. There are no starting problems, no lubrication problems, no noise, no fumes, and no mechanical complexities of any kind. Instead, the Electri-Craft starts at the turn of the button and is silently on its way. There are three speeds forward and three reverse. Low or trolling speed is about 1½ mph for a period of ten hours. Second speed is approximately 4½ mph good for better than sixteen hours. At top speed, the boat will run close to 8 mph with a cruising radius of approximately 32 miles.[13]

Julian Brown continued to improve his product.

Electri-Craft, the electrically-propelled boats produced by the Electri-Craft Corporation have been vastly improved for 1935. They are built in three different models known as the *Angler, Standard* and *Streamline*. The *Angler* is a 15-footer with one cockpit, seating six. The *Streamline*, with its streamline hull, has two combinations of speed because the electric power comes from two sources—eight batteries under the aft seat furnishing power for high and second speeds and two batteries back of the forward seat furnishing power for low speed and lights. On a single charge of the batteries the *Streamline* will operate a total of twenty-three hours at high and low speeds which would be the equivalent of 117 miles. Using second and low speeds the cruising range is forty hours or 195 miles. Among its numerous interesting features the *Streamline* offers a bronze construction suitable for salt water service, heavy skegs protecting the bow, rudder and propellers, leak-proof stuffing box, twin motors, generous storage space and cushions and seat backs of Kapok.[14]

They sold 15', 16' and 17' versions, all built around the same motor. Electri-Craft was in existence for about five years and built somewhere in the neighborhood of 1000 boats total. They would number the boats by stamping a number on their speed control switches. Two of these boats, called *Eeyore* and *Piglet*, named after characters in A.A. Milne's book *Winnie-the-Pooh*, published in 1926, were acquired by the Bowman Grays,

An Electrifying
Message *announcing*

◄ELECTRI-CRAFT►

THE MODERN BOAT

as revolutionary as the first electric light

ELECTRI-CRAFT presents a new boating sensation! An all-electric boat with more individual features than any other small craft afloat!—AND

AT A PRICE BELOW ANY OTHER INBOARD POWERED BOAT

SAFETY · · · · · · · · · · · · · · No fire hazard; a smart seaworthy hull.
ECONOMY · · · · · · · · · · · Operated at a cost of less than five cents an hour.
SIMPLICITY · · · · · · · · · · · Started instantly by a touch of the switch.
DURABILITY · · · · · · · Guaranteed for eighteen months but built to last for years.
PRACTICABILITY · · · · · · · · 15 to 25 hours battery capacity; recharges overnight.
CLEANLINESS · · · · · · No gasoline tanks; no oiling requirements; no exhaust fumes.
SMOOTHNESS · · · · · · · · · Smooth flowing power with no motor vibration.
QUIETNESS · · · · · · · · · · · As noiseless as a small electric fan.
COMFORT · · · · · · · · · · Comfortable, roomy seats with kapoc-filled cushions.

ELECTRI-CRAFT having no motor freezing hazard,
lengthens the boating season by at least two months.

IN ELECTRI-CRAFT
You find ideal water transportation and recreation.

The Answer to Small Boat Luxury

During the 1930s, the Electri-Craft Company of Syracuse, New York, built and sold almost 1,000 electric boats (courtesy Tom Hesselink).

shortly after they built their boathouse in Roaring Gap in 1932. The lake has always since then been restricted to electric boats only, and most of the original 40 or so boats are still operating.[15]

Brown continued to diversify:

If you've ever had to pole a boat through a heavy growth of seaweed or underwater plants of any kind; if you've ever had to clear a weed-fouled propeller; if the channel to your boathouse is so weed-choked that you—but let's omit the profanity and examine a new weed cutter developed by Electri-Craft Corporation. This device consists of a circular saw which operates in a horizontal plane at the lower end of a shaft clamped to the stern of a row-boat. The cutter blade is between two plates which have periodic notches to "back up" the plants being cut. The blade is protected by a vertical guard ring; and the shaft is hinged so that when this ring hits a stone or snag, the entire mechanism swings up. For power, this device depends upon a storage battery, the motor being built into the top of the shaft. In full cutting operation, the motor draws an average of 14 amperes.[16]

In 1938, Dick Pope, recognized as the Father of Florida Tourism, and his wife Julie, added a fleet of Electri-Craft boats to tour the tropical canals at their recently opened Cypress Gardens, Pasco County, Florida. "So silently do the electric boats glide along the flower-banked canals and lagoons at the Florida Cypress Gardens, that one seems floating through a very Fairyland of flowers. Beautiful photographs may be made from these boats. There were in fact 8,000 varieties of flowers from over 90 different countries."[17] These were still in regular use in 1965. Indeed, many Electri-Craft boats can still be found plying the pristine waters of the reservoir lakes of New York's Catskill Mountains, and further north in wealthy St. Regis Lake located in the great Adirondack Park.

But despite such popularity, unfortunately Julian Brown's innovative engineering genius was overshadowed by his succession of marriages, divorces and failed business enterprises, which kept him in and out of the Syracuse courts for the better part of two decades. Eventually he filed for bankruptcy.

The glass-bottom boat had been patented back in 1904 by Louis Larson and Henry J. Woods of Muskegon, Michigan.[18] They became popular in Florida at several areas of natural springs that became tourist attractions, for example, Silver Springs, Wakulla Springs, Rainbow Springs, and Weeki Wachee Springs. The glass-bottom boats at Silver Springs, introduced in 1932, were equipped with electric motors.

In 1938, Barney Connett of Chicago, Illinois, a gasoline service station manager and an inventor and mechanic in his spare time, built a miniature electric one-man submarine called *Maryell.* Measuring 11 ft (3.3 m) long × 2 ft (60 cm) beam, the metal vessel was painted green and yellow, with eyes and gills, to look like a giant trout. With Connett at the controls, *Maryell* covered the 30-mile distance under Lake Michigan between Michigan City, Indiana, and Chicago's Navy Pier in just less than 11 hours. This was just one of Connett's 300 successful dives to depths of more than 30 ft (9 m) and a range of 14 miles (22 km) from its two battery banks. *Maryell* was just one of several versions built by Connett, who aimed at the ideal commuter vehicle, but whose progress was stopped by the war.[19]

If inboard electric boats still did not catch on due to the space taken up by the bank of batteries, electric outboards proliferated with brands such as: Jewel Electric of Chicago, Illinois (1913–1918); Ashbrook Electric, Chicago; Silverstreak (Mayfair Boats), New York; Evinrude-Elto of Milwaukee, Wisconsin (1932); Grimes Electric Oar, Syracuse, New York (1933); H-S, Howarth, New York; Hav-A-Ride, Rochester, New York (1933); Fisher, Fargo, N. Dakota (1934); Electrol (LeJay), (1936); Eclipse (Bendix) of Newark, New Jersey (1937–1940); Touromarine, Red Bank, New Jersey (1937–1938); Silvertrol (Silver Creek Precision Corp), Silver Creek, New York (1946—marketed by Sears and Roebuck as the Elgin in the late 1950s); My-Te, Indianapolis, Indiana (1959); Lazi-Trol (Byrd Industries) of Ripley, Tennessee; Bantam (1964); Bucol (Buc-O Mfg.), Lake Alfred, Florida (1964); Electro-jet (Schnacke Mfg. Corp.), Evansville, Indiana (1964) … and maybe others. Most of these disappeared, although one or two did survive.[20]

The LeJay electric outboard, produced in 1950, was one of the dozen "come-and-go" products which could not quite compete with gasoline outboards (courtesy Tom Hesselink).

One example, the Minn Kota electric trolling motor, began its life in 1934 in Fargo, North Dakota. Oltmann G. Schmidt, inventor of the trolling motor, was known to be a man of many diverse ideas. Prior to the trolling motor, "O.G." invented, produced and sold a copper soldering torch from his home in Wheatland, North Dakota. For the trolling motor he took a starter motor from a Ford Model A, and added a flexible shaft and a

An Accumot-powered boat takes tourists around the Seegrotte near Hinterbrühl, Lower Austria (author's collection).

propeller. Due to its success, manufacturing operations were then moved to Fargo. Because of its proximity to the MINNesota–North DaKOTA border, Mr. Schmidt named the business the Minn-Kota Manufacturing Company. Among its firsts: 1934, the first electric gear-driven motor; 1935, the first electric flexible cable motor, remaining the standard bearer for decades.[21]

On June 8, 1932, a 25-pax electric boat began to give rides to tourists to Die Seegrotte (= Lake Grotto), near Hinterbrühl, Lower Austria, an underground cave system with a large grotto located 60 meters (200 feet) below a former gypsum mine. In 1918 the grotto had been bought by Friedrich Fischer, a Viennese liqueur producer. In 1937–1938 about 50,000 guests were taken in this electric boat through the tunnel to marvel at the underground lake grotto. With the water surface covering 6200 m², pumps were used to keep the water level down.

During World War II, Die Seegrotte was pumped out and its bottom concreted to make an underground factory for developing the top-secret Heinkel He162 jet fighter. The workforce, made up of inmates from the nearby concentration camp, were inhumanely treated. As the war ended, before they evacuated, the SS detonated explosive bombs, killing hundreds of workers. At the beginning of 1946, the Seegrotte was seized by the Soviet occupation forces. But by 1948, the Fischer family returned and cleaned it up so that by Easter 1949, the electric boat tour could resume, using Accumot engines. Today the Seegrotte remains the largest underground lake in Europe, a tourist attraction that draws 250,000 people to visit it each year. Other grottoes such as Han-sur-Lesse, Namur Province in Belgium, run Accumot-engined boat tours.[22]

With the advent of the Second World War, the Italians produced several small battery-driven submersibles which they named "carri" (= chariots). Later on in the war, starting at the beginning of 1942, a British midget submarine was developed. This was known as the X-Craft and was about 25 ft long (7m50). Each sub had a 60 hp continuously rated compound motor, series-and-shunt wound, fitted in the tail with direct drive through a tail-clutch and engine clutch; 110-volt chloride lead-acid batteries provided energy. This installation enabled them to cruise at 3½ knots for 30 miles (50 km) to accelerate to a maximum 7½ knots and to crash dive straight down to a maximum depth of 350 ft (100 m).

The mission of these mini electric subs is best explained by one of their most coura-geous skippers, Commander Jo Brooks: "To sink heavy enemy battleships, we would sneak in, lay very heavy time-activated mines under the big ones, then sneak out again. Sometimes if we had to set the clocks to a short period like an hour, that would only give you about half an hour to get clear. We used to do quite a lot of raids like this. One of the most difficult raids was when we immobilized the *Tirpitz*." The British had informa-tion that the German 40,000+ ton battleship *Tirpitz* was sheltering in the Kaafjord fjord in Norway. It was decided that this was a suitable target and six normal submarines, each one towing one X-Craft on a tow rope, left England to go to Norway. "We set off from the north of Scotland and we were towed up there by bigger submarines, to save battery power. Then we cast off and did the job."

Two of the X-Craft, one captained by Lieutenant Donald Cameron and the other captained by Lieutenant Basil Place, got through the surrounding protection and placed their charges under the *Tirpitz*. The charges were detonated and severely damaged the *Tirpitz*; it did not sink, but it was put out of action for some time. This was the first of many successes by the X-Craft. Before long these mini-subs went over to carry out the same strategy against Japanese cruisers in places like the Timor Sea, off Singapore.[23]

Nazi Germany's Kriegsmarine considered various submarine designs for specialized operations or improving U-boat performance. Many of these designs did not come to fruition for various reasons. Others towards the end had to be abandoned, as the yards were overrun by Allied forces. One of these was Type XXV, intended to be electric propul-sion–only boats for coastal use. The design was 160 tons with a crew of about 58 men and would have had two torpedo tubes fitted at the bow. The submarine was propelled by a single three-bladed propeller and steered by a single rudder. No contracts were granted for these boats.

Electric boats were used in occupied Holland in 1944–1945 for the clandestine trans-port of British and Canadian troops and equipment.

During the German occupation of France, on the Canal du Midi, some barges received precious lead-acid batteries from the state as a substitute for heavy oil and adapted an electric engine. This motorization worked on short trips. *Barge SSS72* of engi-neer Jean Desor was used after 1945 by the Sablières de la Seine (sand dredgers) for a shuttle between the excavations of Grigny and Boulogne, a distance of 40 km every day. The boat transported 275 tons of sand at 6.5 kph (4 mph) in both directions. A 380-volt electric recharging post was established at each end. Later, a third charger was installed on the St.-Martin to enable the barge to transport Paris suburbs. It had 8.8 tons of Tudor batteries and a Sauter-Harlé DC engine option of 15, 18 or 36 kW at 240 volts. The normal operating speed with 15 kW ran at 900 rpm. The functioning at 18 kW could not last longer than two hours. Finally full power at 36 kW for occasional use could not last longer than 5 minutes. The speed was therefore 8.5 kph (5.2 mph).[24]

In Germany, government policy also favored electrics, since there was no native oil. Electric passenger boats continued in use on the Königsee. In 1937 came construction of the 19-m *Berchtesgaden*, capable of transporting up to 93 passengers and crew. Between 1920 and 1990, sixteen such waterbuses were in service on the Bavarian lake. Three electric ferryboats also went into use on the Machsee, an artificial reservoir in Hanover.

In the city port of Bordeaux, not far from the quays, is an ornamental public gardens. Since 1893, a boat called *Le Petit Mousse* ("little sailor boy") had been taking up to fifty passengers around the oval canal, landscaped into the gardens. Originally propelled by hand-cranking, then by pedaling, from 1910 *Le Petit Mousse* was driven by a gasoline engine—first a 5 hp Daimler, then from 1920 by a 15 hp Grégoire.

In 1941 *Le Petit Mousse's* owner, Edgard Mouraz, installed a battery-electric system. From then on, and for the past sixty years, *Le Petit Mousse* has silently carried a total of 3 million people around the canal.[25]

In 1946, when the celebrated stage and film actress, Beatrice "Bea" Lillie, Lady Peel, once dubbed "the funniest woman in the world," bought a magnificent riverside house close to Marsh Lock, Henley-on-Thames, it came complete with 25-ft (7m60) electric canoe and charging station in the form of a thatched boathouse. Known as *Aegina*, the canoe had been built some forty years before by J. Bond for a Mrs. Lowenadler and could carry a maximum of eleven people. In 1920 a new electric motor, built by Submersible and J.L. Motors Ltd. of Southall, Middlesex, and batteries by Pritchett & Gold and EPS Ltd. were installed. While renaming her house "Peel Fold," Lady Peel renamed the canoe *Beazie*. Accompanied by her companion John Huck, she often took friends such as Sir Noel Coward, Ivor Novello, Lord Laurence Olivier, Sir John Gielgud, Sir Ralph Richardson, Ben Johnson—as well as the Duke and Duchess of Windsor—and many other celebrated actors, playwrights and critics, on silent cruises up and down the river. In 1951 *Beazie* was refitted with Exide Type 34 PON 13D unclad marine batteries. Of necessity *Beazie* was fitted with three bulb-horns.[26]

In 1947, Warwick Productions of Kenilworth launched a venture to supply various councils in the Midlands with small fleets of battery-electric hireboats for their public boating lakes. Raybuck (Yard N°29) is still in working order. The same year, Captain Charlie Hirst of Leroys Boathouses, Guildford, Surrey, built a 30-ft, steel-hulled electric boat called *Pilgrim* for day trips up the down the local River Wey. Her steering wheel came—via Messrs. Thomas Ward, shipbreakers—from HMS *Achilles*. Between 1947 and 1981, *Pilgrim*, with three successive skippers, but with her original machinery and 96-cell "Nife" steel-alkaline battery, would make at least 26,000 trips up and down the River Wey on electric power.[27]

North of Göteborg, Sweden, between 1913 and 1948, the battery-electric ASEA-engined *Hamnfärjan I* ferried workers from Marstrand Island to their shipyard on nearby Koön Island. It was built for the Marstrands Mekaniska Werkstad by August Svenningsson. Svenningsson had no plans to work from apart from being given the required dimensions. Ferry no. 1, including the electrical cables, was delivered in July 1913 at a cost of 15,000 Swedish crowns; it carried 36 passengers and remained in service until 1960. It was powered by a 5 hp electric motor and also at first by a 5 hp crude-oil engine since electric power was cut off at 5 p.m. In 1948 the battery-electric *Hamnfärjan II* took over.

Passenger boats on the Königsee in Austria (author's collection).

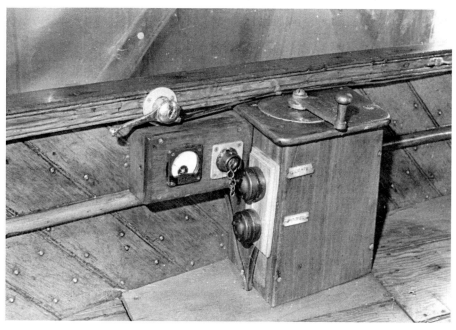

Electric motor and control system installed in the Thames canoe *Beazie* **in 1948 (author's collection).**

It was built in 1948 by Gösta Johansson at Kungsviken on Orust Island. It was more or less identical to its forerunner. Forty battery cells of 2 volts each (generating 80 volts in all) drove an ASEA electric engine delivering 8 hp. Popularly known as "the tram," it would continue the ferry service until 1985. Although the local Kungälv municipality planned to scrap "the tram," a conservation society stepped in so that today, *Hamfärjan II* is the longest-running ferry service in the world.[28]

During 1957 and 1958 the RN built several diesel-electric paddle tugs: *Dexterous*, *Director*, *Faithful*, *Favourite*, *Forceful*, *Grinder* and *Griper*. They were fitted for firefighting, salvage and oil pollution spraying. The electric drive provided quick response to the direct bridge controls, and masts could be lowered by hand turning gear to rest between the funnels when working under the overhang of aircraft carriers.[29]

The Gilpin Motor Board was developed in 1948 by John Gilpin,[30] an inventor in Hollywood, California. Measuring 12 ft (3.8 m) long and 7 inches (17.5 cm) thick and weighing 75 kg, the rudders were mounted on both sides at half the length. Gilpin claimed a top speed of 11.2 kph, with battery autonomy of 8 hours long with overnight recharge. Price: $345. It would be another 60 years before an electric surfboard was produced.

In 1949, Paul Rogers turned the San Marcos Springs, Texas, into a popular tourist attraction and resort he called Aquarena Springs. The name derived from a concatenation of "aqua," referring of course to water, and "arena," referring to a submersible underwater theater that was considered an engineering marvel in a 1952 issue of *Popular Mechanics*. Ralph the Swimming Pig, and frolicking underwater mermaid dancers, became trademarks. Aquarena also offered lake tours in 25-passenger electric-powered glass-bottomed boats. Each seat was padded and there was a glass plate along the center of the bottom of the boat, enabling passengers to lean over the wooden railing and watch the life beneath.[31]

At this period, if one electric outboard was to do more than any other to pioneer and revive electric boating, it was the Accumot, developed by the Preinerstorfer brothers of Gmunden, Upper Austria, at the northern end of Traunsee Lake. During the 1920s, the Preinerstorfer brothers, Franz, Otto and Hermann, ran an electrical and radio business (repair and sales) in Gmunden. Franz and Otto were highly intelligent and interested in everything technical:

> Uncle Franz was almost a genius. He had studied both music and painting in Vienna, creating fine canvasses and composing for organ and violin concertos. Both brothers invented various technical things: an optical arrangement using a system of rotating perforated discs for color photographic toning, both still and moving images (U.S. Patent 2088339); a wireless radio for Gmunden, later Gmunden's Cable One TV, even a prototype color television. Hermann, the youngest brother, was added as an apprentice and so got a very good technical training in an environment always looking for the latest technical and physical achievements. The brothers also took a Siemens & Halske motor and rebuilt it as a 200 watt, 24 volt electric vertical transmission outboard for use in a boat on the local lake.[32]

During the war, Hermann, whose sister had married a textile manufacturer in France with mills in Europe and North Africa, obtained the job as a driver and repairer of the auto electrics of the company trucks. Postwar, although the Preinerstorfer brothers continued their automobile electrical repair business, they kept thinking about the commercial construction of an electric boat motor for private owners.

In about 1947, based in 4, Slagenstrasse, Gmunden, Preinerstorfer began to build the first test engines using components from truck generators. These were above-water engines with an output of about 200–250W. They incorporated the same basic electrical design as would be used in all future units: simple DC series-wound machines whose thick wires made them robust, ideal for safe operation with matching propellers. Initial trials with the power transmission to the horizontal propeller shaft by means of "flexible shafts" functioned, but the solution was noisy and repeatedly led to power cuts in weed-infested waters (the series-wound characteristic gives tremendous torque). Changing over to step-up gear brought a transmission advantage. By 1949, the first sales brochure for the "Akku-Mot," written by the Preinerstorfers' father, Dr. Almoslechner, was published. The 12-volt batteries were made by Feilendorf of Vienna, who supplied that capital city with the entire electric fleet of postal and brewery trucks. The owner, Friedrich Eisenkolb, was a close friend of the Preinerstorfers and also had a summer residence in Gmunden. To regularly recharge these batteries, normally used for trucks, as there was nothing on the market in 1952, using the Accumot philosophy, the Preinerstorfers decided to design and build one themselves. This was a simple and robust unit with tube rectifiers without any shutdown but already with a characteristic control in the transformer, which caused a corresponding constant charging power with increasing battery voltage, and thus with relatively small devices during the night hours. They soon realized that it was a good business idea to offer their specially matched charger with each engine produced. Up to 1990, Accumot would produce thousands of recharging units.

Nine units of 3 kW "Akkumot" Series One outboards were sold in 1952 for boat rental companies in Austria. By 1955, just over 50 units had been sold, some of which are still operational sixty years later.

In 1955 Accumot became one of the first companies in Europe to produce silicon rectifier chargers, while others were still including the old selenium system. These were first used in their "Fantom," a 24-volt, 300-watt robust gearless *underwater* motor with its cooling advantages: twenty such Fantom units were delivered to boat owners for the Austrian lakes. They were of a futuristic design with a vertical control fin and horizontal wings on the side of the engine. With its blue livery and elegant and trademarked Accumot lettering, until 2005, over two thousand engines would be sold, almost exclusively to boat rental firms. Some of these units are still in use. According to Preinerstorfer, "Blue was our family's favorite color and was of course emblematic of the water." Accumot blue would become known worldwide.

In 1958, to offer private boat owners a better performance, the Preinerstorfers of Gmunden came up with their 6-pole "Turbo" with its slightly larger motor diameter. To prevent propeller cavitation and protect from debris, they fitted a streamlined ring. The 30-volt 1000-watt Turbo was sold mainly to boatyards and distributors around the Bavarian lakes, but some units were exported to Switzerland, Miami and even to Caracas. Modified versions of the Turbo (36 v/1600 watts and 24v/750 watts) followed. They largely used Austrian-built batteries such as Bären (Feistritz im Rosental), Elbak (Graz) and Banner (Linz). The sophisticated electrics made it quiet and more resilient, although more expensive. Only a few hundred engines were sold, mainly in Bavaria and Austria, but some machines also went to Switzerland, France, Holland and the USA.

Responding to demand from sports fishermen, Accumot next developed the Minimot, a lightweight, easy-to-use 12-volt 180-watt motor with a pull switch in the machine head. The Mini was followed by the 24-volt Delf—again acquired by thousands of fishermen in the Alpine Lake District, but also sold in Holland, Denmark and Italy.

Lake Neusiedl or Fertő is the largest endorheic lake in Central Europe, straddling the Austria-Hungarian border. The lake covers 315 km² (122 mi²). By the 1960s, Neusiedl, having built up impressive 50-strong fleets of hireboats, required a stronger and more robust unit. As the 300 Fantom fitted to a (18 ft) 5.5 m 4-pax boat was not effective against a strong headwind and choppy waves, in 1961, Accumot developed its 24-volt (500 or 800 watt) Nautilus, which was to continue selling until 2007. Thousands of pieces of this indestructible machine can be found in almost all European countries in boat rentals and private boats. The batteries gave a hireboat up to 6 hours' autonomy a day. With

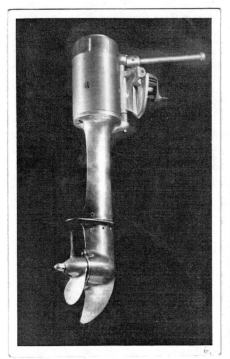

In 1952, the first Akkumot is tested in a dingy (courtesy H. Preinerstorfer).

their traditional aluminum housings, the chargers were especially designed to operate in the increasingly damp boat cabins or even in boxes on the jetty. By the mid–1960s, private pleasure boats were also becoming increasingly popular, and Accumot was there to deliver.

In 1960, Volvo Penta of Sweden marketed their "Aquamatic" sterndrive, an inboard

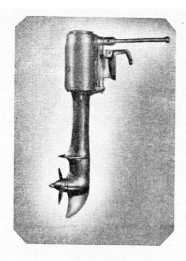

„AKKUMOT"
Elektro-
Außenbordmotor

Seit drei Jahren laufen auf mehreren Seen Österreichs unsere „Akkumot"-Elektro-Außenbordmotore mit bestem Erfolg.

Es entspricht den vielfachen Wünschen der Fahrgäste von Bootsvermietungen, ein mit Motor getriebenes Boot **ohne jede Motorenkenntnis** alleine bedienen und **ohne Bootsführer** fahren zu können.

Die absolute Betriebssicherheit, der nahezu geräuschlose Lauf, die aus dem Aus- und Einschalten bestehende einfache Bedienung und vor allem die niederen Betriebskosten haben unseren „Akkumot"-Elektro-Außenbordmotor als Antrieb für Ruderboote an den Seen schnell bekannt gemacht.

Die Anlage besteht aus:

1 Leichtmetallmotor mit Anhängevorrichtung, zum Heck jedes normalgebauten Ruderbootes passend.
1 Schalter für 2 Fahrgeschwindigkeiten samt Anschlußkabel.
2 Stück Bootsbatterien, zusammen 24 Volt, 90 Amp.-Stunden.
Diese Bootsbatterien wurden für ihren Verwendungszweck speziell entwickelt und haben unverwechselbare Anschlüsse. Die Fahrstundenleistung dieser Bootsbatterien ist größer als die Fahrstundenleistung normaler Kraftfahrzeugbatterien gleicher Größe.
1 Ladegleichrichter.
Der „Akkumot"-Ladewürfel ist an jedes Lichtnetz 220 Volt Wechselstrom anschließbar und ladet in 12 Nachtstunden die Bootsbatterien voll auf.

Eine Voll-Ladung verbraucht 3 Kilowattstunden aus dem Lichtnetz und gewährleistet 8 Fahrstunden am Normalgang oder mehr als 20 Fahrstunden am Schleppgang (für Sportfischer zum Schleppfischen sehr geeignet).

Ein zirka 5 m langes Ruderboot (Rundspant) erreicht mit 2 bis 4 Personen eine Geschwindigkeit von 6 bis 7 Stundenkilometer. Diese Geschwindigkeit liegt etwas höher als die Ruderleistung von zwei Personen.

Mit „Akkumot"-Elektro-Außenbordmotor betriebene Ruderboote sind in Österreich vom Amt für Schiffahrt als Ruderboote anerkannt und unterliegen weder gewerblich noch privat den allgemein für Motorboote geltenden Bestimmungen.

Wir stehen Ihnen gerne mit weiteren Auskünften und eventueller Vorführung unserer „Akkumot"-Elektro-Außenbordmotore zur Verfügung.

Gmunden, Sommer 1954.

H. PREINERSTORFER
Bootsmotore
Gmunden, Schlagenstraße 4
Telephon 141

The first brochure for the Akkumot engine was distributed in 1954 (courtesy H. Preinerstorfer).

engine powering an outboard leg. Accumot responded from 1966 with their 2 kW SD2000 and then in 1970 with their 1.5 kW SD 1500, both still in blue metallic livery. Each had three advance and three astern positions. In 1969, some 70 SD2000s were shipped out to the USA to enter service at the Six Flags theme parks in Georgia and Texas. At these parks, twin units powered each 20-pax boat around an excursion called "LaSalle's River

Adventure," inspired by the historical La Salle Expeditions in the late 1600s, through a wilderness full of animated puppets. The canals were only slightly wider than the boats so that the motors were fitted at the bow and the stern for greater control.

Accumot's next development was with their more powerful 72-volt SZ4000 and SZ4000, basically two engines combined into one, units of which powered private boats and passenger boats in Europe, Lebanon and Iraq. In 1978, two engines were delivered to Lake Kozjak, Plitvice Lakes National Park in Croatia, where they powered a 50-pax boat.

During this period, an electric outboard had been developed in the USA. In 1946, Garrett H. Harris, a 30-year-old home building contractor in Jackson, Mississippi, was tired of sculling his small bass fishing boat around nearby 16 mi (25.74 km) Ross Barnett Reservoir (also known as "The Rez"). So he began toying with the idea of building an electric motor to move his boat along at fishing speeds. Although the SilverTrol electric motor had been invented some 30 years before, Harris found it to be awkward to use, having to turn it on and then steer by hand. He wanted something he could operate *with his foot* to leave his hands free to fish. After months of experiments, Harris finally produced a spring-loaded direction control that he could operate with his foot to guide the boat. And when he took his foot off the pedal, the spring would return the electric motor to the straight-ahead setting. Harris obtained an initial patent for the system in 1947 (U.S. 2545086 A), then continued to patent his subsequent modifications as he made them. Twelve years later, with the boom in bass fishing, Garrett Harris enjoyed a happy coincidence. He became friends with Dick Herschede, owner of the Herschede Hall Clock Co., makers of high-quality grandfather clocks, who had just moved to Starkville. In 1960, Herschede agreed to build and sell Harris's unit, trademarking it as the "Guide-Rite." Soon after, they changed the name to MotorGuide and it became extremely popular with bass fishermen across the USA.[33]

The MotorGuide slowed down the sales of Accumot's Minimot; but the Austrian family soon hit back with their 300 w/12 volt "Hobby," whose innovations included heat-curable epoxy resins as a building material for propellers and parts of structures, which was done using in-house injection molding machinery. The Hobby was much appreciated by anglers and dinghy-sailors: by 2006 around two thousand had been built and sold.[34]

In 1957–1958, the British Admiralty commissioned seven 157 ft (48 m) diesel-electric paddle tugs; each paddle wheel was driven by an individual electric motor, giving outstanding maneuverability. Their main role was to provide berthing assistance to aircraft carriers. The very wide 60 ft (18 m) beam over the paddle boxes allowed the tugs to tuck under the protruding flight decks of carriers without catching their funnels. *Dexterous, Director, Faithful* and *Forceful* were built by Yarrow Shipbuilders at Scotstoun in 1957. *Griper* and *Grinder* were built by William Simons & Co. at Renfrew in 1958. *Favourite* was built by Ferguson Brothers of Port Glasgow. There were four diesel engines per vessel, each with a 24-hour rating of 585 bhp at 1,000 rpm. Each engine was coupled to a 340kW generator. There were two 600-volt DC propulsion motors per vessel, each producing 800 bhp at 212 rpm. The electrical machinery and control gear were manufactured by British Thomson-Houston.[35]

At the same time, Saunders-Roe shipyard at Cowes on the Isle of Wight built a class of eighteen 70-ft (21 m) fast patrol boats, called the Dark Class. Five of these (T201-T205), built entirely of riveted aluminum, were sold to the Burmese government. While they were powered by twin 5,000 hp Napier Deltic engines to give them a top speed of 40 knots, they were also fitted with bespoke alternative power, known as Slow Speed Drives. This was to help cope with the confined jungle waterways in that area of the world and also enable the Burmese Navy to creep silently along the many creeks to combat piracy, smuggling, and illegal fishing.[36]

In 1959, Commander Jacques-Yves Cousteau and engineer Jean Mollard at the French Center for Undersea Research developed what they called a "soucoupe plongeante" (= diving saucer), a one-man mini-submersible. Inspired by the propulsion system of the squid, which sucks water in from the front and spits it out at the back, they developed a battery-electric waterjet system. The SP-350, more affectionately known as *Denise*, was the first generation recreational submarine. Electric lamps were fitted for night diving and to provide illumination for photography at extreme working depths. An electrically operated manipulator arm could be fitted at the front of the craft to pick up objects for the crew to examine through the portholes. The underwater jet-pack scuba used by James Bond 007 in the 1965 film *Thunderball* is said to have been in part inspired by *Denise*.[37]

In 1964, it was decided to refit the 82.4-m (270 ft) tall-masted training ship *Amerigo Vespucci* (built 1931) with diesel-electric propulsion, using a 4-stroke, 8-cylinder FIAT B 308 ESS to generate electric power for one electric Marelli propulsion motor that could produce up to about 1471 kW (2000 hp).[38]

In 1968, on one of his annual holiday trips to Italy, Jette Mortensen, the technical director of the Tivoli Gardens, Copenhagen, made a stop in the Salzkammergut region and saw the Accumot-electric boats there. He immediately contacted Gmunden because the Tivoli had a problem: Many small boats for 2 people went there on a small ornamental Dragon Boat Lake and had had a pneumatic drive since the 1930s. These compression air tanks were only good for a short ride and many lost pressure, leaving passengers stranded out on the middle of the lake. To guarantee an extremely high life expectancy, Accumot developed their "TIVOLI 12 Volt 150 Watt" based on the "FANTOM 24V 300W": This was the first "pod propulsion system" with electrically driven small boats.[39]

The concept of the Tivoli motor was for the boats to run nonstop, from 8 o'clock in the morning until sometimes midnight. After a certain journey time the boats successively entered a channel for disembarking and embarking passengers and new crew. So they were equipped with 12-volt Accumot tube panels and batteries in pairs charged by 24-volt Accumot loading machines. This system worked for decades, and periodically the 50 engines were returned to the Gmunden factory in large crates for servicing.

Even in Abidjan, Ivory Coast, a similar park was built and its 40 boats equipped by Accumot. Accumot also developed a 300-watt model they called the LEG 24 for use in Legoland Parks in Denmark and Sweden. Ninety units were built by the 12-strong Austrian workforce. Since the late 1960s, sixty Accumots have given reliable service at the Phantasialand theme park in Brühl, North Rhine-Westphalia, Germany.

During these years the 8–15-strong workforce at Accumot were building 500 units complete with their recharging machines per year. Through continuous operation throughout the season of the parks, these engines achieved a tremendous mileage. Silent blue Accumots were also seen in Israel, Jordan, the Philippines, Iraq … and even England.

In 1968, Edward and Dinnie Hawthorne of Bourne End on the River Thames fitted a 500w Accumot electric motor onto their 15-ft (4m50) shopping boat *Dynia* so as to no longer frighten their collie dog Laird. Hawthorne had been interested in boating and the

River Thames from childhood. A keen rower, he had taken bow position in the Cambridge Eight who won the Varsity Boat Race in 1940. A mechanical engineer by training, he had worked on aero-engine and gas-turbine development. In the years to come, Edward Hawthorne would do much to promote electric boats on the Cookham to Marlow reach of river and indeed became the doyen of electric boat heritage on the Upper Thames.[40]

Some innovations were made during this period which would eventually play an important part in the development of electric boats.

Taking up Gustave Trouvé's idea, proposed in 1887, of a battery-powered ship deriving its energy from sea water, in the 1950s, Ralph E. McCabe of Forks of Salmon, California, in the Siskiyou County hack country, a lanky, 52-year-old gold miner, inventor and former Detroit auto worker, built no fewer than 36 model boats and tested their electrolytic efficiency at various points in the Atlantic, Pacific and the Gulf of Mexico. For these, McCabe developed a saltwater battery with carbon-graphite plates for the positive, and a nickel-zinc electrode for the negative pole. The saltwater battery could be mounted horizontally or vertically below the ship's hull, the movement of the boat ensuring the continuous flow of seawater. Two of these prototypes, *Mamie* and *The Eighth Wonder of the World*, were each 21 in (53 cm) long with a 4½ in (12 cm) beam and they weighed 2½ and 3 lbs, respectively. Each produced a little over one volt and up to three amperes of current, enough to drive them through the water at speeds up to 5 mph (8 kph). To promote his invention, McCabe planned a series of boat races, but nothing came of it.[41]

In the early 1950s, an English engineer, Professor Thomas Bacon of Cambridge University, was making considerable progress developing the first practical hydrogen-oxygen fuel cell to present large-scale demonstrations. One of the first of these demonstrations consisted of a 1959 Allis-Chalmers farm tractor powered by a stack of 1,008 cells. With 15,000 watts of power, the tractor generated enough power to pull a weight of about 3,000 pounds (1,360 kg). Allis-Chalmers maintained a research program for some years, building a fuel cell–powered golf cart, submersible, and fork lift; but not a boat. The U.S. Air Force also participated in this program.[42]

Over in the States, Karl Kordesch, working at Union Carbide in Parma, created the thin carbon fuel cell electrode. He presented a fuel cell demonstration at the Brussels World Fair in 1958, using a suitcase with a hydrogen-oxygen fuel cell. His development of thin electrodes for fuel cells came soon thereafter. In 1967 Kordesch built a fuel cell/NiCad battery hybrid electric motorcycle. The motorcycle was featured in television commercials for the program *21st Century*, hosted by Walter Cronkite. Kordesch relished telling people how he had to join the actors' union to ride in the commercials. It was fitted with a hydrazine fuel cell, capable of 200 miles (322 km) to the U.S. gallon. Kordesch ran up over 300 miles on the motorbike. In 1970 Kordesch fitted his own Austin A40 with a hydrogen fuel cell (ammonia being too hard to come by), and used the adapted vehicle as his personal transportation for over three years. The fuel cell was installed in the trunk of the car and hydrogen tanks on the roof, leaving room for 4 passengers in the 4-door car. It had a driving range of 180 miles (300 km). Thus, he was the first person in the world to have produced and driven a practical fuel cell/battery electric car. His fuel cell design provided the basis for the 40 kWh alkaline hydrogen-oxygen fuel cell for the General Motors Electrovan, which had a PEM fuel cell, a range of 120 miles (193 km) and a top speed of 70 mph (113 kph). There were only two seats, as the fuel cell stack and fuel tanks took up the rear portion of the van. Only one was built, as the project was deemed cost-prohibitive. General Electric and others continued working on PEM fuel cells in the 1970s.[43]

In 1965, Siemens R&D equipped a boat called *Eta* with a fuel cell propulsion system and demonstrated it on a pond at their Erlangen Research Center in Bavaria. But it was 3 decades later before this technology would be installed in a succession of boats, then ships.

FIVE

Rebirth

What the outboard units made by Accumot of Gmunden, Austria, had achieved for electric boating in Europe, if any one man was responsible for reviving the inboard electric boat in America and beyond, it was Marshall Dixon Duffield, Jr. During the past 45 years Duffy's firm has made and sold some 14,000 electric boats. Therefore his career plays an important part in this history.

His father, Marshall Duffield, Sr., quarterbacked USC's 1930 Rose Bowl–winning team, earning the nickname "Field Marshall." He sold liquor wholesale, built the Rancho San Joaquin golf course, and developed real estate.[1]

Duffy Jr., born in 1952, grew up in a waterfront home beside Newport Bay, California, sailing, tinkering with motors, inventing. He sketched sailboats in his bedroom and built a tank in his yard to test his models.[2]

In the summer of 1969, before his senior year in high school, Duffy grew frustrated with the constant breakdowns of his family's gas-powered runabout. He was advised by his friend Kurt Olsen that one way to solve the problem would be to put a golf cart motor in it. Duffy asked his father for a $300 loan to buy an old cart with an electric motor. Outside a Quonset hut his father owned on 17th Street in Costa Mesa, Duffy and his friend Jack A. Heiser tested the first electric boat engine. They had six batteries in a row and four wires to connect. The experiment sparked and clattered and required constant oil. But it worked. The boat was slow, the motor made a terrible whining sound, and the controls overheated too quickly. A lot needed to be perfected.

In 1970, Duffy started building a youth-class racing sailboat. His boats won every major West Coast sailing event in the class. He also began using the electric boat to squire girls around Newport Harbor. A few months later, an elderly man demanded to know what type of batteries powered the boat. Duffield showed him a row of Trojan Batteries, and the man—who turned out to be Ray Godber, president of the Trojan Battery Co.— ordered his wife to get the checkbook out!

"I don't make them for sale," Duffield recalls saying. "You do now," Godber replied. Godber bought a boat from Duffy Jr., so beginning the world's first electric pleasureboat-building company for half a century. Godber gave Duffy some start-up capital and directed him to engineers at General Motors who could help him to design the production prototype. Before long, with contacts and finance from Godber's brother Dick, orders were coming in so fast for the "water-going golf cart," he had to leave college. By 1973 a tiny fleet of Duffy 20s had started to quietly cluster in Newport Harbor. Duffield used to drop the electric boats off on the docks of interested customers, leave the keys, and ride

Above: The first Duffy in Newport Harbor, 1970 (Duffy collection). *Right:* Marshall Duffield, Jr., 21, next to an Edison (Duffy collection).

a bicycle home. He soon outgrew the 17th Street Quonset hut, moving to a nearby factory. During the next twenty years, the number of boats produced would grow to thousands.

At the same time, W.D. "Bill" Schock of Santa Ana developed the Duffy 18-footer (5m50) into the traditional-looking Newport Electric Packet, powered by a 2.5 hp 36-volt DC motor and six 6-volt deep-charge lead-acid batteries. It came in three versions: the Classic, the Surrey Top and the Hard Top. It was nicknamed the "electric Schock."

Still in the same state, 80 miles northwest of Duffy in Newport Beach, the year 1969 saw the creation of Westlake Village, a planned "Venice-style" community that straddles the Los Angeles and Ventura County line. The appearance of electric boats began when one of the village's new residents, Frank Butler, founder of Catalina Yachts, one of the biggest boat designers and manufacturers in the world, had his yard build a 15-ft (4m50) boat equipped with 4 large batteries and a 1.5 hp DC motor and called the *Runaboat*. Behind the project was Skip Toller, who, with the help of his wife Cheryl, in 1979 set up the ElectraCraft line of what he called "floating golf carts." The first three models were to grow to 8, ranging from the 10-ft (3m) Jonty to 21-ft (6m40) Coastal Cruiser. While 600 boats were sold to Westlake Village residents, before long ElectraCraft were seen in 32 other states and in other protected waterways in England, Holland, Sweden, Japan, Canada, Cayman Islands and China.

In 1970, the Minn Kota electric trolling outboard company was bought by Samuel C. Johnson of Racine, Wisconsin, the owner of the $2 billion Johnson Wax empire. Johnson, who had set up a subsidiary of his firm called Johnson Outdoors, happened to be a freshwater fishing enthusiast, and so he took a particular interest in improving the Minn Kota motor for better bass fishing. Recently, Minn Kota had brought out an electric motor with reverse switch and a foot-operated electric steer remote control, and during the next few years Sam Johnson directed innovation with an electronic variable speed control trademarked as the Maximizer.

Elsewhere, Walter C. Beckmann, who operated the Rhode Island Marine Services, located in Snug Harbor, was recognized for building antique replica harbor tugs. In the 1980s, Beckmann offered his red *Kathy 22*, powered by a 3.5 hp General Electric 5B DC motor, and a fantailed Commodore Twenty with a 1.5 hp 36 volt DC motor. Douglas Little set up Black Water Boats in North Carolina to produce electric canoes and kayaks, implementing submersible motors, building over 100 boats between 1985 and his retirement in 2012. For many years his most popular boat, the single-passenger Black River Guide, was raffled off twice a year as a fundraiser for the North Carolina Maritime Museum in Beaufort, North Carolina.[3]

After retiring from the U.S. Army, while tinkering with boats on his local Lake Barcroft in Virginia, Morton Ray was disappointed by the unreliability of ex-gasoline e-obm conversions. So in 1973, he single-handedly built the first prototype of his electric outboard in the basement of his home in Annandale. This was a 3-speed battery-switching control system, 9" (22 cm) prop and exposed GE motor. "I made the patterns, the furnace to melt the aluminium, the moulds and machined the castings and other parts on a Sears lathe. When we poured the aluminium into the moulds, it was my wife Dot's job to hold one end of the shank! The next year the five speed model with enclosed cowl was introduced. We never ever used a resistor or battery tapping system although we were accused of it. The controls were very efficient." Over the next two decades the Ray electric outboard would enjoy a limited but highly respected production.

Back in the USSR, in 1971, Comrade Vladimir M. Karpachyov, director of the Pskov

Electric Machine Building Plant, beside Lake Peipus near Leningrad (today's Saint Petersburg), gave orders that a prototype electric outboard should be developed alongside their 5 to 30 kW range of DC and AC motors. The "snetok" (Снеток (Корюшка = smelt)— *Osmerus eperlanus eperlanus morpha spirinchus Pallas*), named after a fish that bred in the local lake, was both foldable and could be dismantled into two parts for ease of transport. The prototype was widely tested on the Chyornaya River, 70 km north of Pskov, and in many small lakes such as Uzhinskaye. In time, the Pskov plant would be manufacturing 100 outboards per month for the Soviet Union and beyond.[4]

Over in the UK, in 1975, Rear Admiral Philip Gick, OBE, the 62-year-old director of the Emsworth Shipyard, near Chichester, began to play a key role of the reintroduction of electric boats when he designed and built a 16-ft (4m90) day boat for interior use at His Majesty Sultan Qaboos bin Said's summer palace.

"Percy" Gick had been a war hero. Less than a month after joining 825 Squadron, flying Swordfish biplanes from the carrier HMS *Victorious*, Lieutenant Gick was involved in the hunt for the German battleship *Bismarck* in May 1941. During an initial attack at night, he was the only pilot out of nine to score a torpedo hit, though no significant damage was inflicted. He went on to serve on a total of eight aircraft carriers, and was awarded the DSC and Bar and twice mentioned in dispatches. Retiring from the Royal Navy in 1964, Gick decided to commute his pension, and threw himself into a demanding new project, turning the former logging ponds at Emsworth, near Chichester, into a yacht harbor. Making use of local plant hire companies, he did much of the physical work himself, losing a finger in the process. Within five years he created the Emsworth Yacht Harbour, one of the first such enterprises in the country. Two years later in 1976, Emsworth Shipyard's electrically driven waterjet-propelled *Waterbeetle* was shown at the Earls Court Boat Show.[5]

The Königsee fleet in German Bavaria had continued its services: 26 electric boats with a total capacity of 1,870 passengers were transporting over 800,000 passengers each year. A further 2 e-pax operated on the Rursee in the Eifel Mountains, 2 on the Titisee in the Black Forest, 3 on the Maschsee in Hanover, and 9 on the Bundesgartenschau in Kassel.[6]

In the late 1970s, Oswald Kraütler of Lustenau on the Rhine, Austria, on the Swiss border, built an electric motor for his own boat. Finding that there was no product on the market which satisfied his high demands, he founded a company. In time, the Kraütler family concern would manufacture a range of electric inboards, outboards, saildrives and fixed pod motors, with a power output from 0.5 to 120 kW.

Although the fuel crisis of the 1970s caused car manufacturers to search for alternative power sources, the return of the electric boat took a little longer. The resurgence of interest was encouraged by the import of electric outboards developed in America as trolling motors for fishermen on the lakes, Minn Kota and MotorGuide in particular.

In 1973 the Dudley Canal Trust had organized boats to take tourists through the tunnel of their newly restored canal. But to propel the boats through the tunnel, the method of legging was used. This was extremely tiring for the crew. So in 1975, the Trust took a steel narrowboat (built in 1910), fitted it with a thirty-year-old 6.5 hp electric motor formerly used in a milk float (or delivery truck) and a bank of Exide batteries, and so created *Electra*, the world's first electric narrowboat.[7]

In spring 1978, with the cooperation of the Electricity Council, the Lead Development Association and Derek Davison of Davison & Bros., Long Eaton and Emsworth

Dudley Canal Trust's *Electra* was powered by a milk float engine and Exide batteries, 1976 (author's collection).

Shipyard, an 8-meter Trentcraft was fitted out at Emsworth with electric instead of diesel propulsion. It was an Austrian Accumot engine. During that summer, the *Electra of Emsworth* appeared at the IWA Rally at Reading, and then operated on the Thames and canals based in Little Venice. In May 1979 she was launched at Chertsey by Rear Admiral Percy Gick and his wife, who set out to attend the Tameside Canals Festival at Ashton under Lyne, and on their way home to attend the next IWA Rally at Birmingham. During the summer about five different crew spent a week or two in her and just charged their batteries overnight or occasionally briefly in the middle of the day from any convenient 13 amp socket. These were usually in marinas and boatyards where a berth had been booked in advance, but occasionally at a pub or farm, and on several occasions from a private house whose owner was delighted to welcome a boat that made no noise and had no bad smell. By the end of the summer *Electra* had totted up 600 miles.[8]

Predictions by Japanese, German and American researchers that within the next ten years the cost of solar cells would be reduced to 20p/w, with an increase in output to 10w/ft^2, prompted a 65-year-old former consultant on railway electrification switchgear, Alan T. Freeman of Rugby in England, to make a practical study of the viability of future uses of this form of energy. In 1967 Freeman had converted a Berkeley sports automobile to battery power and during the next ten years he had been silently totting up 16,000 km. After that, Freeman built a ¼-scale miniature car which he was able to power with a 14-watt Ferranti solar cell. This vehicle model was then equipped with five Ferranti 7w solar modules mounted horizontally to produce 28 watts and give it a speed of 6.4 kph.

In 1975, Freeman decided to go afloat. He built himself a simple 8-ft (2.5 m) long catamaran in marine plywood and duralumin. At first, he equipped *Solar Craft I* with

In the summer of 1979 *Electra of Emsworth*, seen on the Ashton Canal near Dunkinfold Junction, clocked some 600 miles (author's collection).

ten Lucas solar modules, each comprising 5 cells connected in series to give a maximum output of 1.3 w. The total weight of *Solar Craft I* worked out at 38 lb (17.2 kg), of which 7 lb (3.2 kg) were the solar panels. Freeman's little boat first sailed under solar power on February 19, 1975, and during the summer a speed of 2.4 kph was recorded. This was the birth of solar-powered boating.

During the following winter, Freeman carried out further modifications, replacing the single solar panel replaced by two Ferranti MST 102 solar panels mounted fore and aft, giving a total output of 28 w. (14 v at 2A), increasing motor speed to 1800 rpm, geared down at 2/1 ratio to 900 rpm. He tested fifteen types of propeller in a home-built water tank—and was consequently able to increase the gear ratio to give a propeller speed of 450 rpm. These changes increased the speed of *Solar Craft I* to 2.5–3 mph and the final two-bladed aluminum prop was 7.5 inch in diameter with a pitch of 7 inches.

On May 10, 1978, this revolutionary craft made a trip of 4.1 miles (6.6 km) in 2 hours on the Oxford Canal at Rugby. It was an extremely sunny day, although Freeman found that his power efficiency was interfered with by the vapor trails left by jet aircraft. Waiting patiently for the price of solar cells to come down, Freeman wrote, perhaps prophetically: "There are approximately 25,000 craft on British Waterways and the speed of *Solar Craft I* can be viewed in context with the maximum permissible speed on the Canals = 4 mph (6.4 kph)...."[9]

In 1980, Max Schick of Vidy, Switzerland, head of a solar energy company, launched his *Sunenergy 1* on Lake Geneva. Solar cells covered its roof, enabling two 12V batteries to give an autonomy of 10 hours for a maximum speed of 6 kph. During summer 1980,

Alan Freeman helms his *Solar Craft I*, the world's first solar-electric boat, 1976 (author's collection).

Max Schick's son Claude and his co-driver Jean-Pierre Siegenthaler tested and monitored the performance of *Sunenergy 1*, exhibiting it at the Comptoir Suisse Show in Lausanne. During the summer of 1981, *La Tribune-Le-Matin* newspaper and *Romande* radio station voyaged on the Swiss lakes and rivers between Yverdon-les-Bains and Solothurn. Throughout this 155-mile (250 km) cruise, which lasted a week, on-board journalists wrote reports and made direct broadcasts about the water and its lacustrine environment. On June 9, 1981, Schick presented a 4-pax 1m40 (4.6 ft) solar boat on a small lake near Sierre, naming it *Geronde* after the lake.[10]

In May 1981, Roger Martire, a 56-year-old paint manufacturer of Puy l'Evêque by the River Lot in France, who had spent ten years developing and then patenting his MAP (= Moteur à Aimants Permanents), a permanent magnet electric motor, decided to test it out, with a small solar panel on a scale model cabin cruiser called the *Espadon* (= *Swordfish*) provided by Yves Basillou of the nearby Cahors Model Club. Tests proved promising, so Martire asked Monsieur Bas to let him borrow and equip a small catamaran pedalo with a larger motor and a mast supporting a removable double solar panel. The 108 solar cells, by Soleco of Narbonne, provided a power of 100 watts, enabling a speed of 3 knots (a little more than 5 kph). Helped by a retired engineer called Paul Gauthiez, Martire was able to demonstrate his MG1, *Solar Glisseur,* on the local River Lot the "Corso Naval fleuri" during the Puy l'Evêque fête. They demonstrated *Solar Glisseur* elsewhere— at the Trois Nautiques at Port Camargue, at La Rochelle and the Minimes, in Monte Carlo Harbor—and exhibited it at the 1982–83 Paris Boat Show. Encouraged, MGI not only mortgaged their homes to attempt to borrow money to start up a boatyard, but

Roger Martire, right, and his son on the *Solar Glisseur,* France's first electric boat (courtesy Roger Martire).

planned bigger craft for a cross–Mediterranean voyage, then a transatlantic voyage. Martire also ambitiously planned to use the MAP motor to power an automobile he called *Solaroto*. "But we were ahead of our time and nobody was prepared to sponsor us."[11]

Other power systems were considered but never adopted. In 1977, a journalist in *Boating* magazine predicted: "Sooner or later, I predict, there will be restrictions on the use of petroleum fuels in pleasure boats. Perhaps by then scientists will have developed a pleasure boat sized nuclear power plant; they've got some running a few of our lighthouses already."[12]

The Arrival of the Lithium-Ion Battery

During the same period, *the lithium-ion battery*, which would totally change the autonomy and speed of electric boats, was being developed. In the fall of 1972, M. Stanley Whittingham, an English-born chemist working with a team at the Exxon Research and Engineering Company, announced that they had come up with a new battery, and patents were filed within a year. Within a couple of years the parent company, Exxon Enterprises, wheeled out a 3W 45Ah prototype lithium cells, and linking it to a diesel engine, started work on hybrid vehicles.

When solid-state physicist Professor John Goodenough became head of inorganic chemistry at Oxford University in 1976, his research group included assistant Dr. Phil Wiseman, Dr. Koichi Mizushima and Dr. Phil Jones. They set themselves the task of looking at the potential of rechargeable batteries, which began by simply "kicking around ideas on a blackboard." "We looked at it in a different way using lithium cobalt oxide at the positive terminal and pulling the lithium out; this produced a huge cell voltage, twice that of the Exxon battery," Dr. Wiseman explained. "It was this spare voltage that allowed alternatives at the other terminal where Exxon had been forced to use lithium metal which was fraught with problems. Instead lithium-ion material could compose both electrodes."

The group's research was published in the *Materials Research Bulletin* in 1980. In 1977, Whittingham teamed up with John B. Goodenough to publish a book, *Solid State Chemistry of Energy Conversion and Storage*. But unlike solar power, it would not be for another fifteen years that the lithium-ion battery would be found in the hull of an electric boat.

Meanwhile, in 1979 Roger Davis of the Original Boat Company of Evesham on England's River Avon cooperated with Midlands Electricity Board and Chloride Industrial Batteries (traditional lead-acid battery suppliers) to build *Electric Blue*, a 50-ft (15 m) narrowboat, followed by *Electric Monarch*. "After many years' experience of diesel boats and hiring to the public, it became apparent that something had to be done to produce a boat which would be as kind as possible to the environment and, yet, provide the pleasure and convenience that users demanded. After evaluation of the alternatives it was decided that the use of battery-electric power offered the best solution."[13]

The fact that the venue was the River Avon was largely due to David Hutchings, an architect with a vision: to contribute to the revival of Britain's neglected inland waterways. He had organized the restoration of the southern section of the 13-mile Stratford Canal in 1964, then the Lower Avon Navigation, and then from 1969 to 1974 the Upper Avon. So it came within his vision that these canals should welcome electric narrowboats. His pioneer plan was for them to cruise between Upton-on-Severn and Stratford-upon-Avon on seven-day holidays and part of their time going around the "ring" through Worcester, Wolverhampton, Birmingham, Stratford-upon-Avon, Evesham, Tewkesbury, and back to Upton. The stages between charging points were arranged to cause the least inconvenience to the user.

Indeed, in 1981, again on Hutchings's hospitable initiative, Michael G. Mayer of the Lead Development Association held a seminar on electric boats for inland waterways on October 6, 1981, at Stratford-upon-Avon, better known as the home of the playwright William Shakespeare. Papers were delivered, including one by Roger Davis of the Original Boat Company, while demonstrations were given of his electric narrowboat, and of Rear-Admiral Gick's electric workboat *Electra of Emsworth*. An Accumot electric outboard was also on show. Hutchings, announcing that the Upper Avon Navigation Trust would be charging only *half* the licensing fee for electric boats moored on that river, stated prophetically: "The rebirth of electric boats with modern technology can play a vital role in getting more people to use and value our inland waters."[14]

Another key pioneer in the British revival was Jestyn St. Davids. Since his childhood, Jestyn Reginald Austin Plantagenet Philipps, 2nd Viscount St. Davids, Baron Strange of Knockyn, Hungerford and de Moleyns, had loved boats. He crewed a Basque cargo boat during the Spanish Civil War, enjoyed a Thames sailing barge on the Essex coast, crewed a square-rigger around the British coast, and stowed away to Guinea on an iron ore carrier. He also became a glider pilot above Dunstable Downs. From his love of diving, down to four fathoms, he had built up a beautiful collection of shells, one of which he turned into his beloved "Captain's Cup."

His Lordship first became involved with electric boats in 1981 at the age of 64: "I heard about work being done by Roger Davis at Evesham. I was sure it was the only thing to do, in the long run. I had a boat built by Davis, sold a small amount of family silver to part-pay for it, hence the name *Silver Sail*. In 1982, with my wife Margerie, we cruised her up from Evesham to our home at Camden Town—her maiden voyage, included going up to Lechlade on the way. Originally she had an Italian Selva outboard mounted on a British Seagull leg, which we soon replaced with twin Austrian Accumots, supplied by John Fryer of Reading."[15] In the next ten years, with Jestyn and his wife Marjorie at the helm, *Silver Sail* would complete 365 days total cruising, covering 3,500 miles and 1560 lock gates. For the most part, recharging was accomplished using modest 13-amp power sockets.[16]

Three months later, on January 26, 1982, a meeting was held in Committee Room 3A of the House of Lords, Westminster, London, arranged by Viscount St. Davids. Twenty-three interested parties from the electric vehicle and boating industries came together at Westminster to discuss electric boat potential. Among those present were Lord Ironside of the Electric Vehicle Association and Lord Lucas of Chilworth. An association was proposed and discussed. Its objectives should be to install charging points, create boat designs, and reduce license fees. Lord St. Davids expressed the need to have a membership class for individual owners—a users' group.

The indefatigable David Hutchings was at the meeting with a plan: "To establish, if possible with Government help, a trial fleet of at least 20 electric narrowboats on the Avon Ring." Prime Minister Margaret Thatcher's UK government decided not to participate, considering it "inappropriate for a Government Department (of Industry) to be too closely associated with the formation of a trade association...."

So it was that a meeting was held on May 20, 1982, at the Electricity Council, Mill-bank, London SW, which marked the official birth of the Electric Boat Association. Seventeen people attended. Giles Baker of Anglo-Welsh Narrowboats was elected as the EBA's first chairman. Lord St. Davids became chairman of the users' group. Michael Mayer became first secretary.[17]

A second meeting at Millbank involved altering and improving the draft constitution to include boats of up to 100 tons. Then on June 16, 1982, the EBA held its first executive council meeting at the Lead Development Association, N° 34, Berkeley Square, not far from Bond Street in London's West End. For the next eight years, the Electric Boat Association's HQ would be "where a nightingale sang."[18]

And the great debate began. Would future electric boats incorporate the ability to recharge from 13-amp sockets as well as from 30-amp sockets? Chairman Baker also envisaged two lines of development: (1) hireboats with a 15–30 hour range, and (2) day launches with an 8-hour range. The EBA would become a clearinghouse for technical information. St. Davids announced that for May 1983 a special "Boat-a-float Show" would be held near his residence at Little Venice and perhaps there should be an EBA presence.[19]

In February 1983, His Lordship published the EBA Private Boat Owners' (or Users' Group) Section Newsletter N°1, in which he suggested: "We ought to meet soon; London is probably the best place. There are not many of us yet, so would my house do? I can supply some refreshments if I plan the numbers."

EBA Secretary Mayer was flooded with electric boat correspondence—a huge, bulging file generating more interest than any other of his lead development work! There was much interest from overseas, for example, with this advert "Electric Boat for Sale, Canot Breton grp 4,5 m Location: Côte d'Azur, France."

Also in 1982, a steam engine enthusiast called Rupert Latham at Wroxham, Norfolk, built his first electric boat, the 18-ft *Papagena*, using GRP construction, a dark blue BKB electric motor made in Birmingham and an advanced electric propulsion system.

As a boy, Rupert Melville Latham was entranced by the boats cruising past Bolney Court, the family's mock Tudor riverside house in Lower Shiplake on Thames. Then in 1964, Rupert's father Jack Latham bought the Wroxham-based Collins boatyard and its hireboat fleet of 31 luxury cruisers, with a vision of providing top-quality cruisers for hire. After serving time as marine engineer in the Merchant Navy, in 1966 Rupert joined the family boat-building business and helped to increase the family's hireboat fleet to 35.

When he was sixteen years old, Rupert advertised a steam engine for sale. It had belonged to his grandfather. This brought him into contact with steam enthusiasts Derek and Janet Mills, who would go on to found the Steamboat Association of Great Britain. By his twenties, Rupert had begun to restore steam launches. In 1974 he found the derelict hull of a naval steam cutter called *Falcon*. He restored the hull and installed an 1895 Simpson and Strickland twin-crank quadruple expansion engine and boiler. In 1980, Latham set up the Steam & Electric Launch Co. in his newly established Wroxham Barns Craft Center. Looking for a hull to mold in fiberglass, he came across a transom-sterned timber launch hull that a friend had bought at the Stalham Boat Auction.

Having added a counter stern and taken a mold off it, Latham approached a young naval architect, Andrew Wolstenholme, who had studied yacht and boat design at Southampton College of Technology. "He came to me just a few days before he was going down to the Steam Boat Association annual dinner realizing that he had nothing to show people on his new project and asked me if I could draw something up. I measured the mold, and then did a drawing of a launch with elliptical coamings, a varnished sheer strake, and using the bronze tiller used on a local sailing half decker (the Y&BOD). I clearly remember him being excited and saying that he hadn't realized she could look so good. I charged him about £35 for my time and the boat was developed just as my drawing."[20]

Rupert called the boat *Frolic*, after an old Edwardian photo he had of a boat of the same name once owned by the Bolton & Paul family. The new boat's single cylinder steam engine was built by David King, a well-known Norfolk steam enthusiast and engineer of the Thames Steam Launch Co. Wroxham Barns was initially Latham's main source of income, and it was only on selling his share to the co-owner of the Wroxham Barns business that he was able to invest in running the Steam & Electric Launch Co. full time. Then a customer who lived on the river outside Horning asked him for an electric *Frolic* for use on the Norfolk Broads. It was very simple, with a wide amidships seat box which housed a single battery to one side and a motor to the other with a belt drive to the shaft—a great little electric boat. The next step for the Steam and Electric Launch Company (STELCO) was to develop a completely new boat. Andrew Wolstenholme designed a 21-footer (6m40), again as a steam boat with electric coming later and not really considered at the design stage. Fortuitously the counterstern lends itself to electric, since adding more weight does not dramatically change drag as it does with a transom-stern boat when its transom is immersed. In the years to come, 150 Frolic 21s were built and would do more to raise awareness of the viability of electric boats than any other, certainly in the UK.

That first electric Frolic 21 was a fleet dayboat built for Robin and Patrick Richardson (Phoenix Fleet) at Potter Heigham, and using an Accumot pod. The Richardsons subsequently went on to create the first electric dayboat fleet using more Frolics, but with shaft drive, and for these, Latham went to a company called Nelco. Its name formed from the surnames of its founders, Nelson and Collin, Nelco Ltd. of Basingstoke made electric forklift trucks, although during World War II they had supplied DC electric motors to the Royal Navy. For his first controllers, he went to Curtis Instruments (UK) Ltd in Northampton, England, who had recently produced their MOSFET (= metal-oxide-semiconductor field-effect transistor), as invented by Stephen Post. The challenge was linking up these two components to perform efficiently.

During this time, the first magazine articles about electric boating began to appear in several British boating periodicals. Indeed, this author had an article, "The Silent Age of Battery Boating" published in *Motor Boat and Yachting*. The article was mostly history, but concluded, "Perhaps the time is ripe for a revival of electric boating."[21] I little knew that the revival had already begun!

Following my article, I received a phone call from Rear Admiral Gick inviting me down to the River Thames to take a ride on his new electric boat, 32-ft *Patricia*. Bossoms Boat Yard of Oxford had made her fiberglass hull using a sleek Saunders electric launch built in 1902 as a mold and then fitted her out with modern electrical propulsion. That little voyage where, like so many people before and since, I discovered the peace and quiet of an electric cruise, gave me a passion beyond history for the future of electric boats. Percy Gick a quick-thinking, open-minded man who without hesitation invited me to attend a meeting of the EBA in downtown London in my capacity as a journalist. On May 21, 1982, *Patricia* was used by the Earl of Avon to open the new Robert Aickman lock on the River Avon, another campaign led by David Hutchings, MBE.

On July 6, 1983, the EBA executive meeting took place during a voyage on board the Clayton Line's newly built 65-ft (20 m) electric waterbus *Stenson Bubble* along the Trent and Mersey Canal near Derby. The boat was named after a small spring on the downstream side of Stenson Lock. One new member was Paul V. Wagstaffe, secretary-general of the Ship & Boat Builders' National Federation, with nationwide and international connections, including a stand at the London Boat Show. The quiet-spoken but dynamic Paul would become one of the association's stalwarts.

Once again, the question was asked about the range of electric boats. On July 26, 1983, together with Kevin Ridgeway, the author piloted Admiral Gick's *Patricia* from Emsworth on the south coast, out to sea across a calm and sunny Solent to Cowes. The 22 miles (35 km) took us 5 hours. This was the first electric boat to cruise offshore since 1886 (see *Volta*). Once in Cowes, His Royal Highness Prince Philip, the Duke of Edinburgh, went on board and, intrigued by her quietness of operation, was given a trip from the Royal Yacht *Britannia* to his ocean racer.[22]

Also that summer, the Original Boat Company's 57-ft (17 m) canal boat *Electric Monarch* was abused by a vacationer, who cruised *some 70 miles (110 km)* from Upton Marina to Wootton Warren without recharging its batteries. Elsewhere, Giles Baker of Anglo-Welsh Narrowboats took his 16-ft (4m90) 9-ton narrowboat from Stoke-on-Trent to Wolverhampton, cruising 3 mph (5 kph) for 28 hours without a recharge.

The more electric boats could be seen and not heard, the better. In 1984, at the Inland Waterways Association's rally on London's canals, the EBA was represented by just six boats. That May the IWA rally on London's Regents Canal included a six-strong EBA fleet. Bellway Marine of Consett, County Durham, equipped their keelboat-dinghy, the *Sunbird*, with an underwater electric pod as an auxiliary. This was an idea that went back to a patent taken out by Kerbey Bowen as long ago as 1893. In July, at Norwich's bicentennial celebrations, several electric boats were demonstrated, one of them carrying a group of minstrels. That November there were further demonstrations and lectures at Norwich, attended by 150 people.

In January 1985 the EBA was represented for the first time at the London International Boat Show, Earls Court. Bossoms Boatyard hosted an EBA stand, backed by the Electricity Council and the Emsworth Shipyard. A buyer's guide, "The Quiet Connection," was handed out. February saw the unveiling of the Steam & Electric Launch Company's 19-ft 6" (6 m) *Mystic* alongside its sister, the 21-ft *Frolic*. Andrew Wolstenhome recalls: "The Frolics didn't hire as well as the more conventional configuration dayboats here on the Broads. With the Mystic I designed a fairly conventional Broads dayboat but keeping her sleeker and also tried to keep the transom lifted well clear of the water so that there was less chance of transom immersion, although on a small boat with people sitting in the sunshine aft it is difficult to avoid."[23]

Other hireboat fleets were being set up. In 1985 restoration began on the first quarter-mile section of the Somerset Coal Canal from its junction with the Kennet and Avon at Dundas Aqueduct. This stretch had not been touched by the railway and was still reasonably intact. Two entrepreneurs, Hedley Smith and Tim Wheeldon, seeing the potential it presented for a marina and boat business, formed the new Somerset Coal Canal Company. Wheeldon then set up the Bath & Dundas Canal, with a hire fleet of Frolics that he named *Dundas Delight, Dundas Dream, Dundas Dabchick, Dundas Isgolden* and *Dundas Duck*.

On October 11, 1985, an electric boat seminar, "Recent Advancements," was held at the British Waterways Board Centre—The Boat Inn, Stoke Bruerne, near Northampton.

There were ten speakers and a demonstration of various boats. Ray Arnold of Castle Narrowboats reported on the design and building of two e-narrowboats the 41-ft (12 m) *Harlech Castle* and the 45-ft (13 m) *Raglan Castle* for use on the Monmouthshire and Brecon Canal in South Wales. Leonard D. Warren of the Handicapped Anglers Trust presented the Allenard inland fishing boat specially designed for wheel-on/wheel-off handicapped anglers. This was reported in Users Group Newsletter N°7. It was during this seminar that the author asked Rupert Latham just how far one of his boats could cruise without recharging its batteries and challenged him to make a long-distance cruise.

Wigan Pier Development, based around the Leeds-Liverpool Canal, was opened in March 1985. To take visitors on round trips via the Pier, Waterways Gardens, Heritage Center and Trencherfield, the Wigan Education Authority commissioned two electric waterbuses from Giles Baker, formerly of Anglo-Welsh Narrowboats, now of Harborough Marine Ltd. in Leicestershire. The first waterbus, named *Emma* after the Lady Mayoress of Wigan and Leigh for 1985, measured 31-ft long by 10-ft beam using Harborough Marine's standard V-bottomed "Camargue" hull. She was powered by a 4 kW motor/52 volts/480 Ah battery, with a cruising draw of 40 amps and seating capacity for 30 passengers. The second waterbus, named *Netta* after the Lady Mayoress of Wigan & Leigh for 1986, measured 39 ft (12 m) by 10 ft (3 m) beam and was powered by a 5½ kW motor/72 volts/540 Ah battery—with a cruising draw of 50 amps and seating for 40 passengers. The Wigan Pier Development was in operation 363 days per year, with one boat in service every day. At the official opening of the Wigan Pier Development, Her Majesty Queen Elizabeth II cruised electric, following which, between April and October, both *Emma* and *Netta* were kept busy nonstop 7 days a week, and if tickets sold were anything to go by—allowing for those who were turned away because of the long lines—an estimated 500,000 had "cruised electric" from Wigan Pier.[24] *Emma* and *Netta* would remain popular tourist attractions at the pier for the next 25 years.

In November 1985, Rear Admiral Gick as EBA Chairman sent out information to John Julius Cooper, the 2nd Viscount Norwich and chairman of the "Venice in Peril" mission. He suggested that non-polluting low-wash electric passenger boats such as the *Emma* and *Netta* could be used in Venice. Viscount Norwich replied that he would pursue the idea.

Between November 22 and 23, 1985, this author teamed up with Rupert Latham of the Steam and Electric Launch Company (STELCO) and we piloted the 21-ft *Cliveden Frolic* nonstop up the Thames from Staines to the Perch Inn, Bisney. We totaled 71 miles (114 km) over 24 hours *without recharging*. We only stopped because the weather had proved bitterly cold in an open boat. Through the use of the then novel device of a mobile phone on board, £1,000 was raised for BBC "Children In Need" live broadcast evening. Nine of the 23 locks were negotiated in the darkness! It was a stunt which gained confidence with a public who feared that e-boats were like flashlight batteries, fading at the wrong moment! Realizing that we could have gone even further, one year later, "Latham & Desmond" took *Frolic 998*, accompanied by *Mystic Z411*, around the Norfolk Broads for 24 hours and upped our record to 101 miles (163 km).

Dutch Beginnings

England was not alone. Giethoorn is a village in the Dutch province of Overijssel, where all transport is along one of the many canals, and which, with its 180 bridges, is known as the known as the Venice of the North. In 1979, Jitze R. Prinsen's restaurant in Giethoorn-Noord was offering some small hireboats, powered by gas engines. For his son's eighth birthday, Prinsen gave his son a small fiberglass yawl. The latest Mercury Marine Thruster trolling outboard seemed a safer way of boating for a child (no tampering with gas). After his birthday, whenever Prinsen Junior went out in his boat, it attracted quite a lot of attention. Following public demand, Prinsen retrofitted his hire fleet with Mercury Thrusters. Even though they went slower, the users were almost unanimous in their enthusiasm.

Following articles in the regional press, Brederwiede Municipality and the Province of Overijssel stated their readiness to provide funding for a study into the feasibility (technical and financial) of the electric outboard for the canals of Giethoorn. Coordinated by the West Overijssel Recreational Department, several existing electric boat motors were purchased and tested. The best available system on the market, the Austrian Accumot, was not only very expensive but only available as a sort of stern-drive engine with separate switching. Taking the Accumot as their example, Prinsen and the Recreational Department looked for a Dutch firm which could produce an electric outboard range. They found this in a renowned electric motor plant in the eastern Netherlands. Together they developed a completed range of full electric outboards developed, produced and marketed under the name "Combi." The name came because Prinzen was working with a partner, Theun Mulder, so therefore they had a "Combination." The engines made entirely out of cast aluminum parts, had a range of 500, 700, 1200 and 2000 watts. The first Combi motor was sold in 1981.

Prinsen recalls: "I had a really titanic struggle against the prejudices of all private and business stakeholders. They did everything to try to thwart my initiatives. One telling example: when we wanted to exhibit our Combi engines at the 1985 HISWA boat show, we were not allowed onto the outboard engine section, and instead had to make do with a stand on the Accessories section. The then chairman of the HISWA was a Mr. Passet, who happened to be an importer of Yamaha gasoline outboard motors…. Thus!!"[25]

Also in Giethoorn, not far from Prinsen's restaurant, from 1924 Albert Klaas n'Baker had been running boat tours around in the boat which he used during the week in his

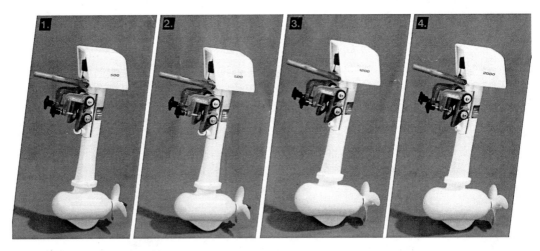

In 1981, Jitze Prinsen of Giethoorn, the Netherlands, produced this first Combi range, at 500, 700, 1200 and 2000 watts (courtesy Combi).

Jinz Prinsen with a 1600 watt Combi, 1981 (courtesy Combi).

profession as a cattle trader. The same year he had opened the Lily Café with two rooms to offer shelter to the artists, who were then taken to the most picturesque spots to paint. In 1958 Dutch filmmaker Bert Haanstra made a comedy film, *Fanfare*, set in Giethoorn. With the surge in tourism, Albert's son Harry Arendshorst expanded the boat fleet to eleven vessels. From the 1980s these boats were retrofitted with homemade units made from the electric starting motor of the Ford Taunus coupled to a battery. Arendorst went on to establish ARKA E-propulsion, building and selling electric drives, inboards and outboards to other Dutch boaters. Elsewhere in the 1980s, Hans Leeuwenstein, a marine engineer of Kalkhaven, near Dordrecht, began to build and sell a converted Yamaha e-drive to clients; he would later add a 360° pod-drive.

In Italy, in 1986, Piero Tosi, of Campo Stringari, Venice, with several decades' worth of experience in field-testing electric motors, began to direct his attention to marine alternative energy. He set up the CCM PAEA (= Centro Commerciale Mondiale Progettazione Applicazione Energie Alternative) to demonstrate the feasibility of electric boats.

Elco Returns

In the USA, still in 1986, Joseph W. Fleming of Ramsey, New Jersey, 58-year-old retired electronics engineer, with his son and daughter as vice-presidents, inspired by the example of Hackercraft owner Bill Morgan, purchased the rights to use the name Elco. His intention was to build replicas of every model produced by the original company.

Elco's original documents and plans had been lost in a 1963 warehouse fire. So Fleming persuaded some friends to let him use their 1898 vintage Elco, the *Diana Banks*, as a model for a new cold-molded hull and fitted out with an up-do-date electrical propulsion system designed by Fleming (= 5 hp DC motor, eight 6v heavy-duty deep-cycle batteries, and infinitely variable speed control). In this, Fleming was helped by William S. Swanson, naval architect and Elco historian, and Andie Mele, a wooden boatbuilder.

The boat was introduced at the 1988 Miami Boat Show to great media and public acclaim, following which Elco extended their range to 21-ft (6.4 m) and 24-ft (7.3 m) electric fiberglass launches with fine wooden decks and interiors. The Flemings claimed that their system offered up to fifteen hours of silent cruising. In reply to a letter sent by the EBA to Elco, Vice-President Margaret L. Fleming wrote: "I think it is wonderful that you have established an Electric Boat Association. If you ever decide to go international, we would like to be your first U.S. members."[26] This was the beginning of an American Association.

Tom Hesselink, formerly of Jarrett Bay Boatworks, who had formed a team of crafts-men at Budsin Wood Craft, was asked to build an electric boat for a resident at Roaring Gap Lake in North Carolina. This community, tucked away in the Blue Ridge Mountains, places a high value on tranquility and tradition.

> All boats on the lake at that time were electric powered boats built in the 1930s, and my customer wanted a similar style. So those early boats heavily influenced my 15' Lightning Bug design; the two cushioned seats which face each other allowing for easy conversation, the convenient side-mount tiller, and the inboard motor were some of the ideas adopted. From there, I redesigned the hull for better efficiency, added the classic wood decks, and incorporated a modern drive system. The built-in cooler, canopy top and trouble-free charging system are some of the refinements added along the way. We now have over twenty-five boats on that lake alone, as well as many more elsewhere.[27]

Budsin Woodcraft would go one to build some 166 Lightning Bugs, four 19-ft (5m80) Piglets, six 22-ft (6m70) Phantoms and one Telescope.

At Henley-on-Thames, England, Colin Henwood, a craftsman boatbuilder, repli-cated a traditional 25-ft (7m60) mahogany and teak Edwardian-style punt, powered it by an 800-watt Accumot pod motor and called it *Voltaire*. "*Voltaire* astounded people when they first took a trip in her, they could not believe that a boat could move silently and she helped a number of our customers agree to have their boats converted."[28]

In January 1987, Bossoms and the Steam & Electric Launch Company exhibited independently at the Earls Court Show.

Canal & Riverboat magazine agreed to publish a monthly full-page column, headed "Electric Boat Scene," which the author researched and wrote up under the pseudonym of "Sparks."

From 1987, *Roath's Pride*, a 32 ft (9m75) vessel using the same mold as *Patricia*, went into public service on Roath Park Lake, central Cardiff. Built by Brummagen Boats, the 40-ft (12m20) *Forward* inspection electric launch, went into operation for Birmingham International Conventions Centre. The traditional 20-ton Norfolk Wherry yacht *Olive* was retrofitted with a 2.2 Kw electric engine and four 12 v 160 AH batteries. The Broads Authority set up a Wildlife Water Trail at How Hill, using a Frolic 21 called *Electric Eel*.[29]

In 1987, Duncan Stewart of Midlands Electricity became chairman of the EBA. Among his projects was to retrofit a cabin cruiser as a testbed for electric propulsion; in doing so they found that by extending the transom, the boat would cruise better. A project was thought up for a London-Paris electric boat cruise—from the Westminster Abbey

Top: From left, Jestyn Viscount St. Davids, an unidentified Electricity Council representative, the author and Rear-Admiral Percy Gick, electric boat pioneers, at the 1987 Earls Court Boat Show in London (author's collection). *Bottom: Patricia* at the 1987 Earls Court Boat Show, London (author's collection).

to Notre Dame.[30] Stewart's chairmanship was short-lived, and when Secretary George Noyes phoned around for a new volunteer, he found most other committee members were busy. I volunteered and was elected chairman, aged 37. Admiral Gick became the EBA's new president.

Over in Newport Beach, California, Duffy continued to build and sell his electric day boats. The early Duffys had been expensive and hard to build, so in 1987 Duffield threw them away and revamped the line to a simple craft easier to maintain. That summer, knowing that among the several hundred owners making up the largest fleet of electric boats in the world, some had a sense of sport, he organized the "Great Electric Boat Race." Boat names ranged from *Watt Fun*, *Charge It*, *La Prima Volta*, *Current Affairs*, *Watts Up*, *LiveWire* and *Electrifying*. Competitors had to answer questions based on local harbor history; corrected answers led them from checkpoint to checkpoint and clue to clue around the harbor course. Clues were stuffed in slit tennis balls and lobbed to competitors, still floating if their intended recipients failed to catch them. Boats started in four colored-coded heats at ten-minute intervals. The first two boats to finish each color-coded heat qualified for the championship slalom race, which had such amusing rules as "your vessel must pass through the buoys with its transom ahead of your bows." It became an annual event.

In 1988 Duffy was joined by an accountant, Gary Crane. They took a boat to the International Marine Trade Exposition and Conference in Chicago. They had no booth, so they set up shop outside the front doors. They gave out all their brochures in two hours—which eventually led to a network of 40 distributors and a production increase

In 1987 Duffy organized a colorful electric boat rally in Newport Harbor (Duffy collection).

from three boats a month, to 1 boat per day. Duffy once said, "I want to make electric boats popular all over the country, not just for rich people in Newport Beach."

On December 2, 1987, a far lower-key EBA/BWB endurance contest was held in Little Venice. Five outboard skiffs cruised in bitterly cold weather for 4 hours. Instead of a mass-produced Mercury, Mariner or Minn Kota winning, the prize went to an ingenious homemade radial armature prototype. It had been welded together at the last minute by a Battery Vehicle Society member, the long-haired, quietly spoken and barefooted Cedric Lynch of the Hornsey-based London Innovation Network. Lynch completed 28 laps, with a massive 5-lap lead over 4 hours.

Cedric Lynch is a lateral thinker, who had been found too bright for ordinary school and educated at home from only 12 years old. He is the son of Arnold Lynch, an English engineer, known for his work on an optical tape reader which was used in the construction of the code-breaking Colossus, the first electronic computer. Working in the cluttered garden shed of his parents' home in Potters Bar, young Lynch was making a modest living repairing motorbikes, mowing lawns and working in a shop when he began to take an interest in electric vehicles. "I was particularly intrigued to see how far electric vehicles could be made to go on a single battery charge. In 1979 Lucas Electrics Ltd. and the Institute of Mechanical Engineers organized a competition to find out how far it was possible to go in a vehicle run on two of their batteries. I hand-made my first motor at home with an armature made from unrolled tin soup cans wound with enameled copper wire. My three-wheeled vehicle came second out of 50 competitors, which success encouraged me to join the Battery Vehicle Society, which regularly sponsored six or seven races a year."[31]

Then for five years Cedric Lynch was the unchallenged winner, using his own motors with a variety of novel control systems. Lynch later recalled, "My earliest attempts were made by hand with the laminations cut from old soup tin cans. By designing the motor in the form of a disc, with an armature consisting of radial copper strips with wedge-shaped groups or iron laminations in the spaces between them and stationary magnets at both ends of the armature, I obtained a much greater efficiency, a lot less friction and much more compact shape."[32]

In the early 1980s the Greater London Council had set up a series of technology networks to support new ideas for socially useful production. One of these was London Innovation Network, set up by Richard Fletcher. In 1986 Cedric Lynch asked LIN to help him commercialize his new design of motor. Many manufacturers of conventional motors were offered licenses to the worldwide patent[33] but found that they could not use their conventional production methods. With further development work, Lynch came up with LIN 1, a motor bicycle which, powered by two 48 Ah batteries, not only won races, but was said to have a range of about 60 miles (100 km) at 20 to 25 mph. Lynch had been adapting his moped engine for a wheelchair application when, encouraged by Rear Admiral Gick and Viscount St. Davids, he was invited to again convert it into an outboard— just nine days before the Little Venice contest. He built a toothed-belt drive system, reduction gear and 12½ in × 12 propeller from mild steel sheet to spin at 400 rpm. When he arrived, the soldering marks were still visible on the prototype as it was hitched to the back of the 15-ft *Chippendale Sprite*, which was steered to victory by naval architect Andrew Wolstenholme.

In 1988 Morton Ray moved his e-outboard manufacturing plant from Alexandria, Virginia, to Cape Coral, Florida, where he developed a lower speed gear case turning a 12.5" (31.5 cm) propeller.

The prototype outboard that Cedric Lynch used in 1987 to win the race at Little Venice (author's collection).

Return to Venice

In Italy, construction began on an all–Italian 210-passenger electric vaporetto. Its hull, built in light alloy by Alutekna SpA at Marcon, measured 23 meters (76 ft) × 4.6 m (15 ft) beam and weighed 25 tons. The battery was lead-acid Magneti Marelli 1450 Ah/220–300 volt/weighing 9 tons. The Ansaldo motor was an air-cooled asynchronous triphase unit normally rated at 25–30 kW, but while only operating at under 10 kW, capable of a peak of 60 kW, required solely for braking. Transmission was by a variable frequency DC/AC inverter. Propulsion was by a Schottel Azimuthal propeller-rudder.

The sixteen hours' daily operation of the boat would be obtained by overnight battery recharging in addition to periodic opportunity charge of 15 minutes every 1 to 2 hours (known in Italian as "biberonnagio") during stops of operation. The plan was to build a small fleet of ten boats for evaluation against the existing "vaporetti." It was estimated by Signor E. Gasparini, chairman of the Working Group, that the charging station for 20 such craft would require a sizeable 2 megawatt installation. This had been designed by ENEL (Italian Electrical Agency, equivalent to the UK Electricity Council) and was already nicknamed "la grande mamma" (= the big mamma)![34]

As chairman/journalist, I was able to launch a number of initiatives. I found a logo, while browsing in my brother's copy of *The Observer's Book of Birds*, in the form of the great-crested grebe (*Podiceps cristatus*)—but I also realized that the word grebe was also an acronym for "generating the revival of electric boats everywhere." At any rate, the fine drawing of our "scruffy duck" (Percy Gick's phrase!) was done by a friend, Andrew Macdonald.

The Lynch motor proved to be a great discovery for our mission. At his Emsworth Shipyard, Admiral Gick organized trials of an experimental low-drag catamaran fitted with a Lynch outboard drive. By matching propeller speed and size to hull characteristics, it was found that speeds of 4 mph (6 kph) could be achieved with 5 passengers using less than 200 watts of power—equivalent to ½ hp.

Lord St. Davids decided to replace the Accumot engines powering his narrowboat *Silver Sail* with two 1.6 kW/24 volt Lynches. At the end of March, with her 3-bladed 9-inch props replaced by 16-inch two-bladers, His Lordship took his 27-footer up and down the Regent's Canal, observing operating current used dropping from 65 amps to less than 25 amps at the same speed, thus extending the range by 2½ times.[35] That summer Lord and Lady St. Davids took their boat on a 411-mile (644 km) cruise from their home on the Regent's Canal up the Grand Union down to Oxford, up the River Thames to Lechlade

and return. When there were any teething problems, St. Davids would go in search of a phone box and ring Cedric Lynch, who would show up hours or days later in his van, never wearing any shoes or socks, and modify what was necessary.[36]

At the EBA management group meeting of April 1988, the idea of an EBA newsletter was agreed on. With my experience in writing the "Electric Boat Scene" for *Canal & Riverboat*, this author would write this for duplication by Roneo machine and postal distribution by the LDA, in particular George Noyes's redoubtable secretary, Olivia Egan. July saw publication of Volume 1, N°1 of *Electric Boat News*, proudly sporting its new grebe logo and the motto "No noise. No pollution. No fuss."

Inspired by an old photo of a floral boat rally which took place in 1901 in Germany, I also suggested that the growing number of electric boat owners on the Upper Thames might be invited to do the same. At first the EBA Committee was not sure whether members would respond, but on June 11, 1988, such a regatta was held at Wargrave-on-

The Electric Boat Association's logo, a great-crested grebe, here used as a pennant at the Wargrave Rally on the Upper Thames (author's collection).

Thames, organized by EBA member Ken Barge, a computer businessman, the lawns of whose home went down to the river. As many as 19 electric boats converged from upstream and downstream.

During a cricket-style picnic on the jetty of Ken's home, they were judged on their decorations with natural, silk and crepe flowers, ribbons, bunting and balloons, Union Jack and Red Ensign flags with 99 guests suitably costumed. The most memorable moment in the rally came when almost the entire flotilla cruised off in convoy and was able to converge between the gates of Marsh Lock, Henley. This photogenic rally gave vivid publicity to electric boats, as so many EBA rallies have done since. "Wargrave" would become an annual event, hosted by Barge until his death in 2000.

The Birth of Solar Boat Racing

In July 1988 "the first ever solar powered boat" race was held at Estavayer-le-Lac (Lake of Neuchatel) in Switzerland. Seventeen boats were entered, fifteen showed up, with about an equal number of Swiss and German teams. Most boats entered the Practical Boat Class, which specified 0.5 to 20 kWh of batteries minimum and maximum amount respectively and 80 to 500 W of solar panels with the amounts allowed linked to each other. Among those competing were Theo Schmidt with his hydrofoil boat, Matthias Wegmann's *Basilisk* trimaran, and Roland Spitteler's Klepper kayak *Sol-Shark* with a 300W outdrive powered by a Bosch IPL motor and NiCad batteries. Despite appalling weather with rain and violent thunderstorms, the Fachhochschule Konstanz's *Corona*, with a 900W motor, completed 17 laps. Soon after this, Schmidt *almost* crossed the Channel in his inflatable catamaran, its 320W solar panel connected to a 300W electric motor giving the boat 5.4 knots in ideal conditions, but then a Wind Force 4 forced him to abandon only 1.5 miles from Cap Gris Nez.[37]

Between November 30, 1988, and February 21, 1989, Alan Colbeck of Australia helmed his twin-hull *Solecist*, its 12 volt Mariner T21 outboard energized by five 45-watt Solarex panels, along the River Murray in South Australia—totaling 1,826 km (1135 mi) after 41 days' cruising. He claimed this as a record.

In 1988, ten years after his 600-mile (966 km) cruise in *Electra of Emsworth*, Rear Admiral Gick set up the Emsworth Trophy for the longest cruise of the year by a boat propelled solely by battery electric power. This was incorporated into the National Cruising Award. The trophy, inspired by the new EBA logo, was a fine painted wooden sculpture of a great crested grebe, carved by retired RN Captain John Powell of Emsworth, and which the Rear Admiral nicknamed "the scruffy duck cup"!

It was time to market the Steam & Electric Company's Frolic abroad. Having read several foreign languages at Manchester University and educational psychology at the University of Geneva, since 1986 Gillian Nahum had been working for Neptune Yachts. There, with help from Cedric Lynch, she had electrified a Tulip launch. She now joined the Steam & Electric Launch Company and between September 15 and October 9, Rupert Latham and Nahum took a Frolic 21 on a 3,300 promotional trip around Europe:

> We began at the Friedrichshaven Boat Show where we gave a demonstration on the Bodensee lake then, lake by lake to Zurich, along Leman—stopping at Vevey, Lausanne, Geneva, Thonon and Evian, then north to Neuchatel (Yverdon), then Thun then over to Vienna and the nearby Neusiedler See. Returning to Konstanz, Rupert and I continued on to Schaffhausen and Freiburg, crossing over to

France, where the Frolic again showed its silence on the River Moselle at Metz; our final stop was made on the River Seine at Paris before trailering back to Wroxham via Dunkirk. During our journey we had realized that there was a market for a more modern boat which looked less like a Victorian replica and more like a contemporary cabin launch.[38]

This was eventually to become the *Deltic*, which is still marketed and built today by Salters of Oxford. Meantime, another Frolic was shipped to the Hamburg Boat Show for exhibition by Scansail Yachts International. One slight marketing problem for them was that over in Europe, "Frolic" was a well-known make of dog food![39]

It was not long after this that I challenged my friend Fiona, the redoubtable septuagenarian Countess of Arran, offshore powerboat racing champion, to take on the unheard-of: sponsor and pilot an electric powerboat which could set a water speed record of at least 50 mph! (See Appendix A.)

At the London Earls Court Boat Show, Latham and Nahum sold eight boats, including one for Sweden, one for Bremen, one to Holland and one to Dubai, the latter airfreighted from Gatwick Airport. Viscount St. Davids became the first recipient of the Emsworth Trophy for his 411-mile (661 km) cruise in *Silver Sail*. Curtis Instruments announced a new range of their popular DC motor speed controllers, the "1209" series, rated at 500 Ah at 36 volts, 450 Ah at 48 volts and 400 Ah at 72 volts.

For some time we had been feeding information to our American friends to the point where, in February 1989, Elco (New York) became the EBA's first U.S. member and talked of setting up an American chapter. This was the beginning of what became the Electric Boat Association of the Americas.

In March 1989, Gillian Nahum, financed by the UK Department of Trade and Industry, went to Japan to introduce the Frolic to the Japanese market, where she observed that there were absolutely no inboard electric boats in that country!

In 1989 Stelco opened its new 10,000 sq ft (929 m²) premises at the Old Foundry, Norwich Road, Ludham, where, if necessary, up to twelve electric boats would be built at the same time. From the new yard emerged the mahogany-cockpit Frolic Traditional. A larger boat now seemed like a natural extension to the range, and Rupert once again used an original 29-ft (8.8 m) teak steamboat hull to make the mold tool for the new Frolic 30. Subsequently Rupert decided that the 30-ft hull was a little tender and not suitable for operation as a small trip boat, so he commissioned Andrew Wolstenholme to design the 31. "I made her as beamy as I felt I could without spoiling her looks, accommodating 12 passengers and allow for a larger cabin complete with toilet, decent galley and two cockpits. She has been sold in reasonable numbers as a full Edwardian cabin launch or as open trip boats. The updated Frolic 31 is still in production both for passenger carrying and for private customers."[40]

Over in America, in April 1989, Duffy took one of his dayboats, *Battery Mate*, on an 11-hour, 60-mile (100 km) round-trip voyage from Newport Beach to Avalon, Catalina Island, before delivering it to its owners.

In June 1989 the British Waterways Board published the results of their low-wash hull design project, undertaken by Professor Archie Ferguson of the Ocean Technology Department of Glasgow University. This had involved towing-tank tests with two models, each alterable at both bow and stern. One was a narrowboat configuration, while the other resembled a typical fiberglass cabin cruiser. The tank was set up to simulate a typical canal cross-section. Following videotaped tests through January and February, the final report was ready by spring 1988. The results showed that to avoid the familiar bow wave and crest, a vertical, cylindrical bow shape was introduced, while the stern was given a truncated cone to reduce viscous drag, but with a skeg to house the propeller, itself surrounded by a U-shaped shroud. The higher the speed—say from 4 up to 6 mph (6 to 9 kph)—the better would be the effect.[41]

An electric boat survey was also set undertaken by an EBA member, Douglas S. Rumsey.[42]Seven manufacturers were producing electric outboards with up to 45 lb of thrust, and by June 1990 the register would number 32 boats in the UK.

On August 9, 1989, an 11-strong all-party House of Commons Environment Select Committee published a report (HCP 237–88/89) based on an investigation by the British Waterways Board. The Committee was appointed in December 1987 with Sir Hugh Rossi in the chair. In the Summary of Conclusions and Recommendations, the 256-page publication encouraged "A changeover from petrol/diesel to electric engines, both by differential license fees and provision of power supply units" (Para 106).

Two significant solar races were held in 1989. The first, held on June 17–18, was conceived by Professor Leonardo Libero of Turin. It extended the length of Lago Maggiore from Angera (Italy) in the south, to Locarno (Switzerland) in the north, a total distance of 37 miles (60 km), divided into 4 stages over two days. A dozen boats completed the distance, the leaders taking a total time of 7.5 hours. There was a close battle between *Korona*, a research monohull by Professor Christian Schaffrin of Fachohschule Konstanz, only just ahead of Matthias Wegmann's *Basilisk* trimaran with its maximum speed of over 6.5 knots, consuming 1400 W (less than 2hp); however, cruising speed was around 5 knots, consuming about 700 W. Race Two was held on Lake Zug (near Zurich), organized by Urf Muntwyler as part of the Swiss Tour de Sol auto race, covering 30 km in two stages the same day. Five racing boats and 10 cruising boats took part. No sunshine and some rain: the winner was A. Bayer with his Canadian canoe *Sonu*. Second came *Basilisk*, averaging 6 knots, completing the distance in 160 minutes. Karl-Heinz Mirwald arrived third with *Korona*, a beautifully made motor launch with solar panels inlaid in teak, the shape of things to come. During the contest, attempts were made to set an official solar speed record over 100 meters. All motive power must come from daylight. But without the sun, Theo Schmidt's catamaran, normally capable of 5 knots, crawled past the stopwatch at only 2 knots.

That August, Matthias Wegmann and Theo Schmidt sun-cruised *Basilisk* from Basel down the Rhine to Koblenz, up the Mosel and Saar until Saarbrücken and back through the canals to Strasbourg, not far from Basel. They estimated a total of almost 1000 km (620 miles). *Basilisk* used a panel with 800-watt full-sunlight capacity linked to a Deltamat variable transmission. Accidents en route forced them to complete the journey using a makeshift propeller hand-carved from pinewood!

In 1989, Dieter Seebacher of Moosburg in Austria built his first Aquawatt electric boat, which he launched onto the Wörthersee in 1992. He would go on to produce the 24-ft *Aquawatt 715*, capable of sprint speeds of 15 knots (17 mph).

In September the British Waterways Board decided to give a 25 percent discount to encourage electric boat owners on their network of canals.

In October, Venice's "vaporetto elettrico" waterbus E1 was unveiled to the world. The ceremony involved speeches from politicians representing four parties, plus a baptism by Monsignor Marco Cé, the Patriarch of Venice! It went on one year's trial.

Meanwhile a STELCO had been progressing well. A Frolic 21, named *Humming Bird*, went into operation on Lake Windermere, the first electric launch to be seen in the

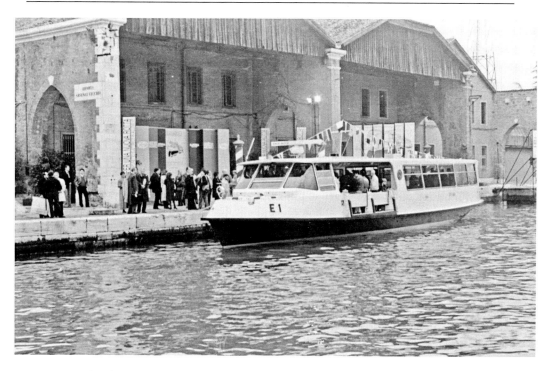

The electric vaporetto *E1* at its launch in Venice, 1989 (author's collection).

English Lake District in 70 years, soon followed by another Frolic 21.[43] Latham had received an order for a new Frolic 31 for the Regents Park Canal—this third model perhaps answering enquiries from France, Spain and Japan for 25-passenger electric launches. They had successfully sold boats for the lakes at Woodstock, Wynyard Hall (*Lady Francis*) and Holkham Hall. They also converted an existing 55-ft (16m70) hull to electric—a graceful old Thames boat called *Humble*, built in 1901. She was refitted with a 3kW Nelco engine.

STELCO was now represented in Oslo, Gothenburg, Stockholm, Amsterdam, Munich, Zurich, Miami and Tokyo. Over in the USA, Elco became dealers for the Frolic 21, as they were often having enquiries for smaller boats than their 24- and 30-ft (7 and 9 m), but having no more building capacity. To date the reborn Elco of New York had sold 17 electric boats.[44]

The first commercial use of a Lynch motor in a boat was in 1990 at Castle Howard, the famous country house in Yorkshire. The Howard family acquired a beautiful 12-passenger trip boat for public use on their Great Lake; Cedric Lynch installed the complete drive system so that the boat only needed 300 watts of electrical power to propel it.

Meanwhile, Emrhys Barrell of Goring-on-Thames, following a degree in naval architecture at Newcastle University, and now a marine engineering journalist, was working with Electro-Marine Technology to convert his 40-ft steel-hulled narrowboat to dual propulsion, linking a Lynch to the three-cylinder Lister engine. This was the beginning of the return of hybrid propulsion, which would become more and more refined in the years to come. Barrell also began to import boats made by Duffy of Newport Beach, such as the Voltaire 18, complete with cocktail cabinet and stereo system. By now Duffy was offering 16-ft, 18-ft and 20-ft models and planning a 10-ft dinghy and a 30-ft cruiser. This importation only ceased due to the fact that the Duffys did not comply with the European Union's Recreational Craft Directive for personal watercraft. This did not affect the six-strong fleet of Duffy 20s being rented to guests and the public by the Marriott Hotel & Marina in San Diego.

In 1990, Kenneth Matthews of Naples, Florida, set up the Electric Boat Association of the Americas (EBAA), choosing a swan as its logo and through the publication *Electric Boat Journal* began to plan annual rallies.

Solar boat-racing continued. For 1990, Longines, the watchmakers, decided to sponsor "A Tutto Sole" (="Sun for All"), a solar boat championship, comprising nine Italian solar boat races, to be held between June 1 and July 29: The venues were Milan, Turin, Venice (Lagoon) and Venice (Adriatic), Lago di Como, San Remo, Lago di Lugano, Lago di Garda, and the Lake of Constance. On June 10, the Berliner Solarboot Cup was held on the Wannsee. This was an 8.5-km course with slalom. Despite heavy rain, the following day, the small flotilla of solar boats was officially asked to celebrate the opening of the border to East Berlin by carrying letters of friendship across the once heavily patrolled waters. On August 25–26, 1990, a Swiss solar boat contest took place on the three lakes of Murten, Neuchatel and Biel, interconnected by two canals. Fourteen boats sun-cruised, of which 7 were prototypes and 7 series-produced. Despite very cloudy weather with frequent drizzle, the winner was Michael Gallay in Scholl's ST90 cat, averaging 6.5 knots.

It was in the autumn of 1990 that solar-boating got underway in the USA. Robert L. Reid, professor of the Department of Mechanical and Industrial Engineering at Marquette University, Milwaukee, Wisconsin, started working with engineering students. "We successfully built a boat in the spring of 1991 which was tested on Okachee Lake

In 1991, the Longines Solar Championships were held on Lake Maggiore, Italy (author's collection).

near Milwaukee."[45] That October, Andy Mele took two days to sun-cruise 193 km (120 mi) up the River Hudson in *Suzibelle*, an Elco replica equipped with Sunwise panels.

Back in Europe, sponsored by Weleda Health Products, Matthias Wegmann went on a second voyage with *Basilisk* from Basel to the Island of Ibiza off the coast of Spain. His itinerary took in canals and the rivers Rhein, Doubs, Saône, and Rhône down to the Mediterranean and along the French and Spanish coasts to Denia. He had completed 98 percent of his voyage, equivalent to 2000 km (1,243 miles), when the unsinkable solar trimaran came to grief during the attempted crossing from the Spanish coast. Extremely poor winter weather left *Basilisk* drifting, and Wegmann was forced to hitch a lift from a passing freighter, abandoning his beloved solar boat to the elements.

In November, the Union Internationale Motonautique, the world governing body for the sport of powerboat racing, officially recognized the category "boats with electric motors," subdividing into 2 classes: "battery" and "solar energy."

Sir James Goldsmith, a billionaire ecologist had Cuixmala, an exotic mosque-like mansion, built off the Mexican Pacific coast, with neighboring guest houses designed for his friends Jacob Rothschild, Jim Slater, Kerry Packer and Charles Hambro, from whence he would take his electric boat out on the former Aztec canals.[46]

In 1990, the Electric Boat Association became officially affiliated with the Electric Vehicle Association, with a plan to organize the "All Electric Transport Show" for May 1991. The Royal Society for the Protection of Birds distributed information on electric boats to all their regional offices.

From June 1990, thanks to sponsorship from a trade syndicate, *Electric Boat News* (volume 3, N° 3) was professionally printed and bound, and included illustrations. In 1990, to celebrate their 70th birthdays, Edward and Dinnie Hawthorne, who had been electric boating for over thirty years, took delivery of *Mystere*, a Frolic 21 fitted out by local boatbuilder David Smith in the style of the traditional mahogany Thames launch in which they enjoyed many trips up and down the river. By this time, Edward had already begun to assemble researches for a definitive history of electric boats on the Thames from 1889 to 1914.

In January 1991, at the Earls Court Boat Show in London, a Frolic 21 called *Cockburns* after the port wine manufacturers carried more than 5,780 passengers around the indoor pool during the two weeks of the show, taking between 6 to 13 passengers per trip: a total of 651 trips in all. Keith Welham was the only driver. She was then delivered to Quinta dos Canais, beside Portugal's Douro River.[47]

In April, the Australian version of *Tomorrow's World*, *Beyond 2000* made a program on electric boats, syndicated worldwide to 60 television networks. One of those watching was a recently retired nuclear physicist, Hans Asijee of Reeuwijk. In 1972, Asijee and his wife Betty had taken the underwater electric Evinrude-700 from their Mirror dinghy and fixed it to their 16 m sailing boat. The waterway leading from behind their house to the lakes in Reeuwijk was not very wide, distance some 1,200 m (1,300 yd), with 3 bridges, making sailing impossible and e-motor-assistance convenient. Due to Asijee's job taking him abroad, nothing happened until his retirement and return to his home in Reeuwijk in 1990.

Inspired by Lady Arran's waterspeed record, Asijee paid a visit to the UK in May of that year, where among those he consulted was this author. In February 1991, Asijee set up a chapter of the EBA, the Stichting Elektrish Varen (Electric Cruising Association). He published a quarterly newsletter, *Electrisch Varen*, initially sent to some 200 members (donors), which would eventually increase to 600 copies. He also organized rallies at Giethoorn which brought together 40 boats. He also acquired a 6 m e-sloop (Poca), imported from Denmark by De Jong in Reeuwijk, equipped with a standard diesel engine. The electric retrofit with Creusen engine and Varta batteries was made by Ecoboat in Gouda. Homan used the same Creusen/Varta installation to build a sloop, and Jachtwerf Arie Wiegmans in Breukelen began to import the Duffy from the U.S.[48]

The watersport company run by Bonte brothers, Dirk and Roel, had acquired Combi from Prinsen, modifying the name to "Combi Multi Traktie." In 1990, the Brederwiede Municipality, in collaboration with the Province of Overijssel, decided that the entire rental fleet of 500 boats for 1993 must be switched to electric drive, as well as the setting up of charging stations for the rental companies, which were subsidized by the municipality, the province and the government to the tune of €295,000. By this time 800,000 visitors had rented electric boats in Giethoorn. That year a fact-finding delegation of councilors from Amsterdam arrived at Giethoorn to see how electric boating could be used on their city's canals.[49]

In 1989 the Combi 500S became the Combi 700 and the engines were given the typical Combi green color which is still used today (in Holland, green is associated with environment-friendly), and a line of thrusters, respectively in 1750, 4000 and 8000 watts. Combis were being sold through distributors in various countries, including England, Germany, Austria, Finland, and South Australia. They are also used for water rides at many well-known amusement parks, such as Legoland UK. Despite this, at the 1990 HISWA boat show they were still not allowed in the outboard section.

By 1990 Duffy's models consisted of the Duffy 18 and Duffy 20. Duffy realized it was time to refresh the models and increase the selection. A lake boat was designed with a catamaran hull shape. This lake boat was needed for those developers who dug a shallow lake and built homes around it. The lake was too small to water-ski on and too shallow to have sailboats. These lakes began popping up all over the country, but mostly in California, Nevada and Arizona. The DuffyCat 18 and 16 sold well to these electric-only lakes during the '90s. They provided a big platform to entertain on. Mostly they added a dimension to the waterfront home that increased the size of their patios. Comfortable seating, refrigerator, sunshade top, tables and stereo; you didn't even have to untie it. Just sit on it and enjoy. Several thousand DuffyCats were built and the line now consists of the Duffy Tri Cat using the patented power rudder drive system.

Back to the Future, an electric slipper stern launch with streamlined hull bottom, appeared on the Thames. Its name seemed to sum up how electric boating, which had enjoyed a golden era a century ago, was now well on the way again. In June, an article appeared in the *IEE Review*, "Electric Boats: Whence and Whereto Now?" It called for a technological input to further develop electric boats, and there was a response from 40 diverse organizations.

In April 1991, 130 delegates attended Eastern Electricity's seminar in Norwich, "New Developments in Electric Boating." EBA membership rose to over the 100 mark, with members in 14 different countries worldwide. Plans were launched for a series of "Information Sheets." That May, 87 EBA members met at Bourne End for the User Group Spring Meeting.

The English Lake District and the Coniston Boating Centre took delivery of two Mystics and two Frolics for a new company calling itself the Windermere Electric Launch Company. Two Mystics were dispatched to the Loch Erne Boat Services near Belfast.

As EBA Chairman, I remained keen to foster sportive electric boating. In May 1991 at the Move Electric conference, I challenged Victor Johnson, UK concessionaire for MotorGuide. So during the weekend of November 9–10, 1991, the *MotorGuide Challenger* created a 24-hour electric outboard endurance record of 80.2 miles (130 km) on the Welsh Harp Lake (or Brent Reservoir), North London. A 17-ft (5 m) aluminum Alustar-52 was equipped with twin MotorGuide Stealth 350V outboards, and twenty 6-volt lead-acid batteries (Oldham-Crompton 3KQII), which were not recharged. The boat was driven in three-lap relays by a seven-strong team, three of them teenagers from the Solihull-based "Youth Afloat" Sailing Center. The run, 47 laps in bitterly cold but sunny and starry weather, working with local "Radio Cracker Neasden," raised £7,700 for deprived children in Brazil. During the run the boat shared the lake with the local sailing club and undisturbed wildfowl. This beat the distance established in December 1987 on the canal of Little Venice by Wolstenholme and Lynch, but that had been limited to four hours with only one battery on board.[50]

From the Frolic to the Mystic, STELCO now produced the 21-ft (6m40) live-on-board, two-berth cabin launch, the Deltic (named after the Deltic locomotive). Its design was commissioned from Andrew Wolstenholme by Adrian Tilbury to add to his Swancraft Fleet. Tilbury gave it a wider 8 ft beam and a slippery superstructure to minimize windage and air resistance. Potentially the most exciting development of the steam and electric range, but the Deltic never sold in any numbers—maybe the cruiser market was still not ready.

On July 6, 1991, at the motorboat base of Rolasco, an experimental race was held for solar boats for the Trofeo dell'Isola. Present as officials were the UIM Président Ralf Fröhling and Raffaele Chiulli of the Sporting Commission of the Italian Motorboat Federation. With 12 competitors (3 German, 1 Swiss and 8 Italian), this was a regularity test won by Giovanni Angiolini's *Solone*.

On July 9, 1991, backed by a grant and a number of sponsors, Curtis Saville set out from Casablanca in his 25-ft (7m60) proa *Solar Eagle* with the intention of crossing the Atlantic Ocean. Sailing south and west, he was hit by a Force 10 storm and 50-ft (15 m) waves for three days. Despite a damaged boat, Saville continued for five days, and on June 30 made landfall at Ad Dakhla on the mainland coast of Africa. Over the three-week period, he had traveled a total of 1,017 miles (1637 km) entirely under solar-electric power. This worked out at an average of 48 nautical miles a day at a speed of 3 to 5 knots. Saville salvaged what he could of the *Solar Eagle*'s photovoltaics and related equipment and a short time later implemented them in powering a 16-foot by 30-inch single passenger pirogue built by Douglas Little of Black Water Boats in North Carolina.

The second year of the Longines Trophy was 1991, beginning on June 15–16 with the Grand Premio Verbana on Lago Maggiore. For the Longines series, each race had two legs of usually 20–40 km (12–25 mi) each, as well as sprints and slaloms. Although detailed rules were not too strictly enforced, the most efficient boats were *L'Offshore*, *Korona* and *Solar Yacht*. Karl Heinz Mirwald of Monaco developed the ST-801, a solar cabin cruiser, equipped with 24 monocrystalline solar panels (12v/43w efficiency). Total cell output was 1 kW. Mirwald claimed an extraordinary autonomy: At 7 kph (4.5 mph), a cruising range of 224 km (140 mi); at 14 kph (9 mph), a cruising range of 45 km (28 mi) for 3.25 hours; and at 12.5 kph (8 mph), cruising range of 87 km (54 mi) for 6.5 hours. On August 24–25, a Grand Prix on the Schwarzee saw 16 boats (Italy, Switzerland, Germany, Holland and England). It was won by the Pierre Scholl Team from Geneva with their ST90, with

Mirwald coming in 2nd at the helm of the ST-801. Venice has a long tradition of nautical festivals; but it was on September 1, 1991, that ten solar boats took part in the regatta on the Grand Canal, as part of the Longines heat organized by the solarnautic club ISPRA. Heats then followed with Genoa-Portofino and Monte Carlo. Unfortunately, soon after that, Longines decided to abandon their championship.

In 1991 Wilson Greatbach, the world-famous innovator of the battery-powered cardiac pacemaker among his 330 patents, even invented a solar-powered canoe for "recreation." Fitting it with solar panels between a bow thruster and stern troller, he took it on a 160-mile (258 km) voyage on the Erie Canal and Finger Lakes in New York on his 72nd birthday.

The January 1992 Earls Court International Boat Show saw no fewer than 9 different electric boats divided into 4 company stands, including the Thames Electric Launch Company (TELCO) set up by Emrhys and Linda Barrell. At the Dusseldorf Boat Show in Germany, visitors inspected *Listo 73*, a solar motor yacht with a Schottel rudder-propeller. She was 7.3 m (24 ft) long, powered by a 2.2 kW quadripole asynchronous motor. Under sunshine, *Listo 73* could sun-cruise at 12 kph for 12 hours, or at 9 kph indefinitely.

In July 1992, Hans and Betty Asijee embarked on a promotional voyage through the Netherlands with their 18-ft (5m50) Poca e-boat *Ilse Femmigje*. Leaving home first to the Braassemermeer, they silently cruised counterclockwise around the waterways of the Netherlands, east—upstream the river Rhine as far as Arnhem, then heading north into

Hans and Betty Asijee in their electric boat *Ilse Femmigje* at Lelystad dock during their 744 km cruise around Dutch waterways, 1992 (courtesy Hans Asijee).

Friesland as far as Sneek, returning southwest beside the Ijsselmeer to Lelystad, and then passing the lakes at Loosdrecht and Nieuwkoop home to Reeuwijk.

> We spent 22 days on the Dutch waterways, total distance 744 km (462 mi), battery-charging every night. Our longest trip in one day was 56 km (35 mi) (Hattem to Ossenzijl), while the shortest was 14 km touring Lelystad Harbor. Our battery capacity of 8.6 kWh (5h) resp 11.5 kWh (20h) caused no problems. The boat needed 1 kW for 8 km/h and 0.5 kW for 6 km/h. Its top speed was 9.5 km/h. Several national and local newspapers were informed, one journalist spending more than half a day with us on board. Most of them were astonished to learn about the possibilities and advantages of e-boating. We met very few other electric boats. The first day two accompanied us to the first lock (in Gouda). Later we counted some at Heeg, where we stayed with friends, owners of Hoora boatyard, who were developing e-propulsion for sailing boats. And in Ossenzijl our boat was moored next to a number of rental e-boats, in that area already becoming popular, like in Giethoorn. Finally, in the boatyard of Arie Wiegmans in Breukelen, we saw one Duffy.[51]

In 1993 the Asijees were awarded the EBA Emsworth Trophy for their extended cruise.

Although this author had spent ten enjoyable but not very remunerative years promoting electric boating by editing the EBA journal *Electric Boat News*, with a young family to support, I was lured away to France to become part of a paid team to set up a Pleasureboat Museum in former wartime submarine pens in Bordeaux. Before I left, I attended the Wargrave Rally, which welcomed some 27 boats and celebrated the 10th anniversary of the EBA. As a parting gift, I was presented with a fine glass decanter on which was engraved the image of the legendary *Viscountess Bury*.

In the first two years in Bordeaux, my mind was far from promoting electric boats, but then something extraordinary happened which once again enabled me to take up the challenge, "mais en France" (but in France).

SIX

The French Connection (1992–)

As I was to discover, following its long sleep from 1910, electric boating in France never quite died out. Indeed, its awakening took place at about the same time as that across the Channel and across the Atlantic.

In 1963, Claude Didier of Gerardmer in the Vosges department in Lorraine in the northeast, decided to fit out a couple of boats with electric outboards. He sent his wife up to the Salon Nautique in Paris, where she visited the stand of "La Soie," dealers in fishing tackle. They were exhibiting Austrian blue Accumot engines and batteries, which seemed just right for the job. That summer, Didier began to rent out his boats. Within five years he had a 10-strong hirefleet. Today, the 40 rental electric boats at Gerardmer are divided into several operators: Loconautique (14 boats), La Chaloupe (9 boats), La Mouette (5 boats), Gaspare (5 boats), and Gigout (12 boats).[1]

Pre-Roman marshland locally known as "Les Hortillonnages," close to the cathedral city of Amiens, had been navigated for a very long time by "Les Hortillons" in their gondola-style punts "barques à corné," 10 meters long by 1m70 beam of oak construction. In 1975, the news of a proposed ring road, which would cut through the floating floral gardens, provoked a 51-year-old photographer, Nisso Pelossof, to set up an association for the protection and preservation of the site and its environment. From 1982, thanks to advice from Claude Didier of Gerardmer, Pelossof equipped eight of the local boats with twin submerged Accumots powered by Fulmen nickel-cadmium batteries, giving 4 speeds and an autonomy of ten hours at 3 kph (1.9 mph). These boats are not only used to take tourists on trips, but to maintain the waterways.

Also in 1976, although the location is lost, a retired sea captain called Garetta built a 5-meter catamaran which he equipped with a 600-watt electric motor.[2] Out of this, on the initiative of the French Ministry for the Quality of Life and Electricité de France (EDF), an 11m50, 24-passenger electric timber trimaran called the *Watt Eau* (a pun on the name of a French painter Watteau) was built by the Pichavant family, traditionally known for their molded timber sailboats at their yard in Pont-l'Abbé, Brittany. The hull was built in red cedar and iroko, with the cabin in mahogany. The whole of the control and propulsion system was studied and assembled by Renault Marine Couach and by Ragonot, subsidiary of Thomson-Lucas Ltd. A 6 kW motor at 72 volts was coupled to a transistorized electronic speed controller—turning at 3500 rpm with a 3:2 reduction gear. Its main three-bladed prop turned inside a reed protecting tunnel, driven by a transverse e-motor of 3kw L-transmission. The batteries were spaced out into each hull 8 horsepower. The boat proved itself able to cruise at 9 kph in calm waters for 6 hours. The

French Press called it "Le Premier Bus Français à Propulsion Electrique" (= "The First French Floating Electric Bus").[3]

Soon after, three more of these trimarans, two in fiberglass, went into operation on the Lac du Der-Chantecoq (Marne), an inland sea of 48 km² surrounded by a nature reserve, the largest artificial lake in Europe. It had been created starting in 1967 to hold the water of the River Marne so that flooding of the Seine at Paris would stop and was inaugurated on January 3, 1974. Nonpolluting boats seemed the perfect solution. Since then the only propulsion allowed on this lake remains electric.

Electric boats continued to appear across France. In the Alps of Haute Provence, downstream from the popular Verdon Gorge is the magnificent 2,500-hectare (6,200 acre) artificial lake of Sainte Croix. It was here that in 1987, the 13m50 (44 ft) *La Perle de Verdon*, designed by Pierre Bachelart and constructed by the Chantier Naval Franco-Suisse in France-Comté, with twin 15 kW Leroy Somer electric motors at 120 volts with an autonomy of 7 hours at 10 kph (6 mph), began to carry up to 60 passengers around the Verdon Gorge. The installation had been researched by Professor Tropette at the Electro-Technical Laboratory of Marseilles. A second smaller boat, *Le Canyon*, soon followed. During each cruise, the pilot used one motor for half an hour, then the other, to avoid overheating.

Not far from the Verdon Gorge is Lake Esparron. In April 1990 electronics engineer Guy Gorius, whose Alize boatyard at Le Jas du Rocher, Gréoux les Bains, began to produce a series of small 4.50 m dayhire catamarans he called *Lagon 45*, equipping each hull with a 1 kW outboard engine. Steering was by electronic joystick. In February 1993, Gorius teamed up with Claude Castelain, French extreme kayak champion, and Macari and piloted an electric trimaran around Lake Esparron for 52 hours covering a distance of 260 km (162 mi) without recharging its batteries. By 2015 the fleet of e-dayhire boats on these two lakes alone would number 70.[4]

In 1990, Brigitte Foucaud set up Saviboat in Saint-Savinien, a small commune in the Charente-Maritime department in the Poitou-Charentes region in southwestern France. From this yard emerged small 2–3 meter (6–9 ft) "tugboats," "ferries" and "paddle-steamers" which families visiting a miniature port could hire out for their children to pilot; for ease of installation and maintenance, "les Saviboats" were electrically propelled. During the next two decades, some 1,500 Saviboats would be built, and with them, the infrastructure necessary for one hundred miniature ports.[5]

In 1990, Jérôme Croyère set up his *Ruban bleu* (= blue ribbon) yard on the Isle de Versailles on the River Erdre at Nantes. Born in 1955, while training as an architect and boatbuilder, Croyère had just finished building his own boat when he got the chance to crew for the legendary yachtsman Eric Tabarly on board his racing yacht *Penduick VI* during the 1975 Whitbread Round the World Race. Back in Nantes, Croyère was working as an independent designer of boats and sites for manufacturing furniture, when his partner, Yvon Menant, suggested they make a pedalo for "freshwater sailors." Croyère drew out the design for what he called the Ruban Bleu (Blue Ribbon):

> The Ruban Bleu was a challenge dating back to the 19th Century for the fastest ocean liners to cross the Atlantic and this of course was a bit of a laugh especially when you see our pedalo. But it seemed a real catchy name for remembering a company's name. My original idea was to make a "pedalo," vaguely inspired by an Italian Riva runabout, but it proved complicated to produce. At the time Yvon Menant was using a small electric trolling motor to go fishing in the local river. Replacing the pedals with a motor seemed a simpler solution. Indeed from the second year we produced only the electric version. Once we had decided to establish our first rental point as the Isle de Versailles at Nantes, we went from success to success.[6]

It is interesting to note that electric boating was rebirthing in three places beginning with the letter "N": Newport Beach, Norfolk and Nantes.

Four years later, by subcontracting to small businesses near Nantes, Croyère's Ruban Bleu yard was selling the 3m60 (12 ft) basic hull powered by a 3 hp (2238 watt) underwater Minn Kota outboard from by two Hoppecke Minitrak batteries; livery was either red and white or green and white. Over 150 Ruban Bleus were already in operation as hire fleets in the Vendée, the Aisne on the Loire near Chartres, and also on the Amsterdam canals.

By this time, the author had been working for two years at the Bordeaux Submarine Base, in southwest France, mostly searching out and assembling, either on loan or by donation, a fleet of historic gasoline- and diesel-engined craft for the Conservatoire International de la Plaisance (International Pleasureboat Museum). *Not one single electric boat was on show.*

One day in 1994, I received a phone called from Professor Jean-Louis Aucouturier, director of the IXL Microelectronics Laboratory of Bordeaux University and founder of the Aquitaine Electric Vehicle Unit. Interested in developing an electric boat project, the professor had contacted the Electric Boat Association in the UK, only to be told that their former chairman, the author, was working in Bordeaux! A meeting was arranged on June 10. This was followed by a second one in the author's rented home in Carignan de Bordeaux, where, over a glass of Scottish Glenfiddich whisky, poured from my engraved glass decanter carrying a picture of the *Viscountess Bury*, it was decided to set up a French Electric Boat Association. At this informal meeting I suggested that, as the EBA had a grebe as their logo, perhaps the new French association could adopt the egret—in French an aigrette can mean either a white waterbird or an electric spark. Another idea was to use the word "bébés" ("bateaux à l'énergie des batteries électriques").[7]

Jean-Louis Aucouturier, founder and first president of the French Electric Boat Association (Association Française pour le Bateau Electrique) (author's collection).

By August, the association was official, the fourth after the English, the Dutch, and the American. Its objective was: To promote the conception, the construction and the use of electric boats; to develop waterways provided with electrical supply; to contribute to the protection of nature and of the environment; to establish links with equivalent foreign associations; and to favorize exchanges with organizations dealing with other types of electric vehicles. Its official address was ADERA, Pessac. Date of the declaration: August 12, 1994.[8]

The first 18 founder-members, led by Professor Jean-Louis Aucouturier, with Christian Marinot of the French Electricity Company (EDF) as the secretary-general, were an assembly of university professors, boatbuilders, racing yachtsman Yves Parlier and this author. All were keen to develop the image and the market for the electric boat in France as abroad.

That September 1994, "Le Rendez-vous de l'Erdre," a boat rally, was held on the River Erdre in Nantes. Backed by EDF, two English electric boats took part, thanks to Monsieur Rabeland of EDF, prior to organizing in Nantes the first European electric boat show. "One of the reasons for this project is to initiate contacts with the English who are the European leaders in electric boats with a view to organizing at Nantes the first exhibition of the electric boat." One of the boats came from Emrhys Barrell of TELCO and the other from Margaret Gadsden, founder of the Day Boats of Aucfer in Saint Jean La Poterie, near Redon, giving electric boat trips.[9]

Back in Bordeaux, a symposium titled "The Electric Vehicle, Second Generation" was held on September 30, 1994, jointly organized by the Laboratoire IXL of Bordeaux University 1 and the Society of Electricians and Electronics Engineers, Aquitaine Regional Group. Among those who spoke at the Amphitheater of the Municipal Athenaeum, this author spoke about the experience of electric boats in English, while Gillian Nahum came over from England as new chairman of the EBA.

Encouraged by this, I also attempted to set up a German Electric Boat Association (Deutscher Elektro Boat Association), and an advert appeared in *Boote* magazine in Hamburg in their October 1994 issue. Stefan Sachs of Öco-Sachs GmbH of Schlechig, who was producing their version of the Lynch motor, organized a meeting on August 23, 1996, but nothing came of it.[10] This would not, however, prevent the reintroduction of electric boats in Germany.

In October 1, 1994, I also wrote to SAS Albert the Prince Hereditaire de Monaco: "During the Monaco Classic week and in particular at the end of the Yachting Dinner at the Hotel de Paris, you most kindly invited me to send you some documentation about electrically-propelled boats. I have recently founded (together with Chatelier Industries, EDF, SAAFT the Electronics Department of Bordeaux University) the AFBE. I am also Honorary Member of equivalent associations in the Netherlands and the USA, therefore I would like to suggest that Monaco could perhaps take an independent initiative."

I learned how the Danish nation had presented Henrik, the Prince Consort of Denmark, with a fully restored and electrified boat, *Anne-Marie* (built in 1946), for use on Lake Esrum, close to the Royal Castle of Fredensborg. Again in 1994, I contacted the prince and suggested he might like to launch a Danish Electric Boat Association. I received a reply from Colonel H.H. Jorgensen, the prince's secretary at Amalienberg, stating: "His Royal Highness has read your letter with interest but from here no initiative will be taken in this matter."[11]

I did, however, eventually succeed with the Norwegians. In 1995, encouraged by this author, Stein T. Viken of Hjelmas, editor of *Praktisk Smabatliv* magazine, liked the idea and planned the Norwegian Electric Boat Association (Norsk Elektrisk Båtforening). Like the British grebe, the French egret and the American swan, Viken chose the tern bird as the Association's logo, the old Norse word "therna" also being translated into a 3-masted schooner. Viken presented the idea in his magazine in spring 1996. Only a dozen people showed an interest. But perhaps because the Norwegians felt at ease with North Sea oil rigs that were making them rich, electric propulsion was not, for the time being, a priority. A Scandinavian association could still be set up, even today.[12]

In 1995, the AFBE's electric pinnace *Egretta* cruises on Bordeaux Lac (author's collection).

But back to the French association, AFBE, which had its first meeting at the EDF-GDF Services office in the Bordeaux suburb of Le Bouscat on October 10, 1994. The plan was to build a pinnace, a traditional boat used in the Arcachon Basin on the Atlantic coast, west of Bordeaux, and to equip it with a 30kW motor and nickel-cadmium batteries. When the project to build an electric pinnace was underway, Gillian Nahum presented a technical approach based on the EBA experience.[13]

The scientific management entrusted to Professor Aucouturier, the research and development of different electric propulsion components was carried out in the IXL laboratory at the general CNRS HQ under the responsibility of Christian Zardini, professor of ENSERB, and Jean Michel Vinassa from the University of Bordeaux 1. Battery options of nickel-cadmium or nickel metal hydride were supervised by Hervé Henry. Taking its name for the AFBE's logo, the 10m50 (35 ft) *Egretta* with a draft of 80 cm (32 in), was molded and constructed in glass-reinforced plastic (grp) by BPSA and Constructions Navales RABA at la Teste and fitted out by the Marine Training College at Gujan Mestras with additions by Arcoa Yachting. State-of-the-art NiCad batteries were provided by SAFT, while the 12 kW motor was developed by Leroy-Sommer of Angouleme and was the same used in the Peugeot 106 electric automobile. Its 1.2 million franc cost paid for by EDF, the state and the European Union, as a demonstration boat, *Egretta* would carry up to 16 passengers.[14]

At the same time, with my experience gained as chairman of the EBA, I had already suggested to the mayor of Carignan, the small village where my family and I were living, that a challenge trophy be set up for electric boat competition carrying the name of the town of Carignan. The trophy was created but never contested. I also challenged the Hélice Club de France to organize a challenger to break the world electric water speed record.[15] I was also thinking up ideas such as a 24-hour record, the Paris-to-the-Sea, Cross-Channel and Rally des Deux Mers (Med to the Atlantic), still waiting to be organized some 21 years later. It was, in retrospect, somewhat premature.

Beyond France...

I am glad to say that despite my sudden departure from my native land, the EBA continued its own mission. Gillian Nahum, who had set up a luxury sales and charter business, first from Hambleden and then Henley-on-Thames (Henley Sales & Charter), became chairman of the association. The stand-in news editor was Emrhys Barrell. Eastern Electricity acquired two boats and installed six charging points on the Norfolk Broads in conjunction with the Broads Authority to support up to 20 boats. That September, a small fleet of electric boats also cruised silently past at the Cookham Regatta.

The 1993 Earls Court Boat Show featured an EBA boathouse right on the Central Feature Poolside, with 4 boats alongside including Colin Facey of Horning's 21-ft *Silent Poppy* becoming the first electric hire cruiser to use the Broads charging points. Well-known television environmentalist Dr. David Bellamy gave interviews about electric boats to a succession of national and local TV, radio and press.[16]

Mike Cooper-Reade of Eastern Electricity became the first recipient of the Lord St. Davids trophy awarded for "a significant advance in the field of electric boating." Presented by Lady St. Davids, the trophy, originally called the BP Challenge Trophy, had been donated by Lady Arran in memory of EBA pioneer Jestyn the Viscount St. Davids.

As had happened a century ago, to the pleasure-boating fleet of electric boats, a service boat was now added. Emrhys Barrell of the Thames Electric Launch Company (TELCO) at Goring-on-Thames was commissioned by the National Rivers Authority to install an electric drive in parallel with the existing Thornycroft 60 hp diesel engine on their patrol boat, *Lambourn*. In this he was helped by a very skilled engineer called Ian Rutter. Rutter had been a BBC-trained outside broadcast engineer and videotape editor who had recently e-retrofitted his own steamboat, *Victoria*. The hybrid set-up was achieved by the coupling of a 5 kW Lynch radial armature motor. A large battery charger, the Chloride 210 36-volt 240 AH, was fitted in the driving cabin. When sixteen electric boats cruised past at Cookham, they were led by the National Rivers Authority converted diesel-electric hybrid *Lambourn*. Soon after, a second NRA launch, *Colne*, would be custom-built by TELCO. In the next 22 years, Ian Rutter would install or retrofit some 200 electric boats, not counting the number of boats he serviced.[17]

In September 1993 the Electric Boat Association of the Americas (EBAA) held its first rally at the Charleston Maritime Festival, in South Carolina.

Solar Boating Becomes Serious

Meanwhile, competitive solar boating had been reaching ever faster and longer goals. In June 1992, seven secondary schools, a university and two private entries had competed in "Minnsolar 92," the first solar regatta in the USA. Amongst the boats taking part on Spada Lake near Seattle was the *Sun Warrior*, built by the students of Marquette University, encouraged by Robert Reid, their professor of electrical engineering.

Meanwhile, over in Japan, solar-powered hydrofoil racing was born. This was first achieved in 1992 by Yamaha Motor Corporation's entry at the Grand Solar Challenge race at Mikata-Goko and perhaps a month earlier in the racing boat stadium next to Lake Hamana in Hamanako. The Yamaha solar hydrofoil completed four laps of the 3-km circuit in one hour—equivalent to 7.4 mph (12 kph). The remaining boats of the

57 Japanese competitors had been designed by professional engineers on behalf of their corporations. Marquette's *Sun Warrior*, which succeeded in finishing 31st, was the only entry from outside of Japan. This was Marquette's first year of racing, and another first-year entry was from Professor Masuyama's students at the Kanazawa Institute of Technology.

In Australia, from December 4, 1992, to January 1, 1993, students and staff of Prince Alfred College cruised their displacement-hulled *SunBoat* a total of 1,080 nautical miles (2,000 km) along the Murray River in Australia, from Yarrawonga to Goolwa. This 10-m open-cockpit catamaran, designed by Malcolm Gray, head of art and design at the college, was equipped with a total of 1152 solar cells giving 60 amps at 24 volts. Almost immediately afterwards, from February to March 1993, Alan Colbeck, 68 years old, sun-cruised *Solecist II*, his 16.7-ft (5.1 m) catamaran with two 21 outboards energized by four 90-watt and four 45-watt Solarex panels, along the River Murray. Averaging 3.5 mph, he bettered the record of Prince Alfred College by totaling 1,137 nautical miles (2,106 km)—an increase of 57 miles (106 km)![18]

With a young sport, the problem may arise of lack of global coordination where speed and distance records are concerned. In August 1994, Bud Roberts, 47 years old, former helicopter pilot, equipped a 25-ft day boat with a 600 watt pv array powered by a 3.5 hp Ray electric outboard engine. He left Knoxville, Tennessee, and sun-cruised southwards on the Tennessee and Tombigbee Rivers into the Intercoastal Waterway on the Gulf Coast. He finished his cruise at Apalachicola, Florida. Roberts's 1,133 nautical miles (2,098 km) established an American record, but was *just 4 sea miles too short* to better the Australian record of Colbeck! Roberts spent 107 days on the water, cruising for 71 of them at an average speed 2.1 knots (2.4 mph). His longest day's run was 42 miles (78 km).

During this time, Professor Robert Reid had started discussions with the Solar Energy Division of the American Society of Mechanical Engineers, of which he was a past chairman, about putting in seed money to start an American collegiate solar-powered boat race, similar to the solar-powered car races. Reid had met George Ettenheim, president of Advanced Energy Competitions, who had run the 1990 solar car race for General Motors and was a member of the GM Sunraycer team that won the 1987 solar car race in Australia.

ASME put up $5,000 seed money and Reid then secured the rest of the funds from Johnson Controls to contract the running of the race to George Ettenheim. The race, "Solar Splash," was first held in 1994 at Pewaukee Lake near Milwaukee, and was to become an annual event (though held since 1995 in the waters of Lake Michigan off the Milwaukee Festival Grounds next to downtown Milwaukee). "Solar Splash" was a two-hour race and a timed sprint. Boats were constructed by students from colleges and universities in Japan, Puerto Rico and the USA. Between August 18 and 20, eleven teams took part on Lake Michigan in Milwaukee, Wisconsin. The entry from the Kanazawa Institute of Technology was the swiftest, recording 23.5 seconds for the 46-yard (200 m) sprint, largely due to its hydrofoil.

Two years after the Yamaha solar-hydrofoil had led the field in the Japan race, several other companies and at least two universities, among them Kanazawa, submitted entries as well. The option was for T-foil or tri-foil configurations. The Roland Corporation which would win the Japanese race for several years to come, used the tri-foil design.

Another form of competition using electric motors, but hardly moving, was bass fishing using electric trolling motors as produced by Johnson Outdoors' subsidiary Minn Kota: the Bassmaster Tournament Trail, the Wal-Mart FLW Tour, and the Won Bass. For these sportsmen Minn Kota had continued to innovate with microprocessor-controlled, then fully automatic trolling motors.

With a successful business also comes competition. During the years, Combi had several dealers in the Netherlands and abroad. One of these dealers, AEE Marine from Enkhuizen, saw the sales rates going up and decided to copy the Combi motor, bringing it on the market as the brand Elva. The case was reported and investigated by the HISWA and a lawyer, but the process would be long and costly. Therefore, the Bonte Brothers decided to leave the case and put their energy in a new and better electric outboard motor.[19]

But it wasn't all outboards outdoors, some wanting the comfort of a cabin. In 1994, Clearwater Electric Boats of Riverside, Connecticut, produced an electric yacht, the *Charger 40* diesel-electric, with a computer-designed planing hull and a range of 50 sea miles (100 km) per charge, designed by Craig V. Walters. At the 1994 Earls Court Boat Show in London, Walton Marine offered the 27-ft (8 m) Slipstream six-berth diesel-electric hybrid motor cruiser, while STELCO presented the John R. Moxham–designed ECO22 and ECO28 Hydraflow low-wash hull.[20]

In February, the Electric Boat Association had its first winter meeting, with an attendance of 42 members. Roy Devereux became editor of the *News*. That summer Phil Horsley of Chloride Motive Power Batteries became the new EBA chairman. A seminar, "Electric Boats—The Future," was organized by Eastern Electricity and the Broads Authority, attended by over 100 boatbuilders. In September, "Silent Sensations," an eb-rally, was held on South Walsham Broad.

After ten years, Rupert Latham took his eighteen-strong Steam and Electric Launch Company staff from Ludham to larger premises at Hoveton; the following year, however, the electric boat pioneer filed for bankruptcy. While Adrian Tilbury of Swancraft took a controlling share and relaunched the company as Stelco, in 1995, Simon Read and Roy Lawson, formerly production manager at Stelco, set up a new company, Creative Marine, re-employing former Stelco craftsmen to continue the Frolic tradition. The new company was based at the "Secret Boatyard," Aldborough Hall Barns in Aldborough, Norfolk.

Andrew Wolstenholme designed the 8m60 (28 ft) *RAPSΩDY*, a double-ender based closely on a prewar C.G. Pettersson cabin cruiser, for a Max Weidtman of Hamburg on the Elbe River. Propulsion involved a Fischer Panda hybrid drive system (essentially an electric boat but with an intelligent on-board generator). The misspelling of *RAPSΩDY* was to reflect her green credentials, with the "h" omitted to suggest the use of rapeseed oil for her generator. The market for her in Germany shrank (vanished!) when rules restricting the use of internal combustion engines on some German waterways were relaxed. The company was sold, and they then went on to develop a range of transom-sterned fast diesel-powered classic launches.

In India, EBA member and commodity broker Malcolm Moss had built *Solar Pichola*, the world's first solar water taxi for Lake Pichola, the historic 14th century lake. Three years before, Shriji Arvind Singh Mewar of Udaipur, chairman and managing trustee of the Maharana of Mewar Charitable Foundation, had a vision of Udaipur as a solar city. He initiated research that led to the development of solar power as a source of energy for transportation systems in Udaipur. A small diesel engine boat with the capacity to carry up to five passengers was converted to operate off batteries powered by 8 × 50 watt solar panels fixed onto the roof that sent the electricity to a single 12-volt 60 amp hr battery that propels a small Minn Kota trolling motor. It now operates on Gajner Lake, besides Gajner Palace, a Grand Heritage Palace of the HRH Group of Hotels in Gajner, Bikaner. Following the success of the *Solar Pichola*, Shriji Arvind Singh Mewar approved the conversion of one of his tourist boats capable of carrying 12 passengers. Malcolm Moss arrived in India with an Öco-Sachs electric motor based on a Lynch motor replacing the gasoline engine of a conventional outboard. The 14 × 70 watt panels and electronics were supplied by AES Ltd of Delhi; 8 × 12 volt deep cycle 65 amp hr batteries store the charge and the *RA II* operates for 2 to 3 hours each day, taking tourists to the spectacular Jagmandir Palace Island at Udaipur in Rajasthan.[21]

At the 1995 London Earls Court Show, the National Rivers Authority and British Waterways displayed a charging pillar complete with credit card reader, to be introduced in the spring.

As important as the design and development of new electric hulls and motors, antique and classic boat restoration was becoming equally popular. Specialist craftsmen at Thameside yards such as Peter Freebody & Co. of Hurley and his former apprentice, Colin Henwood of Henwood & Dean at Henley-on-Thames, were working wonders in perfectly restoring or replicating timber hulls. They were not merely going back to electric boating's Golden Era, but also taking hulls formerly powered by gasoline or steam and retrofitting them with electric propulsion. Freebody's first restoration and retrofit was the 1908 canoe *Cymba*; his first creation was *Tadpole*, a 27-footer (8 m) based on an 1884 design and powered by an original 72 volt DC electric motor dating from that time, with a hi-tech state-of-the-art control system.

Edward Hawthorne, Users' Group chairman, published his seminal book *Electric Boats on the Thames, 1889–1914*. Aware of its historic past, the EBA joined a campaign to save the *Viscountess Bury*, built in 1888 and for 21 years the largest electrically powered passenger vessel operating on the River Thames (see Chapter One). In 1910, after being converted to a gasoline engine, she was taken by sea up the east coast to King's Lynn and then to Cambridge. For the past 80 years she had been a well-known sight, carrying passengers on trips along the River between Cambridge and Ely. She was taken out of service in 1991 and put up for sale. Linda Ashton of Ely and friends formed a trust named the "Friends of the Viscountess Bury," and in 1994 purchased the vessel with plans to refurbish the launch, including converting her back to electricity. After considerable fund-raising, she was fitted with a steel lifting frame, lifted out of the river at Ely, and transported to Lowestoft to Newson's Yard alongside the International Boatbuilding Training College. When inspected there, it was found she was in such poor condition, only a few items could be salvaged; the lines from the hull were taken, and she was broken up—and the rotten timbers burned. However, thanks to Hawthorne, the River & Rowing Museum at Henley-on-Thames were able to conserve her figurehead, the wheel, a cabin door and several other boat parts.[22]

Over in Nantes, France, in 1995, the Ruban Bleu yard launched a new 5m50 waterbus they called the *Zelec* (=Zero electrique). Designed by Joubert Nivelt, it was fitted with 12 Fulmen EDX6 540 Ah forklift batteries which supplied energy to two 1kW Minn Kota motors. Capable of carrying up to 8 passengers, this was the first French e-waterbus in regular service for one hundred years. Working 10 hours per every day of the week, *Zelec* had soon totted up 4,000 km (2,500 mi) and ferried transport over 25,000 people. But as the *Zelec* proved too small for the 50,000 passengers per year, Ruban Bleu then produced the 7 m *Voguelec* for 17 passengers. Designed in aluminum by François Lucas, the *Voguelec* was equipped by twin 3 kw DC motors. By this time Ruban Bleu hireboat fleets were operating from Paris to Port Grimaud in the Provence-Alpes-Côte d'Azur region in southeastern France.[23]

In 1995, "across the Pond" in Longueuil, Quebec, Canada, Phillippe Pellerin founded the Canadian Electric Boat Company and produced his 15 ft 6" (4m70) E-Boat, later known as the Quietude 156 (1997) and Fantail 217. CEBC was to sell over 1,000 boats.

Back to solar racing: Between June 23 and 25, 1995, more than 170 students and 24 solar boats from Arkansas, Connecticut, Louisiana, Maine, Maryland, Massachusetts, Michigan, New York, Oklahoma, Pennsylvania, South Carolina, Wyoming, Wisconsin— and Japan—took part in the second "Solar Splash" on Lake Michigan. The boat of the students of Arkansas University won the sprint with a speed of 25 mph (40.3 kph), and the two-hour race was won by the Japanese with the Kanazawa solar hydrofoil, which completed 15 laps at an average 9 mph (14.5 kph).[24] On July 16, 1995, La Rochelle on France's Atlantic coast organized its first solarboat contest. Eight entries arrived from Berlin, Hamburg, Munich, Neuchâtel and Milan. Unfortunately the race was ruined by bad weather, including a Force 7 gale. August 19–20 saw the sixth running of the Swiss race on the Lake of Neuchâtel. It drew eleven competitors, divided into two classes: off-shore, capable of 50 km (30 mi) in waves of up to 2 meters (7 ft); and inshore for km sprint runs.[25]

The author was very aware that while such international contests were taking place around the world, there was a competitive potential in France. In agreement, AFBE's Vice-President Christian Marinot of EDF contacted André Ribes of EDF-GDF Nantes Atlantique, who in turned contacted Nantes Town Council. The result in 1995 was that in the context of the Rendez-vous de l'Erdre, a symposium, "The Electric Boat Experiences and Perspectives for Development," took place on the barge *Armoric 2* moored beside the quai de la Motte Rouge. The following day, thanks to a suggestion by this author "Les 6 Heures de l'Erdre" (The Erdre Six Hours) was held from 8:30 a.m. to 2:30 p.m. The first event of this type in Europe, it covered a circuit of 1,500 m over five hours. With a Le Mans start, eight to ten boats (Austrian, Swiss, English, American and French) competed around the little Ile de Versailles in four disciplines endurance, maneuverability, silence, and elegance. While the Innovation prize was won by Pierre Scholl of SSP Suisse with his catamaran, the "Prix Gustave Trouvé for Endurance" was won by Jérôme Croyère in the *Zelec*.[26]

That October on the Thames, TELCO organized a media demonstration day at Goring on Thames. *Charles Collier*, a diesel-electric river inspector's launch, went into service on the Broads. TELCO was now marketing its hybrid solution under the name Selectric, to be installed from new or retrofitted to existing boats.

Rupert Latham, as one of the acknowledged experts in the field of servicing the market for the provision of propulsion packages for other boatbuilders, next teamed up with Adrian Tilbury in Salhouse, Norwich, marketing the Dolphin range of electric boats under the banner of Weidtman's "Stelco Electroyacht." The range was based on the Lynch-inspired Cupex disc motor: the 700 Deltic, the 645 Frolic, and the 600 Mystic. The Deltic was pleasing to the German market, which prized the "liege platz" (sunbathing insert in the aft cockpit).

At the Earls Court Boat show, the 700 Deltic was exhibited alongside TELCO's Voltaire 16. That summer, Barbara Penniall became EBA secretary and news advertising manager, standing at her post for the next twenty-one years.

In early December 1995, a crew of 36 boys in teams of six piloted Prince Alfred College's second solar-powered cabin trimaran, the 37-ft (11m28) *Westpac Sunboat II*, from Yarrawonga to Goolwa on the Murray River and marginally increased the record to 2,507 km (1556 mi). In May/June 1995, *Wasser-Häx* (*Water Witch*), the latest solar boat of Matthias Wegmann and Theo Schmidt, made a series of sun-voyages along the River Rhône and the Rhein-Rhône canal to Basel, totaling some 3,000 km (1,860 miles).

Engineer Richard Mesple had joined Mark Wüst in setting up a boatyard for the construction of solar passenger boats, MW-Line at Yverdon-Les-Bains beside Lac Leman. Mark Wüst, who was initially trained as a designer for Omega watches in Bienne, was also a keen sailor, having learned on the Vaurien dinghy. His first electric realization was the *Râ d'eau* built with Professor Lechaire and his engineering team at the "Ecole d'Ingénieur du Locle" and powered by a truck windshield-wiper motor! Now ten years later, sponsored by the Pro Natura Centre of Champ-Pittet, MW-Line's first two 12-passenger boats were called *Solifleur* and *Chlorophylle*, although the model was called the Aquabus 850, a name chosen by Wüst. They measured 8m50 × 2m50 × 80 cm. Their Lynch 24v 8.2 kW motor gave them 9 kph with an autonomy of 8 hours, depending on the sunshine.[27]

In 1996 Jean-François Affolter, of the Institut d'Energie et Systèmes Electriques, based in the Swiss canton of Vaud, led a team to develop prototype fuel cell boats from 100 and 300 W ("Hydroxy 100," "Hydroxy 100 LS"). Two years later the *Hydroxy 300*, a trimaran, and *Hydroxy 2000*, a six-seater prototype, were tested, while a 300W APU PEM fuel cell was used in Roger Langevin's *Branec III*, a 53-ft carbon-Kevlar trimaran yacht taking part in the "La Route du Rhum 02."[28]

Electric boats in Italy were still very few and far between; Ero Mattieri's boatyard in Lezzano beside Lake Como collaborated with the Paris company Zero Emission to produce a 31-ft (9m50) electric mahogany runabout, *Spirit of Volta ZEB(R)*. This zero emission boat used 34 batteries and a submerged 23 hp 18 kW AC motor outside the hull which turned a three-bladed prop. *Spirit of Volta* could cruise at 21 mph (34 kph) for 2 hours, or 11 mph (18 kph) for 6 hours, and took just six hours to recharge. Such a performance was at least a decade ahead of its time.[29]

In Japan, on March 20, 1996, Japanese navigator Kenichi Horie left Salinas (Ecuador) in his 31-ft (9m50) *MALT's Mermaid* on an 8,700-mile (14,000 km) single-handed solar-powered voyage to his homeland. Eleven years before, in 1985, Hori had piloted a 30-ft solar boat some 3,730 miles (6,000 km) from Hawaii to Chichi-Jima, an island southeast of Japan. His second boat was constructed of 20,000 recycled beer cans and bedecked with 130-ft² (12 m²) of solar panels generating 1.5 kW and topping up two rechargeable nickel-hydrogen batteries. He completed the 14,000 kilometers between the two territories in 148 days.

And while Kenichi was voyaging, on Saturday, April 27, the Kingston Foreshore Technology Six-Hour Race was held on Lake Burley Griffin, Canberra, Australia. Two years before, the author had been visited in Bordeaux by Bob Slatyer and asked for his advice on developing electric boating in his native Australia. Twenty-nine teams arrived from Australia, Denmark and Germany, including Alan Colbeck of Callala Bay, New South Wales, 70 years old and sun-cruising with co-pilot Bob Slatyer, aged 76. The Prince Alfred College catamaran also took part. The contest was won by *Incat-039*, designed by giant catamaran manufacturer Incat of Tasmania, which has made fifteen of the world's 23 fast car passenger ferries. Piloted by Bob Clifford, founder of Incat, the *039*, a svelte

The futuristic *CREA 2000* winner of the 1996 European Solar Boat Championship at La Rochelle, France (author's collection).

double-rowing shell adapted from the wave-piercing design, completed eleven laps of the 5.75 km course—a 40-mile (64 km) cruise—and took out the first prize in the competition class for the Fastest Lap and Endurance—3rd lap, 9.54 knots (11 mph).

And still again, while the courageous Japanese Kenichi was cruising, the European Solar Boat Championship was held on the sunny weekend of July 26–28, 1996, at La Rochelle, France. Organized by François Berthet of the French Solar Sport Association and sponsored principally by Charente Maritime General Council, 8 boats (from Switzerland, Germany and France) took part in contests for slalom, maneuverability, towing, sprint and distance cruising.

The winner-takes-all boat was the French trimaran *CREA 2000* (Centre Rochelais pour Energie Alternative), a La Rochelle University project led by Professor Christian Bouly. *CREA 2000*'s speed of 22.63 kph (14 mph) for 300 meters (328 yards) gave her a European record, beating the 17 kph (10 mph) established by the Swiss *Râ d'Eau* some weeks before at the Ulm Solar Championship. Her speed was not, however, fast enough for a world claim. This had been achieved a month before at the U.S. "Solar Splash" intercollegiate contest at Milwaukee, when the Michigan University entry was clocked at 41.974 kph (26 mph). Nevertheless the French sunboat proved herself more versatile when on Sunday she made an offshore cruise of 20 sea miles in choppy seas from Rochefort to la Rochelle and ran for 4 hours 15 minutes. *CREA 2000* could turn in a harbor in under two boat lengths and register a pulling power of 145.5 kg (320.7 lbs) on a strain gauge.

Three weeks later, as a follow-up to our little eb contest in Nantes, for May 13–15, 1996, the author had persuaded the AFBE team to organize a three-day event, taking in an international regatta on the artificial boating lake, Bordeaux Lac. Nine boats representing five nations came to the line for the Six Hours Enduro—which was won by Pierre Scholl and Johan Tischhauser of Geneva, Switzerland, in their 24-ft (7m50 *ST-90*), weighing 400 kg and propelled by a 5 kW motor. At a cruising speed of 6 knots, *ST-90* won the Aigrette d'Or. The silver was won by the AFBE's *Egretta*, piloted by Hervé Henri, while Jérome Croyère in *Zelec* came in third. Also taking part were Guy Gorius in the *Lagon 45*; Claude Didier with an Accumot inboard brought from Gerardmer; a catamaran, *CIPB*, entered by a team from the author's pleasure boat museum; *Luciole*, a 4m50 Budsin Woodcraft imported from the USA, with Tom Hesselink over for the event; and the Frolic 21 *Belisma*, piloted by Brian and Sue Rogers, who had trailered it from their home at Castelnaudary beside the Canal du Midi to represent the UK. Maneuverability trials were held on Day Two. During this time, 156 delegates attended a symposium of the European Working Group on Electric Passenger Boats in a marquee called "le village nautique du lac," where both the Cupex and Accumot motors were on exhibit. The long-term idea of a European Electric Boat Association was discussed and it was stated that there were already 5,000 electric boats in the Netherlands. This event has never been repeated.[30]

Sadly, Hans Asijee, the Netherlands pioneer, did not attend, having retired from the

Competitors at the 1996 International Regatta at Bordeaux Lac. Standing, from left: Jerome Croyère (France), Guy Gorius (France), Sue and Brian Rogers (UK), Johan Tischhauser (Switzerland), Geneviève Vernier (Switzerland), Jean Peters (France); kneeling, from left: unidentified, Pierre Genève (Switzerland) and Tom Hesselink (U.S.) (author's collection).

Stichting Elektrisch Varen for health reasons, with his place taken by former secretary Wim Renssen.

Elco Continues

Over in the USA, the Elco company was acquired in 1996 by another Lake George resident, Chuck Houghton, who was inspired at least in part by the electric boats on Lake George. His great-grandfather, W.K. Bixby, brought the 36-ft (11 m.) *St. Louis* to Lake George in 1903. Indeed, Chuck proposed to his wife on it and gave her an electric 24-footer (7-meter) for a wedding present in 1989. Following the purchase of Elco, Houghton eventually moved from a rented warehouse to set up a 68,000 ft² factory at the site of an old Dutch boatyard in Athens on the River Hudson. There he started to build and sell elegant electric boats again, ranging from 14-ft to 36-ft fantail launches with prices that ranged from $8,700 to $195,000. The Classic models were replicas of Elco's elegant 1890s Edwardian launches, the Picnic models were less formal, and the Sport Utility models had minimum maintenance fiberglass hulls. The company also installed Elco electric drives in boats and sailboats and would restore selective sailboats and motorboats if they were electric or if they are upgraded from gasoline or diesel with an Elco electric drive.[31]

Elco also built the 14-ft (4 m) *Serenity*, a Herreshoff-inspired, 4-passenger launch, with chrome hardware, powered by an Elco ½ hp electric drive. Going back to earlier construction techniques, Elco also introduced a wooden-hulled 16-ft (4m80) electric runabout designed for the rental market. The first of these boats were built for the St. Louis Parks Department for use in the summer of 2003. The company went on to build the only United States Coast Guard–certified, pure electric-powered vessels for commercial use. These 30' (9 m) (15 passengers) and 33' (10 m) (25 passengers) launches, in either the Classic or Picnic finish, are now used commercially on the harbor at Greenport, New York; at the Audubon Environmental Center in Prospect Park, Brooklyn, New York; at the Edison-Ford Winter Estates Museum in Fort Myers, Florida; as a charter boat in Miami, Florida; for guests at the former Rockefeller "camp," The Point, on Saranac Lake, New York; at the Sea Island Company, St. Simons Island, Georgia; and at Mayakoba, an exclusive resort south of Cancun, Mexico. The following year, the *Serenity* boats were transferred to the Lake Placid Lodge in Lake Placid, New York, since that was a much smaller and quieter lake, more suitable for electric boating.

The Friedrichshafen Boat Show in Germany took place in September 1996, and among those boats shown was Kopf AG's *Ra*, a 31-ft (9 m) stainless steel catamaran dayboat with teak platform and solar panel canopy, powered by twin "Cupex" electric motors. Designed by Christoph Behling for Kopf AG in Sulze-am-Neckar, it was developed in cooperation with the University of Stuttgart. The *Ra* went into service on the Danube.

In an article called "Whisper Craft" published in *International Boat Industry* in December 1996, I proudly stated, "Setting aside world sales of thousands of small electric motors, no repeatable statistics exist to enable one confidently to put a precise size on the market for 'customized' electric boats. Informed trade opinion, however, puts the worldwide annual production of such craft in the hundreds of units rather than thousands. Production is primarily located in the U.S., UK, France and the Netherlands, with an estimated 20 boatyards adding to the ever-growing fleet of 'whisper craft,' mostly in the 3–9 meter range."[32]

To start off 1997, the first detailed Provisional List of Thames Charging Points was published in our *News*. Haines Marine produced their *E-Evolution*, a 29-ft (8.8 m) electric cabin hire cruiser with its twin 2 kW E-Drives as developed by Colin Seward of Brimbelow Engineering, Great Yarmouth, Norfolk. Val Wyatt Marine at Wargrave created the Thames Electric Boat Center to bring together and represent several manufacturers in the South of England. Fifteen electric boats paraded at the 10th Wargrave rally. Paul Jackson took over from Edward Hawthorne as Users' Group chairman. Volume 10 N°3 Autumn 97 issue of the *News* published its first pages in color.

MW Line of Yverdon-les-Bains, Switzerland, had continued their progress. The 25 pax Aquabus 1050 was designed by the stylist Fernando Da Cunha Lima in conjunction with Richard Mesple, incorporating a fine hull which could take 1.5 m (5 ft) waves. The motor was an 8.2kW Lynch Sol-Z motor. On August 15, 1997, an Aquabus 1050, the *Aquarel*, started regular service on Lake Geneva. Three more boats were added to the fleet by 1999. In parallel, MW-Line also provided engineering service towards the electrification of other passenger boats. Notably, these included a 50-passenger boat on Lac des Brenets (Jura) and a traditional 60-passenger boat with classic lines, the 20-m (65 ft) *Becassine*, for operation in Geneva from the Quai du Monte-Blanc, near the Grand Casino, with a range of 90 km (56 mi) at 10 knots.[33]

By this time, the author had resigned from his job at the Bordeaux Pleasureboat Museum, and, after a little rest, having learned how to make use of the Internet, he created the "Centre Mondial de Renseignement du Bateau Electrique" (the Electric Boat World Information Center) from his rented home in Carignan de Bordeaux, then researched and emailed out a news sheet he called *International Electric Boat* (*IEB*) to the British, American, French, and Dutch Electric Boat Associations. He was to do this for the next five years. In the absence of interest from powerboating's official governing bodies, he also attempted to build up an "International Records Form" for speed and endurance records. He also produced a report, "A Casebook for Electric Waterbuses," published in 1998 by AVERE (the Association Européenne des Véhicules Electriques Routiers).

In 1997 also came the appearance of a revolutionary concept: a solar-wind hybrid watercraft using pivotally mounted and controlled "solar sails." A "solar sailor" can use both forms of renewable energy available at sea, i.e., the sun and the wind, is virtually silent, creates no water pollution and greatly reduces air pollution and greenhouse gas emissions. The project was conceived by Robert Dane, a doctor in the fishing town and seaside resort of Ulladulla in New South Wales, Australia. Dane had opened a sailing school at the age of 38.

> I was intrigued by the first Advanced Technology Boat race, but felt I could do better. Reading a book about evolution, I observed how dragonfly wings with solar collectors are used for flying. What if I were to mimic the same thing with sailboats? If the weather became too rough, then just like a beetle, the boat could fold its wings away. Modifying a HobieCat racing catamaran, a functioning prototype was built in 82 days and successfully launched at the Advanced Technology Boat Race on Lake Burley Griffin in Canberra in April 1997. It was named the *Marjorie K* after Marjorie Kendall, a dairy farmer and solar power enthusiast who was using sunlight to power electric pumps on her farm and became my first and largest investor. The solar sails on *Marjorie K*, made by local surfboard craftsman Bruce Heggie, were operated by a simple lever and pulley system. During the five-hour endurance race, our prototype completed more laps than any other boat on the day and won the major prize for the Most Innovative Design.[34]

With no wind energy available on race day, the *Marjorie K* completed 13 × 4.4 km laps at 6.2 knots average speed, traveling a total of 35 miles (57 km) in 5 hours on sun and battery power alone. Two days later, in 8–10 knots of breeze, the *Marjorie K* achieved a steady boat speed of 6 knots on wind power alone on a reach while diverting the unused solar power into her batteries. When power was transferred to her electric outboard motor, she quickly achieved speeds of 12–15 knots on the same reach. She also lapped all the other contenders five times, but in doing so had a minor collision with another entrant, and was relegated to second place. Dane's next plan was to make a commercial vessel.

Over in Newport Beach, Duffy gave away some ownership to an employee. Gary Crane was a big part of getting the Duffy Boat Company through the '90s, but eventually Gary grew apart from the company when the factory moved 100 miles inland to the Mojave Desert. The drive was long and hard and he agreed to a buyout arrangement. The move to the desert was initiated by the Southern California AQMD (Air Quality Management District). While the boat was exactly what they wanted to improve air quality, they would not issue the VOC (volatile organic compound) allotments to build it, saying during the 15 minutes the fiberglass was drying in the build process, styrene was emitted into the air, and the AQMD controlled how much of it is allowed to escape in the open molding process. During the rest of the boat's life it does not hurt the environment and offsets a gas-polluting boat, but that didn't matter. When Duffy found the Mojave Desert, the AQMD became much more accommodating, and they even helped Duffy secure enough VOC allotments to build hundreds of boats per year. The move to the desert was painful, having to find workers and train them. The shop in Costa Mesa was now a true factory in Adelanto, California. Located on six acres, it allowed the Duffy boat company to vertically integrate all phases of construction, lowering costs and increasing production.[35]

Duffy always felt uneasy about competition and he always faced the possibility that a large boat manufacturing company would go green and compete. This was the motivation behind the six patents he received over the next five years. First Duffy wanted to perfect his idea of a rotating power drive, knowing this was the best way to push a small boat, allowing much more room to the interior, easier installation, superior maneuverability, quieter operating, and less servicing.

Duffy, along with Alex Kozloff and Charlie Sparkle, built and refined the drive unit for three years and finally developed the final product known as the Duffy Power Rudder (U.S. Patent 6503109 B1). It was a very innovative design. The rudder had in it a spiral bevel gear that drove a prop shaft out the rear of the rudder, and the drive shaft went up inside the boat where the motor was coupled to it. All of this turned and gave the drive great maneuverability. The motor was out of the bilge, where it can corrode. As for the motor, Duffy changed to a much smaller, more modern type called a pancake design. This little powerful unit put out more horsepower than the shunt-wound or series-wound motors and was a fraction of the weight. It also remained much cooler than the other motors, making it more efficient.

The Power Rudder revolution was an expensive, time-consuming adventure for Duffy because to use the Power Rudder each boat in the Duffy line had to be redesigned from the hull up. It took four years to finally finish new molds for every size boat Duffy offers. Today all Duffys use the Power Rudder.

Also as part of the Simple Green Corporation to promote "Environmental Intelligence" as a joint project, Duffy commissioned racing yacht designer Jim Antrim and composite specialist Alex Kozloff to design an offshore boat to make a 58-mile (93 km)

The *Duffy Voyager,* built for offshore distance records, in a promotional postcard (Duffy collection).

trip across the Pacific Ocean from Newport Beach jetty entrance to Catalina Island's Avalon Harbor entrance buoy and back at an average speed of 12 knots. Antrim came up with a wave-piercing water spider measuring 62' (18.9 m) long and 19' (5.8 m) wide, with tiny stabilizing floats. Built in carbon fiber in bright yellow by Westerly Marine of Santa Ana, the Duffy *Voyager* used many of the components which go into every Duffy electric boat. But it was also equipped with GPS, VHF and safety systems. Duffy, as the pilot, commented, "It's kind of funny-looking, but it's very efficient. It's really just a giant box to hold Trojan batteries."

Timed by Ken Matthews of the EBAA, on Saturday, July 11, 1998, Duffy took the helm, and with Heiser monitoring the instruments, the *Voyager* made the crossing in 5 hours 38 minutes 57 seconds, averaging 9.7 knots (11 mph). On August 8, *Voyager,* this time driven by Trojan Batteries director Rick Godber, with Heiser again on instruments, made a sprint from Newport Beach to Long Beach, 12 miles, in 1 hour 30 minutes, claiming an offshore electric speed record of 10.2 knots (11.7 mph). Duffy predicted that with the right tuning, the *Voyager* could run at 13 knots (15 mph) for 100 sea miles, and hit 25 knots (30 mph) maximum. He announced his hope that someone else would build a boat to compete with his for the Catalina Challenge. He also planned cruises from Fort Lauderdale, Florida, to the Bimini Islands in the Bahamas, the Hawaiian Islands, Australia's inland water route and across the English Channel and back to show off the boat's capabilities. Even if these runs were never made, *Voyager* served as good publicity to the company, which was by now offering eight production boats ranging from 14 ft to 21 ft (4 to 6m50) and held its own as the world's largest manufacturer of electric pleasure boats.

And, as Duffy reports:

They have been used in a diversity of locations and events: The retiring president of Disneyland was given a Duffy. They played a trick on him at his gala retirement party on Main Street USA downtown Disneyland. They bought another boat from me that was just a hull, deck, interior, and surrey top. They hoisted it above the crowd a hundred feet in the air, pulled off the wrapping to unveil the cute little Duffy, whereupon the boat came crashing down to the ground, breaking up in a hundred pieces. Sadness prevailed as Mickey, Donald, and Minne cried and cried until out of the smoke came the real Duffy in perfect shape! Who else but Disney would do that or even come up with the idea?

In Idaho at the Coeur d'Alene Resort golf course, one of the greens, N°14, is on an island and the only way to get there after you hit is on a Duffy. At the Mayacoba resort in Mexico you travel with your clubs on a rack in the stern from your waterfront cottage to play golf or dine. On the island of Oahu in Hawaii there is a tiny river flowing from the mountains to the beach and there is a stretch of homes on this narrow waterway that has several Duffys. The ride from one end to the other is less than one half of one cocktail. Beauty abounds and they don't even care. They just drift along in paradise.

Palm Desert in California has three tiny lakes that Duffys are used on. One surrounds a three par golf course with million dollar plus motor coaches. Duffys go from motor home to motor home linking friends, playing golf, tennis and fine dining. Another fleet of privately owned Duffys cruise around Lake La Quinta. Lastly the Marriott Springs resort has a fleet of Duffys that cruise from *inside* the air-conditioned 5 story open lobby and out to the five restaurants where guests eat different cuisines along their tiny lake. One Duffy, on a beautiful high mountain lake with gorgeous views of the Colorado mountains, is used for marriages.

In terms of fleets of Duffys outside Newport Beach–Huntington Harbor, Long Beach and Oxnard Harbor in California have fleets approaching one thousand boats in each harbor.[36]

Duffy continued to produce finely appointed boats such as this 1999 Duffy 30 all-electric (Duffy collection).

By this time, Japanese companies, in particular Sony, had made great strides in the commercialization of lithium rechargeable batteries. In 1997, Tsuyonobu Hatazawa, R&D manager at the Sony Corporation, Kanagawa, invented the polymer gel electrolyte and lithium ion polymer battery. In 1997 Nissan Motors produced its *Altra*, an electric car, equipped with a neodymium magnet 62 kW electric motor and run on lithium ion batteries manufactured by Sony. It would not be long before such batteries would be found in the hulls of electric boats.

Malcolm Moss of England had continued his passion for solar innovation. Constructed by Modular Mouldings of Gweek, Cornwall, *Collinda* was originally designed as a solar boat to test new engines to find replacements for the overheating Occo Sachs motors used in India. It was, however, speedily put into operation to win the challenge to be the first boat to cross the English Channel under solar power. The *SB Collinda* made the crossing on July 22, 1997, taking 6 hrs 15 minutes from Dover to the French coast. The 1.4 kW display of solar panels produced 945 watts, giving an average speed of 3.4 knots. Skipper Moss and his team were presented with the Eurosolar award in 1998.

On August 15–16, 1997: *Wagtail V*, a 29-ft (8.8 m) Lynch-engined electric cruising launch, belonging to Paul and Pat Wagstaffe, prepared by Emrhys Barrell of TELCO, traveled 116 statute miles (187 km) in 24 hours without recharging its batteries. It completed 12 laps of a measured course on the Upper Thames between Goring and Wallingford. An 8-strong relay team of EBA members took turns at the helm. One of these, Tony Ellis, became new editor of the *News*. At the end of the test there was still sufficient energy left in the batteries to carry the boat for a further 16 miles (26 km).

In France, Jérome Croyère of Ruban Bleu at Nantes, continuing to increase his range, launched the 4m60 (15ft) *Scoop* for 7 passengers. The town of Albi commissioned two unusual electric gabares, *Pastel* and *Cocagne*, for service on the River Tarn. Their 9m (30 ft) Aluminox hulls, designed by a Monsieur Gardner, were propelled by a 2 kW motor linked to two Castoldi waterjets. With a passenger capacity of 11, they would carry up to 20,000 passengers per year.

Another innovative 200-passenger waterbus was *Le Vendôme*, designed by Gérard Ronzatti in conjunction with Patrick Droulers, French representative for the Italian firm Ansaldo. A Volvo diesel engine was linked to an 80 kW Ansaldo AC motor that turned a vertical shaft Schottle rudder-propeller. The trimaran's hulls were constructed in the French Massif Central region and the whole assembled at Conflans Saint Honoré on the Seine. This truly European project, bringing together French, Swedish, Italian and German expertise, led to the glass-roofed *Le Vendôme*, managed by the Batobus company, transporting 225,000 passengers on the Seine at Paris between April and October. Three Batobus would follow: the *Odéon*, the *Rivoli*, and the *Trocadero*.

At La Rochelle, Philippe Palu de la Barriere, a mathematician who specialized in computing for yachts, designed and built a vessel that competed in a European solar boat challenge and won it. The event highlighted the potential to run a vessel for an extended period on solar energy alone. Alternative Energies (Alt.En), created in 1996 and funded by the city of La Rochelle, developed and built *Le Passeur Electrique*, France's first solar-powered ferry with a 30 pax capacity. Alt.En were to produce 15 boats for various cities in France.

Between La Rochelle and Niort, in the village of Maillé in the picturesque Marais Poitevin, otherwise known as the Venise Vert, eleven 6m20 (20 ft) hireboats were electro-retrofitted. Saviboat of Saint-Savinien in the Charente launched a new model for their miniature port. The 4m30 (14 ft) *Derby*, designed by Priam-Doizi, was powered by three 100-watt Thruster outboards.

Back in Britain, "Eco-Boat 97," held in September, was a conference and demo on Oulton Broad, attended by 86 environmentalists from all over the world. Nine out of the 16 sessions concerned e-boats. Meanwhile many from the 8,000 visitors took rides on a range of electric boats. On June 27–28, 1998, at long last, Lake Windermere hosted its first e-b rally, with 7 boats at the Steamboat Museum Dock. That September, Waterways Minister Alan Meale, MP, was introduced to e-boats on the Thames at Maidenhead and given a ride in *Wagtail V.* "Silent Sensations" was once again held on South Walsham Broad.

On the Amsterdam canals, the trend began to fit electric propulsion to luxury tourist saloon launches. In 1998, Anton Brands of the Rondvaart Delft cruising company had one of his boats equipped with diesel-electric propulsion. The *Willem de Zwijger* (= *William the Silent*), carrying up to 48 passengers, was the first in the e-fleet. Before long tourists were asking explicitly for this boat for their city tour. Soon after, when Ocean Affairs restored a 35-pax saloon launch built in Switzerland in 1938, they obtained a grant from Amsterdam's Municipal Environmental Department to equip it electrically with a 96-volt system. She was renamed the *Monne de Miranda*, after a legendary Amsterdam alderman from the 1930s. Perhaps the most luxurious of all was the mahogany and teak *De Proost van Sint Jan*, originally built in 1900 and often called "most beautiful saloon boat in Europe," moored outside the Amsterdam Hilton Hotel.

An Austro-Swiss project linking Boesch, Schmalzl and Kraütler set up a 25-kW/ 180-volt speedboat *that could tow a waterskier.* Boesch went on to launch their *Elektro* model. Meanwhile, Seebacher had extended his range to the Aquawatt 550, 650 and 715. In Italy, the Fratelli Rossi yard of Viareggio, Lucca, produced their 15-m (50 ft) 70-pax *Lino Beccati* hybrid, combining a Volvo with a 10 kW/90 volt Micro-Vett motor as used in the Fiat Panda electric automobile. But this initiative proved unsuccessful as the local authority would not provide the necessary recharging point on the quay.

On September 17, 1998, the French made their first offshore voyage. During le Grand Pavois, the La Rochelle Boat Show, where a theme was electric boats, Christian Bouvet and Michel Rabaland took 3 hours 16 minutes to pilot the AFBE's boat *Egretta* on a 24-mile (40 km) round cruise between the Port des Minimes and Fort Boyard.

In Australia, to take his solar sailing innovation further, Robert Dane had contracted Grahame A. Parker BE, a naval architect whose sleek, slim, low-wash River Cats were plying the Brisbane River and Sydney's Parramatta River. Parker was quickly convinced that solar sailing technology could be incorporated into his designs and scaled up to commercial level. With concept drawings from Parker in hand, Dane began to trawl Sydney for money to build a ferry for the tourist market. *Solar Sailor* featured in the July 1998 issue of Massachusetts Institute of Technology's prestigious *Review* magazine. The New South Wales Minister for State Development, Michael Eagan, presented a check for $20,000 to *Solar Sailor*. The grant was made under the Australian Technology Showcase Export Fund. The grant was provided on a matching dollar-for-dollar basis, towards assisting with patenting, ensuring the security of intellectual property would be retained. World Patent 1998021089 A1 for "A pivoting sailing rig" was granted that year.

That same year, Kopf of Germany's 10.4 meter (34 ft) stainless steel *RA 31*, the first international solar boat shuttle, went into operation on Lake Constance, transporting almost 4000 passengers and 2,200 bicycles across the Untersee, the western end of Lake

Constance/Bodensee, between the German village of Gaienhofen and the Swiss counterpart of Steckborn. Powered by two 4.8 kW motors, *RA 31* averaged 9 mph (15 kph), with a maximum speed of 11 mph (18 kph). The 11 m² (118 ft²) roof had a maximum photovoltaic peak power of 1.58 kWp. Because of *RA 31*'s success, Kopf replaced her with the 20-meter (66 ft) stainless steel cat, *RA 66*, called *Helio*, capable of carrying 120 passengers. Its photovoltaic generator was shaped like a tunnel, giving shade and protecting passengers from the rain, and its 52 panels delivered a maximum 4.2 kWp.

The 1999 London Earls Court Boat Show saw an impressive five stands presenting electric boat equipment, particularly STELCO with their Renaissance 31, Capriole 850 and Capriole 700 Elegance. That summer James Keating became the new EBA chairman while Bruce James took over from Tony Ellis as the *News* editor. Windermere and Wargrave enjoyed rallies. Electric narrowboats reappeared in the guise of *Switched Off*, *Catspaw* and *Ratty*.

"Les Rencontres Internationales de la Propulsion Electrique Nautique" (International Meetings for Marine Electrical Propulsion) took place in Nantes between April 9 and 12, 1999. On Monday afternoon, Jérôme Croyère, drove his prototype 15 kW advance-engined 8 meter (26 ft) *Ruban Bleu* trimaran up and down the Erdre River in front of the exhibition tents at estimated speeds of 30 kph (18 mph). Croyère was nicknamed "le Duffy français," having built and sold over 700 boats in one year, in use at over 120 sites in France but also near Barcelona, Berlin, Montreal, and the Italian Lakes. Croyère had now created Ruban Vert, to manage the hireboat business side.

Towards the end of 1999, the city of Strasbourg, France, received its own glass-roofed electric waterbus, measuring 23m50 × 4m80 (77 ft × 15 ft). Built in steel by the Michel boatyard, it was powered by two 30–40 kW motors supplied by 12 tons of lead-acid battery. It would run from 9 a.m. to 10 p.m. making 8 one-hour trips. It was named the *Gustave Doré*, in memory of the Strasbourg-born 19th century painter and illustrator.

On the other side of the world, in Australia, more traditionally, the e-cruise boat *Wagonga Princess* began operating on the Wagonga Inlet on the south coast of New South Wales. The vessel, built in Sydney of Huon pine in 1905, had been powered by steam, gasoline and diesel engines and was converted to electric propulsion in 1996. Charlie Bettini, her owner, was encouraged by a trip on the 1912 retrofitted Baldor 36-ft (11 m.) electric boat *Rubeena*, based on Lake Tyers in Victoria. The Trojan batteries fed a 48-volt Lynch, to give a maximum speed of 9 knots and a range of 6 hours.

In April 1999, to achieve its goal of having a working prototype on Sydney Harbor for the 2000 Olympics, the Solar Sailor Company began the design and construction of *Solar Sailor II*. This was the code name for the 20-meter (66 ft) ferry, equipped with an 80 kW LPG genset on the back deck, to charge the batteries if there was not enough sun or wind. This made it a solar/wind/battery/fossil fuel hybrid. Initial sea trials in Jervis Bay went brilliantly with expected speeds exceeded. Following a slight hiccup with the engines, keeping *Solar Sailor II* at wharf for a fortnight, trials resumed.

Elsewhere on a microcosmic scale was the *Sci-Flier* of Commander Murray Baker, a weapons electrical engineering officer of the Royal Australian Navy, working with the government's Defense Science and Technology Organisation (DSTO). In 1997, Murray had accidentally discovered a 12-meter (40 ft) discarded former 4-man rowing scull amid grass and debris on Black Mountain Peninsula, a suburb of Canberra. Donated by the Narrabundah Rowing Club, the scull was restored and modified by Murray and a team in their spare time. Modifications included stabilizing pontoons, cowlings and a spray cover, plus two large rudders. It was then installed with a 3/95 kW very high efficiency rare-earth magnet, minimal steel three-phase DC, brushless T-FLUX motor and PWM controller, invented by Paul Lillington of Lugarno, Sydney. To the drive chain were added ten lead acid batteries, a modified outboard motor leg and a modified carbon fiber model aircraft propeller. In 1998, Murray and team then entered *Sci-Flier* for the Australian Science Festival's International Bayer Solar and Advanced Technology Boat Race on Lake Burley Griffin in Canberra. On its first lap, *Sci-Flier* set a speed record of 20.83 mph (33.52 kph). *Sci-Flier* would win the speed prize and the endurance prize for three years in the ATBR. When last heard of, the team were looking at increasing that speed by adding a PEM, or proton exchange membrane hydrogen-powered fuel cell, and lithium-ion batteries.[37]

SEVEN

2000–2009

The new millennium would see more and more electric boats using solar power in more and more countries and some totally breakthrough hybrid technologies for extending their cruising range.

Although in 1965, Siemens R&D had equipped a boat called *Eta* with a fuel cell propulsion system and demonstrated it on a pond at their Erlangen Research Center in Bavaria, it was only in 2000, 35 years later, that *Hydra*, innocently proclaimed as "the world's first hydrogen fuel cell electric boat," began to give demonstrations along the Ketelvaart and Leie Canals of Ghent, Belgium. Her low-draft Gottwald-designed hull, built with Teflon coating by Ecoboot, Germany, was equipped with the Europe 21 fuel cell electric generator made by Etaing GmbH.

Etaing was founded in Leipzig in December 1999 by Professor Harald Klein of Linde Engineering and Christian Machens. Energy for the Europe 21 came from ZeTek Mark II alkaline fuel cell modules supplied by Zemar and based on the catalytic conversion of hydrogen and oxygen. *Hydra*'s e-motor is an Oecosachs 48 VDC 8 kW unit, based the Cedric Lynch motor. Thirty minutes to refuel gave *Hydra* a cruising autonomy of 2.2 mph (9 kph) over 16 hours. With official certification by Germanischer Lloyd, the 22-pax Hydra, operated by VZW Eleketroboot, took up over 1,600 passengers on trips.[1] Then in September 2001 Etaing went into liquidation.

The Electric Boat Association continued to hold its friendly regattas at Caversham, Huntingdon, Shrewsbury, Cookham and Norfolk, with shows at Pangbourne and Waltham Abbey. Eco-Boat 2000 was held at Norwich. Tony Ellis returned as editor of the *News*. "Silent Sensations" was again held on the Broads. The indefatigable Barbara Penniall pulled together both a "UK Trade Members Product Guide" and a "Directory of Private EBA Members," plus an alphabetical list of boat names, all distributed with the *News*.

Over in France, on March 3, 2000, a general assembly of the AFBE (French Electric Boat Association) was held. In just six years its membership had grown to 79 members, with no fewer than 17 electric boatbuilders, not only in France: the Lot-et-Garonne, Charente-Maritime, Gironde, Loire-Atlantique, Deux-Sèvres, Vosges, Jura, Morbihan, but also across the border in Switzerland and Italy.[2]

A new world solar boat distance record was established in Australia. Between January 1 and May 13, 2000, Frank Wheeler was out cruising on Sydney Harbor for a total 105 days and clocked up 2790 miles (4,500 km). This was not a continual run, Wheeler staying at home during the night, and casting off in *Sun Pirate III*, his yellow catamaran

Hydra, **the world's first passenger-carrying fuel cell boat, in Leipzig, 2000 (courtesy Electric Boat Association).**

cabin-cruiser, each day to notch up another six hours' cruising. This was despite one quarter of these days being rainy. On one sunny day, Wheeler, an American by birth, clocked 45 miles (73 km).[3]

On the same stretch of water, on September 15, 2000, *Solar Sailor II*'s moment of triumph came when she served as the official media boat following the Olympic Games torch across Sydney Harbor. The torch was carried by a State Transit ferry from Manly Wharf to Circular Quay. Its progress was recorded by those aboard *Solar Sailor II* and seen by billions of televiewers around the world. During the games, she served as the tour boat for the unaccredited media during the Games.[4]

Another solar-powered passenger boat, Kopf's *RA 82,* went into service in May 2000 in the port of Hamburg, Germany. With a weight of 34 tons, a length of 26.5 meters (87 ft) and a beam of 5.27 meters (17 ft), *RA 82* was the then largest PVEB (photovoltaic electric boat) in the world. It had a maximum speed of 10 mph (15 kph), and could cruise for 12 hours or 75 miles (120 km) on a cloudy day—or for an unlimited distance, at 3 mph (5 kph) in sunshine. Its onboard refrigerator and coffee machine were, of course, solar-powered![5]

In 2000, for Switzerland's Expo.02 "Three Lakes" National Exhibition 2002, MW-Line, now a limited company, was commissioned to build four 46-ft (14 m) Aquabus C60 cats, each equipped with 226 ft² (21 m²) of solar panels, to take visitors out to the Jean Nouvel Monolith and back. During the Expo, from May to October 2002, they made some 25,000 voyages and carried over 1 million visitors. After the Expo, one of the boats, renamed *Solar Heritage,* went into service for the Chichester Harbor Conservancy, in

Sussex, England. The other units were sold to charter companies in Evian (France), Lago Maggiore (Italy) and Zaragosa (Spain).[6]

Retrofits continued: The 100-pax 1900 *Angela Louise*, a 70-ft (21 m) former U.S. Coast Guard riverboat, her diesel replaced by a DC motor, returned to work at California's Newport Beach, going on to host and entertain for countless weddings.

On the Amsterdam canals, with internal combustion–engined boats disappearing, the tourist company DUBA Elektra could now boast a fleet of almost thirty e-passenger boats for hire. Her Royal Highness Princess Margriet of the Netherlands launched a second sightseeing tour boat in the restored 's-Hertogenbosch.

Also in Amsterdam, Bellmann began to sell their Aquapella units. Three years before Fred Bellis, an electronics engineer, the inventor of the Infra-Red Movement sensor, lived in Schagen on the Thousand Islands area of West Friesland. Taking one of the Perm 132DC motors manufactured in Germany by his wealthy neighbor Cock Kroeff, the two of them designed and developed an integrated electric boat propulsion system incorporating motor, controller, range display and joystick. The Bellmann became the first electric boat propulsion package to be available on the market.[7]

Duffy continued to sell, but also to innovate with its first diesel-electric hybrid luxurious day cruiser—the Duffy/Herreshoff 30. This was the result of a casual meeting between Marshall Duffield and Halsey Herreshoff during the 1988 America's Cup yacht races about combining a classic appearance with modern technology. The electric motor was a 20 hp Whisper Drive 96-volt DC motor giving a top speed of 8 knots and a cruising speed of 5.5 knots over 15 hours. Production of the boat would be limited to between 8 and 12 boats per year.[8]

Another project with which Duffy was involved was the 19-ft (5m80) *EcoBarca* water taxi for service in Venice, Italy, which went into service from February 2001 to take passengers between the city's railway station and the canal-side Hotel Residenzia de Epoca. The low-wake M-hull form, called Mangia Onda (Italian for "wave eater"), was conceived and patented by U.S. Venice resident Charles W. Robinson, and William F. Burns III of the Mangia Onda Co. in San Diego, and was built by Duffy.[9] The idea was that instead of making waves, which were slowly eroding the palazzi along Venice's canals, this boat would literally eat them up. Power came from a 2.5 hp Leeson permanent magnet motor, spinning a prop at 800 rpm. Energy came from six, 6-volt Sealed Gel "East Penn" batteries manufactured by DEKA.

Duffy explains: "Venice being what it is (Mafia-driven) in my opinion will never go fully electric until lithium batteries are plentiful and inexpensive. Italians love to speed. The Venice port authority was not impressed with our 5 mph speed. They did not pursue going forward with another boat. Venice is sinking due to boat wakes so we thought this would be something they would love."[10]

In the USA, the Wye Island Challenge was established in 2001 by Tom Hesselink, director of the Electric Boat Association of America (EBAA), with two main goals of: (a) demonstrating the viability of electric powered boats, and (b) advancing their performance development. The race takes place in the waters off Maryland's eastern shore near St. Michaels, Maryland (approximately 50 road miles from Annapolis). It has since become an annual event.

England's Rupert Latham had diversified. His former employees, Simon Read and Roy Lawson of Creative Marine, found new premises in North Norfolk, and set about building a Frolic 36, designed by Andrew Wolstenholme, calling it *Estel*. They then built a second 36-footer (11 m) with cabin and toilet facilities, calling it the "Picnic Launch." With a more Classic approach, they then built a Frolic 31 called *Hamsini*, teak-hulled with nickel-plated deck fittings. Latham's new concern, STELCO Yachttechnik, launched the 29-ft (8m80) beaver-stern Sapphire launch *Little Susie*, fitted with low-voltage 3-phase AC motors and inverters.[11]

A new cruising record was established on the Thames. On August 21, 2001, the fully restored Thames Edwardian day launch *Pike*, equipped with a modern Lynch propulsion unit by TELCO, created a new cruising record of 137 miles (220 km) in 30 hours, averaging 4.57 mph (7.35 kph) around a course between Goring and Wallingford, without recharging its batteries. An 8-strong relay team led by Emrhys Barrell and TELCO's engineer Ian Rutter took it in turns at the helm. Barrell and Rutter were rewarded for their dedication when British Waterways commissioned TELCO to provide its 57 ft (17.3 m) narrowboat *Warde Aldham* with their Selectric hybrid drive system. The refit complete at the BW Stanley Ferry workshops, the boat returned to service in BW's North East Region as an engineer's inspection launch.[12]

Finally, thanks to Lars Frederiksen, Denmark became involved with electric boating. During the 1990s, Frederiksen had been a surveyor working for the Danish Coastal Conservation Commission, responsible for that country's 7,000+ km of coastline. Then in 1998 he became involved with electric marine propulsion and set up ASMO Marine in Copenhagen to produce the Thoosa e-saildrive systems installed in yachts.[13]

In the spring of 2001, Gilbert Devos of Roubaix, France, announced his electric outboard, the Propelec, the first French unit since Gustave Trouvé had developed his pro-

In 2001, the fully restored Thames Edwardian day launch *Pike*, equipped with a modern Lynch propulsion unit by TELCO, created a new cruising record of 137 miles (220 km) in 30 hours, averaging 4.57 mph (7.35 kph) around a course between Goring and Wallingford, without recharging its batteries (courtesy Electric Boat Association).

totype back in 1882. Devos rented small boats on his local River Deûle, and wanting a new motor, he called on engineering colleges and mechanical workshops to help him realize his goal. Two models were made available, the 2kW P2000 and the 1.2 kW P1200. Both were asynchronous submerged motors, and that year the small enterprise sold some 50 Propelecs. The enterprise failed to make its mark and went into liquidation in 2014.[14]

Combi in the Netherlands was now making a range of brushless permanent magnet motors (BLPM), based on industrial pumps, complete with their in-house innovative motor controller. The shaft was made of stainless steel and the bracket got the tilt option, and so could now be placed in different positions depending on the transom of the boat. Further, the tiller was moved to the side for better steering comfort. These new Combis ranged from 900, 1500, 2,500, up to 3,500 watts. On the other hand, Minn Kota continued their tradition of outboard innovation to give greater comfort to their bass fishermen: with a wireless remote that allowed trolling motor control from fishing rod, wrist or belt (CoPilot™).[15]

It was about this time that the lithium-ion battery went afloat. Its first planned use was for a top-secret defense application. In 2003, Northrop Grumman had been commissioned to design and build the Advanced SEAL Delivery System (ASDS), a 65-ft (20 m) midget electric submarine, for piggyback operation by the United States Navy. With power from a 67 hp (50 kW) electric motor, when it was found that the silver-zinc batteries were depleted more quickly than planned, the pioneer decision was made to develop a lithium-ion pack. Yardney Technical Products of Pawcatuck, Connecticut, was awarded a $44 million contract modification to provide four lithium-ion batteries for the ASDS program by May 2009. But in April 2006, while this was progressing, the program for new submarines was canceled and Northrop Grumman notified of termination. The current submarine was still in development and use from Pearl Harbor when on November 9, 2008, while being recharged, the lithium batteries caught fire and burned for six hours.[16]

The first use of the lithium-ion battery in a full-scale pleasure boat was taking place at the same time in Germany. Stefan Gehrmann of AirEnergy in Aachen had already equipped and test-flown a self-launching electric sailplane with a lithium battery. *Johanna*, an 8m Petterssen design boat, based on Starnberger Lake, Germany's fourth largest lake in southern Bavaria, was already using a short-range lead-acid drive system. Its owner approached Gehrmann in October 2003 with the idea to upgrade with a li-ion battery. Gehrmann recalls:

> I started with the calculation and cells selection and tried with Chinese cells (thunder sky). The samples I got at first were not too bad, but when I received the full quantity for the battery the cells were very poor and only a handful were as good as the samples. I searched for an alternative and came into contact with Kokam, then the leader in small Li-Ion cell RC applications. They were working on 100Ah cells but the R&D chief did not want to sell any because he was not yet satisfied with performance. Luckily I came in contact with Kokam's owner J.J. Hong who then arranged that we nevertheless got 120 cells for the boat. Actually we were the first in Germany, probably Europe who ordered and received large Li-Ion cells from Kokam. Parallel to the battery design and assembly we developed the BMS, because in those days there was no BMS on the market. The specs speak for themselves: nominal Voltage: 207V; capacity: 200Ah; energy: 41.4kWh; weight: 320kg. In spring 2004 we installed the prototype battery into the boat and batteries actually worked fine for almost ten years, then we upgraded the boat with 240AH cells and it is now owned and used in Berlin.[17]

By sheer coincidence, also beside Starnberger Lake, a new electric outboard was being developed: the Torqeedo from Christoph Ballin and Fritz Böbel. When Christoph

Ballin, a former McKinsey consultant, started working as sales and managing director of the garden tool-manufacturing company, Gardena, he moved from Hamburg into a little weekend cottage alongside a canal that runs into Starnberger Lake. The cottage came with a boatshed. As Lake Starnberg is a "green" lake, Ballin had to get himself an electric boat. He bought himself an old wooden hull and refurbished it, helped by his wife. He then put what he thought was a new electric motor onto the back.

> At Gardena, I had a colleague, Dr. Friedrich G. Böbel PhD. Fritz, who is a highly qualified electronics engineer, was then in our company's R&D, Purchasing Production and General management. [In 1994 Böbel was recipient of the Fraunhofer Society's applied research award for microelectronics.] On weekends, Fritz would visit us for a coffee because his daughter was vaulting nearby. When I showed him our nicely refurbished boat, instead of praising me, Fritz complained that the technology of the engine was fifty years old. I replied that this was all that was available on the market, to which he countered that with the current technology, we could do three times better. I replied that if this were true, we ought to start our own company. When Fritz called me on his way home from picking up his daughter, I knew he was hooked![18]

Realizing the potential, Herrn Ballin and Böbel left their jobs at Gardena and put all their money into the new company. At this stage they worked from home and also in the garden of Ballin's canal-side cottage. During the next four months, Böbel researched new motor technologies, propeller design from commercial shipbuilding *and lithium batteries*. Combining these technologies he arrived at an overall efficiency up to 51 percent, i.e., more than half of the energy stored in the battery arrives after all losses behind the propeller and is available to move the boat. This was by far the highest value from anybody on the market worldwide and was very important, as it provided more range and power from a limited battery supply. They also found a very old U.S. patent for a 3 hp foldable Evinrude gasoline outboard. They were not aware of anyone doing or having done it. They knew they could make their motor extremely lightweight and use lightweight batteries. So integrating the batteries into the motor was not a far step, and enabled putting the motor in a backpack. This particularly appealed to Böbel, a lover of hiking and canoeing.

The result was a motor, using electronically controlled outrunners with rare-earth magnets, which had around 24 times the torque of a motor of the same weight and volume that was state of the art 15 years ago. This development was made possible by recent developments in electronics (getting a little PCB that regulates 35 thousand times a second and that can take 40 Amps) and in material technology (rare-earth magnets becoming cheaper in the last 7 years). So while torque motors had already been known in research for 20 years, nobody had produced them on an industrial level.

At this time they decided to form a company. "We tried several name combinations with the word torque. It must not already be a protected word, but also one for which you could still get the important internet-domains without needing to add suffixes to it, etc. We combined Speedo and it worked: Torqeedo! Then we felt it sounded a little generic, could have been anything, so we added the Starnberg, Germany, to our logo, to indicate it is a real company that has a real base."[19]

For their livery, Gardena, Ballin and Böbel wanted to get away from orange and gray, the colors of their previous firm. But from market research, they ended up with very similar colors: "high-tech" silver, "power" orange and "standard component" black. The first Torqeedo prototype was produced in April 2005. It already had twice the overall efficiency of the market leader. Ballin recalls, "It took us quite some effort to install the mechanical and electronic gear necessary to measure propulsive power (the power that

Fritz Böbel, left, and Christoph Ballin with their Torqeedo outboard in 2005 (courtesy Torqeedo).

is actually available to drive the boat measured after propeller losses) and overall efficiency. We then did a lot of testing throughout the winter, which involved hacking up the ice on Lake Starnberg to get through to unfrozen sections."

Production began in February 2006 with plans to sell the first batch in Germany, Austria and Switzerland. The following year, Torqeedo Inc. was set up in Munich, a suburb of Crystal Lake, Illinois, followed by a dealership in Great Britain. At the same time, the first of a series of international patents was awarded to the innovative Böbel. Dynamically, Torqeedo created a sales force in 7 countries (Germany, Austria, Switzerland, UK, Ireland, USA, Canada) and via distributors in another 30 countries. A series of models came out of the Starnberg factory: the Travel and the Cruise, Power, BaseTravel, Ultralight 402 and Cruise R.

The Ultralight outboard was "the first genuine kayak motor." It weighed 7 kg including its high-performance LIMA battery, had an integrated GPS range calculator and an output equivalent to a 1 hp gasoline outboard. Each unit came with a motor mount, motor unit, lithium manganese battery, and remote throttle control with integrated board computer and magnetic on/off switch.

Torqeedos were soon being put to the test. At the Watertribe Everglades Challenge, called by many the toughest small-boat race in the world, Nick Hall from England used the Travel model for a 24-hour race from Key West to Key Largo—160 km (100 miles) covered in a kayak with pedal, sail and an electric motor containing a battery whose energy compared to 26 grams (1 ounce) of gasoline.

It was also at this time that Hermann Preinerstorfer, the brains behind the legendary Accumot outboard motor, decided to close down his 60-year-old family business. In recent years, Accumot had made some great technical strides, combining electronics with neodymium permanent magnet AC motors, with their 4–7 kW 48-volt SDI and SDE units. But Preinerstorfer decided to take a well-earned retirement and see more of his family. "Over the years, the outboards made by our Accumot family business were copied. It was always a waste of time to take such copyright infringements to court. We preferred to stay ahead by working on new projects."[20]

In May 2002, the EBA held its first-ever all-electric boat show in Hartford Marina, Huntingdon: twelve boats attended on the River Great Ouse. This was to become an annual event. In 2003 Sylvia Rutter, formerly with the BBC, and wife of TELCO engineer Ian Rutter, became the new editor of *Electric Boat News*, starting with Volume 16, N°1. During her ten-year editorship, the *News* was transformed into a full-color publication, to which this author regularly contributed international content. The EBA celebrated its 21st anniversary in June 2003 at Bisham Abbey. Twenty-six boats, ranging from the 6-ft (1m80) *Jubilee* to the 38-ft (12 m) *Lisbeth*, assembled and cruised from Bisham upstream to Temple Lock. The author returned from France to take part in the event.[21]

In April 2003, Australian EBA member Charles Fitzhardinge of Solarboat in Sydney, who had been specializing in all electric boats, crossed the 40-mile-wide Gulf St. Vincent from Adelaide to Port Vincent in his 19-ft (5m80) electric launch *Geehi*, built by Duck Flat Wooden Boats of Adelaide and powered by a 24V Lynch motor with auxiliary solar panels.

Progress continued with fuel cell prototypes worldwide. On October 22, 2003, in Kressbronn (Lake Constance), MTU Friedrichshafen unveiled the first standard yacht with a fuel cell propulsion system certified by German Lloyd (GL). The 40-ft (12-m) Beneteau yacht was named *No. 1*. The fuel cell module incorporated in *No. 1* was manufactured by Ballard Power Systems. Converting the fuel cell modules into a complete propulsion system was carried out at MTU. The company IPF, a power station operator based in Reilingen, was responsible for fitting the system into the yacht; the company also owned the yacht. The fuel cell propulsion system, which had the product designation "CoolCell," was used to propel the yacht in calm waters and to maneuver the craft when in a harbor. The system also delivered the onboard power supply. The yacht's international debut was in August 2003 in Japan.[22]

In Switzerland, Jean François Affolter and the L'Institut d'Energie et Systèmes électriques in Vaud, tested out the MW-Line built 3 kW Hydroxy 3000, fueled by hydrogen from a bottle of 76 liters (30 gallons) at 200 bars. The running of the cell was entirely automatic.

Over in the USA, in January 2004 Duffy took one of his 8-pax 30-footers and installed four Anuvu Power X fuel cells, each capable of generating 1.5 kW. Side-by-side assembly into an 8 hp fuel stack used reformed hydrogen on-board from sodium borohydride pumped at 6 psi through a special catalyst chamber to produce hydrogen, which was gravity-fed to four fuel cell stacks producing a total of 4,000 KW at 48 volts, netting about 3.2 KW to the charging system. This was linked to a 20 hp e-engine, with rheostat controls and a bank of 8 Trojan batteries. "We were the first passenger carrying vessel to use hydrogen to propel the boat using no fossil fuels. We ran for over a year almost every day." It was a project funded by the DOT and the DOE through a grant at the University of Long Beach in 2000.

It so impressed politicians, business folk, environmentalists and media alike that Anuvu Inc. was able to finalize details to be the San Francisco Water Transit Authority's contractor for the world's first fuel cell–powered commuter ferry. With $2.6 million in federal grants, the WTA was charged with building a 149-passenger ferry to run between "Frisco" and Treasure Island by 2005. It would be a 79-ft (24 m) double-decker, designed by John J. McMullen Associates of Hilton Head, South Carolina. The ferry's fuel cell was fed hydrogen via a metal hydride battery. Whenever the ferry was docked, the battery would be restocked with hydrogen via a tube. The fuel cell was housed in a metal container on top of the boat near the wheelhouse, while the battery was stored at the back of the boat for ballast.[23]

Another technology that was being applied to hybrid marine propulsion was a regenerative inboard electric motor patented[24] by David E. Tether of Tarpon Spring, Florida. Basically this is a brushless 144-volt DC motor that uses powerful permanent magnets instead of field windings and an electronic commutator instead of brushes. Dennis and Denise English were the first customers to have the Solomon Wheel system installed in a production boat by the factory, a French Lagoon 410 called *Waypoint*. In 2003 the Englishes made a record-setting, gale-filled maiden voyage in October from France to Annapolis, USA.[25]

In 2005 Solomon's Andy Christian and Alex Pesiridis used a Solomon ST-74 as just one component in a fuel cell yacht. The *Haveblue XV-1* was a Catalina 42 mk II sailing yacht. The vessel already had three systems producing DC electricity: the ST-74, 640 watts of solar panels, and a Rutland 913 Windchanger. The vessel's ultra-pure fresh water was produced by a customized Spectra Newport 400 reverse osmosis water maker. The next element, provided by Texaco Ovonic Hydrogen Systems LLC, was a metal hydride hydrogen storage system for the *XV-1* demonstrator. Management issues at Haveblue prevented the completion of this promising project.[26]

Back beside the Upper River Thames, a new venue for exhibiting and demonstrating electric boats had become the Boat Show at Beale Park near Pangbourne on Thames. On May 26, 2004, His Royal Highness the Prince of Wales took a trip down the Thames on board the Environment Agency's harbormaster's electric launch *Windrush* to celebrate the tenth anniversary of the Thames Landscape Strategy. The same launch had been used at Her Majesty Queen Elizabeth's Golden Jubilee. It was reminiscent of the days, over a century ago, when royalty had enjoyed electric boating on the Thames.

Finland in northern Scandinavia now contributed to electric boat progress when in 2004, Janne Kjellman began to build and market the Electric Ocean (later Oceanvolt) electric SD8.6 saildrive system for an increasing number of Finnish-built yachts such as the *Maestro 40* and the *Finn Express 83* designed by Eivind Still.[27]

Charles Fitzhardinge of Australia, who had been building and supplying electric ferries to Singapore, also delivered four Duffy Cat 16 electric boats for use on the lake system at the new Malaysian capital Putrajaya. On the lake at the Imperial Summer Palace near Beijing, China, five electric dragon boats were giving rides to tourist groups, while a fleet of 150 small dayboats was lined up for hire.

In both 2005 and 2006, Piero Tosi of Venice, founder of the World Commercial Center for the Promotion of Alternative Energy (Centro Commerciale Mondiale Progettazione Applicazione Energie Alternative) twice circumnavigated the Italian peninsula in his solar electric boat *IMES* ("Imbarcazione Mobilità Elettrica Sostenibile" = Sustainable Electrical Mobility Boat). During these long-distance cruises, Tosi was able to communicate the ecological message to 52 Italian ports, always welcomed by the local authorities as ambassador for the city of Venice for the Sustainable Nautical Mobility. Back in Venice, Tosi organized a small e-boat rally on its canals.[28]

In 2006, Thibault de Veyrinas bought the French Ruban Bleu concern from Jérome Croyère: the following year fifty boats were built. Meanwhile Croyère set up the boat-building firm of Vert-Prod at la Trinité-sur-Mer in the Morbihan department in Brittany, and based on 25 years' experience in manufacturing and rental of electric boats, produced the 6-pax 4M50 *Sensas* (as in *Sensationnel*) with a particularly stable hull and a propulsion system whose industrial parts made it reliable with an autonomy up to 8 hours. Energy for the Ruban Vert boats is provided by Enercoop, a French electric utility cooperative company which only uses renewable energies such as solar, wind, hydro and biogas. Croyère's passion remains yacht racing, often with his brother Antoine, financed by his Ruban Vert rental business of 63 boats on 4 rental sites.[29]

In 2005, electric vehicle specialist Monte Gisborne (B. Tech) of Brechin, Ontario, Canada, fitted a 20-ft (6 m) pontoon with 738 watts of solar panels on the roof. Neglecting to install the stabilizer rendered the boat unsteerable. "A family of loon water birds gathered around the boat and appeared amused by my antics, so I decided to name the boat after them." Modifications having been made to the Loon, Gisborne took his family on a six-day 105-mile (170 km) test voyage down the Trent-Severn Waterway. Setting up the Tamarack Electric Boat Company, in 2006 the Gisbornes made a 6-day cruise along the Rideau Canal from Kingston to Ottawa. Gisborne sold his first boat to an entrepreneur in Belize, Central America, who wanted to take people on guided tours to see the indigenous species of howling monkey, but found out that only zero-emission boats were permitted. With TEBC producing and selling 7 Loons to Canadian and Mexican customers, in 2007 the Gisbornes' next cruise, taking 12 days, was along the New York State canals—Oswego Canal, Erie Canal, and then across Oneida Lake. The trip took the same time as it would if traveled by a gas-powered boat. Media attention was extensive and the trip ended with great fanfare in Waterford, New York. From November 2008 production began on the *Kathleen Wynne*, the first prototype Osprey 30-passenger solar boat, the largest such boat built in North America, which went into service at Toronto and Region Conservation's Lake St. George Field Centre, an outdoor educational facility located in Richmond Hill. Backed by the New York State Energy Research and Development Authority to the tune of $500,000, in 2011 Gisborne set up a boatyard in Rome, New York, whence he produced the 22-ft (6m70) New Loon, with its patented retractable and integrated "Sunrise" roof and Torqeedo motor. It was launched in Xiaogan, China. By November 2013 a Loon was running from Fort Lauderdale, the Venice of America.[30]

Gideon Raphael Goudsmit of Amstelveen, in the Netherlands, had the ingenious idea of using the underwater propeller drag of a yacht while it sailed along, to recharge the batteries supplying energy to its onboard electric motors and all service batteries, then retracting the props to give the yacht more sail speed, then lowering the props again to propel the yacht while under power. A prototype was built and went on a test voyage of over 10,000 sea miles of the Wild Coast. It has to date accumulated some 40,000 sea miles and has used the generator for only 72 hours with a fuel consumption of 280 liters. Most of these hours were accumulated while sailing through the doldrums on the way north. A patent for the "Retractable Motogen" was applied for in the spring of 2007 and granted in 2010. The system could be applied to sailing yachts from 30 to 90 ft (9–28 m), whether monohull, catamaran or trimaran. Goudsmit launched a company, Green Motion® in Durban, South Africa, to build the FastCat 445 as the first in a range of African Cats.

Six 160-amp 25.5-volt lithium iron phosphate batteries provided the two motogens

Faircraft Loynes developed this Broads hybrid-electric cabin cruiser, 2006 (Paul Wagstaffe).

with their energy. Their positioning closer to the center of gravity of the vessel made the yacht safer and more comfortable. The large, three-bladed lightweight slow props, rotating at 1100 rpm, had a higher efficiency than the normally used folding or feathering props, and this was possible because of their being retractable. Their forward-facing position, tractor-style, increased propulsion and regeneration by 10 to 20 percent. On top of the mast, a 400-watt wind generator was mounted to keep the batteries charged when moored and under sail. The advantage in mounting the unit on top was threefold: less noise; higher efficiency; and a good-sized wind vane. This wind generator was spray-painted in glow-in-the-dark paint for added visibility. Six 345-watt solar panels also topped up the batteries. An induction stove, air conditioning and an electric oven were installed to make the yacht completely fossil fuel–free. The warm water from cooling them was ducted to the bathrooms, reducing the electricity normally required. To prove its abilities, the GreenCat 445 was sailed to the Netherlands. The GreenCat 605, designed by Simonis Voogd, followed three years later. Built in carbon fiber and lighter lithium batteries, the tenth 445 weighed 2500 kg less, which made it even more energy efficient and faster. By 2015, eleven 445s had been sold, six of them fully electric.[31]

Almost simultaneously to Goudschmidt's innovation, Matthieu Michou of WATT&SeA in La Rochelle worked with Yannick Bestaven, Vendée Globe skipper, to adapt a very similar system for his 60' yacht *IMOCA*, which competed in the 2008 round-the-world Vendée Globe sailing race without using fossil fuels.

In 2005, Shanda Lear and her husband Terry Baylor of Newport Beach, within walking distance of Duffy Marine, presented the Lear204, an innovative approach to an electric day boat. Shanda Lear is the daughter of Bill Lear of the Swiss American Aviation Corporation, who in 1962 had presented the Learjet, his innovative approach to a corporate jet aircraft; it became a best seller. Between 1930 and 1950, the inventive William P. Lear Sr. was granted over 100 patents for aircraft radios, communications and navigation

Gideon Goldsmidt's patented Green eMotion prop system uses the trailing props to recharge the batteries, 2010 (courtesy Electric Boat Association).

equipment—particularly the autopilot. In 1967, with the Learjet selling into the hundreds, Bill Lear moved to Reno, Nevada, where among his later inventions was an antipollution steam turbine engine, an 8-track tape player for automobiles, and the Lear Fan, an aircraft built entirely from composites.

Bill and Moya Lear's daughter, Shanda, grew up around the aircraft industry and obtained her pilot's license when she was only 17. But Shanda's great love was singing, particularly jazz, and in this milieu she met and married Terry Baylor, lead trumpet player on the early Righteous Brothers albums and on their first tour. Terry is also an experienced aerospace and marine pattern maker and designer. During the past forty years, he has worked with Columbia Yachts, Erickson Yachts, Arthur Marine and Willard Boat Works. He also developed the pattern and all the tooling for the 1975 Lyle-Hess designed Nor'Sea 27 ocean cruising sailboat. In recent years, Lear-Baylor of Garden Grove, California, had also done tooling and pattern making for industries such as Boeing, NASA, Disney and Universal Studios. With this background, it was inevitable that the Lear204 should incorporate proven aerospace standards—an approach never previously seen with electric boats on either side of "the Pond."

On the premise that a boat under 20-ft (6m) long will not hold much usable weight without leaving a wake, the Lear204 measured just 20 ft .04" (6 m) long × 8½ ft (2.6 m) beam and 22 inches (56 cm) draft. It was designed to cruise at an optimum 5 mph for over ten hours on one charge. Six 8D AGM maintenance-free batteries provide energy to an advanced 36-volt 5hp DC motor with a solid-state microprocessor-driven motor controller. To recharge the batteries, a microprocessor-controlled charging system is integrated into the boat. Lear-Baylor Inc. was granted a U.S. patent on the 5-bladed, 1,000 rpm propeller, made out of pressure cast urethane. The high-lift rudder had been specifically designed for low-speed maneuvering.

While a fixed hardtop version was available, for just 11,000 dollars more, the retractable hardtop came down (and went up) at the push of a button, securing the boat in 45 seconds and so doing away with a time-consuming canvas cover. With the top down, the boat height from the water at only 39 inches, it could withstand high winds and go under bridges. There was also the EZ2CY double-track window system. Add to this: seats contoured to the body, wide-beam legroom, swim ladder, premium sound system, fridge-freezer and many other amenities and you get "the second generation Lear vehicle." The Lear204 made its official debut early in 2005 at the Dunes in Newport Beach, California. The retractable roof model retailed at U.S. $60,000. It arrived in Europe in 2008, four years later, 43 years after the first Learjet executive aircraft arrived in Europe. It was marketed by the Duna Club of Budapest, Hungary.[32]

Johnson Outdoors of Racine brought out their Escape® Fun Boat, featuring a very easy-to-use "flip-the-switch-and-go" 12-volt electric Minn Kota for kids, in the tradition of the French Saviboat or the British dodgem boats of the 1950s. It had a built-in electric water cannon that shot up to 30 feet (10 m) and an autonomy of six hours. So that the bass fisherman could have his hands free, Minn Kota developed a foot-controlled unit with integrated GPS-controlled trolling motor navigation system (Ulterra™).

On July 26, 2005, to celebrate National Parks Week, the His Royal Highness the Prince of Wales and the Duchess of Cornwall made their first public appearance in Norfolk as husband and wife on board the Broads Authority solar-powered boat *RA*, which took them on a tour of Barton Broad.

On Lake Windermere a solar-powered launch went into service, *Ransome*. Developed by Gordon Hall of Coniston Launches, it used an ST Solomon, while a Fischer-Panda generator cuts in if required.[33]

In 2005 Charles Fitzhardinge provided the drive unit for *Nomad III*, at 35 feet (10m60) the largest solar-powered pleasure craft in Australia. This was a unique live-aboard solar Mundoo Class cabin cruiser built by Duck Flat Wooden Boats for

Like his great-grandfather, in 2005 His Royal Highness Charles Prince of Wales and Camilla, the Duchess of Cornwall, cruised electric on board the solar boat *RA* (courtesy Electric Boat Association).

In 2005 *Nomad III* was Australia's largest solar powered pleasure craft (courtesy Electric Boat Association).

the Murray River. It was powered by an ETEK Lynch design motor running at 48V with a Sevcon MilipaK controller. The owners, John and Gabby Francis, made the maiden voyage traveling 250 miles (400 km) upstream to their home at Renmark in the wine-making Riverland of South Australia.[34]

Solar racing was now extended to Fryslân (Friesland), a province in the northwest of the Netherlands. Bouwe de Boer, co-operator of the energy policy in the province, thought up a 220-km (137-mile) race circuit based on the route taken by the Frisian Eleven Cities ice-skating race, passing through 11 historic cities linked by lakes, river and canals. The first race in 2004 saw 24 participants, but only four teams finished. The competition was open to all businesses, universities and students researching in the field of solar energy. Thanks to this challenge and to technical innovations, efficiency of solar boats progressed a little more each year. From June 26 to July 1, 2006, teams of students from all over the world enrolled for the Frisian Nuon Solar Challenge. Among them was *Energa Solar*, an entry from the faculty of ocean engineering and ship technology, Gdansk University in Poland.[35]

In 2006, the Netherlands developed *its* first fuel-cell boat. It was built by Ecofys of Leeuwarden and boat builder Ganita with subsidies from Friesland and the Dutch Economics Ministry. The 7.4-m (24 ft) *Hydrogen Xperience* was powered by a built-in Ballard Nexa 1.2 kw fuel cell and could cruise at 6 to 8 kph (3–5 mph) for two to three days, using 120 liters of hydrogen. The Air Liquide hydrogen gas was stored under the floor in four 200-bar tanks, each weighing 150 kg. More conventionally, in Reeuwijk in South Holland, there was a small but growing fleet of 15 battery electric boats. By 2010 this would grow to 115, by 2013 to 127, and by 2015 to over 150 vessels.[36]

In July 2006, Scotland hosted its first electric boat with *Bata Greine* ("boat of the sun" in Gaelic), a 43-ft (13 m) twin-screw catamaran built by Kopf SolarDesign and originally called *Ecosol II*. Its service was to take up to 12 passengers, including wheelchairs, from the Duncan Mills Memorial Slipway, Balloch, for rides up and down Scotland's Loch Lomond's 39 km (24 miles).

At Dubai, the most populous city in the United Arab Emirates (UAE), ironically built on the profits of the oil industry, a traditional water taxi known as Abra was retrofitted with an Austrian 4.3 Kw Kraütler motor for use at the Madinat Jumeirah Resort in Dubai beside the Arabian Sea. Following its success, tenders were requested by the Dubai government for the building of a solar-powered Abra watertaxi for taking tourists around the Creek. On December 13, 2016, the Roads and Transport Authority (RTA) announced the formal operation of a solar-powered Abra at Al Mamzar, the first of its kind in the Middle East. This could lead to hundreds of electric Abras taking millions of passengers across the waters.[37]

Observing and reporting on all this technological progress worldwide made me very proud. Electric boating had come a long way in twenty years. In 2007 a new trophy was added to encourage electric boating for which I feel partially responsible. In 2003, I had researched and published the story of *Mansura* (1912), the world's first hybrid cabin cruiser, as developed and skippered for thirty-six years by John Delmar-Morgan, a British electrical engineer (see Chapter Two of this book). During the course of my research, I received the full cooperation of Julian Delmar-Morgan and David Barrett of Duff, Morgan. At the EBA's 21st anniversary in June 2003 at Bisham Abbey, I had traveled over from France to attend. I met up with Delmar-Morgan, who showed me the horse's-head tiller which had once belonged to the original boat.

Together, we formed a plan to present a trophy to encourage and develop hybrid-electric motor boating, particularly offshore. The trophy would be a bronze version of the horse's head. El Mansura is a relatively new Egyptian city along the banks of the River Nile that was founded in 1220 AD. The name El Mansura means "the victorious," and it is known as the "city of victory." By a strange coincidence, the Mansura Trophy was mounted on a plinth whose wood had been recycled from Admiral Nelson's flagship, HMS *Victory*. Thanks to the enthusiasm and hard work shown by Jack Edwards of Delmar-Morgan's original yacht club, the Royal Thames, working with the Royal Yachting Association, the trophy was opened to both industrial concerns and private individuals. It was open to cruising vessels of any nationality and to vessels not exceeding 122 meters (400 ft) length, capable of accommodating at least one adult person on passage. The propulsion system of vessels entered for competition, in addition to sails if installed, must embody electric power derived from wind, solar radiation, fossil fuels, biomass, fuel cell or other sources of electrical energy generation.

Among the favorites for the inaugural 2007 edition of the Mansura Trophy were three hybrid-electric motor yachts. From France came Bénéteau's Lagoon 420, being series manufactured (more than 300 units scheduled) at the CNB in Bordeaux, southwest France. Then there was Pacific Asian Enterprises's *Nordhavn 72*, coupling a Detroit diesel with a Siemens electric. Thirdly the Dutch African Cats FastCat 435 *Vector K*—a combo of wind generators, solar panels, diesel auxiliary and brushless electric motors. Australia's *Solar Sailor* also entered. But they were not the only ones.

More traditional was the 21-m (70 ft) Dutch dektjalk *Liberté*, built in 1908 but recently converted to a 120-hp DAF/35 kW electric hybrid system. Similarly, on eastern England's Broads, there was the 60-ft (18 m) *White Moth* wherry yacht, built in 1915 but recently hybridized by Rupert Latham with a Panda 6000 DC generator and an 8 kW electric motor. One traditionalist on the Upper Thames had even hybridized his dayboat *Irene* to run on steam/electric power. There were also home-converted vessels: the 27-ft (8 m) ketch *Carolann*, built in Teignmouth in 1937, had been hybridized by David Graham of Bideford to cruise around the Bristol Channel.

More modern, Emrhys Barrell of TELCO, the Thames Electric Launch Company, and his engineer Ian Rutter, had produced several one-off hybrid boats—river police patrol boats and canal inspection narrowboats—with their Selectric system. One of these was the *Warde Aldham*, a 57-ft (17 m) narrowboat coupling a 43 hp diesel with an 8 kW electric.

The overall winner of the Mansura Trophy was Lagoon Catamaran's 420 Hybrid Catamaran, while the runner-up was the Sydney *Solar Sailor*. The ceremony took place at the Royal Thames Yacht Club in Knightsbridge and the trophy was presented by His Royal Highness Prince Philip, the Duke of Edinburgh.

It was perhaps ironic that a trophy whose oak plinth had been recycled from the timbers of Lord Horatio Nelson's flagship HMS *Victory* should be won by a French entry, and even stranger that that French entry had its yard in Bordeaux, not far from this author's residence. When, during the ceremony, I boldly informed His Royal Highness that it was a good thing that the French had won and was asked why, I replied that it would enable the British to win it back the next year.

"You are the type of person that provokes wars," glaringly replied the Royal, known for his sharp remarks.

As this trophy was taking place, something extraordinary was happening out at sea.

In 2007 His Royal Highness Philip, the Duke of Edinburgh, right, presents the Mansura Trophy to M. Loic Lagrange, left, of France—they can have the bronze, but not the plinth, made from the wood of HMS *Victory*. Jack Edwards presides (courtesy Electric Boat Association).

While solar-powered boats had so far mainly been limited to rivers and canals, the 14-m (46-ft) catamaran based on the Aquabus C60 design, the *Sun21*, was crossing the Atlantic Ocean from Seville to Miami, and from there to New York (Project Transatlantic21).

Among the crew were solar veterans Matthias Wegmann and Mark Wüst. This was the first crossing of the Atlantic powered only by solar energy, but not the last (see Appendix B). By then, the electrical engineer Yvan Leuppi and naval architect Andreas Kindlimann had joined the MW-Line team and were respectively in charge of electric engineering and naval architecture. Following the success of *Sun21*, MW-Line built two extended versions of the Aquabus C60, measuring 17 m (56 ft) long, one of them for the World Expo in Zaragosa (2007). In August 2008, SolarWaterWorld AG launched the 60-pax SOLON, an Aquabus C60, Berlin's first solar passenger boat, for sightseeing cruises on the River Spree and nearby lakes.[38] The same company also set up the world's first solar-charging station for solar-powered boats in Berlin-Köpenick, where a rental service of Suncats (12, 21 and 23) and the 20-pax 9m50 *Chassalli*, an exact replica of an English saloon boat built around 1880, takes people on a solarpolis tour.

In 2007 *Sun21* arrives in New York after crossing the Atlantic Ocean (courtesy Electric Boat Association).

Finally, the English built their first fuel-cell boat, almost half a century after British fuel cell pioneer Professor Thomas Bacon of Cambridge University demonstrated a fuel-cell Allis-Chalmers tractor. In September 2007, the 16-meter (52 ft) canal boat was launched in Birmingham, the English Midlands. It was named the *Ross Barlow*. Barlow was a 25-year-old student who worked on the Professor Rex Harris's Birmingham University protium project team and tragically lost his life in a hang-gliding accident in 2005. With metal hydride storage systems developed with EMPA laboratories in Zurich, the PEM was installed in the boat's bow. The following year the project set up the UK's first hydrogen filling station, installed by Air Products, where the hydrogen is generated by electrolysis using solar or wind turbines. In June 2010 the *Ross Barlow* made a 65-mile (104 km) journey from Birmingham to Chester, taking four days to cover the distance with its 58 locks.[39]

The ghost of Trouvé continued to walk in downtown Paris. In 2007 two new 75-pax waterbuses in Paris Canal Saint Denis gave free shuttle service for employees commuting to their offices in the 19th district of Paris over a 1.1-km route from Corentin Cariou Metro station to the deck at Millénaire Park, a journey of around 7 minutes.

In 2008, Nigel Calder, a British boating journalist and marine electrical systems expert, coordinated a project through the European Union to develop an "optimized and fully integrated" marine hybrid-electric drive as "a necessary first step towards the complete replacement of the internal combustion engine." The three-year project was named HYMAR (= Hybrid Marine). Calder's idea was that with a group of European partners from seven countries, a long list of technological refinements would eventually be produced to improve the efficiency of hybrid-electric propulsion for commercial and recreational vessels up to 24 meters (80 feet). The funding proposal was written by Calder to be part of the European Commission's Framework Program 7, a working committee of the International Council of Marine Industry Associations (ICOMIA), and for a sum of €2.2 million. Among the components to be developed: dynamically shifting motor and generator controllers, an energy management module, a torque-adapted self-pitching propeller, a rim-drive motor-propulsor and nozzle, a design for a keel-mounted hybrid drive that builders could purchase as a bolt-on unit, and an advanced TPPL (thin-plate, pure-lead) battery designed specifically for hybrid propulsion.

Other advanced batteries would be tested, as well as suitable biofuels and fuel cells with the hybrid platform if they became available at realistic prices.

European partners in the HYMAR project were Bosch Engineering (Germany) for the controller; Steyr Motors (Austria) for the motor; Mastervolt (Netherlands) for the power electronics; Bruntons Propellers (UK) and INSEAN (Italy) for the propellers; Enersys (UK) for energy storage; Malö Yachts (Sweden) for the test boat and ancillary services; and Electric Marine Propulsion (Florida, USA) for marine hybrid implementation experience. Electric Marine Propulsion was participating through a newly established European firm, E-motion Special Projects (ESP), headquartered in Brockham, Surrey.

In 2008, Calder tested a preliminary HYMAR experimental system, from EMP, in a floating laboratory, the 46-ft (14 m) yacht *Nada*, built by the Malö yard, in Swedish waters. The initial system on *Nada* included a prototype 22 kW brushless permanent magnet DC generator, a prototype 16 kW brushless permanent magnet DC electric motor, and a 14 kWh bank of "Odyssey" thin-plate pure-lead (TPPL) batteries. Testing proved that the underlying assumptions and predictions of the project were fundamentally correct. They the progressed to a test boat, the Hallberg Rassy *42 Armorel,* optimized for energy efficiency and based on design principles which allow any compliant equipment to be used regardless of supplier.[40]

HYMAR was not alone. Traditionally E.P. Barrus Ltd. had been importers of Johnson gasoline outboards since the 1920s and diesel inboards. From 2008, they began to work with Graeme Hawksley of Hybrid Marine Ltd. to produce a parallel hybrid saildrive system based on the Yanmar 4JH57 marine diesel engine from 30 hp to 110 hp range linked to a 10 kW electric engine.

In 2007, Fred Bellis of Bellmann teamed up with his rival Marien Schoonen of ID Technology, combining their products Aquapella (2–5 Kw) and the AC-engined Silent-Prop (up to 30 Kw) to form Bellmann Drive Systems. During the next decade, they would make and sell some 2,500 systems at home and abroad. In 2009, Bellmann was bought by Mastervolt International, who financed their R&D until they pulled out in 2015, at which point Marien Schoonen renamed his firm Bellmarine, still based in Gouda.[41]

At the same time, Scott McMillan of Golden Valley, Minnesota, a propulsion engine maker, began to produce the first generation of Electric Yacht units. In 2010 the second generation, Electric Yacht's QuietTorque family of systems, were introduced, ranging in power from 5kW to 20KW. Today the QuietTorque has over 350 installations, mostly in North America, ranging in power from 2.5kW to 40kW. These systems are installed in boats from 18-ft (5m40) monohulls to 68-ft (20 m) catamarans.

By 2008, some 39 participants took part in the second solar-boat race in Friesland, the Netherlands, resulting in 24 teams reaching the finish within 24 hours. The 2010 race got a lead sponsor and the name changed to the DONG Energy Frisian Solar Challenge. Forty-three teams participated, and although the racecourse became harder by extending the stages, the solar boats were much faster. Among those participating were Mark Scholten and Gerard van der Schaar, who in 2007 had taken the bold decision to use a 40 kWh Kokam-manufactured lithium-ion battery as their competing boat *Furia I*'s energy source. Their victory proved them right. The following year, Scholten and Schaar set up MG Electronics in Leeuwarden to develop battery management system for lithium batteries.

For future races they called themselves the CLAFIS Private Energy Solar Boat Team, producing 7 m (23 ft) × 114 kg (25 lb) hydrofoil versions of *Furia*, averaging 22 mph (35 kph) but capable of a top speed of 30 mph (48 kph), so taking 1st and 2nd places in race after race: the Dutch Open Solar Boat Challenge, 2009; DONG Energy Solar Boat Challenge, 2010; Dutch Open Solar Boat Challenge, 2011; DONG Energy Solar Boat Challenge, 2012; and several others. *Furia* also became the holder of a worldwide speed record for ⅛ mile with an average speed of 23.996 knots (27.62 mph). The UIM (Union Internationale Motonautique) approved this record.[42]

Others were working along the same lines. In 2008, when Simon Patterson of Patterson BoatWorks Ambleside beside Lake Windermere commissioned naval architect Nigel Irens to design him an efficient hull for a super yacht tender, he used a 144V 140ah LiFeBATT lithium-ion phosphate battery system. With twin 200DC Lynch engines, the carbon-fiber *Elektra* was capable of 17 mph (15 knots) for an hour or a 70-mile (110 km) range at cruising speeds.[43]

In 2008 Ting Hai Shipbuilding began to build solar-electric passenger vessels with touchscreen/visual display control systems for Taiwan. Two years later, Kaohsiung Port City decided to replace its 15 diesel boats used on the Love (or Ai) River with solar electric "Love Boats." The lithium-battery power drive was provided by Lite-On Clean Energy.[44]

Unknown to such enterprises, English engineer Alan T. Freeman's pioneer *Solar Craft I*, which had been stored in the inventor's garage for thirty years, was donated by his widow to the Motorboat Museum in Basildon, Essex.

The Electric Boat Association of Australia was founded by Charles Fitzhardinge, Steven Mullie and others in Sydney in 2008 to promote the development in electric boating.[45]

In 2008, the 64-ft (20 meter) *Hornblower Hybrid* catamaran became the first known multi-hulled hybrid ferryboat in the United States. Retrofitted by Bayside Boatworks in Sausalito, it was used to transport visitors to Alcatraz National Park. Three years later, the 168-ft (51 m) *New York Hornblower Hybrid* became the first hydrogen hybrid, combining a 32-kW proton-exchange membrane fuel cell by Hydrogenics, two Helix Wind 5-kilowatt wind turbines, and a 20-kilowatt SunPower solar array. The interior boasted recycled and sustainable materials including LEED certified carpet, LED lighting, and countertops made from recycled vodka bottles. The *New York Hornblower Hybrid* became available for public cruises for up to 600 people, having completed the U.S. Coast Guard sea trials and certifications.[46]

So far, fuel-cell boats had been one-offs. In 2008, three Austrian companies—Fronius of Sattledt, Bitter, and Frauscher—linked up to realize the first fuel-cell boat for series production: the 6 m (20 ft) Frauscher 600 Riviera was unveiled in April 2009 at Schloss Orth on Lake Traunsee in Austria. Funding was from the EU program "Regionale Wettbewerbsfähigkeit 2007–2013," resources from the European Fund for Regional Development

(EFRE) and the local state of Upper Austria. The 600 Riviera was powered by a 4 kW Kräutler electric motor, giving it a speed of 11 kph and a range of 80 km. The Fronius fuel cell allowed for 4 kW continuous power, 48 DC output and an efficiency of up to 47 percent. Bitter GmbH supplied a hydrogen high-pressure cartridge system, the STS 261, with distributor stations providing users with hydrogen simply and at the point where they need it. Refueling was done using a standard 350-bar filler coupling on the one hand, plus simple exchanging of an empty cartridge for a full one on the other. The heart of the system was the replaceable cartridge consisting of a compound tank with downline pressure reduction unit. The "Future Project Hydrogen" team projected 10 boats for commercial use within a boat rental or a resort hotel. A use-frequency per boat and season requires filling of 50 cartridges or cartridge changes. In the end, serial production was postponed.

Forty years on, Duffy continued to innovate with their 24-ft (7m31) 16-pax M240Hybrid, a pontoon boat with M-shaped hull form and a Power Rudder drive system. The driver used duel speed joysticks, enabling it to turn 360° in its own length. With four solar roof panels, M240Hybrid could also use a 2 kW generator as wind-generators for batteries.[47]

In December 2009, the 87-pax fuel-cell double-ender cruiser *Nemo H2* (named after the Captain of the *Nautilus* in Jules Verne's *20,000 Leagues under the Sea*) went into service on Amsterdam's canals. Built at Hasselt, she measured just under 22 meters (72 feet) long × 4.25 meters (14 ft) beam, with two stern thrusters, one at each end. She was capable of a maximum 8.6 knots, and averaged 7 knots during 9 hours. *Nemo H2* was the product of the Fuel Cell Boat BV consortium, financially supported by a subsidy of the Dutch Ministry of Economic Affairs and bringing together a pair of Dutch companies: Alewijnse Marine Systems, who provided the electronic systems, two 30 kW PEM fuel cells with 70 kWh battery; Linde Gas Benelux, responsible for the production, storage and distribution of hydrogen, 24 kg in 6 cylinders stored at 35 MPa. Operated by the cruise company "Lovers," the *Nemo H2*'s hydrogen was produced by electrolysis with a current provided by wind turbines based beside the North Sea. Unfortunately she was to meet with a succession of safety problems and did not run very often.[48]

By this time Stitchting Elektrish Varen became part of SEFF, a newly founded organization in Friesland (a district in the north). Membership was no longer necessary, while an Internet website proved very successful.

In September 2009, ODC (= Odysée = Odyssey) Marine, managed by Xavier de Montgros, delivered its first Chinese-built boat, the 10 m (32 ft) *Ecocano*, to Azur Cruises for trips along the canals of the Mediterranean port of Sète, "the Venice of the Languedoc," and the oyster farms around nearby Lake Thau. During the next decade, ODC, a French boatyard based near the northeast Chinese seaport of Dalian, would use their host country's technology to produce a dozen 50–150 passenger e-waterbuses per year. The *Ecocano*, powered by twin 20 kw motors units, also became the world's first passenger boat to be powered by lithium-ion-phosphate batteries.[49]

In 2008, Marseilles decided to replace its 12 m (40 ft) double-ender passenger ferry *César*, powered by a 45 hp diesel engine, which had been carrying people from the Town Hall to the Places aux Huiles for the past 38 years. The replacement was a double-ender with a prop at both ends driven by two electric 12 kW brushless electric rudder-propeller engines, SAFT nickel-cadmium batteries of 400W/135 Ah, supplemented by 25 m² of roof-mounted solar panels. Developed by Jean & Frasca Design and built for Alternative Energies by the Gatto Shipyard of nearby Martigues, *César* went into operation in 2009.[50]

This year saw the return of the hybrid tug (see Chapter Two). Foss Rainier Shipyards contracted with AKA, in collaboration with their Hybrid Technology partner XeroPoint Energy, to provide the propulsion and control systems for the world's first hybrid tug. The *Carolyn Dorothy* went into service in the very busy San Pedro Harbor, California. Once she had proved herself, Foss progressed to a second hybrid tug, the *Campbell Foss*, whose lithium-polymer batteries, made by Corvus Energy Ltd. of Richmond, British Columbia, gave it greater autonomy. The genius behind Corvus, Stewart Neil Simmonds, holding over 70 battery-related patents, helped to produce the first lithium-ion batteries for the EV market until he found the marine sector more challenging. *Campbell Foss* began operations on January 29 at the ports of Los Angeles and Long Beach doing ship assist and vessel escort with container ships, oil tankers and oil barges. Both tugs would later be refitted with EST-Floattech Type 25–62024V LiPo batteries with energy densities of 105 kWh and 294 kWh respectively.[51]

Since the outset, the propeller had reigned almost supreme for e-boat propulsion. But in 2009, two paddleboats went into regular service, one in Scotland, the other in France. The aluminum-hulled *New Era*, her twin Lynch motors driving her twin paddle wheels, began to operate trips in the Beauly Firth and the Caledonian Canal, Scotland, with passengers enjoying the sight of dolphins and seals and taking in the beautiful scenery around the Beauly.[52] At the same time, Grégory Debord's boatyard at oyster-farming Port Meyan near Gujan Mestras, on France's southwest Atlantic coast, produced a paddleboat, *Le Chanaz*, named after the picturesque little town beside the Savières canal, near Lake Bourget in France's Savoy region.[53] It had all come a long way since 1883 when Gustave Trouvé and Cloris Baudet of Paris had equipped their clients with electric paddle-wheel systems (see Chapter One).

EIGHT

Wider Still and Wider
(2010–2014)

The Credit Crunch of 2007–08, also known as the Global Financial Crisis, is considered by many economists to have been the worst financial crisis since the Great Depression of the 1930s. Although electric boatyards and marine engineers were not spared the worst effects, in the decade since, they have certainly made up for it in no uncertain manner. Almost every type of vessel from robotic marine cleaners to surfboards and personal water craft up to skiboats, cabin cruisers, luxury yachts, as well as fishing trawlers, ro-ro car ferries, lifeboats, massive ocean liners and container ships have been electrified in a way that we eccentric pioneers of the early 1980s had never dared to dream of. One of the key features has been the increase in both the manufacture and the energy density of the lithium-ion battery and its range autonomy.

But at the time of the crisis, even Duffy had to temporarily reduce his workforce by half, down to sixty, and focus on boosting his rental and refurbishing business to make up for falling sales of new boats.

Following its bankruptcy, Switzerland's MW-Line might have disappeared completely. But in 2010, Yvan Leuppi, naval architect Andreas Kindliman and Swiss economist and electric boat enthusiast Guy Wolfensberger restarted operations and renamed the company Grove Boats, after Sir William Grove, who invented the fuel cell and was involved in the first experiments with electric boats in 1840. While some of the MW-Line facilities in Yverdon were taken over by Grove Boats SA, production was moved from Switzerland, where salaries were too high, to Croatia. The innovative Marc Wüst remained with the company. Richard Mesple went to work for the company SI-REN, belonging 100 percent to the city of Lausanne, with the objective of producing more than 100 GWh/an.

At the 2010 Miami International Boat Show, Mercury Marine, who had been making marine gasoline outboards and sterndrives for over half a century, finally entered the hybrid technology market. They exhibited a 42-ft (12 m) *Maxum* express cruiser, a vessel equipped with both Cummins QSC 550hp diesel engines, high-efficiency 100 hp electric engines, and Zeus pod drives with power from a 60-kWh lithium-ion battery.

Mike Gunning, an avid sailor and skier with 25 years as a volunteer ski patroller, founded Electric Yachts of Southern California after 40 years in banking and computers. Gunning's firm would install their system in 90 yachts in California and over 150 on the West Coast from Canada to Mexico. In addition to Electric Yacht products, Electric Yachts of Southern California sells Torqeedo, Thoosa, Polar Power, and Elco products.

Some adventurers went on marathon journeys in electric boats. The saga of one, *Tûranor PlanetSolar*, is described in Appendix B of this book. But there were others. Between April and August 2010, *Ecotroll*, a 39-ft (12 m) hybrid aluminum electric boat, made a 7,700-km (4,780 mile) journey up the River Saone to Paris to Le Havre, across the Channel to Devon, the Irish Sea, Scotland, the Faeroe Islands, and Greenland, and return. Crewed by Eric Broissier and France Pinczon du Sel, who were accompanied by their two small children, *Ecotroll* was designed by Jean-Pierre Brouns and built by at the Meta shipyard in the Rhône-Alpes region of France. Two 60 hp NanniDiesel engines were coupled to two 7 kW electric motors supplied by solar panels, three small wind generators, and a 60 m² cone-shaped kite sail.[1]

Some concepts remain concepts. In 2011, Randy A. Mitlyng applied for patent for an electric powerboat whereby two wind turbines in sides of the boat housing were driven by the oncoming wind and, in turn, recharged the onboard batteries; although granted U.S. 8152577 B1, Mitlyng' idea was never built.

Solar electric boat passenger services reached as far as Chile when a 16-pax solar-powered water taxi went into operation on the several rivers around the city of Valdivia in that country's beautiful Lake District. After three months of reliably plying its trade, *Solar 1* was joined by a second boat. The locally built Alowplast hull was powered by an Austrian 4kW/48-volt Kraütler electric motor deriving its energy from Black 230/7 photovoltaic panels made by Solon. Today, the fleet has grown to three taxis. They work 7 days a week, 8 hours every day. Taxis depart every 15 minutes and cover three different routes, connecting different strategic points on the riverbank via 26 piers. The local politician has just inaugurated another two public docks, allowing the operators to increase their fleet. During the southern summer season, there is almost no need to recharge the boats overnight from the 400 sq.m floating solar station on the river. The taxi-fleet's center of operations has an office, a café-shop, a delicatessen outlet, public toilets and general viewing platforms. The station produces enough solar power to sustain itself, plus feeding about 1000 kw/h free electricity back into the grid every month. In addition, the Chilean station has been converting about 5,000 liters (1,100 gallons) of salty river water into drinking water and purifying 7,000 liters (1,500 gallons) of black water and all the gray water they produce via several biologic sequence batch reactors.[2]

Norberto Ferretti, co-founder of Ferretti Yachts and president of the Ferretti Group of Italy, also decided to enter the hybrid field. The result was the 75-ft 6-in (23 m) *Mochi Long Range 23*, built in Pesaro with its trans-planing hull, priced at £1.5 million. Presented as the first "Zero Emission Mode" motor yacht over 65 feet (20 m), the MLR23 obtained RINA "Green Star Clean Energy and Clean Propulsion." Twin 550hp MAN D0836LC engines were linked to twin 70 kW ZF electric motors. Using a NAVIOP touchscreen system, the helmsman could choose between 5 different ways at the swipe of a finger: from traditional diesel function to the zero emissions mode, using different combinations of diesel engine, electric engine, inverter, batteries and generator.[3]

Ferretti was not the only convert. Azimut-Benedetti of Turin followed with the 51'4" (15.64 m) *Magellano 50*, complete with their Easy Hybrid system linking twin 23-kW electric motors to twin Cummins MerCruiser QSB 5.9 diesels, to move the luxury yacht at up to 8 knots under battery power alone, in near-silence. At £2 million, the Benedetti *Tradition Supreme 108* hybrid housed two 35 kW electric motors connected directly to the regulators/inverters of the main diesel-electric propulsion. The electric motors were powered directly by generators allowing navigation up to a speed of about

6 knots. Over in Poole, England, Sunseeker built a hybrid-powered *Manhattan 70*, fitted with twin MTU 1,250hp M94 engines linked to a combined electric motor/generator. In France, Beneteau Power developed the hybrid version of its *Swift Trawler 34*, by collaborating with American Elco for a 425-horsepower Cummins turbo diesel. It was linked to a 72-volt, 20-horsepower belt drive electric motor/generator, a bank of 12 absorbed glass mat batteries, a 7.5 kW diesel generator, a beefed-up battery charger, a battery management system, and helm control panel.

In Hong Kong Harbor, China, the first sea trials took place of *Solar Albatross*, Solar Sailor Holdings' 24-m (79 ft) 100 passenger-carrying catamaran ferry with its stowable SolarSails. After more than 10 years of development and hard work, Robert Dane and his team in Australia had produced another solar sailing vessel, but this was the first time that a true commercial hybrid vessel was propelled by wind power, solar power, stored electricity and fossil fuel. The hull, built by a local Chinese shipyard, was embedded with solar cells both to collect the sun's energy and to use wind power. The SolarSails were stowed flat on the roof of the boat when not in use, although they continued to collect solar energy from the sun and store it in batteries in the two hulls of the catamaran. *Solar Albatross* was the fourth hybrid boat to enter service at Hong Kong Jockey Club's Kai Sai Chau Golf Club, ferrying golf club patrons to and from their three-island-based 18-hole courses off Hong Kong Island. On the Chinese mainland, the WuXi Suntech Group's *Guosheng*, a 31.5-m (103 ft) SolarSailor ferry-cat, became the largest SolarSailor built to date. Carrying 186 passengers, the SunTech *Guosheng* was launched during World Expo. The VIP boat cruised up and down the Huangpu River from June to October, used and viewed by up to 70 million Shanghai visitors.[4]

The use of flexible solar cell–clad sails made of silicon is another option. Italian designers Marco Ferrari and Alberto Franchi, both students of yacht and cruise vessel design at Politecnico di Milano, developed the 180.5-ft (55 m) *Helios*, a solar-powered luxury sailing yacht concept design, for the Young Designer of the Year 2015 contest. The surface area covers about 2,500 panels that can generate approximately 355 kWh of power for its batteries. While the exterior styling of the deckhouse is modern and is shaped from the soft curves of an oyster shell, the reduced 13-ft (4 m) draft, thanks to the lifting keel, enables *Helios*, accommodating 10 guests and 8 crew members, to cruise electrically in shallow waters.[5] Another yacht concept which takes in this photovoltaic sail technology is the 130-ft (40 m) *Kira*, designed by Mexican-born Sebastian Campos Mölier.

The challenge to series-produce a hybrid electric cabin cruiser was taken up by former cardiologist and yacht concept designer Japec Jakopin of Seaway, a pleasure boat design and development company based in Slovenia. Since the end of 2007 the Seaway team of designers and engineers had been working on a 5-mode hybrid in cooperation with Iskra Avtoelektrika, Bisol, Podgorje and Volkswagen Marine. After computer-based studies and simulations using CFD (computational fluid dynamics) and Velocity Prediction software, a full range of tank testing trials were performed. Based on the 4 geometries tested in the tank, a full-scale hull shape was developed. Similar research effort was devoted to the development of the hybrid, battery and solar drive technology.

A fully functional prototype was built by Seaway and tested during nine months in a range of displacement, trim, propulsion variants and weather conditions. This included several European countries, the Mediterranean, the North Sea, large lakes and the rivers and canals of northern and southern Europe. This extensive automotive-style development and testing program, a first in the boating industry, resulted in a reliable and user-friendly product in spite of the use of new technology. During the initial months of 2009, Seaway performed the production engineering for the Greenline Hybrid 33 and installed the associated tooling. A preliminary run of 6 pre-production yachts was built in August and September of the same year. Serial production started in January 2010. The Greenline Hybrid 33 was exhibited at major European boat shows and won 4 boat-of-the-year awards (Amsterdam, Stockholm, Düsseldorf and Slovenia) and 2 environmental awards. During this time, it had received over 60 orders. Two charter companies, Le Boat and Bénéteau, turned to Seaway to add to their fleet. Seaway had sold 300 Greenline Hybrid 33s by 2013, claimed to be the best-selling 10-m boat in 2010 and 2011.[6]

In 2011, Le Chantier Naval Franco-Suisse, who had built their first electric boat some 24 years before, and whose two solar-powered boats, *Vénus* (75 seats) and *Sauconna* (110 seats) had since then been enabling tourists to discover the nearby Saut du Doubs gorge, produced a 15-m (50 ft) hybrid-electric cruising restaurant for the Lot River, east of the Aquitaine. *L'Olt*, named after the ancient word for the Lot, is powered by two EMC e-motors of 22kW each and a back-up i/c motor. On board are one hundred seats, of which 64 are table settings, and an upper deck. The boat was financed by the Lot Regional Body as part of the renovating the river, which had been closed to navigation since 1928.[7] Elsewhere, Adrien Chevillotte began to build up a fleet of Torqeedo-engined hireboats for fishing on inland lakes located in the Somme, Normandy and Ile de France regions. Planet Nautic now has 40 such boats ranging from 2 to 70 hp in power.

Apart from Italy's luxury hybrid motor yacht builders, in Venice, shipbuilder Moreno Vizianello had begun to collaborate with Fabio Sacco of the city's waterbus company Alilaguna, with its white and yellow livery, to produce *Energia*, a 14-meter (46 ft), 40-pax ferryboat. *Energia*'s electric motor was joined in parallel to a classic internal combustion engine to charge the batteries of the boat during its journey across the lagoon between the airport and San Marco. *Energia* went into operation in January 2011, and was soon joined by sister ships *Murena* and *Razza*.[8]

Not far away, Alberto Pozzo and Alessio Zanolli, based in Rovereto, Province of Trento, northeast Italy, produced the little *GardaSolar*, an elegantly curvaceous 3.85-m (12 ft), joystick-controlled, solar-hybrid four-seater dayboat. Built of 100 percent recyclable composites, there are two versions—the pedalo-style E-Light and the sportier E-Xclusive with a 1kw motor giving a top speed of 15 knots. The next model is the GS4. Interest in this purely Italian boat has been shown by India, the Bahamas and Dubai.[9]

Austrian and American technology combined in 2011 when Steyr Motors, known for their "parallel" hybrid drive system worked with Mastervolt to innovate compact "serial" hybrid gensets which combine a 2-cylinder parallel twin marine diesel engine, based on the company's monoblock with a highly efficient permanent magnet generator. Mastervolt electronic power modules integrated the functionality of the generator, a charger, an inverter and the possibility of driving an electric propulsion motor. By doing so they effectively combine energy that comes from either the diesel engine, the battery pack, or shore power when available, and use it for all possible combinations of AC loads, DC loads, battery charging and propulsion. Controlling these energy flows was fully automatic.[10]

It took some boatyards a little longer before they were converted to e-propulsion. Since 1954, Princecraft of Princeville, Quebec, Ontario, Canada, had been building gasoline-engined aluminum boats. They had 300 employees and dealers throughout North America. But from 2011, they began to offer three boats designed for propulsion by Torqeedo Cruise electric outboards: the 15-ft (4m50) Brio 15e and the 17-ft (5 m) Brio 17e pontoon boats were specifically designed to be more compact and lighter than traditional versions. The 14-ft (4 m) Yukon DLe fishing boat was also reconfigured to better fit an electric outboard. Solar panels extend battery autonomy.[11] Torqeedo Cruise 2.0 outboards were also fitted by Gene Carletta of Blue Planet Catamaran, North Carolina, on his latest 32E model.

By this time the legendary Elco name had passed into new ownership in New York financier Steve Lamando, planning to step up its technological innovation. He began with the Hunter e27 and Hunter e36 Hybrid sailing yachts, fitted out with an Elco EP4000 AC electric motor, Valance lithium-iron-magnesium phosphate marine 12-volt batteries, Super Wind 350 wind turbine, Kyocera 135 Solar Panels and a Polar DC Marine 14 kw generator. Elco claimed this as "the First Totally Integrated, Eco-Friendly Electric Motor Propulsion System for Sailboats Up to 55 Feet" (17 meters). The system gave the Hunter e36 yacht a range of more than 800 sea miles at 5 knots under battery power. The EP4000 has only one moving part and is completely sealed, making it highly water-resistant to guard against moisture damage or corrosion.[12]

Another new application came with a sail-training e-boat. This was developed by Tanguy le Bihan of E3H in Lorient, Brittany, in northern France, in partnership with the French Sailing Federation, Nautisme en Bretagne, Nautisme en Finistère and the French Sports Ministry: "Sail training is a serious responsibility. Staying close to his pupils, the instructor needs a lightweight, spacious and easily maneuverable boat which enables him to intercept rapidly and to take several passengers on board. For this reason the 5m50 (18 ft) *Costo* has no stern to climb over. With a 3 cm (1.1 inch) draft of just 0.3m, its 4kW motor gives it a top speed of 9.5 knots, enabling the instructor to pilot the *Costo* at 6 knots for an entire day without the need to recharge its 48V lead-acid battery."[13]

But with all this activity going on either side of the Atlantic, had anything happened in Africa? In 2006, the management team at Chobe Game Lodge, Botswana, linked up with Freedom Won SA to become the first lodge on that continent to operate an entirely electric safari fleet. Chobe National Park is also known for its large elephant population, with upwards of 120,000 elephants in the Chobe area. Alongside *Freedom 3*, the electric Land Rover, *Freedom 4* was an electric skimmer boat. The electricity that charges the long-life lithium batteries to power the fleet comes from the hydroelectric plant at Victoria Falls and is thus fully renewable energy. During the next decade, powered by 30 kW WEG22 motors, another four vessels followed.[14]

In Gambia, from 2011, 50-ft (15m50) monohull *The Solar Queen* (KFK-52), built by Köpf Solarschiff GmbH of Sulz-Kastell of Germany, began its voyages for eco-tourism, operated by Englishman Mark Thomson of "Hidden Gambia" in Gambia, West Africa. Built in Germany, she was shipped to Banjul in 2 separate containers. Once bolted together, she was successfully reassembled by Köpf technicians, then cruised the 280 km (174 miles) up to Mark Thomson's main operation, the Bird Safari Camp, with its solar-powered amenities, near JanJanburegh on MacArthur Island. *The Solar Queen* was named after the famous 1951 Humphrey Bogart/Katharine Hepburn film *The African Queen*. It can carry up to 12 passengers through the mangrove habitat along the lower end of the West African country's river between Bintang and Farafenni (via Tendaba). Tendaba Camp is opposite the BaoBolong Wetland reserve—a must for the keen birdwatcher. Although a battery-electric launch, built by Gustave Trouvé of Paris, had amused the veiled harem of Sultan Mouli-Hassan of Morocco in the late 1880s, *The Solar Queen* became Africa's first solar-powered boat for inland waterways (the African Cats fleet having been designed for offshore cruising). When Mark Thomson surfed the Internet to check out the authenticity of his claim, he says "The only other 'solar boats' I could find in Africa were those used by the ancient Egyptians to transport their dead pharaohs to the Pyramids").[15] The solar-powered boats at the Chobe National Park followed suit. Regrettably, as a result of the actions of Alhagie Bithaye and certain members of the Gambia Police Force, *The Solar Queen* was impounded on November 25, 2012, and has been withheld since. On August 25, 2014, the boat sank while in police custody, and at the time of writing, it is still at the bottom of the Gambia River, gradually rusting away.

Amsterdam continued to remain a nerve center for the development of electric boats. In July 2011, Anton Schiere, a pioneer of the electric credit card and secretary of Stichting Elektrisch Varen with its on-line "Platform Elektrisch Varen," was waiting to board the sea sloop *Beau't* to report on its retrofitting as an e-boat, when he took this photo. It was then used by the SVUVA (Foundation for pollution-free boating Amsterdam), via the media to persuade that city's authorities to force the 5 tourist boat-operating companies to convert their diesel fleet to electric.

By the fall of 2013 a zero-emission status was declared, requiring all private and smaller sighting boats to go electric by 2020, and the larger 20-meter (65 ft) vessels to be emission-free by 2025 at the latest.[16]

For airline passengers at the city's Schiphol Airport with a minimum transfer time of 5 hours wanting to experience Amsterdam in a spectacular way, the solution was *The Floating Dutchman*, aka Amfibus. This hybrid-electric amphibious bus, for up to 48 passengers, makes a round trip from Schiphol, first on land, and then plunges into the water

In July 2011, Anton Schiere of Platform Elektrisch Varen was waiting to board the sea sloop *Beau't* to report on its retrofitting as an e-boat when he took this photograph. It was the used by the SVUVA (Foundation for Pollution Free Boating Amsterdam) via the media to persuade that city's authorities to force the five tourist boat-operating companies to convert their diesel fleet to electric (Platform Elektrisch Varen).

for a 45-minute cruise along the canals to the city center, passing by Skinny Bridge, Royal Theatre Carre, Oude Schans and the Oosterdok … then back to the airport. Operated by Rederij Lovers, the 198 battery-electric Amfibus (020), based on a Volvo chassis, was built by Dutch Amphibious Transport Vehicles (DATV), of Nijmegen, Gelderland. It was christened by Alderman Eric van der Burg of the city of Amsterdam and Maarten de Groof, EVP and CCO of Schiphol Group.[17]

In Otoshibe, Japan, where local fishermen were threatened by the increase in fuel prices, thanks to government funding, hybrid-electric fishing boats were developed. As part of a two-year-old program, the Japanese marine industry also tested biofuel-powered marine engines, computer-engineered propeller designs and low-energy LED lights on squid boats, which use bright lights to lure their catch. Elsewhere, Ohiori Capital's Eco Marine Power, based at Fukuoka on the west coast of Kyushu Island, working with Solar Sailor of Australia, planned a hybrid passenger ferry they called Tonbo, Japanese for dragonfly. The 10-m (32 ft) 200-pax vessel's 6.5kW lithium modules will be recharged by a biofuel generator and/or from solar panels on its roof which could be raised or lowered, allowing the vessel to pass under bridges.

For this, EMP has further developed the SolarSail concept into EnergySail, a rigid sail device, fitted with flexible solar panels, beneath which are sensors, safety devices and equipment panels; the mast can be rotated and lowered. The EnergySail can be used even when a ship is at anchor or in port, and has been designed to withstand high winds or even sudden microbursts. The EnergySail has primarily been designed for Eco Marine Power's Aquarius MRE System and is suitable for a wide range of ships, ferries and other vessels. Not only for Tonbo, but on a smaller solar-electric commuter ferry or eco commuter ferry design called the Medaka. EMP is also studying how large-scale renewable energy technologies can be incorporated into ship designs and looking into the use of renewable energy on-board Unmanned Surface Vessels (USVs).[18]

Although lithium is the flavor of the day, other batteries have begun to make silent waves in the industry. The Furukawa Battery Company of Japan linked up with Eco Marine Power (EMP) for use on vessels by ClassNK (Nippon Kaiji Kyokai). Their sealed VRLA (valve regulated lead acid) battery, the FC38-12, would be used for small marine solar power applications (i.e., up to around 5kWp). It is a return to lead, but in a much more sophisticated form.

Is there a limit to the applications of the e-boat?

Raonhaje in South Korea developed the *Ego*, a compact semi-submarine which can be enjoyed as both a motorboat and a two-seater submarine. Passengers can either enjoy the sun above, watch the fish below, or take the stairs to the submerged central hull to watch the undersea world. Both the 2.7-m (8 ft) *Ego* LE (luxury edition) and the *Ego* SE (standard edition) are run by 2 × 2kW e-pods with a battery-powered BLDC (brushless DC electric motor) and used a Trojan T-890 8-volt battery pack.[19]

Until now, tournament waterskiing had been the domain of the gasoline-engined towboat. In 2011, Correct Craft, who had been building gasoline ski-boats for over eighty years, teamed up with e-motor specialist LTS Marine of Montreal to innovate the Ski Nautique E, a twin-engined powerboat capable of towing a succession of 3 to 4 skiers at a silent 35 mph on one charge of its lithium-ion battery pack. The boat proved itself at a water ski tournament in Orlando, when the Correct Craft 100 percent electric Ski Nautique E towed two champion skiers in a head-to-head slalom exhibition. Correct Craft planned to reduce the recharge time from 4.5 hours to 15 minutes. The Correct Craft e-towboat joined Boesch of Switzerland, who had already been building e-ski-boats since the late 1990s, but whose latest boat, the 560, powered by an 80 kW (108 hp) electric motor, could reach a top speed of nearly 55 kph (34 mph), and the 620 Sunski with 120 kW (162 hp) capable of 60 kph (37 mph).[20] In 2013 Nautique's Super Air Nautique 230 pulled pro wakeboarder Kyle Rattray through multiple sets with little discernible difference, consuming 124 kW at 24 mph. The 230 E had enough power for four wake "sessions," or about 45 to 60 minutes of run time.

Another marque with a legendary track record for water-skiers is the Italian firm, Riva, a company now owned by Ferretti. The latest Riva, the Iseo, had an option of Ferretti's Hybrid Propulsion ZEM, offering a consumption of just 1.2 liters per mile at 30 knots. The in-line electric motor provided additional thrust of up to 44 knots, and at slow speeds, under electrical power alone, it had a range of 40 miles.

Paris, France: The Salon Nautic 2011 (French Boat Show) at the Porte de Versailles saw an impressive fifteen e-boats on show, some of them already described above: the Aquabus C60 of Grove Boats on show at the entrance to the Salon; the Greenline 33; and the Costo sail-training boat.[21]

British cinematography inventor William Friese-Greene had once stated: "So the invention goes through the stages: 1st: Rubbish, impossible! 2nd: Impossible! 3rd: Possible and probable. 4th: Yes, possible, but is there any money in it? 5th: Yes, there is money in it (that is the stage of worry); 6th: Plenty of money in it; 7th: Oh, I have heard of that invention long ago!"[22] With electric boating the latest stage was n°5: "Possible, and maybe, at last, some money in it."

Fuel cells continued to enter into use. In 2010 engineer Rolf Eichinger of Büchenback, Germany, developed a fuel-cell drive for his 9-m pleasure boat. He called his drive the *Fodiator* (= flying fish). Entrak in Wendelstein, who had been developing drives and energy supplies for aircraft and boats, contacted Eichinger. By 2012 Fodiator and Entrak had presented the first 5 kW commercial prototype, tested in Eichinger's 9-m (30 ft) sailing yacht moving up to a speed of 10 kph on the Brombachsee (lake) near Nuremberg in Franconia. Soon after, Fahrland Boat Charters, based near the Brombachsee and the district of Weißenburg-Gunzenhausen, planned a boat marina in Ramsberg with its hydrogen fuel station, using wind-powered hydrolysis. Two launches and a 14-m (46 ft) luxury houseboat could be ready for charter in June 2013. Eichinger and Entrak soon developed Fodiator fuel-cell systems ranging from 1.1 to 10 kW. At the exactly same time, Turkey had taken on the same challenge. In 2011, Istanbul Technical University (ITU)'s the *Marti* (= seagull) had been developed by a 32-strong team of technicians, with funding from various organizations, including Istanbul Metropolitan Municipality and the United Nations Industrial Development Organization (UNIDO). *Marti*, with a capacity of 6 passengers and 2 crew, has gone into use on the Haliç estuary in Istanbul, shuttling between various wharfs and the Rahmi M. Koç Museum—which, fittingly, is a museum dedicated to the history of transport, industry and communications. Using 8.5 kW from a PEM fuel cell, the 8.13-m (27 ft) catamaran can run for 10 hours on 5 kg of hydrogen at a maximum speed of 13 kph (7 knots).[23]

German outboard maker Torqeedo was going from success to success. Their awards included the German Startup of the Year 2008 (Germany), ETT Cleantech Summit 2009 (Europe; selected as one of Europe's 25 hottest Cleantech Startups), IBEX innovation award (USA), Innovation Award of the DAME Jury (NL), Pittman Innovation award (USA), Hiswa innovation award (NL), West Marine Vendor of the Year (USA). The company employed 27 people in R&D, production management, sales and marketing, finance and administration and service. Production is outsourced to suppliers predominantly in southern Germany. Some 20 people were working on Torqeedo full time on the payroll of production partners, but not included in the 27 Torqeedo employees.[24]

Other firms stepped up the kilowatt power output of their outboards. In 2011, All4Solar of Trinity Park, Queensland, Australia, who had been producing their Aquawatt 20 hp (13 kw) and the 30 hp (22 kw) electric outboards, announced a 35 hp model (22 kW), powered by 80 V Li-po4 batteries; they claimed that this was the most powerful electric outboard motor in the world. It was a claim that they would not hold for very long.[25]

From Hong Kong, China, ePropulsion Technology Limited developed two outboards: a 1 kW *Spirit* and the 6 kW *Navy*, both using in large capacity Li-po batteries.

In 2012 the Scottish government's Clyde and Hebrides ferry strategy commissioned Ferguson Shipbuilders, Port Glasgow, to build three hybrid ferries. The 150-pax/22-car MV *Hallaig*, named after a poem by Sorley MacLean, and run by CalMac, now serves the lifeline route between Sconser on the Isle of Skye and the Hebridean Isle of Raasay. She was also the first ship to be fully built and delivered on the Clyde in over five years. The lithium battery banks are charged overnight but with a view to ever-greener technology, Ferguson Marine continues to explore greater efficiencies which will include in-service recharging, taking on self-generated power from the island ports.

In May 2014, she was followed by MV *Lochinvar*, named after a poem by Sir Walter Scott, and serving the Tarbert-to-Portavadie route. The third vessel, MV *Catriona*, was launched in December 2015 and went into service in 2016 between Lochranza on the Isle of Arran and Claonaig on the Kintyre peninsula. In keeping with the now established tradition, she was named *Catriona* from the title of the 1893 Scottish novel by Robert Louis Stevenson, sequel to the much-loved *Kidnapped*.[26]

Back in Friesland, the Netherlands, the fourth Dong Energy Solar Challenge 2012 was won by *Gowrings Continental BV* (T82) in a record time of 10 hours, 40 minutes. The second boat was clocked in just over 4 hours later. In third place was an American team from Cedarville University. By now some of the competitors, such as the Adela boat, had entered hydrofoils. Altogether some thirty teams from as far afield as Brazil, the Netherlands, Germany, China, Belgium, Finland, and Poland took part.[27]

Inevitably, mighty China entered the electric boat market. In early 2011, the Genencor solar boat unit was established in Xiamen in southeast China's Fujian province. By December, Xiamen Hansheng Yacht Co., Ltd., Xiamen Guan Yu Technology Co., Ltd., and Xiamen New World Technology Co., Ltd., had formed a new company, Li Technology Co., Ltd. Within several months the first solar-powered passenger boat was launched on Lake Yungdang in Xiamen. The 15-meter-long and 6-meter-wide boat has a roof entirely covered in flexible monocrystalline silicon solar panels that offer a high conversion efficiency of 22.4 percent.

From South Korea, a new player in the electric boat business is Leo Motors Co., Ltd. ("Leozone") of Seoul, led by Jung Yong ("John") Lee. John Lee received his doctorate in industrial design from the University of New South Wales, and a Master's degree in industrial design (vehicle styling) from RMIT University, Australia, and had worked on several e-automobile projects, including the Polymer Battery, Dual Motor System, and alternative energy vehicle design. Together with his Chief Technical Officer Kean Seab Kim, Lee made a succession of innovations. In 2011 Leo Motors was able to enter a Memorandum of Understanding (MOU) with the Chinese Company Shenzhen Rui Li Da Shebei (SRLDS), Ltd., to share its 56 patent for around US$6 million. Using Leo's technology, SRLDS set up an Electric Vehicle (EV) manufacturing plant in Beijing. In September 2013 LGM, Inc., a subsidiary of Leo Motors, Ltd., registered in Las Vegas, was granted 70 million won (US$63,000) by the Korean Ministry of Maritime Affairs and Fisheries to research electric propulsion for small boats. The following year they received a further subsidy from the government to develop an electric jetski.

With the permanent closure of the Motorboat Museum in Basildon, Essex, England, *Solar Craft I*, inventor Alan Freeman's pioneer craft, was donated to the Planet Solar Foundation. Raphaël Domjan took the little catamaran back to Yverdon-les-Bains, where it was to be restored for posterity.

From the outset, although the electric boat was primarily a vessel for sports and leisure activities, it could also be used in the workplace, evidenced by the turbo-electric tugboats. In 1966, the city of Utrecht, concerned to save its monumental bridges and roads near the canals from heavy freight traffic, introduced what they called a *Stroomboot* (= *Beerboat*) to supply bars, pubs, restaurants, hotels and other catering businesses with beverages, from the waterside. In recent years, frozen and perishable fresh products had also been delivered by the *Stroomboot*. The Beerboat, however, reached its full capacity. In early 2010, Utrecht introduced the new electrically propelled *Stroomboot*. Two years later, the waste of central Utrecht has been collected by the electrically driven *Ecoboot*, based on the *Stroomboot*. The electric crane arm of this zero-emission cruising trash truck, picks up each garbage bin from the canal side, then tips it into one of the eight on-board containers, depending on the type of waste. It can also load heavier waste, up to half a ton, from the canal banks. Its full capacity is 15 tons, more than a truck. The 17-m (55 ft) vessel, built by the Bocxe shipyard in Delft, has four Fiamm battery packs, each of 480 volts, with overnight recharging. These batteries are used to power the 55 kW Siemens electric motor and all equipment on board the boat. The city of Utrecht has invested half a million euros in the *Ecoboot*, part obtained by grant from a European fund called "Connecting Citizen Ports 21." The extra costs for the electric drive are funded by the Freight Action Plan of the municipality. If the results are positive, inland cities in Belgium, France, Germany and Switzerland may launch their own ecoboats. The Berlin Institute of Technology is already investigating this potential.[28]

The Danish company ASMO had expanded their 3.5kW–12 kW Thoosa propulsion units for pleasure boats, Triton AC 22 kw and commercial use up to 90kW or even higher. In 2012, to reduce shipping costs to the USA, they arranged for their U.S. distributor, Annapolis Hybrid Marine in Maryland, to assemble and manufacture Thoosas and Tritons in a plant in St. Petersburg, Florida, and renamed their operation Clean eMarine Americas.[29]

Minn Kota continued to make "hands-off" bass troll fishing even easier by bringing out the world's first wireless remote-controlled GPS-based trolling motor navigation system, which they would extend to communicate with a Hummingbird fish finder (i-Pilot® Link™).

Others had joined the electric water-ski towboat challenge. Goldfish, based in Norway's Oslorjord, combined with ReGen Nautic of Dania Beach, Fort Lauderdale, USA, to produce the all-electric 23-ft (7 m) eFusion, capable of accelerating 47 knots in just 10 seconds and fully rechargeable in 30 minutes. Capable of towing a water-skier for almost one hour, the eFusion is powered by the E200, a 145 kW permanent magnet brushless electric outboard motor weighing just 45 kg (100 lb), built by UQM Technologies of Colorado, USA. It gives equivalent to 180 horsepower at 8,000 RPM, but with a concomitant price tag of $30,000! Running, it is cooled by a closed-loop glycol system, which is itself cooled by sea water. The 25 kWh battery pack was built using Dow Kokam lithium cells packaged by Corvus Energy of Canada. The eFusion won the innovation award category of the 2012 European Powerboat of the Year award at the Dusseldorf Boat Show. While Goldfish announced that they would to deploy up to 10 additional eFusion boats in 2013, ReGen Nautic's President Pierre Caouette announced, "We have installations in much larger vessels, one with twin 200 HP electric motors, one with twin 300 HP electric, but these might not qualify as they have a generator to recharge the batteries." A 180 HP eFusion version was developed for Campion Marine of Kelowna, British Columbia, Canada.

In Auckland, New Zealand, 2012, NewPower Integrators developed the E-workboat catamaran for marinas, oyster and fish farms, and marine reserves. Two 10kW water-cooled BLDC motors through surface drives and draws power from a lithium-ion-phosphate (LiFEPO4) battery of 6kWh capacity. This gives the boat a top speed of 22 mph (35 kph) and range of approximately 20 miles (30 km). The E-workboat joins the 15 hp longshaft 10kW E-outboard as a second commercial marine E-drive system.

Following the success of Britain's first hydrogen fuel cell boat, the *Ross Barlow*, in 2013, the 36-ft (11 m) steel *Hydrogenesis* went into regular operation at Bristol in southwest England. It was ordered Bristol City Council as part of its Green Capital initiatives to make Bristol a low-carbon city. With twin Lynch motors, it was designed and constructed at Richard Rankin's yard in Weston-super-Mare for Bristol Hydrogen Boats, a consortium comprising Keith Dunstan of Bristol Packet Boat Trips, Number Seven Boat Trips, and Jas Singh of Auriga Energy. The hydrogen fuel, incorporating SmartFuel modules and a dockside refueling station in Bristol Harbor, were supplied by Air Products. *Hydrogenesis* operated six hours a day between Temple Quay and the SS *Great Britain*. She carried passengers at the annual Bristol Harbor Festival. Having gone over to bottled hydrogen, *Hydrogenesis* is, at the time of writing, available for private hire.[30]

Over in Canada, *Au feel de l'eau*, a 12-pax Torqeedo-engined water taxi started plying its trade across the Outaouais River between Ottawa and Gatineau. It shuttles between the two banks some 38 times a day. Lasting 5 minutes, it offers passengers a unique view of both Parliament and the Canadian Museum of Civilization.

With the increasing concern for planetary pollution, some e-boats were put into practical use. During October 2012, *Riding Currents—The Last Straw*, a 22-ft (6m70) Duffy electric day boat fitted with four solar roof panels and an extra bank of Trojan T-145 batteries, made a 13-leg, 354-mile (570 km) cruise down the southern Californian coast from Santa Barbara to Ensenada, Mexico. Its mission: to advocate the elimination of plastic pollution from marine ecosystems. *Riding Currents's* two-man crew were surf-boarding friends, Mark Ward and Billy Dutton. At various points along the "electric surf safari," Dutton and Ward pulled trawls used by the Five Gyres Research Institute for collecting samples of floating debris. They were also working with Heal the Bay, taking water samples at predetermined points, to assisting in monitoring water quality along the coast. At each port of call they visited schools to get across the message out about the dangers of plastic waste and its harm to the ocean. By the end of their voyage, *Riding Currents's* cabin was piled high with plastic. During their voyage they kept a log on Facebook.[31]

In 2012 Carter Quillen of Florida, a heating engineer, bought a 20-ton, 50-ft (15.24 m)

Hero was among those electric launches restored and revived by Rupert Latham and his team at Classic Boatworks (author's collection).

concrete yacht, removed its rotten wooden rigging, and retrofitted it as a solar-electric cabin cruiser. Its 5kW solar array gave it a cruising speed of up to 5 mph (8 kph). Renaming it the *Archimedes Sun Pirate*, Quillen cruised it from Jacksonville to Pensacola including the Atlantic Intracoastal Waterway, conducting a series of sustainable energy workshops en route.[32]

The EBA had continued to organize rallies for their members on the tranquil waters of British rivers. Among those attending were some of the most exquisite late Victorian and Edwardian launches, restored or replicated—like the finest varnished teak and mahogany furniture afloat, but with fiberglass hulls and the latest electric propulsion systems. These fine craft were afloat thanks to the painstaking craftsmanship of yards such as Freebody of Hurley, Henwood and Dean of Henley-on-Thames, Creative Marine and Latham's Classic Boatworks of Woodbastwick, working with experienced designers such as Andrew Wolstenholme. They bore names such as *Adelaide, Caramane, Cymba, Lady Charlotte, Estrel, Humble, Hero, Lillie Langtry, Mystical Maid,* and *Pike,* to mention a few. Those deserving won the Simmonds Trophy at the Thames Traditional Boat Rally.

One example, the *Lady Charlotte* (ex–*Flying Fox*, 1914) had been restored and electrified by Henwood and Dean. In 2012 this river launch was lifted out of the water, the cabin removed and the riveted steel hull sent to Southampton, where engineer Michael Williams carried out a long and punishing job restoring or replacing the plates and rivets. Work on the building of a new cabin began at the boatyard, and the two components, together with a silent 10kw electric motor installed by the Thames Electric Launch Co., were reunited in the spring of 2013. Working closely with Simon and yacht designer

Colin Henwood of Henley in the magnificently restored *Lady Charlotte* (© Michael English, used by kind permission of Henwood & Dean Boatbuilders, Henley-on-Thames).

Andrew Wolstenholme, Colin Henwood and his team produced a unique and beautiful launch. *Lady Charlotte* would win *Classic Boat* magazine's "Powered Boat of the Year" Award, and at the Thames Traditional Boat Rally she won the Osland Trophy for structural restoration and the Simmonds for electrically powered craft.

Another example is 34-ft (10 m) *Hero*, a Victorian counter stern launch. Originally built as an electric launch, she was later converted to a gasoline engine, then in 1969 to steam power. At Classic Boatworks, while the team brought her teak and mahogany back to pristine condition, Rupert Latham fitted a 4kW direct drive motor and deep cycle gel batteries under the cockpit floor, providing ample and comfortable seating for up to 9 passengers. Boats such as these can be hired out for events via Henley Sales & Charter, run by Latham's former colleague, Gillian Nahum.

Some rallies are unique. On June 3, 2012, on downtown London's River Thames, electric boats joined vessels of all shapes and sizes to celebrate Her Majesty Queen Elizabeth II's Diamond Jubilee. At the front of the procession was the magnificent red-and-gold Royal Rowbarge *Gloriana* with a team of 18 oarsmen, also discreetly equipped with two Lynch electric motors connected to a pair of Sillette-Sonic saildrives to provide an additional 14 kW of driving power.[33]

In 2012, the author's full biography *A La Recherche de Trouvé. La Quête d'un génie français oublié* (= *Looking for Trouvé: The Quest for a Forgotten French Genius*) was published by Pleine Page of Bordeaux, France. It devoted several pages to Gustave Trouvé's pioneering work on electric boats (see Chapter One). Following its publication, on October 13, 2012, Monsieur Jacques Barbier, the mayor of Descartes, unveiled a commemorative metal plaque in the Saint Lazare Square, former site of Trouvé's childhood home.

Two months later, the Académie Nationale des Sciences, Belles Lettres et Arts de Bordeaux, founded in 1712 by King Louis XIV, presented the author with Le Prix Jacques Paul, "pour couronner votre oeuvre" (to crown your work). In my speech I stated that the prize was as much for Trouvé as for me.

As if by coincidence, to the very same Parisian waters of the River Seine where Trouvé's boats had first been marveled at, several months later, a 17-m (56 ft) Aquabus C60, called the *Felix de Azara*, named after an 18th-century Spanish naturalist, went into silent summer operation in the established fleet of the capital's passenger boats (Croisières en Seine, Batostar/Paris Canal). The *Felix de Azara* offered trips around the Ile Saint-Louis, up to the Eiffel Tower, and as of 2015 up the Canal de la Villette. Among those who enjoyed a cruise on her was the president of the French Republic, François Hollande.[34]

Torqeedo, nicknamed "the Outboard Duffy," went from strength to strength. In 2012 the venture capital company of the Bosch Group, Robert Bosch Venture Capital GmbH, acquired a minority stake in the Starnberg firm. The move was made as part of a round of financing that Torqeedo undertook in preparation for further growth and the development of new innovative products. The R&D team, led by propulsion specialist Jens Biebach, formerly of Dresden Technical University, and Marc Hartmeyer, now came up with a 325V DC high-voltage Deep Blue system of a 40 hp and an 80 hp outboard. At the New Orleans International WorkBoat Show, Torqeedo received the DAME award for its Deep Blue. At the same time Torqeedo established a partnership with Johnson Controls for the all-important lithium batteries.[35] It seemed that there was no corner of the world where Tornedos could not be used.

In December 2012, German engineer Norbert Droessler of "Photovoltaics Peru S.R.L." cruised a Torqeedo boat across Lake Titicaca, South America, at an altitude of 3,810 m (12,500 feet) above sea level. At that altitude, gasoline outboards cannot provide their full power due to the thin air, so the Travel 1003 could keep up with boats powered with 5–6 hp fuel engines. Again thanks to Droessler, the Amazon Delta finally saw an electric boat. A German NGO, "Chances for Nature e.V," began to use a Torqeedo Travel 1003 on their research patrol boat in the Rio Tapiche area, about 75 miles (120 km) southeast of the Peruvian Amazon city of Iquitos. They are using the Travel 1003 on different boats, as well as on a traditional 33-ft (10 m) thatched roof boat traditionally using a noisy 15 hp gasoline outboard. To charge the battery, a photovoltaic system was installed on the main building of the camp. Despite the environmental aspects, they can travel daily in the area and totally autonomous of any fuel supply.[36]

In Brazil, the 24-m, 18-pax motor yacht *Tucano* has been fitted with solar panels and auxiliary electric motors. It is used to take tourists on cruises through the rainforest along the Amazon River.

In 2013, Combi Nautic, which had been providing e-outboards for several decades, was acquired by Peter Jager of Vollenhove, near Giethoorn, previously in the mega-luxury yacht business but with a love of electric boating. Jager trademarked the name and set up a fully equipped workshop with service department so that all units were "made in Holland." In 2015 Combi released a new line of electric motors, respectively 1,000, 1,500 (24 volts), 2,000 and 3,000 watts (48 volts), with streamlined underwater housing, and their i–Combi, a digital key that allows the user to enable multiple combinations for the rental. They have also incorporated a built-in electric motor propeller shaft knife to prevent fouling by weed, fishing lines and plastic. By examining existing products, they have developed their own controller for the Combi 700 and 1200 DC motors, improving output. Combi has also produced a 50 kW/65 hp unit.[37]

Combi's continues to produce new engines in the Netherlands (courtesy Combi).

Was there no corner of the planet were a Duffy was not put into service? In Finland's lake district, *Lady of the Lake* (Lake Haukivesi to be precise), went into operation for a local nature tourism company, Lakeland GTE, managed by Arto Keinänen. Cruising silently across Lake Haukivesi, the boat has access to the Kolovesi National Park, where motorboats are prohibited, and enabling up to ten passengers to observe the rare, endangered Saimaa ringed seal.[38]

Electric boats had arrived in Norway, Sweden, Finland and even Lapland: Located alongside Lapland's Lake Inari, north of the Arctic Circle, Mauri Rautiainen of the Finnish Fantan Catamaran Ltd. boatyard has designed and built three hybrid-electric passenger boats calling them Inari after the 3000-island lake. The local Laplanders, impressed by their silent running, have nicknamed them "valkoinen kummituksia" (= "white ghosts"). The 16-m (53 ft) 25 kW *Inari III* had a passenger capacity of 120 people. Its hull was built of aspen wood coated with grp and epoxy. The hybrid system was developed by Randax Ltd. located in the northern Finnish city of Oulu, and part of the Future Manufacturing Technologies Group research group led by the city's university, the second largest in Finland. Energy was generated by a 1.9 liter, 55 kW Volkswagen marine diesel TDI 75-4, integrated at the end of the crankshaft where a reduction gear would normally be. Each hull of the catamaran had its own propeller, which was driven by a Randax permanent magnet motor directly coupled to a straight propeller shaft. The 50 kWh Li-ion batteries were from European Batteries Ltd. *Inari III* cruises at 7 knots with a maximum speed of 12 knots, remaining stable in 2 m (6 ft) waves. As the 80-km (50 mile) lake is completely frozen over from November to June, the boat has only five months to make its silent cruises.[39]

Although it was fascinating for this author to keep tabs on e-boat development around the blue planet, it was a very special event when they also arrived at his home city of Bordeaux, Aquitaine, southwest France. From May 2013, that city, with its elegant electric tram network, and Vélib rentabike system, began to offer its "Bordelais" citizens the first of two new h/e 19-meter (62 ft) aluminum river cats to take them safely across the often strong currents and floating debris of the wide Garonne River; their fine-entry armored bows can deflect any natural tidal debris. Built by Dubourdieu of Gujan-Mestras, out on the Atlantic coast, the first boat was put through five months of sea and river trials before she obtained her navigation certificate. Their 140 kWh lithium batteries were provided by the local SAFT company. Christened *L'Hirondelle* (= Swallow) and *Le Gondole* (= Gondola), the 45-pax vessels soon got the nickname "Les Batcubs" (Bateau = Boat; CUB for Communauté Urbain de Bordeaux). It had been many decades since our "Claret City" had two regular and highly popular fleets of gasoline-powered waterbuses, quaintly known as the Gondolas and the Bees, plying their trade. Ferrying up to 800 passengers per day, the two e-boats have become a common site.[40]

The Batcub ferryboat, built by Dubourdieu for the unforgiving currents of the Garonne River in Bordeaux, France, 2013 (© Keolis Bordeaux Métropole).

Since the 1980s, e-boat conferences and seminars had been organized in particular countries. But in October 2013 the net was considerably widened at "PlugBoat 2013," held in Nice, France, led by Frédéric Vergels of the Belgium-based Electri-city. One hundred delegates came from 17 countries to listen to more than 60 PowerPoint and Poster presentations on virtually every aspect of electric boating, including reliability reports of existing passenger ferries or computer-modeled boat designs. There were feasibility studies made by university graduates from as far afield as Aachen, Hanover, Delft, Waseda, Vaud, La Rochelle, Warsaw, Genoa and Rijeka. It was estimated that the worldwide total of electric boats of every description *now passed the 50,000 mark*, Torqeedo alone having sold some 40,000 li-ion powered outboards. ICE and/or solar hybrids are being equipped with LiFePO4 batteries, although sodium-nickel-chloride, nickel-metal-hydride, NiCad and lead-acid batteries are still considered as options. Hydrogen fuel cells, super capacitors and induction recharging systems are also progressing. PlugBoat then concluded with a short Mediterranean cruise of 5 electric boats, one of which, the ODC hybrid-

Seaway of Slovenia's fleet of Greenline hybrid electric cabin cruisers, 2013 (SVP AVIO).

electric, having voyaged over from Corsica, took many delegates across the Bay of Nice. Plans were made for PlugBoat 2015 to take place in Friesland, northern Netherlands, where there are 900 e-boats and 115 charging points on electric-only routes, out of a total in the Netherlands of between 6,000 and 10,000, of which some 1,500 are for daily rental and over 100 for tourist excursions.

In Slovenia, Seaway Yachts of Puconci, famous for its award-winning Greenline 33 hybrid-electric cabin cruiser, of which over 300 had been delivered to 28 countries in the first three years, now developed the transoceanic Greenline Ocean Class for cruisers over 50 feet (15 m). With its solar-lithium-twin 800hp hybrid-diesel drive, the Greenline Ocean Class can cruise for 20 nautical miles in emission-free silence, but on the other side of the coin, will also do 22 knots flat out with twin 800hp engines. Greenline also offered the 40 Hybrid yacht. In July a taxi version of a Greenline 33 went into service at the Fonda fish farm park in the bay of Portorose, North Adriatic. In February 2017 Greenline launched its 36 Hybrid, combining a Volvo Penta D3 220-hp diesel engine with a 10-kW Siemens. It has been named the Adriatic Boat of the Year.

Carl Kai Rand of Copenhagen, Denmark, who studied boat design at the Rhode Island School of Design, along with Kasper Eich-Romme and Anders Mørck launched their 10-pax Picnic version of their GoBoat boat. Built out of Kebony sustainable timber, equipped with recycled wind turbine blades, and with its unsinkable kernel made of recycled plastic bottles, the Rand boat is self-bailing: any water that gets into the interior is conducted back into the surrounding water automatically without pumps. With its 23 percent efficiency, the boat's solar cell table will remove the need for recharging the Torqeedo even on clouded days. Small fleets of these dark blue boats soon went into service in both Copenhagen and Stockholm harbors from jetties also made of Kebony sustainable timber.[41]

Late in 2013 the irrepressible Torqeedo acquired Moonwave Systems of Jena hybrid-electric drive for 40–70-ft (12–21 m) sailing catamaran yachts using their Deep Blue engine.

Switzerland's Grove Boats (ex–MW-Line) had been modernizing the design of their Aquabus line and delivered several units to French customers. Its initial focus market was Lac de Gérardmer (private tourism operator), Lyon harbor (Company Nationale du Rhône). One, a Kraütler-engined Aquabus 850T, was even delivered to French Guyana for the Iracoubo commune, 75 km (45 miles) away from the Kourou European Space Centre, where another modern technology is being introduced … but without the noise and pollution of a space rocket!

At the same time, like the Dutch canal refuse collector, Grove Boats were diversifying into a new line of electric-powered vessels to collect floating rubbish in harbors and marinas. They called them "SeaCleaners." Innovated by Marc Wüst, the first unit was a 20-ft (6 m) catamaran, equipped with 2 × 1.8kW Kraütler pods, the "SeaCleaner 400." One, sold in 2013 in the United Arab Emirates, earned Grove Boats numerous prizes (Mansura Trophy medal in 2013, Energy Globe in 2014). Further such cleaner craft have been developed: in 2014, the "Marina Cleaner" was launched, a fixed craft producing a surface current to softly attract floating rubbish into a collecting basket and also able to filter oil spills. Then in 2015, Mark Wüst headed another visionary project, the "Mini SeaCleaner," an unmanned remote-controlled solar catamaran that will navigate in the tight spaces of a marina to collect floating waste.[42]

Another unmanned surface vessel (USV) has been produced by Solar Sailor of New South Wales, Australia: the Steber Solar Sailor Bluebottle, tasked for ocean monitoring and surveillance. A Bluebottle, operating on energy available at sea—solar, wave and wind and coupled with the fact it is unmanned—represents an ideal platform for low-cost ocean surveillance both above and below the surface. With 500 watts average electrical power 24/7, there were three models: the 5m9 (20 ft) Big Blue, Blue Stinger and 1m9 (6 ft) Blue Nemo.[43]

The unmanned Wave Adapted Modular Vehicle (WAM-V) is being used by the San Francisco Baykeeper organization, to map shorelines and raise awareness of the impacts of global sea level rise. With the overhead Street View Trekker camera system loaned by Google Maps, the WAM-V is powered by twin Cruise 4kW electric outboard motors rigged with Power 26–104 lithium batteries linked to solar panels. As a trial, it completed a mapping project of American Samoa.

NINE

In Recent Months (2015–)

In 1894, when Thomas Commerford Martin and Joseph Sachs published their book *Electrical Boats and Navigation*, in New York,[1] they were presenting the state of the art technology of their time. While Chapter One of this book chronicles some sixty years, Chapter Two thirty years, as this history has progressed, more and more successful applications of e-boats are taking place. It therefore seems only right that the past three highly productive years should be given a chapter of their own, and even this is at the time of going to press!

A measure of success is that despite world oil prices hitting an all-time low due to overproduction, indirectly reducing the cost of running i/c boats, the zero-mission political movement is far stronger than it has ever been. So it was that in 2014 the World Wildlife Fund now saw the importance of electric boats for conservation. From 2015, *Solaris* began to transport scientists, environmentally minded tourists, and student groups on tours to see the wildlife across Academy Bay around places like Puerto Ayora on Santa Cruz Island in the Galápagos. This was the result of a joint project between the World Wildlife Fund and the Galápagos National Park (a branch of the Ecuadorian government). Confiscated from an illegal fishing operation, *Solaris* has been retrofitted for $35,000 with a Torqeedo motor with energy from lithium batteries supplied by eight solar roof panels. Boats are the primary mode of transportation in the Galápagos Islands. In the last few years the number increased to 60,000 visitors each year and the pressure continues by the ever-expanding tourism industry. Yet there are many drawbacks. Fuel has to be imported from the mainland, which is very costly, and motors spill fuel and oil into the water—and that's in addition to the pollution created by engine smoke. WWF and the park are looking into setting up several solar charging stations that would make it so each boat didn't need solar panels.[2]

If this pilot program goes well, a huge switchover could take place. Torqeedo's Big Blue may be retrofitted to inter-island ferries, and the giant barges that cover the couple of hundred feet between the island of Baltra, where the most popular airport is, and Santa Cruz, where the most people live, could one day be replaced by solar boats.

The same approach to watching wildlife has been taken by Finland, where the tourist company NorthSailing (Nordur Sigling), based in Húsavík, has retrofitted a German-built 1951 oak two-mast schooner, formerly a Baltic trawler, with a variable-pitch prop regenerative 144kW Baumuller e-motor. The batteries are also charged on the mainland with electricity harvested by renewable sources. The official launch was by Sigmundur David Gunnlaugsson, Prime Minister of Iceland. The *Opal* is an international project:

Caterpillar Propulsion (Sweden) and Wave Propulsion (Norway) designed the propeller, and the Icelandic company Naust Marine designed the electrical and control system in collaboration with Clean eMarine (Denmark) and Anel AS (Norway). Other partners in the project are Lakeside Excursion (Faroe Islands), Bellona (Norway), Icelandic New Energy and Innovation Center Iceland. Lithium Storage (Switzerland) specifically designed and produced the batteries. Skippered by Heimir Hardarssen, this motor-sailer is now giving 3–4 hour whale-watching tours in Skjálfandi Bay, northeast Iceland. Its silent running is more echo-friendly to the whales' sonar. North Sailing is already restoring and electrifying another traditional 60-ft (18 m) whale-hunting vessel, salvaged from the ocean floor, with a 109 kw motor. Another eight vessels could be "improved."[3]

In line with this, later in 2017, the 50-ft welded aluminum 47-pax E/V *Tongass Rain* is scheduled make its seagoing trials from Juneau, southeast Alaska. Electricity for its lithium batteries comes from rain used by the Juneau Hydropower micro-grid, set up by Keith Comstock. The hull, designed by Scott Jutson Marine in Vancouver, is under construction at Armstrong Marine in Port Angeles, Washington. It has been certified by the U.S. Coast Guard for 150 nautical miles "for safe harbor" in 6.5-foot (2 m) seas at 12 knots. *Tongass Rain* will be used for eco-education, where passengers can go on whale-watching trips and also admire sea mammals, birds and the distant glaciers of Tongass. Alaskan fishing industry will be watching performance to see if the same system could be used for salmon drifters, gill netters, and crabbers.[4]

Even in Tahiti, tourists wishing explore Punaauia and the French Polynesian islands and lagoon of the island of Tahiti can hire and drive a 30-ft rigid inflatable with electric trolling motor; they board the boat at the Taapuna quay, which is located approximately 15 miles (25 km) from Papeete. They are then able to view coral reefs and other underwater flora and fauna.

Following the successful operation of Foss Maritime's two hybrid tugs in California, in 2015 the Rotor®Tug RT *Adriaan* began service for Kotug in Rotterdam. It is 32 meters (105 ft) long with a gross tonnage of 463. Like her American cousins, the tug was retrofitted in 2012 with the XeroPoint Hybrid Propulsion System with Corvus Energy's lithium polymer batteries. *Adriaan* is equipped with three Caterpillar 3512 C-HD main engines rated at 1765 kW at 1,800 rpm. Each powers a motor generator attached to a fully Azimuthing Schottel Rudder Propeller SRP 1215 with a fixed-pitch 94-inch (2.40 m) diameter propeller. There are two auxiliary 200 kW Caterpillar C9 gensets and one 36 kW Caterpillar C4.4 emergency genset.[5]

One electrical engineer who had helped pioneer electric boating in France is Guy Gorius of Alize Electronics Greoux les Bains, in the Alpes-de-Haute-Provence department in southeastern France. Now thirty years later, Gorius has worked with Jean-Luc Tardy of Signe-Ltd., whose E3H (for Efficient Electric Evolved Hull) was incorporated into the *Costo*, to develop the solar-electric Obiboat®. Measuring 4m50 (15 ft), this 7-passenger catamaran with Minn Kota engines was designed for calm inland waters with a rigid/Bimini solar roof and a 70-cm (28 in) polycarbonate crystal circular glass bottom. One of the first Obiboats went into operation in Madagascar and northeastern Mozambique.

In 2015, Clemens Dransfeld, a designer and engineer of Kreuzlingen, near Lake Constance, Switzerland, who had already made a success with Peter Minder of the local Heinrich boatyard with their successful "Tender" runabout, made the changeover to electric propulsion and used an 80 hp Torqeedo Deep Blue i (inboard). Their Tender 06e won the Best of Boats award at the BOOT&FUN trade show in Berlin, selected from a total of 166 different boats from 18 countries launched during that season; 11 journalists from various countries had put the boats through their paces in 333 tests in predefined conditions.[6] In contrast to this sportsboat, a workboat equipped with a Deep Blue was used to maneuver barges on the quarry lake Rogau near Frankfurt. These barges consistently carry over 60 metric tons of gravel.[7]

Still from Switzerland, Michael Köhler of Niederkassel has developed Solarwave 62, an oceangoing yacht in which both the propulsion and all household appliances are exclusively solar-powered. To test the system, in January 2010, a prototype went on a rigorous 3-year sea trial, which involved crossing the whole of Europe by river, sailing the dangerous Black Sea, the stormy Aegean and the Mediterranean. This experience of more than 140 weeks was also enjoyed by hundreds of guests and visiting journalists. Köhler then linked up with Dr. Orhan Celikkol at the Nedship shipyard in Turkey to produce a carbon composite luxury catamaran to use his Solarwave technology. The yacht's roof is clad with a 15 kW photovoltaic array connected to a series of 100 kWh batteries. With two e-motors (41 kW continuous and 62 kW peak) on board, the yacht can cruise at speeds between 7 and 13 knots without the need to utilize additional fuel sources during sunny conditions and light winds.[8]

After service from Yvoire on Lake Geneva, Switzerland, in April 2016, the 50-pax ODC Marine *Nyami* was shipped over for service by the Martinique Navigation Company in Fort-de-France Bay, on the Caribbean island of Martinique, the first of a silent fleet of five.

David N. Borton, Ph.D., 71 years old, had taught solar energy engineering for 33 years at Rensselaer Polytechnic Institute in Troy, New York. In 2014, Borton adapted a 1906 design to build a 39-ft (11m80) boat, whose cedar strip planking was assembled from October through May with help from middle school and high school students in the Schodack School District in Rensselaer County. He then fitted it with 5kW of solar panels, serving two battery banks. The lithium batteries powered twin Torqeedo Cruise 4.0 electric motors, while conventional lead-acid batteries powered the onboard facilities. That summer the *Solar Sal*, crewed by Borton and his wife Harriet, cruised at 8.3 mph (13.3 kph) from Lockport along the Erie Canal in New York, passing through 72 locks and traveling a total of 650 miles (1,046 km) to deliver 4 tons of recycled cardboard to a paper mill in Mechanicville. Borton is planning to build more boats.[9]

The increasing versatility of electric boats is evidenced by the 63-ft (19 m) catamaran *Spirit of the Sound*, used by the Maritime Aquarium at Norwalk for examining, monitoring and teaching about Long Island Sound. Designed by Incat Crowther of Australia, *Spirit of the Sound* was built in Mamaroneck, New York, at the Robert E. Derecktor, Inc., shipyard, with construction managed and integrated by Alternative Marine Technologies (Amtech). Her hybrid-electric propulsion system was made by BAE Systems, Inc., Corvus Energy and Northern Lights Hybrid Marine. The *Spirit of the Sound* replaced the Aquarium's 40-foot (12 m) 34-year-old diesel-powered trawler, R/V *Oceanic*. Derecktor is now under contract from the City University of New York and the Science and Resilience Institute to build another hybrid-electric research vessel. This latest vessel will be built to USCG (United States Coast Guard) subchapter T regulations and will be used for research and educational purposes, operating out of Jamaica Bay, New York.[10]

In the American and Dutch tradition, solar powerboat racing continued to grow. Hosted by the Yacht Club de Monaco and Solar 1, there was an endurance race of 30 laps around a rather choppy one-nautical-mile circuit on the open sea outside Port Hercules;

a test of maneuverability skills on a slalom course in the YCM Marina; and one-on-one speed duels. Fifteen boats designed and built especially for the event by engineering students from six countries across Europe and Russia competed for the Monte Carlo Cup. Russia followed two weeks later, on July 26, 2014, when a regatta was held at the Luzhniki side of the Moscow River and sponsored by the local Skolkovo School of Management's alumni, the Department of Science, and the Moscow Innovation Development Center. Race teams came from Russian universities and a Dutch solar boat team. Most impressive was Synergy's Team Beluga solar hydrofoil, which had competed at the Monaco Solar Regatta, although the winners were the student team of Samara State Technical University, with Aleksei Belkin of Ryazan Radio Engineering University placing second. The team from Ogarev Mordovia State University announced they were setting up a design office in the field of alternative energy. A second race took place in St. Petersburg on September 19, on the River Neva by the spit of Vasilyevsky Island, and included a team from the city's Polytechnic University. Eugene Kazanov, the president of the organizing committee of the Solar Regatta, stated that 80 to 90 percent of the boats were made up from Russian component parts.[11]

The DONG Energy Solar Challenge 2014 Solar Championships in 2014 lasted 10 days, and by a total of forty crews, including teams from Belgium, Brazil, China, Indonesia, and Germany, raced the Friesland route of more than 220 km. The CLAFIS *Furia Mark III* won for the second time. The TU Delft solar boat team entered their latest 5.57-m T-T hydrofoil, weighing just 90 kg and using 1750 Wattpeak, comparable to the power used by a frying pan. Piloted by Tim Heijnen, the boat's time totaled 12:01:00 for the race. Separately, with Luuk van Litsenburg in the cockpit, the solar hydrofoil clocked a record 51 kph (32 mph) on a test run measured by his team.[12]

The Friesland event has sparked off developments in other parts of the world. In Auckland, New Zealand, since designing the trimaran hull of the *Furia I* for the 2008 Friesland Solar Race, yacht designer Tim Clissold has developed his 7-m *Elotri* (Electric Trimaran) hull, used in the 23-ft *Solar Star*, built in Arizona. In 2012 its prototype navigated the Erie Canal, and then ran for 17 hours nonstop during the Solar Spectacular on Tempe Town Lake in Phoenix.[13]

The technology of the Friesland racing hydrofoils and their lithium batteries has also been taken to Sweden, where it is being incorporated into the *Candela*, a 25-ft (7m50) carbon-fiber retractable hydrofoil-hulled electric speedboat, capable of a range of 3 hours at 28 mph (45 kph) and a top speed of 45 mph (72 kph). The Speed Boat AB design team, led by Gustave Hasselskog of Lidingö, Sweden, comprises experts from France, the Netherlands, and Denmark. By the fall of 2016, the Swedish Energy Agency, Energimyndigheten, decided to support *Candela* with a 4.9 MSEK grant to enable them to develop a serial production model. At time of writing, the Candela speedboat can now rise up regularly onto its foils and make regular extended trials with a range of close to 2 hours in 25 knots and a hull that makes no slamming in 1-meter waves. Serial production is planned for the end of 2017.

With the trend towards the autonomous driverless electric automobile, it was perhaps inevitable that boats would follow suit. In October 2014, 15 university teams from Australia, Japan, Singapore, South Korea and the United States competed in the inaugural Maritime RobotX Challenge. Jointly organized by the Association for Unmanned Vehicle Systems International (USA) and the National University of Singapore's (NUS) Faculty of Engineering and Science Centre, the challenge consisted of fitting out a standard 16-ft

The solar-powered hydrofoil TU *Delft* (bottom) and the *Furia*, two of the successful competitors in the Friesland Solar Boat Race, 2015 (TU Delft).

(4m88) rigid inflatable catamaran, powered by two electric trolling outboards, with sensors, computers and software. The roboboats were required to complete a highly sophisticated orienteering course in Marina Bay in both searing heat and torrential downpour conditions. The winning team comprised students from MIT's Department of Mechanical Engineering and Computer Science and Artificial Intelligence Laboratory (CSAIL) as well as students from Olin College of Engineering.[14] The second RobotX Challenge, organized by RoboNation and the Polynesian Voyaging Society, was held in December 2016 on Sand Island, Honolulu, Hawaii; 200 students from 13 universities in Australia, Japan, the USA, Singapore and South Korea took part. The winner was the team from the University of Florida.

Alongside this, in the Netherlands, mechanical engineering students at the Energy & Automation Lab at Centre of Expertise of the Rotterdam University of Applied Sciences are working on autonomous and zero-emission floating drones to clean up the plastic soup in the oceans. Their laboratory is in the port area of the former shipyard of the Rotterdam Drydock Company (RDM). Their Smart Energy Systems Demonstrator is called an Aquabot; part of Project Aquabots is a battle between two teams of mechanical engineering students. They battle each other with their autonomous and zero-emission floating drones to clean up the plastic soup in the oceans.[15] In February 2016, a demonstration of two Aquabots, *Eindmass* and *Anna*, revealed that there is still work to be carried out on the onboard software before the Aquabots become a practical reality.

In May 2016, Damon McMillan and a team launched *SeaCharger*, an 8-ft (2.3-m), 60-lb. (27-kg) autonomous underwater pod monohull decked by two 100-watt solar panels, into the Pacific Ocean from Half Moon Bay, California. Forty-one days later they stood in a harbor on the Big Island, Hawaii, as *SeaCharger* came to shore, completing a journey of 2,413 miles. *SeaCharger* used off-the-shelf electronics as much as possible. The brains of the boat were an Arduino Mega, an Adafruit GPS, a satellite modem from Rock Seven, a compass from Devantech, and a battery protection/charging circuit from AA Portable Power Corp. Information was sent back to the team every two days. In July, McMillan then re-programmed the boat and sent it on its way to Aotearoa, New Zealand—a distance of 4,400 miles (7,080 km). Disappointingly, in January 2017, after 155 days at sea, during its journey from Lae, Papua New Guinea, *SeaCharger's* rudder failed—just 300 miles (482 km) from its final destination. It was rescued by the crew of Liberian freighter *Sofrana Tourville*.[16]

A project called IntCatch, funded by six major European universities and 14 other private and public companies and institutions and coordinated by London's Brunel University, are using fleets of r/c controlled AI electric water-drones to collect and analyze water quality in some of Europe's most important rivers and lakes. The project started in June 2017 in Peschiera del Garda near Verona and is scheduled to continue until the end of January 2020.

During the previous decades, solar-powered boats had always made use of the technology available. In 1983, Professor Martin Green and co-workers at the University of New South Wales had made the first silicon cell to convert electricity to sunlight with more than 18 percent efficiency (18 percent of the incident sunlight energy converted to electricity). In 1985, they increased this to 20 percent, the photovoltaic "4-minute mile," using a cell structure that used the same type of expensive processing as in microelectronics. Inventing the "buried contact solar cell," by 1989 they had increased efficiency to 25 percent. In May 2016, with Dr. Mark Keevers, Professor Green developed a new solar cell configuration which has pushed sunlight-to-electricity conversion efficiency to 34.5 percent—establishing a new world record for unfocused sunlight and nudging closer to the theoretical limits for such a device. Green's team is currently using nanotechnology to continue to improve solar cells, with the target of making solar cells with 74 percent efficiency. The effects that this will have on the autonomy of solar boats should not be underestimated.[17]

As this book goes to press, a number of battery companies are claiming exponential progress with new types of battery, with energy densities climbing to a mercurial 50 Wh/Kg (Advance Battery Concepts' bipolar lead-acid), 300Wh/kg (Dyson-Sakti 3's solid-state lithium battery), and approaching 1000 Wh/Kg (grapheme-based super capacitor lithium-oxygen prototypes). Linked to 100 megasiemens/meter wireless motors, the range autonomy for GPS-guided e-boats looks very promising indeed.

With its production still in Dalian, northeastern China, ODC Marine launched its diesel-electric Nyami range, designed by French architects, with a passenger capacity from 12 up to 200 pax. The Nyami *Agrion*, a 14-m (46 ft) solar-electric 70-passenger ferryboat, operates from Evian les Bains beside Switzerland's Lake Geneva. Her twin 40kW motors give *Agrion* a cruising speed of 6 hours at 6.5 knots, with a top speed of 8 knots. ODC is nearing completion of a fourth 100-pax hybrid to join her sister ships in Corsica.[18]

One of the grails of electric boating has been the fast recharge—instead of in several hours, in several minutes. Magnus Eriksson, a submarine designer and engineer of Stockholm, determined to bring Swedish marine technology to the surface. With Joachim Skoogberg and Hans Thornell, Eriksson set up Echandia to take an electric Pod motor and retrofit a Djurgarden 8 yacht as a test bed which they renamed *Electra*. One of the innovations was the ability to super-recharge the batteries in ten minutes. With funding to the tune of €800,000 by the Swedish Energy Authority and Stockholm City Council, Echandia Marine set up Green City Ferries to retrofit the *Movitz*, a 23-m (75 ft) 100-pax ferryboat with 125 kW electric Pod motors, using super-advanced swift-recharge nickel-metal-hydride (NiMH) 180 kWh batteries from the Swedish company Nilar. As systems integrator, Eriksson's round-the-clock support of the project in the summer of 2014 allowed the system to be installed within a few months and on schedule. From August 2014 the *Movitz* was operating a central route between Solna Strand and Gamla Stan, the heart of Stockholm's Old Town. The supercharging station was in downtown Stockholm. The ability to supercharge for ten minutes and then to operate for an hour is an extremely important development for the passenger ferry industry, which operates on a strict timetable. Furthermore, it reduces the need for large battery packs. The ferry can charge while passengers embark and disembark. During 2016, operators around the world were observing *Movitz*'s performance.[19]

In January 2015, Feadship, a cooperative venture between two shipyards, Royal Van Lent Shipyard and Koninklijke De Vries Scheepsbouw, launched the 83.5-m (274 ft) *Savannah* by CG Design. They claim it as "the world's first hybrid superyacht." The "Breathe" propulsion system has been optimized to five operation modes from diesel to diesel-electric combinations to fully electric—courtesy of a 30-ton lithium-ion battery bank capable of holding a million watts of electricity. Another departure is the installation of a single Wärtsilä main diesel engine running the electrically powered screws. These consist of a single central propeller nacelle and an in-line Azimuthing thruster set in the slipstream.[20]

Benetti has produced a hybrid diesel-electric version of its Supreme 108 tri-deck motor yacht with *My Paradise* with its diesels now linked to two 35 kW electric motors.

In southwest Turkey in 2015, following their establishment four years before, Naval Yachts/Naval Studio, headed by Dinçer Dinç and based in Antalya, on the Mediterranean coast of that country, launched their 50-ft (15 m) *GreeNaval* aluminum hull hybrid motor yacht, fitted with the twin Electric Yacht QuietTorque™ 30.0 system, with its 4 different propulsion options.[21]

Again in aluminum, the Symphony Boat Company of Duluth, Minnesota, has incorporated a 20-ft aluminum hull with bio-based bamboo and Okume timber fittings produced by Lamboo® Technologies of Litchfield, Illinois, to create the Torqeedo Deep Blue 80i 66 kW-engined Six-1 Conductor, capable of a top speed of 27 mph.[22]

As an electric auxiliary for a classic boat replica, none is perhaps more noticeable than for a full-scale replica of the French 44-m (144 ft), 32-gun three-masted frigate, the *Hermione*, which in 1780 ferried the Marquis de Lafayette across the Atlantic to Boston to help the Americans in their war for independence from the British. In 1997, the French decided to build a full-scale working replica of this seminal craft in one of the two dry docks beside the Corderie Royale at Rochefort. One challenge to the builders was that the French had no blueprints of the boat. The project's marine historian eventually tracked down British-drawn plans for one of the three sister frigates of the *Hermione* in Greenwich, England! While the original took less than one year to build, the replica took 18 years. Before she could navigate, *Hermione* was obliged to be equipped with two Pod motors, 300 kW each, with a permanent magnet electric motor developing 300 kW at 1500 rpm. These would facilitate her movements in harbors and enable her to respect international regulations. These MML55 units, as well as the control system, were supplied by Masson Marine of Saint Denis les Sens. In April 2015 *Hermione* crossed the Atlantic under sail, arriving in New York in June, returning to France in August.[23]

Much younger but still worth mentioning, Finland's oldest ferry, the *Föri*, which had been plying its trade across the Aura River between Turku and Åbo since 1904, has been converted to all-electric propulsion by local boatyard Mobimar using two Visedo Marine permanent magnet motor drives and two Visedo Marine DC/DC converters to control the ferry's DC grid.

The same month, Andrey Igorevich Melnichenko unveiled his £260 million hybrid-electric superyacht *Sailing Yacht A*. Melnichenko, whose net worth is estimated at £6 billion ($9 billion), founded the fertilizer producer EuroChem. Measuring 469 ft (142.81 m), with three freestanding carbon fiber rotating masts 300 ft high (100 m), *Sailing Yacht A* is the world's biggest sailing ship, with eight decks, an underwater observation room, and an onboard electric submarine. The steel hull was developed by Dykstra Naval Architects and designed by Philippe Starck to accommodate 20 guests and a crew of 54. It was built at the Nobiskrug yard at Rendesburg, Germany. Propulsion consists of a variable-speed hybrid diesel-electric package made up of two MTU 3,600 kW diesel engines, and two 4,300 kW electric motors, driving shafts ending in highly skewed 5-bladed Andritz Hydro/Escher Wyss controllable-pitch lineshaft twin-screw propellers. *Sailing Yacht A* is expected to cruise under power at 16 knots with an expected range of 5,320 nautical miles and will have a top speed of 21 knots.[24]

Another retrofit was to *Enza*, the 30-m (98 ft) racing-sailing catamaran once skippered by the legendary New Zealander Peter Blake. Renamed the *Energy Observer*, she has been converted into a zero-emission motor yacht for a global circumnavigation by a team of naval architects and the CEA-Liten research institute in the French city of Grenoble, working with Fred Dahirel and Marsaudon Composites in Lorient. Her re-equipment includes two 220 volt e-motors, small vertical-axis wind turbines, kites, solar panels and battery-recharging propellers, with an autonomy of four hours. *Energy Observer* fits into the OceanoScientific® program sponsored by UNESCO, whose purpose is the study of a dozen parameters to the ocean-atmosphere interface on maritime or rarely explored routes in order to enable the international scientific community to better understand the causes and consequences of climate change. This data, collected automatically every six seconds, will be sent free via satellite to researchers worldwide. Crewed by experienced yacht racing skipper Victorien Erussard, and Jacques Delafosse, a documentary filmmaker and professional scuba diver, the *Energy Observer* will soon embark on its round-the-world trip to 50 countries, with 101 stopovers and 2,000 days of sailing including the Mediterranean, then the Caribbean, the Galápagos, the west coast of the USA, Asia, etc.[25]

More than 150 exhibitors were on display at the Electric & Hybrid Marine World Expo, June 23–25, 2015, at Amsterdam RAI. Each showcased the very latest ideas, concepts, technologies and components for electric and hybrid marine applications.

REAP Systems Ltd. (Renewable Energy & Advanced Propulsion), led by Dennis Doerffel, in collaboration with the University of Southampton and eight industrial partners including Marine South East, have developed hybrid electrical vessel propulsion with integrated motor assist (HEVIMA). With sufficient crowd-funding, the first trial may be for hybrid water taxis in Venice, Italy.

Mark Wüst of Grove Boats once again helped to advance hydrogen fuel cell boat progress with a Hydroxy 3000, the *ZEN* (Zero Emission dans la Navigation), a 7-meter (23 ft) catamaran powered by an Alcoa aluminum-air battery as developed by the Israeli company Phinergy, and installed by Heig-VD University, under the supervision of Prof. Jean-Francois Affolter. The idea of releasing energy contained within metal such as aluminum or zinc was not new, but in the past nobody had succeeded in developing a system that could utilize this energy efficiently or over any extended time. Then Arie Zaban and Ernst Khasin, two Israeli electrochemists at Bar Ilan University, overcame the main obstacles presented by metal-air technology through their innovative nano-materials research. In 2008, the technology rights were transferred to Phinergy. In 2009, back at Alcoa, an electric vehicle with an aluminum-air battery achieved a record distance of 330 km (186 mi), at which point continuation for a similar distance required no more than a "refuel" with water to recover the electrolyte in the battery. The aluminum-air battery used in Hydroxy 3000 contains just 33 lbs (15 kg) of aluminum, which provides about 25 hours of additional navigation time, for a given navigation profile. Initial tests were made on Switzerland's Lake Neuchâtel.[26]

Superyacht designers continued to welcome hydrogenetic propulsion on board. In July 2015, PI Super Yachts of Devon launched its trimaran *Dragonship 25*. Designed by Gillian Gray Naval Architects, it incorporates Hydrogenesis "Blue Box" technology powering electric propulsion and solar PV panels on the coach roof and integrated into the Autosail wingsail. PI Super Yachts CEO Will O'Hara has called it the "Baby-Dragon," ultimately planning an 80 m (263 ft) trimaran called the *Dragonship 80*, that will also feature the Autosail and Hydrogenesis systems, as well as a folding-wing keel that narrows its width for entering ports.[27]

Michael Stusch of H2-Yachts has conceived of a 62-m (200 ft) superyacht, rigged with a fully electric system with a liquid organic hydrogen carrier (LOHC) as the energy storage and low-maintenance management for all systems to give it a range of over 6,000 nm at 10 knots. Andrea Valllicelli and Fincantieri Shipyard are ready to build a 75-meter (250 ft) fuel cell SWATH yacht, for which Nuvera has been commissioned to produce and deliver eight of its Orion™ fuel cell stacks (total power 260 kW).[28]

From the mega to the micro, until now surfing and wakeboarding had depended on the whimsical wind and waves of the sea, but with the advent of small high-density lithium batteries and compact motors, a new era was born. This came in the form of the MXP-3 seventy-nine, an electric surfboard, developed by Markus Schilcher of DK Constructions in Oberammergau, Germany. His Waterwolf MXP-3 is a board that untethers the user from wave and wind conditions and lets him "make your own wave." It's a sport that's best described as electric moto-surfing with a top speed of 26–30 kph (16–18 mph). Weighing in at 53 lb (24 kg), the MXP-3 is powered by a 5 kW, water-cooled motor driving a custom-designed stern propeller. The 20 Ah lithium-ion battery, which is housed in a watertight case, provides enough run time for about 20 to 30 minutes of water play or 8 km (5 mi) of range before requiring up to a three-hour charge. However, a couple more exchangeable batteries provide a day's moto-surfing. The moto-surfer controls his MXP-3's output and speed via a Bluetooth handheld throttle, referring to the top-mounted LCD screen for speed and battery information. As a safety precaution, the board has a magnetic emergency kill switch that's activated at the pull of the wrist leash. Should the rider fall off, the tug of the strap pulls the magnetic connector out, cutting power immediately. The MXP-3 comes in five colors: petrel, blue, yellow, red or white.[29]

At the same time, Philip Werner at Lund University, Stockholm, Sweden, a professional wakeboarder known for organizing large wakeboard events in Malmö and elsewhere, set up Radinn AB (Radical Innovation). Werner assembled a team of engineers to develop an "extreme sport" jet-propelled wireless-remote electric wakeboard, with a 30-minute life from its 64 lb (29 kg) fast-recharge replaceable lithium batteries for full-speed operation at nearly 50 kph (30 mph) and, of course, longer if you go a little slower. The thrust of its waterjet is 700 nm. The carbon and Kevlar composite e-wakeboard is 1.90 meters (7 ft) long by 80 cm (32 in) wide. There is an on-board computer system Mobile-app for iOS and Android, a GPS, and magnetic safety switches. Combining the speed and agility of wakeboarding with the freedom of surfing, the Wakejet Cruise allows for riding in the ocean, sea, lake or even up a rapid.[30]

The third company to launch a range of electric surfboards is Iñigo Sobradillo Benguría's start-up, Aquila (= Eagle), a spin-off from the R&D company Bizintek Innova, based at Erandio, in northern Spain's Basque region, whose local Bay of Biscay is known for its surfing. A Mosfet wireless system controls the brushless motor with energy from swiftly replaceable Samsung 18650 lithium-ion battery packs, normally used for power tools. Three Aquila boards are available: the 2m30 (91 in) Manta is aimed at beginners and those who enjoy relaxed cruising over flat water. Its top speed of 33 kph (21 mph) is the lowest of the three options, but it also has the longest battery life at 30 minutes. The 2m45 (98 in) Carver, designed for high-speed slaloming across the surface of the water, has a top speed of 71 kph (44 mph). Aimed at freestyle riders, the 1m85 (73 in) Blade is designed to provide optimal maneuverability. Weighing only 18 kg, it has a top speed of 53 kph (33 mph).[31]

Finally, Sashay GmbH of Hamburg, Germany, led by Benjamin Sashay Köhnsen and Dr. Ing. Olaf Jacobsen, has designed and are beginning to manufacture the Lampuga range of electro-jet powered *inflatable* surfboards, which can reach speeds of up to 29 mph (52 kph). A modular design lets you swap the jet drive between four different hull styles—from the standard 6.5-foot (2-m) Air, the Boost, the Rescue and the Shuttle. Once used, the surfboard can be deflated and stacked in the back of your automobile.

For decades, noisy waterbikes had been annoying beach goers. In 2010 Jérémy Benichou persuaded the Mayenne Laval Technopole, based in France's Loire region, to back him in the development of a silent electric waterbike. Setting up Aqualeo, he produced the Gliss-Speed, a 2.49-m (8 ft) two-seater joystick-controlled electric water Go-Kart that manages a speed of almost 30 kph, using a 2.5 kW motor and 3 kW lithium-ion battery pack. Autonomy is between 2 to 4 hours. Aqualeo's Benichou has set up a distribution network in the Caribbean, Dubai and Oman, resulting in the sales of over 300 Gliss-Speeds.[32]

The *Jetfoiler eFoil,* is a single-hydrofoiling electric surfboard developed by ex-kiteboard professional, Don Montague and his team at kai concepts in Alameda located on Alameda Island and Bay Farm Island, adjacent to and south of Oakland and east of San Francisco across the San Francisco Bay.

Another small watercraft is the SeaScape 12. Having developed BionX to sell electric drive systems for bicycles, in 2011 Austrian-born Frank Stronach of Aurora, Ontario, Canada, and Manfred Gingl of Weiz, Austria, decided to transfer their technology to a personal watercraft they called the SeaScape 12 (12 ft/36 cm) for both fresh and saltwater venues. Weighing in at 485 lb (220 kg), the SeaScape 12 has four selectable electric-assist levels in "eco" or "performance" mode: Eco-Mode 30 percent (Cruise: Assist Level 1) or 60 percent (Tour: Assist Level 2), or Performance Mode 100 percent (Ambition: Assist Level 3) or 300 percent (Power: Assist Level 4). Overall length: 3,645 mm. The manufacturers expect to build thousands of units.[33]

Another fun application arrived in the form of the Quadrofoil Q2, a 3-m (9.8 ft), 100 kg (220 lb) electrically-powered pleasure hydrofoil. It was designed and built in Slovenska Bistrica, a town south of Maribor in eastern Slovenia, by a team of Slovenian engineers led by Simon Pivec, together with fellow engineers Marjan Rožman and Marjan Arh. They used biomimicry to develop the shape of the minimum-drag aluminium C-foils. The Quadrofoil Q2 is a seafaring coupé, with two faux-leather seats, steering-wheel-mounted acceleration and brake controls, and a touchscreen display on the wheel, which keeps you informed about battery power, range, speed and consumption. It also functions as a detachable key, without which the engine can't be started. The company claims that its hollow composite hull is "unsinkable." By 2015, there were two versions. With a 3.7 kW motor and 4.5 kWh batteries, the standard Q2A Electric lifts out of the water at 7 mph (12 kph) and can accelerate to a top speed of 18 mph (30 kph) and a battery range of 31 miles (50 km). The Q2S Electric Limited Edition, with its £17,586 price tag, has a 5.5 kW motor and longer-lasting 10 kWh batteries, and is said to be good for a top speed of 40 kph (21 knots) above the water and a range of up to 62 miles (100 km) per two-hour recharge of its battery. A limited run of 100 Q2S quadrofoils was planned to ship in May 2016, while the Q2A was available in mid–2015 for $18,500. The current foils are suitable for speeds up to 80 kph. In cooperation with Fakulteta za Energetiko (Faculty of Energy Technology) in Krškothe, the company is developing its own outboard motor and propeller with variable pitch, which it believes will be one of the most efficient in the world. The propeller and 12 kW outboard were ready later in 2015, and presumably a version will be available in the not-too-distant future with a top speed more than double the current version. In February 2016, Invertor d.o.o., Quadrofoil's authorized dealer for Croatia, signed a new agreement, making them the first authorized distributor in the EU. The first mass production Quadrofoil came off the factory line on July 3, by which time the company announced it had signed up an international network of 11 dealers.[34]

Alain Thébault, French skipper of the 50-knots multihull sailing hydrofoil called the *Hydroptère*, has been working with Swedish partner Anders Bringdal, the first wind surfer in the world registered for an average speed of 50 knots, on a twin e-motor quadrofoil commuter craft called *Les Bulles de Mer* (*The Sea Bubbles*) for use on the rivers of the world's main cities (Paris, London, San Francisco). Following sponsorship by Henri Seydoux of the drone manufacturing company Parrott, design and construction of the prototype by Décision SA began in Lausanne, Switzerland. The first prototype *Sea Bubbles* was launched in March and the first trials took place in La Ciotat Bay in the Mediterranean, followed by tests on the River Seine in Paris. The use of *Sea Bubbles*, capable of 18 kph, for daily commuting, should take the strain from the cities' circular roads. Initially, there will be drivers, but eventually the *Sea Bubbles* can become autonomous.[35]

Added to this gaggle of small fun e-boats, even if more static, is the FloatBall, a 10-seater Torqeedo Cruise 2.0-engined boat looking like an igloo: it features flat-screen TVs and 4G WiFi, a hydraulic ceiling, and panoramic windows, and can be equipped with LED backlighting that provides a night view. In 2006, Peter Jacops formed the Whisper Boat Building Academy for the Deaf in Khayelitsha, and before long they had come up with what they called Time Whisper Ball. With the help of catamaran builder Wayne Robertson Yachts, some sixteen of them were built and floated around the V&A waterfront in Cape Town, South Africa, during the 2010 Soccer World Cup and for 6 months after it. The Academy won the South African Boating Award 2010 for most innovative product of the year, renamed *FloatBall*. A business was created in 2013 by a group of entrepreneurs in the nautical, sports and digital media markets, led by Brazilian Giovanni Luigi, former CEO of Yacht Collection and a Mastercard director. More than 15,000 families already have experienced FloatBall voyages in Rio de Janeiro, Brazil. Additionally, thousands more from 80 different countries had the experience of sightseeing during the 2014 FIFA World Cup in Brazil this year. In 2014, Zoo Miami, in partnership with Aquatic Sports LLC, took delivery of a FloatBall fleet at the Amazon Lake at "Amazon and Beyond." More fleets to come.[36]

Off the coast of Africa, on the island of Madagascar, from November 2015, the solar catamaran *Zanarano* (= water baby in Malagache) went into service on the Pangalanes Canal from Tampina, a fishing village located on the east coast of the island. Led by Jean-François Guy, supported by the NGO Man and the Environment, its propulsion system, developed in Brittany, uses a 4 kW outboard and 12 AGM batteries.

Once again Venice, Italy, with its involvement in electric boats going back over a century, stepped up. On April 14, 2013, i/c motorboats were banned from Venice from 10 a.m. to 3 p.m., part of a larger attempt to halt the eroding and sinking of the world-famous city. Man-powered gondolas, electric and hybrid electric motorboats were exempt. A representative from Italia Nostra, an association working to preserve the city, said: "We hope it'll make Venetians more aware of how lovely the city could be if we insist on boats only with electric power."[37] Currently, there are around 7,000 small craft registered to traverse Venice's waterways. Eventually, officials would like to see a switch to electric-powered or man-powered vessels. Soon after, Electrosmartboats of Venice proposed a scheme to make their canal city more sustainable. Part of this is the VEBS (Venice Electric

Boat Sharing), a pilot program that was due to start in 2016 and replicating the principle of car sharing already existing in many European cities. Using 6-m (20 ft) electric boats, inhabitants of the Venice Lagoon will have the chance to experiment a new, clean type of transportation for their daily needs. Cleaning up Venice will also involve retrofitting goods transport barges and garbage collection boats with serial hybrid, electro-diesel).[38]

Alongside this, Moreno Vizianello had continued his shipyard's collaboration with the waterbus company Alilaguna. In the summer of 2014, he launched the Siemens diesel-electric *Scossa* (= Shock), propelled by an 180 kW 3,000 rpm Siemens with 32 19-volt Valence batteries and a 200 kW at 2200 rpm (equivalent to 272 horsepower) diesel SISU 74 CTIM and a ZF Aquadrive. Almost immediately afterwards, work began on what became known as the Hepic. With funding from the Veneto Region, during 2015 construction of "HEPIC—Hydrogen Electric Passenger Venice Boat" was run by a joint venture called "Hydrogen Park Water Green Mobility." The H2 park in Marghera has been in existence for ten years and here is a new application. The technology is provided by Enel Distribuzione (Italy's electricity provider) for the electricity infrastructure and Dolomitech, producer of thirty hydrogen buses used at the World Nordic Skiing held in Val di Fiemme in 2013. The 40-pax, 15-m (50 ft) *Hepic* is fitted with a 200-kw triphase AC motor, alimented by 70 kWh lithium batteries in three packs; each pack has a weight of 350 kg (772 lb), for a total weight of embarked traction batteries of 1050 Kg (2314 lb). For the 60 kW PEM, the hydrogen is stored on-board at a pressure of 350 bar in 4 large carbon fiber cylinders, each of 2 meters (6.5 ft) in length and 40 centimeters (16 in) in diameter. With its specially designed four-bladed propeller, *Hepic*'s top speed at full load is 30 kph (20 mph). The *Hepic* was launched in December 2016 and is expected to undergo shakedown trials this year in the Venice lagoon.[39]

On the occasion of the visit to Venice of Ms. Chiyo Ikeda, senior staff member of the Tokyo metropolitan government, a workshop sponsored by Hydrogen Park and Veneto Innovazione was held in Marghera on November 23, 2015, with the aim to discuss the future of hydrogen technologies. Ms. Ikeda provided an overview of Tokyo's investment plan toward realizing a hydrogen-based society, to be implemented within the next five years for the 2020 Olympic Games in Tokyo. Soon after, the Japanese automobile manufacturer Toyota, who had launched their Mirai, the world's first hydrogen-fuel-celled sedan, newly elected world "Green Car" of 2016, signed an agreement with the city of Venice, whereby the latter would undertake auto-sharing trials in return for fueled boats such as the Hepic being used at the 2020 Games.[40]

As it had being doing since the 1990s, the French town of Nantes continued to pioneer electric boating. In 2015 it launched the 8m50 (28 ft) fuel-celled ferry *NavHybus*, propelled by two combustible hydrogen fuel cells. It was realized by a 7-strong consortium, including Ship Studio, Ruban Bleu, Nantes Polytechnic, and Jean-François le Bert of Mission Hydrogène. *NavHyBus* is part of a bigger project of Mission Hydrogène working with the local Loire Region called FILHyPyNE: to create a 12-m (40 ft) multi-purpose fuel-cell fishing vessel. A 200 kW electric motor will be fueled by a hydrogen fuel cell generation of about 210 kW and electric batteries. Such a fishing boat could carry a reservoir of 120 kg (265 lb) of hydrogen.[41]

With the potential of more and more transports using fuel-cell technology, in 2014, Vuosaari Harbor at the Port of Helsinki, Finland, set up a hydrogen fueling station supplied by the national gas company Woikoski Oy, for private cars, buses—and boats. Some 20 years after Stein Viken had courageously set up a Norwegian Electric Boat Association,

Ulf Tudem of Sandefjord, Norway, began work on a battery-powered 30-knot, zero-emission, air-supported electric ferryboat, project-named the BB Green. Spearheaded by his company Effect Ships International, a three-year collaborative R&D project was in part funded by the 7th Framework Program of the European Commission Fast. Four EU countries are involved, with a €3.3 billion budget, 2.3 billion of it from European Union. Following tank testing of two ultra-low-resistance ASV candidate hulls at SSPA in Gothenburg, Sweden, the demonstrator prototype was built in Devinycell, a carbon and Vinylester resin sandwich at the BJB/Latitude Yachts, located in Riga, Latvia. The full-scale BB Green vessel measures 22 m (72 ft) × 6 m (20 ft) and could carry from 60 up to 100-pax (with or without bicycles). It has a fast-recharge 400 kWh lithium-ion titianate battery pack developed by Emrol bvba of Belgium. Echandia Marine Sweden is the electric drivelines integrator. The vessel has three main propulsion units: two 280 kW (continuous rating) contra-rotating motors for pod propulsion, and one electric motor to power the ASV lift fan system, where less than 50 kW would be required. The power requirement for the lift fan is between 40 and 100 kW depending on loading, sea conditions and speed. In a normal scenario, approximately 80 percent of the vessel's operational displacement is supported on a cushion of air, reducing the hull/water resistance by as much as approximately 40 percent. A commercial BB Green vessel, with a 400 kWh battery, operated at high speed (25–30 knots), will typically have a range between recharging of approximately 14 nm (26 km). Provided sufficient shore power, the battery may be recharged in approximately 20 minutes. Launched in Latvia in June 2016, by late October, *Ariel BB Green* was unveiled in Stockholm, Sweden, and showed herself capable of an impressive top speed of 35 mph (56 kph), creating considerable interest from ferry operators in northern European countries. On April 28, 2017, the decision was made to build the commercial version of *BB Green*, a 90-seater, at Rotterdam shipyard. It is expected to go into service in Stockholm in September 2018—its speed should reduce the intercity trip to 40 minutes. A second-generation fuel-cell *BB Green* is now being designed.

The Griffon Hoverwork *995ED*, another air cushion vehicle also known as the hovercraft, whose origins go back fifty years, finally embraced electric power. Designed by a team led by Mark Downer in Woolston, Southampton, southern England, the 8.6-m, 8-pax sees two standard hybrid power modules containing a 67-kW Ford Tiger diesel engine providing lift through highly efficient fans and supplying the two 45-kW lightweight axial thrust electrical motors. No batteries are involved. The *995ED* went on trials in August 2016 and is still looking for clients.

Also in Norway, the 80-m (263 ft) *Ampère*, the world's first fully electric passenger/ro-ro cargo ship, went into operation by Norled between Larvik and Oppedal in Sognefjord. *Ampère* has the capacity to carry 120 cars and 360 passengers and runs 34 times a day with a crossing time of 20 minutes. Between its trips the Siemens 1MWh lithium-polymer battery pack on board enables a ten-minute recharge. Built by Fjellstrand shipyard, it is propelled by two 450 kW electric motors. *Ampère* was put into operation in May 2015, and has traveled a distance equivalent to more than 1.5 times around the world at the equator.[42]

Also magnificently "retro" in multiple varnished wood, the Boesch 710 Ascona de Luxe Electric Power, powered by an 80 kW or 100 kW three-phase Piktronik Synchronmotor and 159 Ah lithium polymer batteries, was one of six different models available.

Torqeedo's next step for its advanced Deep Blue propulsion system was to team up with both Frauscher Bootswerft GmbH of Oberosterreich, Austria, for the latter's 740

Mirage Air that premièred in July 2015. The Deep Blue motor concept is also available for Frauscher's boat models 650 Alassio, 680 Lido, 740 Mirage, 740 Mirage Air and 750 St. Tropez.[43] Simultaneously Torqeedo also teamed with Nimbus Boat Sweden AB to develop the world's first Coupé Cruiser with serial hybrid propulsion. Sweden's Nimbus 27 e-power had been the first large electrically-powered boat from the drawing board to the market. Now the 11-meter Nimbus 305 Coupé e-power, fitted with twin 80 hp Deep Blue Hybrid motors, will be fed by banks of automotive-grade lithium batteries to provide energy for propulsion of the 6.5-ton boat, and more than 50 kWh of electric power are available also for auxiliary equipment on board. A cruising range of up to 20 nautical miles is possible without using a generator, which is always available for extended range.[44] Ever innovative, Nimbus Boats Sweden AB has also signed up with Scandinavian fuel cell company PowerCell Sweden AB to equip an electrified Nimbus 305 Coupe with fuel cells. The aim is to provide the demo vessel with two PowerCell MS-20, a fuel cell system based on the stack PowerCell S2, totaling 50kW, which is equivalent to about 70 horsepower, or a Power Cell S3, 100-kW, which corresponds to 134 hp.

In 2014, Swedish ferry operator Ballerina commissioned an electric ferryboat to transport residents between Stockholm, Nacka and Lidingö. The 23-ft (7-m) *ES Sjövägen* was designed and built in Denmark by Faaborg Vaerft together with Principia North AS and Wilhelmsen Technical Solution and built in DIAB's Divinycell H composite. Saft li-ion batteries give energy to two 125-kW motors. In 2015, the boat received the Stockholm County Council's environmental award.

In sharp contrast, Mark Isaacs, entrepreneur from Bay St. Louis, Mississippi, created an electric boat *to fit on top of* his Toyota hybrid-electric sedan: the 8-ft (2.4 m), 65-lb SolarSkiff, powered by a Torqeedo 1003 outboard, can take its pilot sitting in his foldable deckchair at a speed of 5 mph.

It also looked like Torqeedo had a potential rival. Some names never die. Dating back to 1893, 122 years later, in 2015 Elco Motor Yachts of Athens, directed by Steve Lamando, announced it had entered the electric outboard market with units ranging from 5 to 25 hp alongside six patented electric inboard motors ranging up to a 100-hp equivalent. To promote the new engines, Elco launched the Elco Electric Elite Fishing Series. The first stop was Lake Varner in Georgia in June 2015, where with 40 Jon boats taking part, Elco debuted its 9.9 hp electric motor. The Elco was by far the fastest motor on the water; the winners of the tournament, Bobby Hood and Jason Burkholder, took home the 9.9 horsepower motor. Elsewhere twin Elco EP-1000s powered a 40-foot (12 m) dredge tender operated by the New York State Canal Corp. The motors are powered by 36 AGM batteries. Another was the Elco-powered Beneteau Swift Trawler 34 Hybrid. This utilizes the same 425 hp Cummins diesel, transmission, shaft and prop as the standard model. In line with the shaft, a clutch-driven Elco EP-2000 electric motor delivering the equivalent of 20 hp is installed.

So far, the fishing industry has not fully benefitted. In November 2015, Leo LGM of South Korea unveiled five new electric vehicles, including two prototype fishing boats (1.15 ton, 90 hp (67 kW). and 1.85 ton, 20 hp.) at a product launch event in Busan, the largest marine city in Korea. They then took the vehicles to the Grand Pavois yacht show at La Rochelle, France. The newly developed electric power trains had undergone three years of field tests. LGM presented their patented Cartridge Battery (CB) Replacement System, which splits the battery into smaller, lightweight cartridges optimized for easier handling. They also presented The Internet of Things platform for e-boats which is networked and connected with an Android Operating System. These were ready to function under the command of artificial intelligence. Auto Pilot Applications make autonomous sailing possible. Leo's AI-connected positioning application was based on digital GPS, which uses both satellites and mobile networks. LGM's power train is CAN (Controller Area Network)-based, which enables mobile diagnosing between mobile devices and Leo's boats.

Another fishing boat, *Karoline*, aka the Selfa Artic Elmax 1099, has a Siemens 195 kW battery pack on board as well as an electric propulsion motor. While being docked, the vessel will be charged via a 63-Amp 220 V course, with a normal charging time of 6–8 hours. Following testing in Tjeldsundet, Norway, in September 2015, *Karoline* was placed in Troms, Norway, and included in the daily operations of Øra AS.[45]

Karoline is now in service and Selfa Arctic has moved from Selsbakk to the company's factory in Harstad to concentrate on battery production. Combined with PBES in Columbia, Canada, directed Perry, formerly with Corvus Energy Ltd., Hanse Yachts, and Grand Banks Yachts Ltd., PBES is also setting up production facilities in China.

Another solution is in Urk Harbour in the Flevoland Province of the Netherlands: MDV1 *Immanuel* is a revolutionary new 30 m (100 ft) fishing trawler. Built by Hoekman Shipbuilding for the Romkes and Hendrik Kramer families, she is part of the Dutch fishing industry's "Duurzame Visserij" (sustainability fisheries) master plan. Several years ago in the Dutch flatfish fishery in the North Sea, catching one kilogram of fish used up nearly four liters of gas oil. MDV1 *Immanuel* will consume less than half a liter. Her 600 kW propulsion consists of one 500 kW Oswald permanent magnet electric motor turning at 140 rpm and one 100 kW diesel genset. At the end of a perfectly horizontal propeller shaft, her three-bladed wing-profile Kort nozzle rudder-propeller drives measure 3 m (10 ft) in diameter. The "schroefrende" aqua-dynamic bow and hull shape, plus a coating of Sigma Glide anti-fouling, further reduces resistance. Even the novel fishing technique requires much less boat speed and creates less disturbance to the seabed: the nets float just above the bottom. There is also research into the twin rig pulse technique, an unprecedented fishing technique consisting of a trawl net with mild electrical impulses when the fish respond.[46]

In the town in the Gaspésie-Îles-de-la-Madeleine region of Quebec, Canada, Danny Boyle of Ocean Marine in Chandler, is building a hybrid lobster-fishing boat with plans to go 100 percent electric by 2018, and then to entirely replace the ageing local lobster-fishing fleet.

In 2014, perhaps ironically, the offshore petroleum rig industry also received its first diesel-electric supply vessel. Designed by Havyard Design and Solutions in Fosnavaag, N° 126, the Havyard 833 WE ICE platform has c-Hull lines, recently employed in a smaller PSV design (Havyard 832 L WE), and for windmill service, vessels are developed for reduction of fuel consumption and increased comfort for crew in both calm and heavy seas. Measuring 89m70 (294 ft) long, it was constructed at Havyard Ship Technology's yard in Leirvik in Sogn, Norway. Norwegian Electric Systems developed and delivered a QUEST® 2 (Quadro Energy Storage Technology) battery system for the vessel, which will be the first vessel to be equipped with this system. The battery pack supplies power to the main switchboards via an AC/DC converter. When not working for the petroleum industry, the boat would be based at Spitzbergen to carry out patrols in territorial waters of the Artic.[47]

Could even a lifeboat be electric? In February 2015, Verhoef, the Dutch pioneer of aluminum crane-launched freefall lifeboats in areas where rescue from the lifeboat will not take a long time or a long sailing phase, has now successfully performed full-scale tests along the Dutch North Sea Coast with the first freefall lifeboat, powered by an electric motor and an advanced type of li-ion battery set. Tests showed already the immediate benefit, the highest level of reliability and improved human comfort, as the electric-powered engine does not make any noise.[48]

In spring 2016, the Royal N.V. Texels Eigen Stoomboot Onderneming (TESO) put their sustainable ferry *Texelstroom* into service between Den Helder and the islands of Texel in the Netherlands. The 443 feet (135 m) long, 1,750-passenger, 350-vehicle double-ended ferry, built at the LaNaval Shipyard in Bizkaia, Spain, has an advanced energy management system—operating principally on gas, but also with a Corvus lithium-ion battery energy storage system and solar auxiliary power and the capability to run solely on diesel.

Soon after, Corvus announced that, based on experience from 50+ vessels currently utilizing a Corvus ESS, totaling over 35MWh installed and 1 million operating hours, they had developed their safety-proof Orca Energy Storage System (ESS) with its cell-level thermal runaway isolation. It has already been selected by Halvorsen for the retrofit of the 1990, 211-ft (64.4 m) Norwegian fisheries and environmental research vessel MS *Johan Hjort*.

In Denmark, the shipbuilder Søby began construction of the world's largest battery-operated ferryboat. It will be used to transport vehicles and passengers between Ærø Island and the mainland of Denmark. The Finnish electric drive train specialist VISEDO has been selected as the sole electric-system supplier, while the Swiss manufacturer Leclanché will provide a 4.2 MWh lithium-ion battery system. The e-ferry will be constructed in Denmark, and her sea trials will be conducted during April and May 2017. The initiative is part of the Danish Natura project and is one of the top five projects in the EU Horizon 2020 initiative, a program with a total budget of €21 million.[49]

After five years of campaigning, Le GREENBOAT®, an 18-m (60 ft) long passenger boat with 1m10 (3 ft) draft, its hard chine bows resembling the regional pinnace, has gone into operation on the water of the Bassin d'Arcachon. Godfather to the boat is ex-footballer Jean-Pierre Papin, who achieved his greatest success while playing for Olympique Marseille between 1986 and 1992. Le GREENBOAT® can carry 52 passengers and 20 bicycles. Its hull was built at the Dubourdieu Shipyard at Gujan-Mestras using timber from the regional Landes Forest: layers of pine and on-board furniture in acacia. Motorization is hybrid-electric with two 120 kW BAUDOUIN 4W105S diesel engines coupled to two 37 kW LEROY SOMER LS160 electric motors, giving top speeds of 15.5 knots and 5 knots, respectively. There are 50 kW of Regen batteries. The boat has been in part financed by COBAS, the local Arcachon community. Emmanuel Martin of Dubourdieu plans to convert Le GREENBOAT® to zero emission, working with Symbiocell specialized in hydrogen propulsion.[50]

Once again, automobile technology has been transferred to autoboats. In 2009, Croatian engineer Mate Rimac developed the 600 hp prototype BMW E30 Green Monster electric sportscar, capable of reaching 100 kph from standstill in 3.3 sec and a top speed of 280 kph (174 mph). In 2013 Rimac teamed up with Jure Valant of Bulgarian start-up Cadia Yachts to build the Cadia 34E electric yacht, as designed by Mauro Sculli of Italy and built by Elan Motor Yachts of Obrovac beside the Zrmanja River, Croatia. The 10.2-meter (33 ft) hardtop yacht, weighing in at only 3630 kg, will have a maximum speed of

The Greenboat ferries passengers across the Bassin d'Arcachon (courtesy Dubourdieu).

30 kn (55.5 kph/ 34 mph). Range at full load is calculated to be up to 3h (133km/82 mi) with cruising speed 24 kn (44.4 kph/27.6 mph). A pair of 654 kW electric motors, using 350 kWh of batteries would generate 848 nm of torque.[51]

Adapting the technology of Formula E automobile racing team Amlin-Aguri, headed by Japanese racing driver Aguri Suzuki, VanDutch luxury yacht builder announced a high-performance electric yacht, named the VanDutch 40 Electric.[52]

The Netherlands continue to lead the way. The province of Friesland is aiming to be "the cleanest state in the country" regarding CO2 emissions within ten years from now. As proof, according to the Stifting Elektrysk Farre Frysland, the total number of electric boats of all sorts has grown from 4,699 in 2011 to 13,000 in Spring 2017.

Ambitious targets were set, such as eventually having 10,000 electric vehicles in Friesland. According to the Stifting Elektrysk Farre Frysland, the total number of electric boats of all sorts has grown from 4,699 in 2011 to 13,000 in Spring 2017, including the addition of over 100 charging points.[53]

Several Frisian shipbuilders have specialized in electric boats and a lot of joint research is being conducted by the industry in cooperation with scientific institutions.

HappyWhale was founded in 2015 by two boat-loving financial brokers, Jan Vriesinga and Edo Meijerman, with the goal of organizing the building of the largest single fleet (200 vessels) of electric boats in the Netherlands. Design, building, and exploitation, but also maintenance and service, will all be in the hands of boat rental firms, waterside restaurants and hotels, to boost the local economy. The standard boat design chosen is a 23-ft (6m90) aluminium sloop to be powered by a 4 kW AC Kraütler pod motor. The first batch of 45 HappyWhales, built by the Friesland yards of Hoora, Rensol and Insol, were built during the summer. One innovation is that, using software, the performance of each boat in the fleet, the state of its batteries, engine temperature, and prop problems, can be remotely monitored via Microsoft Cloud from the HappyWhale HQ in Gröningen.

Alongside this, SEFF, the Frisian e-boating Foundation, has launched the "Mienskip Frys-lân" (= Friesland Community) where various groups (schools, neighborhoods, friends, local communities) are invited to collectively engage in building affordable electric boats, designed by Vripack of Sneek with professional help and supervision provided when needed. Mienskip was launched at Boot, Holland, February 2016. The first two Mienskips were an aluminum version by students of ROC Friese Poort Sneek, the other by the Two Provinces Water Company (Yachtcharter Leeuwarden Sytze Kooi) in Leeuwarden. Another is being built in wood and another still of recycled plastic bottles.

Another Friesland initiative began when on June 24, following lobbying by the SEFF, a newly excavated route was opened between Heeg and Oudega designated electric-only. Creation of a second electric-only route the Reidmarroute is planned along the villages of Blauwhuis, Greonterp, Wolsum and Westhem. Outside Friesland, special pathways built include Rosmalen, Beuningen, Nesselande and Nieuwkoop. Such measures will be in full swing by 2018 when the province becomes the cultural capital of Europe.[54]

Based in Heeg, Friesland, "De Stille Boot" (= the Silent Ship) boatyard has retrofitted a number of boats with fully electric and hybrid electric power, including yachts, tradi-tional Dutch "sloeps" and motorboats. For this they use the shaftless Torque-Jet ring motor with energy from lithium batteries and Solbian flexible solar panels as manufac-tured by Thousand Suns. Their Solar Boat was designed by naval architect Willem Nieland using towing tank and e-outboard towing models. Its 8-meter (26 ft), 1200 kg hull is fitted with sixteen Solbian SP series flexible lightweight solar panels, glued to the deck. These panels have a 22.5 percent efficiency, the highest on the market today. Twelve of them are standard 100-watt panels, while 4 are tailor-made panels to follow the form of the boat. Total peak power is approximately 1400 W. On a clear day, all the energy will be supplied by solar power, giving it virtually unlimited range in those conditions. The engine is a highly efficient 25 kW electric inboard, coupled with a specially designed car-bon fiber propeller for maximum hydrodynamic efficiency. Both are designed in con-junction with the Naval DC Company. As for performance, the Solar Boat's lightweight, energy-efficient hull needs just 1–1.5 kW to give it a cruising speed of 10 kph (6 mph) and a planing speed of 30 kph (19 mph).[55]

In 2015, the city of Amsterdam reaffirmed its decision to ban 2-stroke engines on private boats from 2017 and achieve its "zero emission" target by 2020. Commercial vessels operating in the city (there are about 530 canal boats yearly transporting some 3 million passengers for sightseeing) will have to achieve zero emission by 2020 to be able to continue operating on the city canals and surroundings.[56]

In answer to this legislation, the Lovers Company is having its fleet of 90-pax tour boats retrofitted, mostly with Bellmarine electric drive. The *André van Duin*, originally built in 1979 with a 165hp DAF diesel, is now 100 percent electric, using a 40 kW liquid-cooled, asynchronous Bellmarine motor and a 350 kWh C20 battery pack. The 72 ft (22 m) *Wim Kan*, built in 1982 with a 105hp DAF diesel, was retrofitted with a Schottel rudder-propeller. Lovers' hydrogen fuel-cell boat *Nemo H2* has been retrofitted with a Bellmarine AC motor and a Schottel rudder propeller. Alongside this, from April 2016, the 't Schmidtje tour boat company added the sixteenth electric boat to its fleet. The 80-pax, 20-m *Jan Huijgen*, built by the Bocxe Shipyard in Delft, is powered by a 50 kW Bell-marine Modular N80-2 electric drive, with a C20 250 kWh battery, weighing just 6 tons of the 30-ton all-up weight of the boat. With its teardrop-shaped hull, the *Jan Huijgen* is capable of a top speed of 11 mph (17 kph).

Indeed, it is Bellmarine of Gouda, with their 10-strong staff, who will continue to retrofit the older tourist boats and equip the brand-new boats (totaling 250 vessels, with an average length of 8 to 25 meters and weight of 53 tons) with their drive systems up to 80 kW, although their lower-powered engines can do the same task when linked to the versatile Schottel rudder-propeller. They are also developing an automatic speed controller with Raymarine of Velp to comply with the 7 kph speed limit on the Amsterdam canals.

The Swiss government has followed suit by banning 2-stroke engines from their lakes by 2017.[57] The Chinese government has also announced that they will no longer allow ICE boats in reservoirs, lakes, or rivers which exist as valuable sources for drinking water. With the COP21 Paris Agreement, other lake regions will follow suit.

Emrhys Barrell and Ian Rutter of the Thames Electric Launch Company continue to innovate. Their Ecodrive system, developed in 2015 for narrowboats on the British canal network, utilizes the latest brushless AC motors, for maximum efficiency and low noise. A 16 kW motor also employs regenerative charging, as found in all modern electric cars, removes the need for a separate diesel generator, saving a significant cost and space. The system consists of the 48V electric motor/generator, mounted on the swim. A bank of batteries supplies power to the motor when traveling under electric power. The batteries also supply power to a 5kW inverter, providing 240V. This can supply main power when the boat is traveling, but more importantly it will supply 240V when the boat is moored, without the need to run the main engine or a generator, particularly noisy when the moored boat is using its household appliances. The first boat to be so equipped is the *Olinda* on the Leeds and Liverpool Canal.[58]

Alternative Energies of La Rochelle, France, continued to serve the hybrid electric fleet. In 2014 they entered into collaboration with naval architect Sandith Thandasherry of the Navgathi shipyard, based in Kochi, a city in southwest India's coastal Kerala state, to form NavAlt Solar & Electric Boats. Navgathi had already made a 20-seater solar-powered boat for a tourism operator in Bhatinda in Punjab. The scaled-up Rs. 1.7-crore creation, with its 40 kW engine, would be a 75-pax solar ferry for Kerala State Water Department, the 1.5 mile (2.5km) stretch of Lake Vembanad between Vaikom and Thavanakadavu. In November 2016, after attending the trial run of solar-powered ferry *Aditya*, Transport Minister A. K. Saseendran said the government was planning to operate at least one solar-powered boat each in every district, eventually a fleet of up to 50 vessels. *Aditya*, used in the singular means the Sun God, Surya. In January 2017 *Aditya* won the Silicon Valley Challenge 2017 held at New Delhi.[59]

Ganesh Chaturthi is the Hindu festival that reveres elephant-headed deity. Ganesha. The festival ends on the tenth day, and near Mumbai the tradition is for the Lalbaugcha Raja idol to be carried in a public procession with music and group chanting, then immersed into the Arabian Sea, thereafter the clay idol dissolves and Ganesha is believed to return to Mount Kailasha. This August 2017, for the first time in over four hundred years, a 12-tonne 19ft^2 (1m8^2) electrically operated raft will carry this out by tilting at an angle of 45° so that idol slides down into the sea.

In 2015 AltEn fitted out two 69-ft (21 m), 98-pax hybrid-electric waterbuses, the *Estello* and the *Longo Mai*, for regular service across Toulon's Mediterranean coast harbor from Saint Mandrier to the city's new marine station.

Leroy-Somer of Pessac, France, and UK-headquartered Control Techniques and Mayday Electronics of Portsmouth have joined forces to produce a hybrid propulsion system for the Construction Naval Bordeaux for its client, the Corsican boat excursion company NAVE VA. The 165-pax passenger vessel, supplied to NAVE VA for visits to the Scandola nature reserve in Corsica, is equipped with two 800 hp motors, allowing it to achieve a speed of 20 knots in diesel mode. In electric mode it has a maximum speed of 8 knots and an endurance of 6–8 hours at a speed of 6 knots. Recharging takes a maximum of 6 hours, and uses a harbor three-phase supply or the on-board electrical generator.

For the first time since World War I, hybrid-electric surface boats will be used by a navy. During 2016–17, the first of six 24-m multi-mission barges will be built for the French Navy. Designed by Mauric, built by H2X shipyard at La Ciotat, fitted out by AltEn, the prototype 53-ton CMM will then be maintained in operational condition for three months by Cegelec Defence and Naval South-East (Toulon). If successful, the remaining five CMMs will be built for deliveries in 2019 and 2020. Two units each will be assigned to Toulon, Brest, Cherbourg and a sixth at St. Mandrier Mediterranean Pole at schools (PEM). The contract includes an option for two additional units to operate overseas, the *Caribbean* and *New Caledonia*. The CMMs will cruise in harbors or close to inshore naval bases. They will carry out various missions: underwater work, transportation equipment, pollution control, and diver training. Their job profile will also significantly increase the comfort of sailors, reducing noise during long periods of work, and removing the exhaust gases. Recently, France's Defense Minister Jean-Yves Le Drian has negotiated multi-billion–Euro sales of twelve 90-m submarines to the Australian Navy and of almost sixty Dassault Rafale fighter planes to the Egyptian, Qatar and India Air Forces. So this pioneer fleet of CMMs may soon make silent waves with other navies.[60]

In Taiwan, more than 100 diesel launches on Sun Moon Lake (日月潭) in Nantou County are to be replaced with electric boats over the next 14 years to help improve the environment and quality of service. A subsidy program to encourage ferry operators and boat owners to convert from diesel to electric is to run until 2027. Participants can receive a subsidy of up to NT $7.1 million (U.S. $236,270) or less than 50 percent of the cost of rebuilding a boat or installing the required equipment. The owner of the first boat covered by the program this year has received a subsidy of NT $6.1 million. The catamaran, the *Guo Yi No. 2*, which started operating on Sun Moon Lake in February 2016, is powered by lithium-ion batteries that only need to be recharged every eight hours. This allows about 12 round trips per charge.

In February 2017 Taiwan city of Kaohsiung retrofitted its 75-ft (23-m) Cijian Island passenger ferry with a Finnish Visedo electric propulsion system. Visedo worked alongside Taiwan's Ship and Ocean Industries R&D Center, also known as SOIC, to complete the retrofit. Kaohsiung's new "e-ferry," *Ferry Happiness* is halving daily fuel consumption while transporting 15,000 passengers every day to Cijian Island. If successful, the Kaohsiung City Government plans to retrofit the remaining 11 diesel ferries to help reduce pollution levels around Taiwan's largest harbor. There are also plans for a hybrid-electric tugboat.

While electric boats have a successful future, as is shown in the earlier chapters of this book, it also has a rich past. In May 2015, an expanded paperback version of this author's biography of electric boating's founding father was published. Titled *Gustave Trouvé, French Electrical Genius*, this 240-page illustrated edition was at last able to present the inventor who signed his name Eureka to the English-speaking academic world. In homage, Tom Hesselink of Budsin Woodcraft in North Carolina called the latest model in his line of fine varnished timber electric launches the *Trouvé*.

Tamás Stickl of Gárdony, Hungary, developed the 4 kW Evolution 629, an open six-seater sports boat. Thanks to its special underwater hull, this boat promises a top speed of 11 to 12 kph and a range of 52 km or 6.5 hours at 8 kph.

In March 2016, the *Elize-Rixe*, an electrically propelled fully equipped water villa designed by Lieuwe Koonstra, was launched in the Frisian village of Opeinder. She is powered by 7.5 kW ARKA pod motors, supplied by eight solar roof panels through a lead-acid battery pack to cruise for 6 hours at a speed of 9.5 kph (6 mph). There remains still enough energy for household use.

Boat-shaped automobile bodies and varnished wood bodywork go back to the 1920s, but for the Milan Design Week of April 2016, Toyota launched their 3-meter boat-shaped Setuna (= "moment" in Japanese) electric sportscar. Its construction, featuring Japanese cedar for the exterior panels and Japanese birch for the frame, uses a traditional Japanese joinery technique called *okuriari*, which does not use any nails or screws. The Setsuna can be driven, but it's so conceptual—with no plans at all for production—that Toyota hasn't included the requisite equipment to make it street-legal in Japan, Italy, or elsewhere.

For 2016, in Sezana, Slovenia, Iztok Pockaj, wealthy manufacturer of gaming equipment, set up Alfastreet Marine and asked Armin Koren and Paolo Dose from the company Venetian Design, and the architect Andrea Agrusta from the naval engineering company Naval Heads, to produce an electric boat called the *Energy 18 Open*, whose 10kW motor and 25 kWh battery enable up to 8 passengers to ride at a speed of up to 15 kph.

In spring 2016, the 51.36-m (165 ft) sailing schooner *Rainbow II*, designed by Dykstra Naval Architects, was launched from the Holland Jachtbouw at Zaandam. A retro yacht with mahogany Art Deco–style interior, she can be operated entirely on her Hy-Store li-ion batteries, including sailing, navigation and hotel load. A lightweight 50 kW Hy-Gen variable speed generator, combined with the 50 kW main engine integrated flywheel generator, provide the power. Fully charged from sailing, *Rainbow II's* batteries can be charged up sufficiently for a full day of cruising at 7 knots. This schooner's maiden voyage was to the Baltic for the summer, followed by winter in the Caribbean.[61]

Cor and Lodewyck Beghuys of Supiore in Amsterdam developed a 5.25-m (17-ft) €50,000 luxury runabout, the *Superiole Uno*, its solar panels discreetly integrated on the front deck. The *Uno's* speed is electronically limited to 10 knots (18.5 kph, 11.5 mph). In 2016, airline captain Christian Smulders of Lillebror Marine in Loosdrecht Amsterdam produced the fine entry aluminum *E78 Tourer*, weighing in at only 1850 kg, whose liquid-cooled, reduced belt transmission e-motor of 40 kW derives its power from a 40 kWh, 27 kWh lithium pack.

Security consultant Jan van Eck of Wateringen, the Netherlands, launched his 40-ft (12.55-m) *DutchCatTwelve* catamaran concept, designed by Vripack naval architects with a beam of 16 ft (4.90 m) and a draft of just 2.6 ft (0.8 m), coming in six propulsion options: 100 percent electric from twin 10-kW Krautlers with a 48-kWh WhisperPower gel battery, series or Parallel hybrids or twin 30-hp Yanmar diesels. Alongside this, each owner can select the interior layout, cabin or fabric schemes. *DutchCatTwelve* was nominated as European and HISWA Powerboat for 2017.

Bavaria Yachtbau, one of Germany's largest shipyards and builders of catamarans and motorboats, are working with Transfluid Trasmissioni Industriali to develop the hybrid Bavaria E40 for operation in diesel, pure-electric and diesel-electric mode during navigation at the push of a button.

In March 2017, LGM and Hyundai Yachts, a division of the automobile maker, went into partnership to develop and market electric yachts, taking part in the 2017 Busan Boat Show in Korea using a joint booth. As proof of further development, LGM took a 650-hp Riva Ferrari speedboat and converted it to electric propulsion while maintaining its acceleration of 40 knots in several seconds. On April 19, 2017, LGM, Ltd., signed a contract with SOH, Inc., for approximately US$6.3 million to provide electric passenger boats: nine public boats for tourists, including four 12-seaters, three 20-seaters, and two 50-seaters. LGM's electric inboard and outboard propulsion systems now range from 40 to 670 hp (500kW), and include their Sailing Generation System for sailing yachts, which uses power generated by the wind to recharge batteries while under way. Leo Motors has also developed a proprietary Zinc Air Fuel Cell Generator (ZAFCG), which will free EVs from range limit with zero emissions. The Korean company has also formed a joint venture company with China for production of e-boats. In the United States, Leo plans to open an electric power yacht workshop this year. The workshop will convert up to 45-foot luxury ICE yachts into electric.

In early June 2017, LGM delivered their first high speed electric fishing boat to the Korean government in a ceremony at Daecheon Harbor, South Korea. The government then transferred the high-speed electric fishing boat to S.W. Hwang, secretary general for the Association of Fishermen Union. Hwang would deploy the high-speed e-fishing boat for deep-sea fishing, testing the power, safety, dependability, and utility while assessing for further improvements. He would then promote sales of the electric boat to Korean fishing communities. The Korean government's subsidy program for conversion of electric boats is intended to deploy more electric fishing boats to resolve problems caused from the former tax-free gas program for fishermen. The tax-free gas costs about half of regular gas, allowing Korean fishermen to fish at lower costs than competing countries.

A latecomer is Croatia where the Croatian government approved its national park to sign contracts worth almost 10 million Kunas for the construction of three, 54-Pax tourist solar-electric boats for operation on the Veliko Jezero and Malo Jezero (Big Lake and Small Lake) from the beautiful island of Mljet. The boats will be built by the Zagreb company iCat, in cooperation with the Riva Company from Sibenik.[62]

Solar racing continues to grow. The Dutch leg of the World Cup for Solar Powered Boats took place in Friesland in early July 2016. The course was over 124 miles (200 km) and covered 2 provinces. The race was held for various classes of solar-powered craft and was spread out over an 8-day period in five different stages, such as mass sprint and endurance racing. Venues were Amsterdam, Lemmer, Drachten, and Grou, finishing in Leeuwarden. Alongside the teams from the Netherlands, consisting of mainly engineering students and innovative sustainable companies, teams from Indonesia, Brazil, Poland, Belgium, Bahrain, Turkey, America, Finland, Hungary, and China competed. The winner was the *Clafis Victron Energy*, although on Day 5, with the venue moved to the wider less windy Nije Kanaal, TU Delft set a speed record of 50.5 kph (over 31 mph).

The teams then headed south for the Monaco Solar Boat Challenge. Teams which did not have a solar-powered machine had the opportunity to assemble one from scratch, supplied in kit form as the 6-m (19.7 ft) U20 by Marnix Hoekstra and his colleagues at Vripack of Sneek in the Netherlands. The U20 had already received the Green Environmental Award special mention from the international motorboat federation UIM.

At the end of three days of competition combining a fleet endurance race, a timed slalom course and one-on-one duels, the Dutch teams *Clafis Victron Energy* Solar Boat

Team and Dutch Solar Boat proved their supremacy, winning in their respective classes (Open Class and A Class) for the third year running. Another highlight was the YCM International Speed Record, organized in collaboration with the UIM (Union Internationale Motonautique) over a distance of one-eighth of a nautical mile. *Clafis Victron Energy* Solar Boat Team, piloted by Gerhard van der Schaar, set a new top speed of 49.10 kph (30.51 mph), beating its own record set in 2015 by 4.7 kph. The Yacht Club de Monaco then announced a new challenge for 2017. Instigated by engineer Marco Casiraghi, the 50-sea-mile Monaco Offshore Solar Race will be between boats which can accommodate three people and for which the technical specifications have been drawn up in collaboration with the UIM.

Minn Kota continues their innovative approach for the freshwater and saltwater fisherman. In 2016, they won the award in the "Electric Motor/Battery Powered Propulsion" category, with their Riptide® Ulterra™, enabling the saltwater fisherman, using the i-Pilot® remote, to deploy, trim and operate his corrosion-resistant motor from anywhere on the boat. The unit features automated stow/deploy and power trim, which raises and lowers the depth of the motor with the push of a button.

Torqeedo's CEO Christoph Ballin recently stated: "Our mission to make electric boating possible for the largest number of boat owners and sailors is gradually becoming reality." The Torqeedo range now extends to the Deep Blue Hybrid, whose clean energy is generated by wind and solar, and, while under sail, by the rotating propellers. Efficient, modern diesel generators are used as a backup to supply additional energy when needed. This system is now at work on PHW 1 (Plugin Hybrid Water), a black-and-yellow 12-pax watertaxi in service on the River Meuse in downtown Rotterdam, southern Netherlands. The 80 hp Deep Blue motor works with two generators, delivering 20 kWk with a top speed of 25 kph. PHW 1 is the first hybrid in a 16-strong fleet. If trials are successful, others will be retrofitted. The Port of Rotterdam Authority, which is striving for a sustainable port, has also ordered a new inspection vessel, the RPA 8, which is equipped with hybrid propulsion and is expected to be taken into service in 2017, with construction taking place at the Kooiman Group shipyard in Zwijndrecht, the Netherlands.

The Torqeedo Cruise 10.0 R can deliver 12 kW peak/10 kW continuous power, making it the most powerful boat motor that can be used without a license in Germany, with potential use for tenders, ferryboats, barges and excursion boats. The Cruise 4.0 FP pod motor will propel a sailboat of up to 4 tons at over 11 kph (7 mph). The Deep Blue SD Torqeedo is the world's first high-performance saildrive system from serial production, delivering 40 hp-equivalent power for the large luxury yacht segment. Weighing less than 70 kg and designed without a shaft drive, Deep Blue SD is very easy to install and maintain. In 2016 Torqeedo announced that they had sold 70,000 units in their eleven years of operation. In April, Torqeedo was awarded the Most Eco-Friendly Marine Business 2016 at the 21st China International Boat Show in Shanghai. On June 20 of that year, 13 top journalists from German mass media plus the chief editors of leading European boat magazines gathered for the first "Electric Days" at Lake Starnberg near Munich. Motor manufacturer Torqeedo had teamed up with the four shipyards Nimbus (Sweden), Frauscher (Austria), Designboats (Switzerland) and Kaiser Boote (Germany) to present the future and present of electric boating with seven boats on the water during two days of test drives.

In the fall of 2016, Torqeedo announced that it had teamed up with Hanse Yachts of Greifswald in Germany and Jefa of Copenhagen, Denmark, to produce an e-motion rudder drive, first tested with a Hanse 315. The core of this innovative concept is a specially adapted 4 kW (8 hp) Torqeedo Cruise 4.0 with folding propeller, designed into the rudder blade itself. The streamlined system replaces the combustion inboard or saildrive and removes the need for a separate thruster; the Jefa rudder blade's range of motion was extended to a total of 100 degrees. While docking, the stern can easily be maneuvered into the proper position. This is highly useful in windy conditions or in narrow slips.[63]

After four years' development, two French naval architects, Marc Van Peteghem and Vincent Lauriot Prévost of Perspective Yacht Design in Vannes, France, backed by entrepreneur Francois Alexandre Bertrand, launched their Platypus on the market. *Ornithorhynchus anatinus*, also known as the duck-billed platypus, is a semiaquatic mammal. Platypus is a 19-ft (5.7 m)-long blue catamaran which, controlled like a jetski, can surface cruise out to a desired diving spot, then make a third mobile davit hull pivot downward, so turning riders into divers, submerging them a few feet below the surface for a view of the underside of the waves. If the chosen diving spots are near the coast, then the Platypus can be equipped with twin 2 kW Torqeedo motors powered by an 8 kW Absorbed Glass Mat (AGM) battery providing a range of 25 miles (40 km) and a maximum speed of 5 knots (5.7 mph/9 kph) in surface navigation mode. The 2 × 2.4 kW model is powered by a 10.5 kW lithium-ion battery and gets a range of up to 30 miles (48 km) and top speed of 10 knots (11.5 mph/18 kph).

In a similar vein, the *Aeon Explorer* has been developed by Planet Earth, a community-owned venture in Kailua-Kona, northern Hawaii. Users lie prone on the solar-electric watercraft, looking down through an acrylic window in the underside of its nose—they can also look forward to see where they're going. Propulsion is provided by a single e-propeller in the rear, while a dual-joystick system is used for steering and throttle control. Additionally, LED spotlights on the underside of the craft help illuminate the depths at night, and can also attract wildlife. The *Aeon Explorer* team is currently running a crowd-funding Indiegogo campaign for a goal of $100,000 to ramp up production of the vehicle.

In sharp contrast, a Torqeedo Travel 1003 has been integrated into a pedal-electric dinghy called the *Ludy*, developed by Vigliano at Ludyvert in Quiberon in the Morbihan region of France. Also in France, Aqualeo's Jérémy Benichou is using a Jérémy Torqeedo pod to develop a Gliss-Speed electric waterbike capable of 50 kph.

To crown their achievement, in November 2016 Torqeedo received the overall 26th DAME Design Award at the METS Trade Show in Amsterdam. The chairman of the jury, Bill Dixon, observed in his award statement that "this engine is in price and performance 'equitable' with conventional internal combustion saildrives."

By Appointment of Her Majesty Queen Elizabeth II, the Royal Barge *Gloriana* has also been retro-fitted with twin Torqeedo Deep Blue 40 Saildrive motors alongside two pairs of BMWi3 battery packs. Luxury catamaran manufacturer Privilege Marine of Les Sables-d'Olonne has presented its first Privilege Series 5 Hybrid Catamaran that will feature a 2 × 50-kW Deep Blue Hybrid system.

Batteries continue to increase in energy density. MG Electronics is utilizing in their brand-new line of batteries based on NCA. NCA chemistry (lithium-nickel-cobalt-aluminum oxide, $LiNiCoAlO2$) with 2.5 and 5 kWh capacity batteries weighing 15 and 27 kg. Their energy densities are 6 kg/kWh, and for the double-capacity, therefore more weight efficient battery, no more than 5.4 kg/kWh. Max discharge current is 1.5 C and max charge current is 1 C with a 2,000-cycle lifetime. Torqeedo's Power 2.7 kWh battery, weighing 24.2 kg, has an energy density of 9 kg/kWh. And Torqeedo's at METS 2016 newly unveiled BMW3i 33 kWh battery weighs 7.8 kg/kWh. Until now the industry standard weight (except for MG, whose special Solar Challenge lithium packs were always super light at round 4.5 kg/kWh) was between 7.4 and 11 kg/kWh, so these new products are breakthroughs. No wonder that in May 2017, the Nimbus 305 Drophead E-Power utilizes batteries that are the latest Torqeedo BMW3i technology

In 2016 Combi electric outboards, with thousands of units sold around the world, celebrated their 35th anniversary. For the future, they prepared a liquid-cooled 10 kW AC that can be linked up to 4 motors (Master/Slave) for inboard applications or as a saildrive, and an asynchronic sensorless 3.5 kW outboard. Two other longtime key players in the e-boat movement have joined forces. Grove Boats of Yverdon-les-Bains, Switzerland, have become distributors for the Ruban Bleu, based in Nantes (Brittany), the European leader for electric boats used for rental, hotel resorts and for private individuals looking for a smooth and fancy electric leisure boot. Over 1,400 units are operating throughout Europe and Ruban Bleus products portfolio covers a range of elegant units with a capacity from 4 to 11 passengers. Grove Boats is currently working on a 27-ft (8-m50) 12-pax pure electric taxi for use on the River Seine. Based on their Aquabus 850T hull, designers Flahault & Chantet of Saint-Herblain–Nantes have conceived a vessel whose wooden decking and cabin more resemble the Classic cabin runabout. Instead of the customary solar panels, li-po energy to the twin inboard motors of 10kW each will enable the Grove to reach the 10 mph (16 kph) required for winter navigation on the Seine.

As the Electric Boat Association enters its 35th year with over 400 members, its journal is now an online publication for members with tablets and smartphones. In recent months, key electric boat builders representing the Netherlands and Belgium, France and Switzerland, Austria, Germany, Scandinavia and Slovenia and the United Kingdom and have been exploring the potential of a combined European electric boating industry sector to improve its visibility. Initial meetings were held during exhibitions in Amsterdam (2015) and Dusseldorf (2016). The European boating industry has inquired with its member organizations in the Czech Republic, Poland, Italy and Spain about possibly interested companies in these countries. England's role following Brexit remains to be seen.

For example, at the international conference "Ports, Maritime Transport and Insularity," which took place in Piraeus, Greece, on March 10, 2016, a European Community project for an e-ferry was presented. A working group made up of Denmark, Greece, Germany, Switzerland and Finland had obtained 15 million Euros to design and build a medium-sized prototype, powered by wind-source electricity and whose 4.3 MW battery pack will enable it to travel up to 21.4 nautical miles on one charge, so making it suitable for journeys between small island groups, and along coasts and inland waterways. Tests are due to begin in the summer of 2017.

In January 2017, SINTEF (Solar Fuelled Electric Maritime Mobility), an independent non-profit research institute based in Norway was awarded the $1 million 2016 Energy Grant from the United Nations Department of Economic and Social Affairs (UN-DESA), in partnership with the China Energy Fund Committee to demonstrate the feasibility and the social, economic and environmental benefits of solar electric ferryboat transport in Tunisia. In 2016, the UN-DESA Energy Grant had received over 150 applications. The winner was selected through a rigorous review and objective assessment of these applications, undertaken in multiple stages, guided by an Advisory Council and a High-level Steering Committee. Ban Ki-moon the out-going UN Secretary-General said at the awards ceremony. "The transport sector is responsible for nearly a quarter of energy-related greenhouse gas emissions. It also has significant public health impacts. The answer is not less transport—it is sustainable transport. We need transport systems that are environmentally friendly, efficient, affordable, and accessible." A Grant will be awarded annually from 2015 until 2019.[64]

The hybrid combination is being used in many ways. Jean-Marc Simiand of Guyancourt, Île-de-France, France, a 53-year-old Renault engineer and avid sailor, is preparing his 44-ft (13m40) catamaran *World ECO Sail* for a three-year circumnavigation of the planet. The hull, built by Fountaine Pajot, is a customized version of Berret Racoupeau Designs' High End Hélia 44 Evolution. In addition to the 70m² sail area, twin 10 kW Piktronik Podmaster Prop electric motors are powered by 20 kWh Winston 48-volt lithium-ion battery packs drawing power via Mastervolt converters from six 345W SunPower solar panels—and turning two Bruntons Autoprop screws, bring the overall weight of the cat to 190 kg. With a cruising speed of 6 knots, and a range of 70 nm at 5 knots, Simiand plans to cast off from Cape Verde, Africa sometime in 2017.[65]

Solar-boat racing continues. The fourth edition of the Belgian Ecorace-Challenge was organized in early May 2017 on the straight-line Leuven-Dijle Canal with entries from Leuven, Antwerp and Delft competing. Across the border, in the Akkrum, Friesland, with Dong replaced by Eneco as sponsor, the three-year-old Young Solar Challenge, where high school students build then race their own boats saw 24 teams. The best speed was set by Bogerman Sneek—1 minute 18 seconds—and endurance by Oultremontcollege, at 1 hour 9 minutes. World Speed Record holders TU Delft, sponsored by Stork and Femto are planning to win in Monaco in July then to cross the English Channel in record-breaking time. Their new boat was unveiled on June 8, 2017, at Scheveningen.

Although Elon Musk of Tesla has not yet produced an electric powerboat, Scott Masterson of Orlando, Florida, has come very close to it by converting his Bayliner Bowrider 175 into an all-electric speedboat. Masterson pulled out the 3.0-L Mercruiser engine in favor of a 147-hp three-phase AC induction motor that is oil cooled for temperature regulation, then input a Curtis Model 1222 controller for power steering, and incorporated 32-kwh battery pack made up of 10 Tesla modules which are posted under the seats. Other general specifications include a range of approximately 25 miles, a 12-hour charge time at 120 volts, and 4-hour charge time at 240 volts. It has a cruising speed of 25–30 mph, and a top speed of 53 mph (86 kph). The boat weighs about 1,900 lbs (862 kg). His latest unit delivers 147 hp.

In November 2016, when the eighth edition of the Vendée Globe nonstop, solo, unassisted round-the-world yacht race set sail from Les Sables-d'Olonne, among the 29 competing yachts was the 60-ft (18-m) *Foresight Natural Energy* of Conrad Colman, a New Zealand skipper based in France. Using an Oceanvolt management system, the Kiwi intended to be the first to complete the circumnavigation without using fossil fuel. Energy on the boat is provided by a photovoltaic film integrated into the mainsail and by the trailing-prop hydogenerator, to top-up 9 batteries that give power to the on-board instrumentation. Phil Sharp, British yachtsman, has been working with the Energy Future lab at Imperial College London, in preparation for the Barcelona World Race; his yacht will use a fuel-cell system to provide on-board energy. On February 25, 2017, Colman finished his Vendée Globe in 110 days, 1 hour, 58 minutes, thereby achieving his goal.

The United Nations taking an interest in electric boats is perhaps the cherry on a rich cake. SINTEF (Solar Fueled Electric Maritime Mobility), an independent non-profit research institute based in Norway was awarded the $1 million 2016 Energy Grant from the United Nations Department of Economic and Social Affairs (UN-DESA), in partnership with the China Energy Fund Committee, to demonstrate the feasibility and the social, economic and environmental benefits of solar electric ferryboat transport in Tunisia. The UN-DESA Energy Grant had received over 150 applications. The winner was selected through a rigorous review and objective assessment of these applications, undertaken in multiple stages, guided by an Advisory Council and a High-level Steering Committee. Ban Ki-moon, the out-going UN Secretary-General, said at the awards ceremony, "The transport sector is responsible for nearly a quarter of energy-related greenhouse gas emissions. It also has significant public health impacts. The answer is not less transport—it is sustainable transport. We need transport systems that are environmentally friendly, efficient, affordable, and accessible." A Grant will be awarded annually until 2019.

In April 2017, the *Tapiatpia*, an 18-pax solar powered passenger boat went into service along the 60 km of the Pastaza and Capahuari rivers, in Ecuador, tributaries of the Marañón River in the northwestern Amazon Basin between Peru and Ecuador of South America. The stretch is territory belonging to the Achuar Indians. An Achuar legend says that the Tapiatpia was a giant electric eel that transported the animals of the forest. A traditional Amazonian canoe was built and then fitted with a curved pv roof by Oliver Utne, founder of Kara Solar, funded through the Fundación Pachamama, by the government of Finland, in collaboration with ESPOL University of Guayaquil in Ecuador and the Massachusetts Institute of Technology (MIT). On April 20, after a 23-day, 1800-km journey, the crew aboard *Tapiatpia*—the first regular solar ferryboat on the Amazon—arrived at Achuar territory in Ecuador, so linking nine communities previously dependent on gas-engine canoes. Utne plans a network of boats piloted and maintained by trained Achuars.

Duffy of Newport Beach states:

We are continuing to expand our electric boat line with creative new interiors for our 14–22 foot boat line. Next, we will be launching in summer 2016 a longer, larger all electric boat line. There will be a version for sightseeing and charters. Another will be a larger version of our popular all electric bay launch. Finally we will be offering the boat with a hybrid system. This boat will have the ability for enjoying overnight cruising with a galley, head and comfortable cabin. The first launching will be the cabin cruiser hybrid version. We are also developing a larger, more powerful power rudder to push boats up to 10,000 lbs displacement at 7.5 knots. It is a displacement boat, not a planing hull.

We are working together with a 2011 start-up company called Pure Watercraft of Seattle. Their engineers, Chris Gil and Michael Schaefer, have successfully developed a 20 kW electric outboard capable of producing equivalent thrust as a 35 horsepower gas outboard as well as a safe, dependable 90 lb. lithium battery pack in two sizes. First application is on rowing coach's boats that we build for Stillwater boats out of Boston. They are the premier coach's boat and now with electric power, the most efficient and quiet one too! The package of battery, motor, electronics and drive unit is designed to compete economically with gas outboards. The upfront costs are initially higher than gas but come down to an equal value over a five to seven year period depending on usage. We have a significant amount of orders for this boat from schools all over the U.S. They began taking pre-orders in April 2016.

Of the 14,000 Duffy Boats worldwide, 3,500 have been sold in Newport Harbor alone! Duffy Electric Boat Rentals of Newport Beach holds the world's largest Duffy electric boat fleet!

Marshall Duffield himself, 63 years old, is now an active Newport Beach town councilor,

In 2016, the Duffy *Bay Island* shows the sheer elegance and delight of cruising electric (Duffy collection).

concerned about losing the marine servicing businesses and public waterfront spaces to over-intrusive condo development, and about dredging the harbor. "My story is that I popularized the use of the electric boat. No doubt we made several technological contributions but that had very little to do with why or how we sold so many. What we offer is a way of living."[66] The same can perhaps be said about every electrical engineer and boatbuilder who, during the past 130 years, has and is still delighting passengers with the relaxing calm and the silence for which electric boats are so very much loved.

On October 15, 2016, to commemorate the life and work of Gustave Trouvé, a marble plaque positioned on the exterior wall of his former workshop was officially unveiled by the mayor of the 2nd Arrondissement of Paris and this author. It was from here that the inventor carried his experimental electric outboard motor on a short walk down to the Seine to begin trials which were to change the world of boating.

TEN

Towards the Sustainable Electric Ship

With the introduction of highly efficient and economically favorable diesel engines in the middle of the 20th century, turbo-electric propulsion, as described in Chapter Three of this book, *more or less disappeared* from merchant marine vessels.

Then several innovations contributed towards a return to electric propulsion. The first was the development of variable speed electric drives, first by the AC/DC silicon controlled rectifier (SCR) or thyristor as developed by power engineers at General Electric (GE), led by Gordon Hall and commercialized by GE's Frank W. "Bill" Gutzwiller. The SCR, together with AC/DC converters, in the late 1970s were first used on the sub–Arctic icebreaker *Kapitan M. Ismaylow* and the Finnish research vessel *Aranda* with alternating current propulsion motors and cycloconverters, as fitted by the Asea-Brown-Boveri (ABB) Group with the Finnish shipbuilder Wärtsilä.[1]

In 1986–7 the cruise ship SS *Queen Elizabeth II* underwent a major refit at the Lloyd Werft yard at Bremerhaven in Germany. Fifteen different proposals by 7 manufacturers were considered, but despite initially looking cost-prohibitive, diesel-electric was decided to have the greatest reliability, flexibility and environmental friendliness (in terms of reduced noise and vibration). Further analysis after this option was selected uncovered even greater advantages over the geared diesel option. A saving of 250 tons a day (at 28.5 knots) was now anticipated. Nine MAN diesel engines would drive two 44 MW General Electric motors turning five-bladed propellers. This refit, costing $162m, was hugely successful and allowed the ship to sail on for another 20 years as the Cunard flagship, the only transatlantic liner and the fastest and most powerful merchant ship in the world.

The azimuth thruster using the Z-drive transmission was invented in 1950 by Joseph Becker, the founder of Schottel in Germany, and marketed as the Ruderpropeller. It was patented for ships in 1955 by Friedrich W. Pleuger of Hamburg and F. Busmann (Pleuger unterwasserpumpenGmbH), U.S. Patent 3033125.

The idea that an electrical rudder propeller drive could gain commercial traction was first conceived in the 1970s, but it was not until February 18, 1987, that Strömberg Oy filed the patent application for it. Pekka Salmi, a Finnish engineer, realized its great potential for ice-going vessels. He approached Wärtsilä Marine with the idea. Project development was initiated in close cooperation with ABB, with Salmi as project manager working with Erkki Ranki, Kari Laukia, and Ulf Rosovist. The Wärtsilä Arctic Research Centre drew up the first research plan in 1988. Their idea was to build a prototype to be installed on the waterway service vessel *Lonna*. In June 1989 the project was accepted. Construction of the pod had already started in the machine department. The project switched to *Lonna*'s sister vessel, the 1979-built *Seili*, but when Wärtsilä Industries went bankrupt in autumn 1989, work was put on hold. A merger that formed ABB took place, and when Masa Yards was established in 1989–90, the project was resumed. With the 1.5 MW unit, dubbed "Azipod" (a portmanteau of "azimuth thruster" and "podded propulsion unit") installed, *Seili* took to the frozen sea in January 1991. Before the conversion, the ship could not break ice astern at all, but with the Azipod unit she could run astern in level ice as thick as 0.6 meters (2 feet). The vessel could also easily be steered when running astern in ice.

This idea, to use the Azimuthing propulsion and to operate the vessel with stern first, was patented by Masa Yards in March 1991 as DAS, the Double-Acting Ship. The results were so encouraging that Kvaerner Masa-Yards and ABB Industry signed an agreement for further development and sale of the Azipod in spring 1992.[2]

The next units were retrofitted on two Finnish oil tankers, *Uikku* (= grebe) and

In 1990 the *Seili* became the first boat to be equipped with the ABB Azipod propulsion system (ABB).

Lunni (= puffin), in 1993 and 1994, respectively. Nearly eight times as powerful as the prototype, the 11.4 MW Azipod units considerably increased the icegoing ability of the vessels that were already built with independent icebreaking capability in mind. The M/t *Uikku* was the first Western oil tanker to navigate the entire Northern Sea Route. The first three Azipod units were of the so-called "pushing" type in which the propeller is mounted behind the gondola. In the subsequent installations, ABB adopted the more efficient "pulling" configuration similar to propeller-driven airplanes.[3]

Another breakthrough came in spring 1998 when the Carnival Cruise Lines ship, the 262-m (860 ft) *Elation*, was delivered by the Kværner Masa-Yards Helsinki shipyard, with twin Azipod electric podded propulsion units.[4] She was soon followed by the *Paradise*. During their subsequent cruises, the advantages were so convincing, such as cutting their turning radius by half and saving fuel, that podded propulsion almost overnight became a standard on new cruise liners and paved the way for competitors such as the "Mermaid" system developed by Rolls-Royce with Cegelec in 1999.

In 2000, the U.S. Navy announced plans for a new generation of electrically propelled guided missile destroyers, which became the Zumwalt Class. Two Rolls-Royce Marine Trent-30 gas turbines drive Curtiss-Wright electric generators to two propellers driven by electric motors. Due to budgetary problems, only three were built.

By 2003, the 345-m (1,132 ft) *Queen Mary 2*, at 151,400 tons the largest and most expensive passenger ship ever built to that date, is an integrated electric propulsion ship. She is fitted with four 16-cylinder Wärtsilä 16V46CR EnviroEngine marine diesel engines generating a combined 67,200 kW (90,100 hp) at 514 rpm, as well as two General Electric LM2500+ gas turbines, which together provide a further 50,000 kW (67,000 hp), all of which is converted into electricity used to power electric motors that drive four 21.5 Mw Rolls-Royce Mermaids.

Alongside integrated electric ship propulsion, other systems have been tested. In 2007, the keel was laid at the SSB shipyard in Oortkaten for a 100-pax hydrogen fuel-cell ferryboat to operate on Lake Alster and the River Elbe, within the port of Hamburg. The "green ferry" was part of the €5.2m *Zemship* project, which involved 9 German and Czech partners and was led by Hamburg's State Ministry for Urban Development and Environment. Proton Motors of Puchheim built the drive train using an existing bus fuel cell in the project, adapted for marine requirements, including layout of the drive train, design of mechanical interfaces and safety analysis. Fuel came from compressed hydrogen, at 350 Bar. Although propulsion was by two hydrogen fuel systems making use of 12 hydrogen fuel tanks, the ferry could also fall back on a 560 V lead-gel battery should an alternative power source be needed. A refueling station for the ferry was built at Hellbrokstrasse at a depot of Hamburg's public transport operator Hochbahn, directly on Lake Alster, with hydrogen being taken directly from an LH2 storage tank at 8 Bar pressure. The FCS *Alsterwasser* began its trials on inner-city waterways in Hamburg in the summer of 2008, and by 2014 had logged up 4000 operating hours and transported more than 50,000 passengers on Lake Alster.[5]

Following the Hamburg project, further fuel cell–powered ferries were planned for Bratislava and Prague in the Czech Republic. But while the FCS *Alsterwasser* obtained hydrogen refueling within the lake area, deep sea vessels faced a different challenge.

This challenge was overcome with 92-m (300ft) *The Viking Lady*, a fuel-cell offshore supply vessel. The project was initiated by Det Norske Veritas, Eidesvik and Wärtsilä in 2003. It was developed in three phases and was funded by the Research Council of Nor-

Between 2008 and 2014 the fuel cell ferryboat *Alsterwasser* logged up 4,000 operating hours and transported more than 50,000 passengers on Lake Alster (Proton Motor Fuel Cell GmbH).

way, Innovation Norway and the Eureka Network. It was also supported by the German Federal Ministry of Economics and Technology. Designed by Wärtsilä Ship Design and built on the western coast of Norway by West Contractors, *The Viking Lady* was delivered to its owner, Eidesvik Offshore, in April 2009.

The vessel is powered by a complement of LNG fuel and an onboard fuel cell. This comprises a dual-fuel liquefied natural gas (LNG)/diesel-electric power plant. If required, it can be reconfigured to operate on methanol. Electricity for the propulsion is supplied by four Wärtsilä 6R32DF engines with an output of 2,010 kW each. Its four main generators are Alconza NIR 6391 A-10LWs, each producing 1,950 kW of power. Its emergency generator is a Volvo Penta D9-MG-RC, which is capable of producing 160V of power. The vessel's engine uses the molten carbonate fuel cell and LNG to produce all power requirements. The fuel cell operates at 650°C and generates 320 kW of power. Hydrogen gas is the most favorable fuel for the cell, but the technology has been developed to also work with methanol, LNG, biofuels, and landfill gas. Due to the combined use of the fuel cell and a gas engine, the vessel can reduce sulfur oxide by 100 percent, nitrogen oxide by 85 percent, and carbon dioxide by 20 percent. The ship also has two Rolls-Royce AZP 100FP propeller systems. It was claimed that *The Viking Lady* is the most environmentally friendly vessel ever built. After its delivery, the vessel was chartered to a French oil company and ran for more than 18,500 trouble-free hours.

In 2003, Wallenius Wilhelmsen Lines' car carrier, the 228-m (748 ft) *Undine*, with a capacity of 7,200 cars or a combination of 3,700 cars and 600 trucks, was equipped with an experimental 20 kW Wärtsilä solid oxide fuel cell to test out the regulatory requirements for using methanol as its fuel. During trials, although the methanol fulfilled its role, it was realized that the fuel cell installed was satisfying only a small proportion of the *Undine*'s auxiliary power. The group's ships require between 2 and 3 MW of installed power. The fuel cell was removed, and larger fuel cells were envisaged.

At the same time, 2009 Nippon Yusen KK and Nippon Oil Corporation developed the first cargo ship to use supplementary solar power. The experimental 60,000-ton, 200-m (660 ft) M/V *Auriga Leader*, a car carrier ship used by the Toyota Motor Corporation, is fitted with 328 solar panels to generate 40 kilowatts of solar power, which covers only 0.2 percent of the ship's energy. The aim of the boat was to provide statistical research in how solar power can assist in powering a ship at sea.

Subsidized by the Ministry of Land, Infrastructure, Transport and Tourism, Mitsui OSK Lines preferred to stay with diesel-electric hybrid for their 6,400-vehicle automobile carrier. Built in 2013 at the Kobe Shipyard of the Mitsubishi Heavy Industries, Ltd., the 200-m (656 ft) *Emerald Ace* combines a 160 kW solar generation system, jointly developed by MHI, Energy Company of Panasonic Group with lithium-ion batteries that can store some 2.2 MWh of electricity. The diesel-powered generator is completely shut down when the ship is in berth, and the batteries provide all the electricity it needs, resulting in zero emissions at the pier.

A.P. Moller-Maersk Group's (Maersk Line) Triple E, the world's biggest ship, is hybrid-electric. Triple E stands for Economy of scale, Energy efficiency, and Environmentally improved. With each ship measuring 400 m (1,312 ft) long, and capable of transporting over 18,000 TEU containers, the twenty-strong Triple E fleet was built by Daewoo Shipbuilding and Marine Engineering (DSME) of Seoul, South Korea. They are powered by two 32-megawatt (43,000 hp) ultra-long stroke two-stroke MAN diesel engines, driving two propellers at a design speed of 19 knots (35 kph; 22 mph). Three 3 MW Siemens shaft generator motors (SGM), enabled by a waste heat recovery system (WHR), act as variable consumer or power generation units. MV *Mærsk Mc-Kinney Møller* was the first to enter into service in 2013, followed by another nineteen ships, each with a first name beginning in M: The latest, *Mathilde Mærsk*, went into service in July 2015.

The *Allure of the Seas*, built at the STX Europe shipyards in Turku, Finland, and currently operated by Royal Caribbean International, uses integrated electric propulsion. Measuring 362 m (1,187 ft) long × 73 meters high, she can carry a maximum of 5,400 passengers with a crew of 2,384. Her propulsion system integrates 3 × 13,860 kW (18,590 hp) Wärtsilä 12V46D motors and 3 × 18,480 kW (24,780 hp) Wärtsilä 16V46D units coupled to 3 × 20 MW (27,000 hp) ABB Azipod, and 4 × 5.5 MW (7,400 hp) Wärtsilä CT3500 units. When her slightly larger sister ship, the *Harmony of the Seas*, with a maximum of 6,000 passengers, was launched in May 2016, she became the biggest ocean liner in the world.

From 2018, the world's largest emission-free electric ferries, *Tycho Brahe* and *Aurora*, formerly diesel-powered, will be operating completely on battery power between Helsingør (Denmark) and Helsingborg (Sweden), a distance of approximately 2.5 miles (4 km) carrying more than 7.4 million passengers and 1.9 million vehicles annually. The combined battery power of 8,320 kWh for the two ferries is the equivalent of 10,700 car batteries. ABB have supplied the complete power and propulsion systems and in particular, at both ends, the first automated shore-side charging stations using an industrial robot, to optimize the connection time and therefore maximize the charging period. All pre-docking procedures are based on 3D laser scanning and wireless communication between ship and shore. During the last 400 meters of the ferry's approach the robot will reach

The Azipod has been scaled up to the world's largest ships (ABB).

out and pull the shore cable from the ship. The cable reel releases the cable and the robot moves the connectors to the corresponding connectors below the robot. After the connection is made, the robot moves back to the home-position and the roll-up doors closes. The robot will reside inside its own building when not in use. The drydocking of the first vessel, *Tycho Brahe*, began April 2017 and, when work is completed, it will start operating as a fully electric ferry immediately. *Aurora* will undergo the same process in October 2017.

   In the summer of 2015, Sandia National Laboratories signed a cooperative research and development agreement with Red and White Fleet, whose diesel-electric ferries ply San Francisco Bay, to design, build and operate a high-speed hydrogen fuel cell passenger ferry and hydrogen refueling station. Designed the by Elliott Bay Group, the 30 mph 150-pax ferry, called *SF-Breeze* (= **S**an **F**rancisco **B**ay **R**enewable **E**nergy **E**lectric vessel with **Z**ero **E**missions), would use about 1,000 kilograms of hydrogen per day taken from a refueling station, which by dispensing 1,500 kilograms (3,306 pounds) per day, would make it the largest in the world and serve San Francisco's fuel-cell electric cars, buses and fleet vehicles in addition to the ferry and other maritime vehicles.

The latest generation of British naval warship, designated the Type 26 Global Combat Ship, will use a CODOG (combined diesel-electric or gas turbine) propulsion system, with a 36MW MT30 turbine from design partner Rolls-Royce, unspecified MTU diesel generator sets, and a gearbox via David Brown Gear Systems, Ltd. GE will be the overall integrator for the diesel-electric system. Current plans state a top ship speed of 28+ knots, with 60 days' endurance and a range of 7,000 miles (11,000 km) at normal steaming speed of 15 knots/ 28 kph.

The 284-m (932 ft) HMS *Queen Elizabeth*, the newest aircraft carrier of the British Navy, and the largest warship ever built in the UK, was named by Queen Elizabeth II on July 4, 2014, and scheduled to be commissioned in early 2017. She is powered by two Rolls-Royce Marine Trent MT30 36 MW (48,000 hp) gas turbines and four Wärtsilä 38 marine diesel engines (2 × 12V38 8.7 MW or 11,700 hp & 2 × 16V38 11.6 MW or 15,600 hp). Her fully integrated electric propulsion system uses four Converteam 20 MW advanced induction motors turning two shafts and fixed-pitch propellers. The second aircraft carrier, HMS *Prince of Wales*, is scheduled to be launched around 2017, followed by commissioning in 2020.

In the USA, at 186 m (610 ft), USS *Zumwalt* is the U.S. Navy's largest and most advanced stealth destroyer. Financed to the tune of U.S. $35m, its technology was developed by Florida State University's Center for Advanced Power Systems (CAPS), also involving scientists and engineers from the Massachusetts Institute of Technology, Mississippi State University, Purdue University, University of South Carolina, the University of Texas at Austin, and Virginia Tech. USS *Zumwalt* has an onboard GE 78-megawatt power station supplying electricity to an advanced integrated power system (IPS). This in turn powers giant GE 15-phase induction motors connected directly to the propeller shafts and routes electricity to a vast array of sensors, weapons, radar and other critical systems on board. GE had been able to free up as much as 80 percent of the ship's power previously dedicated to propulsion by simply getting rid of the gearbox. By a reversal of the direction of the rotating magnetic field in the motor, the shaft can turn in the opposite direction to give astern power.

China Shipbuilding Trading Company has unveiled a model of its first ever electrically-propelled trimaran warship. Construction of the 465-ft (142-m) ship by the China Shipbuilding Trading Company, which will be developed for the People's Liberation Army Navy, will start in late 2017 or 2018. The Chinese warship will utilize an integrated electrical propulsion system (IEPS) that will provide power to drive three pumpjets. The frigate will have a top speed of 30 to 35 knots and its operations will be based in the East and South China seas.

Inevitably, a proposed replica of the legendary ill-fated ocean liner, the Olympic-class RMS *Titanic*, the 269.15-m (883 ft) *Titanic II*, to be built at Jinling, China, for a planned launch in 2018, would be driven by Wärtsiläs and propelled by three 10 MW azimuth thrusters.

Peter Boyd, chief operating officer of the Carbon War Room, an international organization that encourages businesses to reduce their carbon emissions, has stated, "Shipping is a big sector. There are 100,000 ships that account for 3 percent of greenhouse gas emissions. In GDP terms, shipping would be the sixth largest country in the world."

Today, ABB is the largest manufacturer of electric podded propulsion systems with over 250 units delivered to over 100 ships and cumulative operating hours exceeding 7 million. In 2015, ABB introduced their Azipod D for shipping segments such as offshore drilling, construction and support vessels. The Azipod D requires up to 25 percent less installed power, which is partly due to the new hybrid cooling that increases the performance of the electric motor by up to 45 percent. ABB's Azipod D propulsion power ranges from 1.6 megawatts to 7 megawatts (MW) per unit.

Rolls-Royce Marine in Norway has been testing a propulsion system based on permanent-magnet technology. The *Gunnerus*, based in Trondheim, a research vessel for the Norwegian University of Science and Technology, has been fitted out with two permanent-magnet 500kW azimuths, including new frequency converters and control system. Like its tunnel thruster counterpart, the new azimuth unit operates on the rim drive principle with the permanent magnet motor surrounding the propeller blades in a slim ring. This creates a compact, efficient unit which, say the developers, increases power output by 25 percent from the same-size propeller.

Another innovation for the future is wireless charging and mooring, already used for cars, buses and trains. For maritime use, Wärtsilä Marine Solutions and Cavotec are developing the world's first combined induction charging and automatic mooring device. The integrated system will be capable of transferring more than 1 MW of electrical energy—some 300 times more than that of current chargers used by electric cars.

Diesel-electric propulsion is also an advantage for the installation of wind turbines and their connecting cables. For example, Siemens has provided the diesel-electric propulsion, integrated automation systems and remote and thruster controls for the 123 m (404 ft) *Nexus* (= connexion in Latin), being built for Van Ord in Germany by Sietas. Total power is approximately 10 MW, with the two propulsion drives delivering 2 MW each, for operating as a cable-laying vessel for constructing offshore wind parks. The first project for the *Nexus* will be the Gemini offshore wind park that will be built 85 km (53 miles) off the coast of Groningen. The 600 MW wind park will consist of 150 wind turbines with a capacity of 4 MW each. After construction, the park will deliver electricity to more than 1.5 million people. Another, the *Sea Installer*, is being built in China to set up a wind farm off the Danish coast.

To spare the Nærøyfjord (a famous fjord in the west of Norway listed on the UNESCO world heritage list) from exhaust gases, the 40-m (130 ft) *Vision of the Fjords* carbon-fiber catamaran ferry has two 749 kW motors, two 150 kW electric motors, a controllable pitch propeller (CPP) and a 576 kWh ZEM battery pack. The vessel was delivered in May 2016 for silent operation by Brødrene on the 32-km route between Flam and Gudvangen. On reaching the scenic part of the fjord, *Vision of the Fjords* switches to battery power and runs at a speed of 18 kph to allow its 400 passengers to enjoy nature in complete silence.[6]

For a 90-m (295 ft) ferry being built at the Cemre shipyard in Altınova/Yalova, Turkey, Wärtsilä is providing its latest hybrid battery technology to improve efficiency, reduce the exhaust emissions and lower the noise level. This involves 20 generating sets, electrical and automation (E&A) systems and a sanitary discharge system. With a capacity of 178 cars and 1,000 passengers, the new ferry is expected to be in use by UK operator Wightlink to serve the Fishbourne-to-Portsmouth route by 2018.

As this book goes to press, several long-term marine ship projects are underway, using sustainably obtained electricity.

The Kongsberg industrial group and the fertilizer manufacturer Yara International have commissioned the first 100 percent autonomous electric cargo ship in the world. Capable of transporting a hundred containers at a speed of 12 to 15 knots (23 to 28 kph), the 70-m *Yara Birkeland* (Yara's founder was famous scientist and innovator Kristian Birkeland) will transport fertilizers between Brevik and Larvik in Norway. According to the joint statement of the two partners, the *Yara Birkeland* with its 120-km of autonomy from its 3.5–4-MWh battery pack will avoid about 40,000 trips by diesel trucks, more than one hundred per day. Kongsberg is responsible for development and delivery of all key enabling technologies including the sensors and integration required for remote and autonomous ship operations, in addition to the electric drive, battery and propulsion control systems. The *Yara Birkeland* will make its first trips with personnel on board in the second half of 2018 before moving to remote operation in 2019 and to 100 percent autonomous operations from 2020 onwards. To ensure safety, three centers with different operational profiles are planned to handle all aspects of operation.

Eoseas is a 305-m (1,000 ft) five-hulled pentamaran cruise ship concept by STX Europe in collaboration with Stirling Design International (SDI). To reduce power consumption by 50 percent, the ship would use four dual fuel LNG diesel-electric gensets, each providing 8 MW of power for propulsion and hotel load. There are four screws, two pump propellers with shaft lines on the outriggers, and two pump propeller pods on the central hull. An 8,300m² array of photovoltaic panels fixed on the side and upper decks provide maximum power of 108 MW and an average of 270 kWe. The onboard organic waste gasification plant generates 300 kWe syn gas, which is used in the generator sets. The ship is equipped with an innovative sail concept patented by STX France. The sails, mounted on five masts and over 12,440m² in size, significantly use wind energy for propulsion. STX France conducted 13 tank tests with different hulls and propulsion configurations during 2008 and 2009, achieving 17 percent improvements over conventional propulsion / hull systems. *Eosas* may be built by 2020.

Another project is the 100-ft *Mayflower Autonomous Research Ship* (MARS), which will cross the Atlantic in 2020 to mark the 400th anniversary of the original *Mayflower* voyage from Plymouth, England, to Plymouth, Massachusetts, USA. The crewless trimaran will use state-of-the-art wind and solar technology for its propulsion, enabling an unlimited range. Its solar cell, actually required for effective motoring, is too large to fit on the trimaran, but the hull system increases the solar cell area by 40 percent in calm conditions. It will carry a variety of electric UAVs (unmanned aerial vehicles) that will be flown to conduct experiments during its voyage. Once launched, *MARS* would be controlled by a computer, or by a captain sitting behind a virtual bridge onshore. It would sail out of Plymouth via remote control and then switch to autonomous control once out at sea. Conceived by Brett Phaneuf of MSubs, *MARS* has been designed by John and Orion Shuttleworth and, funds obtained, will be built at Plymouth University.

Another concept that would be propelled by a diesel-electric pod systems is the *CF8* (= "cars and family in 80 meters"). Designed by Sea Level Yacht Design in Muiden, the Netherlands, this 80-m (262 ft) superyacht features a 950 ft² swimming pool that can be converted into a dance floor. It has its own artificial waterfall and a showroom to hold eight luxury electric automobiles. With an 80-m beam and 30-m draft, CF8 will have a cruising speed of 18 knots.

In September 2016, the Dutch shipyard Feadship of Haarlem announced the 74.5-m (245-ft) *Choice*, designed by Tanno Weeda, at the Monaco Yacht Show. The mothership

Eoseas **is a 305-meter five-hulled pentamaran cruise ship concept, planned for 2020, whose hybrid power comes from a combination of diesel-electric, solar and wind (Stirling Design International).**

is a cruising platform, away from which two 24.5-m (80-ft) detachable electric tenders, *Freedom Won* and *Freedom Too*, each with two double suites, a single cabin and a lounge, can separate and accelerate off to marinas or places the mothership cannot reach. While attached, the tenders provide additional electric propulsion and stability to the slower mothership. Other ways to leave the mothership include a two-passenger drone located at the top of the yacht and an amphibious beach house apartment.

Japan-based Nippon Yusen KK (NYK) is developing a "green" container ship that emits 69 percent less CO2 than existing models. The so-called NYK *Super Eco Ship* 2030, which is currently in design stage, will be 353 meters (1,160 ft) long and mainly powered by fuel cells. NYK says the ship's fuel cells (40 megawatts) will use liquefied natural gas as a hydrogen source. In emergency cases, solar sails will supply additional energy. The ship will be built using newly developed friction-resistant material in order to boost its eco-friendliness. NYK plans to complete development of the futuristic vessel by 2030.

This should not be confused with the Japan Peace Boat NGO's hybrid wind and solar-powered *Ecoship*. Architectural naval design company Oliver Design has based the *Ecoship* design on biophilic principles, incorporating cutting-edge technology to deliver a 20 percent reduction in propulsion energy, a 50 percent decrease in electricity load, and a 40 percent reduction in C02 emission in comparison to similar vessels built before 2000. Some of the most notable features include: ten masts to harness wind energy for propulsion, solar-panel-covered sails, a 6,000 m² top-deck solar farm, a closed-loop water system to reuse, purify and repurpose water, and waste heat recovery systems whereby it is hoped that 80 percent of the energy normally lost in the air and in the water can be reclaimed for use. Its maiden voyage is scheduled for 2020, with the vessel offering educational voyages, serving as a "floating sustainability laboratory," contributing to research on the ocean, climate and green marine technologies.

Wallenius Wilhelmsen Logistics, the Norwegian/Swedish shipping company, announces that their E/S *Orcelle* would be made from aluminum and thermoplastic composites, rather than carbon steel, as they are lighter, more fatigue-resistant, easier to shape, more recyclable and require less maintenance. *Orcelle* has three solar sails, each with an area of 1,400m² (15,070 ft²) and made from composite material, which can be rotated and positioned to catch the wind. Their 800 m² (8600 ft²) of photovoltaic panels generate a maximum of 2,500 kW of solar electricity; when not used for propulsion, the sails would be folded back against the upper deck of the ship to maximize the amount of solar energy they receive. More electricity-generating components are located underneath the ship. Joining the sponsons to the keel of the main hull are 12 horizontal fins, three on each sponson. These are configured to move up and down as the ship moves through the water, with the movement converted into electricity by hydraulic motors. The solar and wave energy is planned to be stored in the form of hydrogen, obtained by electrolytic splitting of seawater. The hydrogen would be converted back to electricity in on-board fuel cells with a total output of 10,000 kW. *Orcelle* will have two Azipods, one at either end of the main hull, and each incorporating a motor, gearbox and propeller. Conceptual work began on the *Orcelle* in 2004, with the ship first presented a year later. Since then, WWL envisages an in-service date for an *Orcelle*-like ship around 2025.

Norsepower, in partnership with Maersk Tankers, Energy Technologies Institute (ETI) and Shell Shipping & Maritime, is preparing to retrofit two 30-m tall by 5-m diameter Flettner Rotor Sails on a 109,647-ton Maersk tanker to carry out trials until the end of 2019 and measure fuel reduction and operational experience. A reduction of 7–10 percent is predicted.

Recalling Jules Verne's *Propeller Island* (see Chapter Two) is the Floating Ecopolis, otherwise known as the *Lilypad*, capable of holding 50,000 people, with electric systems including maneuvering, 100 percent sustainable. For a smaller version of this, the BMT Nigel Gee design consultancy of Southampton has teamed up with Yacht Island Design of Nottingham to create a four-legged island called Project Utopia. Measuring 330 ft (100 m) in length and breadth, and spanning over 11 decks with the equivalent volume of a present-day cruise liner, there is enough space to create an entire micro-nation. BMT Nigel Gee describes the Utopia as not a sea-going yacht, but a structure which uses sun, wind and water to generate electricity. Each leg supports a fully Azimuthing thruster, and with four such units, Utopia is able to move around between desired locations at slow speeds. A large central structure bisects the water surface, acting as the conduit for the mooring system, as well as housing a wet dock for access by electric tenders. In addition to tender access, the design features multiple helicopter pads. BMT Nigel Gee conceives the vessel adapted as floating resorts, casinos, or a "personal island."

Drone ships may be the next generation of shipping. With an average of 900 fatalities per year, the mortality rate in shipping is 90 percent higher than in comparable land-based industries. Studies have shown that the majority of these accidents are caused by human error. Unmanned vessels take this factor out of the equation and make the operation of these ships more cost-efficient. Rolls-Royce has also launched a $7.2 million autonomous ship project intended to pave the way for drone vessels. The Advanced Autonomous Waterborne Applications Initiative will produce specifications and prelim-

Measuring 330 feet (100 meters), *Utopia* **is a floating community which will move around using its four Azimuthing thrusters (BMT Nigel Gee).**

inary designs for next-generation ship solutions. The project will run through 2017, and the Rolls-Royce unmanned ship could potentially store more cargo and expend less fuel. The project known as MUNIN—Maritime Unmanned Navigation through Intelligence in Networks—is a collaborative research project, co-funded by the European Commissions under its Seventh Framework Programme. But Munin is in Norse mythology also the name of one of Odin's ravens that each day flew around the world without guidance, gathering information, and in the evening safely returning the information—its "cargo"—to its master, the Norse god Odin. MUNIN aims to develop and verify a concept for an autonomous ship, which is defined as a vessel primarily guided by automated on-board decision systems but controlled by a remote operator in a shoreside control station. Budget: Total: €3.8 million; Funding: €2.9 million. The MUNIN consortium consists of eight partners with both scientific and industrial backgrounds located in Germany, Norway, Sweden, Iceland and Ireland. It is coordinated by the Fraunhofer Center for Maritime Logistics and Services CML in cooperation with MARINTEK. On June 10–11, 2015, the project partners and more than 50 guests met at the final event of the research project MUNIN, led by Fraunhofer CML. After nearly three years of research in the draft of the autonomous ship, the work concluded at the end of August.

A three-day Autonomous Ship Technology Symposium took place in mid–June 2016 in Amsterdam; Hosted at the Electric and Hybrid Marine World Expo. The projects MUNIN and The Advanced Autonomous Waterborne Applications Initiative, being led by Rolls-Royce, have shown that the technology is not far away.

Since August 2013, a group of highly qualified engineers and technologists led by Hans Anton Tvete, senior researcher in the Department of Maritime Transport, DNV GL in Høvik, Norway, have been working diligently on the project *ReVolt*, a 60.23-m (198 ft) *unmanned*, emission-free and battery-powered ship concept for short sea shipping with space for 100 containers on board. DNV GL is one of the world's leading ship and offshore classification societies (in the top 3 certification bodies), and a leading technical advisor to the global oil and gas industry. The *ReVolt*'s 3000 kWh battery, as developed by SINTEFF, a Norwegian-German (former Swiss) firm, uses a rechargeable zinc-air (Zn-air) technology, offering significantly higher energy density than regular batteries. *ReVolt*'s batteries are considerably less costly to manufacture than li-ion batteries and there are no toxic materials applied. The zinc-air battery was developed in the mid–1990s by John F. Cooper and colleagues at the Lawrence Livermore National Laboratory (LLNL) in California. The 3000 kWh unit will give the ship a range of 100 sea miles. At an average speed of 6 knots, the vessel faces less water resistance than other ships, which usually travel at about 8.7 knots. The slight loss of speed allowed the engineers to fit a straight vertical bow, further reducing water resistance along the ship's entire profile and ultimately saving energy. At the time of writing a 3-m (10 ft) scale model of *ReVolt* has undergone trials.

From 2016, Norway's Maritime Executive announced that it was moving ahead to construct a fleet of plug-in hybrid ships to service its marine industries. In a joint program with the Norwegian government, Oslo-based DNV GL has launched the Green Coastal Shipping Program, which aims to create the most environmentally friendly vessels in the world. The ships will use LNG and batteries as energy sources. "We envision a fleet of offshore vessels, tankers, cargo, container, bulk and passenger ships, ferries, fishing and aquaculture vessels, tugs and other coastal vessels, run entirely or partly using batteries, LNG or other green fuels," said DNV GL's Narve Mjøs, who is the program director for the Green Coastal Shipping Program. The first project is a cargo ferry plug-in hybrid for short ocean voyages. The second is a battery-powered coastal tanker project. The third project is a hybrid vessel for commercial fishing operations, while the fourth will convert a cargo ship into a hybrid battery and LNG carrier. Converting existing vessels into LNG carriers has been seen as cost-effective to many small operators. In addition to the low-emissions vessels, the program will develop a green port facility that uses less energy than usual and has a minimal carbon footprint. It will make use of electric heavy-duty vehicles and cranes and will have dockside charging stations to service the plug-in hybrid ships.[7]

Sondre Henningsgård, managing director of Norway's Maritime Battery Forum, has stated:

> By 2025 all new projects in the Norwegian domestic coastal fleet should be electrified where possible and hybridized and use zero or low emission fuels when necessary. By 2025 Norway should be well on its way towards a zero emission coastal fleet, and be the most environmentally friendly coastal fleet in the World. The general idea for the coastal fleet is that by 2050 it should be as close to zero emission as possible. Hence, most new ferries in Norway are now being electrified, and use LNG or Bio-fuels. The newest is of course the hydrogen hybrid ferry set to be sailing in 2021, and Yara Birkeland, a fully electric and autonomous vessel which will sail manned from 2018 and unmanned hopefully from 2021, twenty boats will be in service and 16 boats nearing completion. In addition, most ferries in the fjords will be electrified within the next decade. Probably cruise ships will also have to comply with emission control in the fjords. The future of electric (mostly hybrid) ships is looking very good. As for smaller boats, Norway has not yet really started the uptake of personal leisure boats running on battery, but this will surely come at some point.[8]

As one example, Norwegian ferry operator Fjord 1 is building six pure battery ferries to meet Norwegian Government requirements for zero-emission technology. From January 2018, Fjord1 will be operating the two new battery ferries on the 1.5-mile (2.4-km) route between Anda and Lote on the west coast of Norway, and will be the first ferry connection in Norway where the Road Administration requires the use of zero-emission technology. Construction of the new ferries has begun at the Tersan Shipyard in Turkey. The Norwegian ship design company Multi Maritime has developed the design, in close cooperation with Fjord1, and they will both have a cargo capacity of 120 cars and 12 trailers with the capability to carry 349 passengers. A unique feature of these new ferries is that they will be automatically controlled during the crossing under the supervision of the captain with Rolls-Royce supplying the automated control system. These take their place alongside seven other electric and plug-in hybrid ferries under construction by several yards for Multi Maritime. Analysis shows that some 84 ferries in Norway are ripe for conversion to electric power, while 43 ferries on longer routes would benefit from conversion to hybrids.

Another, *Elfrida*, 46-ft (14-m) long, the world's first electric boat for fish farming has gone into operation for Salmar Farming AS, Norway, to transport feed and equipment, to repair and relocate fish cages or make inspections. Siemens teamed up with the shipbuilding company Ørnli Slipp, the BlueDrive PlusC electrical propulsion system ensuring the effective operation of the ship even under the severest conditions. *Elfrida* will be charged directly from green energies as all of the country's electricity comes from renewable sources. The fishing fleet alone consumes around 400 million liters (105 million gallons) of diesel each year. The conversion to electric propulsion could reduce its fuel consumption by 80 percent.

As part of this program, lithium-ion (li-ion) batteries using li-ion Super-Phosphate® (SLFP) chemistry—as developed by SAFT with its Seanergy® marine energy storage system offering the highest levels of safety, performance and reliability—will be used the Norwegian Maritime Executive (NMA) for use in a variety of hybrid and fully electric propulsion applications.

APPENDIX A

The World Electric
Water Speed Record

Although most lovers of electric boats prefer a leisurely 5 to 10 mph, as is the case with every type of transport, once somebody goes faster, somebody else wants to beat them.

As long ago as October 8, 1882, to show the speed with which an electric boat could move in a race situation, a "Trouvé" electric boat was launched onto the River Aube and was steered onto the race circuit only five minutes before the start. It left at gunfire and spectators noticed, not without astonishment, that in this famous race, the EB covered more than 3,200 meters (3,500 yards) in 17 minutes, averaging 11 kph (6.8 mph) and slowing down to make four turns around the buoys! This boat was also demonstrated on the Seine at Rouen.

Although difficult to verify, in 1888, British electric boatbuilder Moritz Immisch's designer-builder W.S. Sargeant took the 30.5-ft (9 m) *Malden* 56 miles downstream at an average 10 mph (16 kmh), before this launch went into service on the Blackwater for police patrol on the River Dee. (Elsewhere it is "reported" that a Monsieur Flaurin constructed a 52-ft (16 m) electric launch with a 60 hp electric motor, capable of traveling 30 nautical miles at a 10 knots (18.5 kmh) top speed, and 200 nautical miles at 5 knots (9 kmh). This boat is reported to have weighed only 3 cwt!

Nothing really happened until the 1970s, that is, when the Electric Division of Eagle-Picher, Inc., in Joplin, Missouri, was producing state-of-the-art batteries such as the silver-zinc or nickel-zinc couples. To promote these batteries, Division President James Dines decided to attack a range of speed and distance records. A driver-builder called Jack Reed was employed, and a lakester was built out of the fuel tank of a jet aircraft. Reed's tubular steel chassis was covered by an aluminum body and used plastic windows. *Silver Eagle* was powered by a General Electric series-wound motor, and weighed just 1,140 lbs, mainly due to its silver-zinc batteries. In August 1972, Jack Reed went out on the Flats and covered the flying mile at 237 kph (146.4 mph) in *Silver Eagle*, hitting a top speed of 152.59 mph (245.5 kph). This land record is one of twenty-one records established by this vehicle for electrics—14 national and 7 international.

Before long the speed started to climb, but without disturbing the silence of the Salt Lake. On August 19, 1974, Mike Corbin set a new world record for the flying kilometer of 165.367 mph (266 kph) battery powered Yardney-Corbin motorcycle *Quick Silver* at Bonneville. Its silver-zinc batteries had been supplied by the Yardney Electric Company of Pawcatuck, Connecticut. This machine, weighing just over 700 lbs and 9 ft in length, stored

13.5 kWh in its 100-cell battery, which delivered 1,000 amps at 120 volts to 2 jet engine starter motors rated at 100 hp each. In a previous practice run, *Quick Silver* had unofficially reached a speed of 171 mph (275 kph). A few days later, on August 23, 1974, the officials at the Bonneville National Speed Trials clocked the *Battery Box*, powered by lead-acid batteries, over the flying mile and kilometer at 175.061 mph (281.733 kph), with Roger Hedlund at the wheel.

Breaking records on land was one thing; breaking records on water was slightly more challenging. In 1978, *Miss Nickel Eagle*, piloted by Floyd Darryl Goade, an electrochemist working at Eagle-Picher's Battery Division in Joplin, Missouri, became the first electrically engined powerboat to create a speed record for the quarter-mile of 54.54 mph (87.77 kph), and for the measured kilometer of 45.76 mph (73.64 kph), with a peak speed of 58.91 mph (94.81 kph).

The 14-ft (4 m) three-point hydroplane hull was built by Bill van Steenwyk at Festus, Missouri, and fitted with a 180-lb series DC motor specially built by the General Electric Company to turn up to 6,500 rpm at a nominal 196 volts input, giving 94 hp. The nickel-zinc battery was developed at the Electric Division of Eagle-Picher, Inc. It was built in four sections to be series-connected after installation. Each section contained 38 cells and weighed 80 lbs. Total battery voltage was 200 under a full-power motor load of 350 amps. The driver controlled the speed of the boat with a General Electric SCR motor controller, also specially designed. The battery was good for little more than two minutes per charge,

In 1978 Darryl Goade piloted *Miss Nickel Eagle* to a world electric water speed record of 45.76 mph (courtesy EaglePicher).

and was only designed for a maximum of ten charges. Fourteen charge cycles were used in testing, and they went into the official timed runs with the battery past its prime.

As an historian of powerboat racing and an electric boating enthusiast, this author believed that one way to improve the latter breed was to adapt a tradition of the former: record-breaking. He discovered that, although scaled down, electric model powerboats had shown the way. In 1968, the British magazine *Model Boats* ran a series of articles titled "Fast Electrics" by Philip Connolly, in which electrically powered model powerboats were explained and advocated. The development of the nickel-cadmium fast-charge SAFT battery, superior to the traditional lead-acetate batteries, coupled with the public outcry against noise and pollution made by gas-engined model powerboats on public ponds and lakes, did much to escalate popularity in the "Electrics." NAVIGA (the European Union for Ship-Modelling and Ship-Model Sport) had soon organized 1kg and Unlimited Classes, although the British MPBA always preferred the 2½ Class. The longest lasting multi-race for British electric boats lasted some 10 minutes. The champions of electric model boat racing at the time were Rod Burman, Daniel Holder and David Harvey, using special silver-zinc batteries, developed at enormous cost in France. On June 17, 1978, Rod Burman set an unrestricted water speed record for electric radio-controlled boats over 110 yards (100 m) at 32.85 mph (52.86 kph). Ten years later, in June 1989, *Morena*, a 3-ft (92 cm) electric monohull designed, built, and controlled by Nick Rees, was clocked at an average 45 mph (73 kph) for two passes down a 110-yard straightaway course on a lake at Llandryd Wells in Wales. Herr Christian Lucas had designed and built a 3-ft (92 cm) three-point radio-controlled hydroplane capable of 70 mph (110 kph) on every run. Its 3 kW engine was powered by bank of Nicad batteries.[1]

To break the ten-year-old Record of *Miss Nickel Eagle* would require an experienced and wealthy powerboat enthusiast. In 1965, Fiona, the Countess of Arran, having witnessed the Paris Six Hours circuit marathon on the Seine from the yacht of the British naval architect Commander Peter du Cane, bet a friend that the following year she would be one of the starters. True to her word, in 1966 she was the sole woman competitor and finished 14th out of 90, in a monohulled boat named *Badger I*. Bored by circuit racing, Lady Arran soon progressed offshore. In *Badger II*, a 20-ft Don Shead design, she quickly set a new speed record of 55 mph (89 kph) for Class III offshore powerboats. For the 1970 season she was at the helm of *Badger III*, a Cougar catamaran. Lady Arran then turned to a young naval architect, Lorne Campbell, who designed a series of three-point hydroplanes in which she competed in offshore races. In 1971, Lady Arran piloted her powerboat *Highland Fling* across Windermere in a hailstorm to lift the Class 1 record to 85.63 mph (137.8 kph). In 1980, the Countess, in her sixties, piloted her 26-ft *Skean-Dhu* (Gaelic for the small dagger worn in a Scotsman's stocking) with its twin 225 hp Mercury outboards, to 102.45 mph (164.88 kph) on Windermere, an achievement that earned her the highest accolade in powerboating, the Segrave Trophy.

During that period, this author had written a number of magazine articles about Fiona Arran and had become something of a friend. Now, as chairman of the Electric Boat Association, I challenged my friend, at 71 years old, to take on the unheard-of: sponsor and pilot an electric powerboat that could set a water speed record of at least 50 mph (80 kph)! Plucky as ever, even though not quite knowing what an electric boat was, she at once contacted her naval architect, Lorne Campbell of Broadstone, Dorset, and asked him to come up with a new design. He drew out a 15-ft (4m50) three-pointer hydroplane with an innovative anhedral tunnel exit. For the motors, Cedric Lynch was asked to scale up his revolutionary radial armature permanent neodymium magnet motor and to build as many as would give a power output of 60 hp.

Various battery manufacturers were contacted, with varying responses. On November 23, 1988, E.T. Royds of Oldham-Crompton Batteries replied pessimistically: "In order to produce the current required, 790 Ah for at least ten minutes, the boat would need to carry around 1 ton of batteries. We therefore very much regret that we are unable to help on this occasion as the only likely publicity would be the recovery of the Countess of Arran from the watery depths!"

At the time, the Union International Motonautique, the official governing body for the sport of powerboat racing and record-breaking, had no category for electric boats. In March 1989, the UIM Sports Commission adopted a new category for electric boats: "Hull free; all power derived from on-board batteries, allowed to take on fuel between runs, but only 20 minutes to elapse between runs."

During the summer of 1989, the hull was built by Nick Barlow of MayDay Marine, Woolston, Southampton, using a composite of gaboon plywood, Kevlar, carbon fiber and resins to make a lightweight challenger that weighed only 210 lbs (95 kg). Elsewhere two contra-rotating three-blader surface propellers were made in nickel-aluminum-bronze. While all of Lady Arran's previous powerboats had been dark blue picked out in white, her electric challenger was to be white picked out in electric blue. While on summer vacation at her family's Rossdhu Castle beside Loch Lomond, her Ladyship was given a Gaelic name for the boat—"an stradag" (= the spark). Its official Registration number was E.1.

In the shed of his family home in Potters Bar, 33-year-old Cedric Lynch beavered away on his own, building and ironing out the teething troubles of his motors, each of which must put out 15 hp. As he came up against problem after problem, a succession of as many as a dozen British engineering companies helped out with special component parts and treatments, such as Morganite graphite-silver brushes. Despite this sophistication, the dashboard was fitted with the simplest of on/off buttons for power (green and red).

Meanwhile, Tungstone Energy Products had agreed to prepare a batch of their hi-tech SB40 batteries to go either side of Lady Arran's cockpit. Developing 12 volts at 35 nominal Ah, normally used as RAF jet aircraft starter batteries, they could yield up to 1,000 amps in only minutes: the perfect solution for a sprint record.

An Stradag was assembled in the stable block of Lady Arran's stately home, Pimlico House, near Hemel Hempstead, Hertfordshire. In early October, the owner-driver of this revolutionary speedboat found herself feeding and providing hot drinks to a seven-strong team. As the boat was not ready, it was decided to forego its record attempt, scheduled for the annual Powerboat Regatta on Lake Windermere, scene of her Ladyship's former triumphs.

Soon after, the challenger was ready for its maiden trials. Lorne Campbell was the first to try the boat, but when he hit the green button, nothing happened. Cedric Lynch, who had never driven a powerboat in his life, climbed into the tight cockpit to check. Once he had removed his cardboard restrictors, the engine inventor accelerated the boat down the somewhat restricting length of Cosgrove Lake in Buckinghamshire, and with his four engines turning at 4,500 rpm, reached a speed of 40 mph (65 kph) on the fourth run. Seventeen days later, following further modifications, filmed and videoed by five separate crews including the BBC, Lady Arran piloted her open-cockpit An Stradag up and down the Welsh Harp Lake (Brent Reservoir), and averaged an unofficial 45.5 mph (74.8 kmh), 1 mph faster than Miss Nickel Eagle's record of eleven years before.

On a cold late November day, Lady Arran, *An Stradag* and the team then went to the Holme Pierrpont Water Sports Center near Nottingham for the record attempt. The night before, one of the batteries had literally exploded while being charged. Fortunately there was a replacement! On the morning of November 22, 1989, a chilling 30-knot wind was gusting down the Measured Olympic Rowing Course. The media was out in force: three television crews, six national and several provincial newspapers, and a battery of photographers. And yet, this unique boat had only run for 10 minutes and had still not rehearsed the tight maneuver of recharging its batteries and getting back into the time traps in under the officially required 20 minutes. With the Royal Yachting Association timekeepers, representing the UIM, at their posts, Lady Arran was towed out into the center of the lake. Her first downwind run was timed at 49.7 mph (79.9 kmh). Towed back to the jetty, the 5-ft Benning Belatron traction unit took 12 minutes to recharge the SBS40 batteries to 80 percent of their full capacity. Meanwhile Lady Arran warmed herself up with a glass of rum, commenting to the press, "Why not? It's the proper Navy drink!" Minutes later, she was back on course, silently piloting the unique challenger into a choppy measured kilometer, and coming out of it with a time of 51.97 mph (83.62 kph). The average of 50.825 mph (81.80 kph) gave her the world electric water speed record.

Thanks to publicist Bob Huntley, in the days pre-Internet and Facebook, *An Stradag* gained media coverage in 88 outlets, from the national and regional newspapers, to the international boating and electrical press. The article in *The New Scientist* was titled "Electric

In 1989 Fiona, the Countess of Arran, piloted her hydroplane *An Stradag* to a record 50.825 mph (81.80 kmh). Painting by Arthur Benjamins (author's collection).

Boat Rides on the Current—and leaves all others in its wake."[2] It became the star feature at the 1990 London International Boat Show, and the title "The World's Fastest Electric Boat" was accepted as an entry in the *Guinness Book of World Records*. The publicity gained was immeasurable. But apart from some sponsorship from Harwin Electronics and anonymous donation from the USA, the £25,000 bill for the e-hydroplane had been footed by Lady Arran. Cedric Lynch believed that, with a couple more batteries, he could further increase the output of his four motors, enabling the speed of at least 100 kph (62 mph) to be reached. But Lady Arran decided to call it a day and see if the Americans could take the record back. Our team dispersed, somewhat frustrated.

There were, however, many spin-offs, in particular UIM Article 592, whereby the Sporting Commission proposed that electrically propelled boats were accepted as an international series divided into two classes—battery-powered and solar-powered. This proposal was voted in at the UIM General Assembly on March 17, 1991 (22 votes for, 5 abstentions). In July a contest was held on the River Po, Italy, to further establish rules for racing. In October 1991, Lady Arran challenged both Fabio Buzzi of Italy and Bob Nordskog of America, world champion powerboat drivers, to build challengers that would break her two-year-old record. Both accepted but never did anything.

However, the challenge was taken up in Washington State, USA. The original idea was to get the electric speed record back for the U.S. Led by veteran powerboat driver John Paramore, a small group of home-built electric car enthusiasts—Burton Gabriel, Fred Saxby, Don Crabtree and Dave Cloud—joined forces with another longtime powerboat speedster, Norm Boddy. To get things going, Paramore obtained ABPA permission to race electric boats head-to-head as an exhibition event at scheduled outboard races around their home state of Washington. For 1994, they chose five races sites and ran 8 two-mile (three-kilometer) sprint races from June to September. Even after running at speeds between 30 and 40 mph (50–60 kph), the electric raceboats had power surplus at the end of each race. By the end of the series, they had publicly proved that electric powerboats could plane, corner buoys and tramp up to speeds of 50 mph (80 kph).

Finally, in the kilometer trials held on October 8, 1994, at Lincoln City, Oregon, Norm Boddy of Edmonds, Washington, capped the season by setting a new world electric boat record, driving his hydro *Hardly Normal* to a speed of 55.913 mph (89.964 kph). His motor was a 48-volt Prestolite forklift unit mounted on a Mercury Speedmaster outboard racing lower unit. His runs both ways were made without recharging, but Boddy lost a little speed because he came off the plane on the turnaround and was too close to the trap entrance to be at top speed on re-entry.

The 1995 six-race season in Washington saw Norm Boddy competing in a 14-ft (4m20) Blackwell hydro, the first powerboat custom-built for electric racing. Although Boddy easily won the National Drivers' Championship with speeds of 60–70 mph (95–110 kph), it was Dave Mischke who lifted the world record. On October 14, again at Devil's Lake, Mischke piloted the 72 kW 13-ft-9" (4m10) hydro, designed and built by David Cloud of Seattle, to a new 70.597 mph (112.63 kph) average. Energy came from twelve 12-volt Optima lead-acid batteries powering an outboard Prestolite 48-volt DC pump motor developing around 96.5 hp. For 1996, e-boat racing saw Steve Cloud in the red record-holder dueling regularly with Brad Boddy in race after race, regularly achieving over 70 mph (110 kph) on the straights. Unfortunately, during the previous three years at the annual speed trials on Devil's Lake, none of "the boys from Washington" had been able to reach the magic 80 mph (130 kph), although Boddy had been testing at speeds between 78 and 82 mph (125–132 kph) during previous two weeks. But as Steve Cloud stated: "We have no plans to break our own record. We have sold our new boat that has tested well over the record to a guy in Florida. We still have the original record holder boat and will not attempt a new record until after someone breaks our record…."

In 2001, Malcolm Pittwood, Paul Hannaford, Phil Evans and Novie Dzinora of the British Speed Record Club commissioned Farrow & Chambers, Ltd., Grimsby, to build the hull of 20-foot (6.1 m) e-hydroplane they had called *Lightning Strike!* They planned to regain the record for the UK, but the challenger was never completed due to lack of funds.

There was always *An Stradag.* After the Earl's Court Boat Show, Lady Arran loaned her to the Motorboat Museum in Basildon, Essex, of which this author was founder and honorary keeper. In 1993 she sold it to Don Sidebottom of the Lakeland Motor Museum at Cartmel, Lancashire. Here it was shown until lack of exhibition space relegated it to a nearby warehouse, eventually Sidebottom decided to sell it off. At first, his reserve price of £4,000 was not reached. But then at the beginning of 2005, it was bought by Henry Engelen, a caterer and former Go-Kart racer from nearby Penryth. Engelen was originally from a Dutch family, but of English nationality. His condition for purchase was that the boat could be fit with a new battery and engine to run again. Following several offshore races, Henry Engelen had no intention in just keeping it as a museum piece. He wanted to make it "live again"!

When the author heard about this, the maddest idea came to me. Why not persuade Engelen to make a new attack on the world record? With his agreement, I started making phone calls to members of the former team. After sixteen years' research and applications of his innovative engine in narrowboats, patrol boats, Go-Karts, commercial vehicles and auxiliary gliders, Cedric Lynch, now working at Arvind Rabadia's Agnimotors concern, felt that he could build four new motors capable of delivering a total 135 hp, over twice the power of the previous units. Once this decision had been made, other members of the original team agreed to return to the non-remunerative record team, in particular naval architect Lorne Campbell and Emrhys Barrell of the Thames Electric Launch Company with his colleague, former BBC electrical engineer Ian Rutter. To refit the boat, it was decided to transport it south, to the Henley-on-Thames boatyard of Colin Henwood, normally used to building antique and classic electric boats. Much of the hull modification and renovation work was done by Chris Pattinson.

The venue for the record attempt would be Coniston Water, better known for the unlimited speed records created by Donald Campbell in his turbojet-engined *Bluebird K7* before its 320 mph final fatal loop-the-loop crash in 1967. A Records Week had been scheduled for the first week in November. As Henry Engelen was not the same diminutive size as Lady Arran, a search was made for an RYA-qualified pilot who could fit into it tight cockpit. The "jockey" chosen was Helen Loney, a 24-year-old member of the Windermere Motor Boat Racing Club. Although Helen was only 8 years old at the time of the original 1989 record, both her grandfather George and her father Paul had been very successful club racing drivers on Windermere since the 1960s. Obviously this was bound to rub off. But until now, Helen's only experience was clocking up race victories in a 90 hp Yamaha outboard-engined V-bottom Phantom, *Tempo.* In addition, Helen's husband Chris Loney, also keen on powerboating, both classic and modern, was able to use the technology at his family firm, Lonestar Advertising, to create a website for the project: electricrecordteam. com.

By the beginning of October, *An Stradag*'s frame had been adapted to take the new and slightly larger motors built at Agnimotors's new factory in Gujurat, India; this time they would use chain drives taken from the Honda C0 motorcycle. These were installed, together with twelve slightly heavier spiral-wound Exide batteries and 4 Curtis 1231C Mosfet controllers. Instead of the crude "go" and "stop" buttons of 1989, there was now a foot-operated accelerator pedal, plus on the dashboard behind the new curved windscreen, four ammeters, one voltmeter and a Garmin Quest GPS for measuring the speed.

On Thursday, October 6, 2005, Emrhys Barrell gave the refitted *An Stradag* its first test since November 22, 1989. Floating and rising up on the plane and leaving a roostertail spray in its wake, but the quarter-mile Taplow water-ski lake was not long enough to allow acceleration. Five days later, the e-hydro was clocked at 55.5 mph (34.4 kph), 5 mph better than its 1989 record. Nine days later, Helen Loney made her first test-drive at Chasewater in Staffordshire. The GPS had clocked her at 62 mph (39 kph) before a bearing failed. Following the rebuilding of the bearing and modification of the Curtis controllers, the e-hydro was trailered up to the Record Pits alongside Coniston Water, where owner Henry Engelen had rigged up a small white marquee to protect both the boat, now in white and red livery, and the team from the autumnal weather. While 30 companies had supported the original boat, the number of logos on the refitted boat showed an equally strong commitment.

To date the recharging had been carried out on dry land. For Coniston, the strategy was to recharge from 15 batteries (battery-to-battery) on board a "mother" boat, stationed ½ kilometer after the measured distance at the south end of the lake. The vessel selected for this task was the *Mobiboat*, an electric outboard–engined craft ingeniously designed for use by handicapped people. Both *An Stradag* and the *Mobiboat* became objects of great curiosity by other engineers and drivers there to challenge for records in the noisier gasoline or diesel classes.

Although water conditions on October 31 were too rough for *An Stradag*, Helen Loney went out in her 16-ft *Tempo* and, while familiarizing herself with the measured distance, clocked up her first-ever speed record of 54.78 mph in the 1.5-litre Super Clubman Mono Class (she was later to increase this to 57 mph). The morning of Tuesday, November 1, saw a calmer Coniston Water. The 4 mph *Mobiboat* went sedately down the lake to take up its position. Half an hour later, Helen's husband Chris Loney, driving their Delta V6 runabout *Red Admiral*, towed the e-hydro and his wife to just over ½ km before the time traps, marked by two vertical orange marker buoys. On board, Helen had her cuddly toy duck mascot "George." With a perfect roostertail, at 8:50 a.m. the red-and-white e-hydro accelerated through the course, clocking an impressive 70.610 mph (113.6 kph) with the on-board GPS peaking at 71.8 mph (115.5 kph).

We all waited anxiously while the speedboat docked with its mother boat and the recharging plug was inserted. Amazingly, the time between Helen's two runs was 18 minutes, as in 1989. The return run was made at 9:08 a.m. at a speed of 65.561 mph (105.5 kph) with the GPS at 66.2 mph (106.5 kph). We phoned Lady Arran, now 87, who was delighted with the news, especially as it was another woman pilot. The average speed of 68.09 mph (109.55 kph) should have meant a new international record and an increase of 17 mph (27 kph). But then the Americans protested!

In 1995, an American e-hydro, piloted by David Cloud of Seattle, claimed to have clocked an average 70.597 mph (113.62 kph) on Devil's Lake, Oregon, USA. *His boat had not recharged between runs.* But then, Dave Cloud had not paid the necessary dues for his speed to be officially homologated by the UIM. When Cloud heard about *An Stradag*'s new

Helen Loney and the *An Stradag* team at Coniston, Cumbria, England (author's collection).

record being claimed as the fastest, he protested that the British had illegally recharged. This resulted in the UIM's rejecting the British bid—even though they had officially accepted *An Stradag*'s 1989 record, including recharging between runs.

Come what may, from May 2006 any new electric water speed record challengers would not be allowed to recharge *An Stradag* between runs. This has not stopped the British. Henry Engelen was planning a different and third woman in the driver's seat, Sarah Donahue. Target speed was 80 mph (130 kph), following which a second and more powerful *An Stradag II*, target speed 120 mph, would be developed. Nothing came of this. Meanwhile the Loneys' Electric Record Team bought a new hull, which Helen Loney tested during 2007 up to speeds of 120 mph (190 kph).

Ironically it was one year later, in 2008, that the world electric water speed record was lifted to 98.8 mph (160 kph) by Englishman Michael Bontoft, who ran a machine shop in Castle Rock, Washington, USA. The boat, called *Bridget's Watt Knot*, after Bontoft's wife, had 42 lithium-polymer batteries encircling the craft in two rows. Bontoft ran his boat at Devil's Lake in Lincoln City, Oregon, USA. Bontoft grew up helping his boater father Alfred "Alf" Bontoft compete in offshore powerboat racing. He was there in 1976 when his father lost his life during the Cowes-Torquay offshore race. It was the first fatality to happen at the event, which had been taking place annually for 17 years at that time. The younger Bontoft went on to expand his racing horizons. He continued as a racing mechanic for Cougar Powerboats, Ajac Hawk Racing, and Tom Gentry's American Eagle Race Team, where he built the engine-testing facility. He was part-working for Ron Jones Junior's Composite Laminate Specialties in 2007 building composite boats when he stumbled across the idea for an electric boat while googling on the Internet. When he saw the record speed of only 50 mph, he thought he could build something that could go faster. His partner, wealthy dentist Lohring Miller, thought so too.

First of all, they built a ¼ scale model and achieved a speed of 90 mph. It then took Bontoft about eighteen months and almost $30,000 to build his boat out of fiberglass, carbon fiber and honeycomb. He built it at Composite Laminate Specialties, a specialty fiberglass fabricator owned by Ron Jones, Jr., grandson of unlimited hydroplane designer Ted Jones. There, Mike was able to tap into generations of boat building and design experience. For batteries he chose 42 low-weight lithium-polymer starter batteries donated by a Korean company, Enerland Division of A123 Systems. When these were combined into six packs, roughly 22 volts lithium were given off, with a total voltage of 133. These batteries were then distributed around the craft. The only drawback of this multiple approach was that they had to charge each battery individually with highly specialized chargers. The electric motor was a rebuilt Prestolite brushed DC unit normally used in forklift trucks. For the right prop, they had help and advice from Bob Wartinger, seasoned record breaker.

Because of *Bridget's Watt Knot*'s cramped size, Bontoft had to lie down in the hull to maneuver it, with just a columnless steering wheel and throttle. He also had an on-board GPS speedometer. On the first test run down Washington's Silver Lake, the boat did about 78 mph (126 kph). A few adjustments helped Bontoft to increase the speed so that on the last test run, it reached an unofficial 101 mph (163 kph).

On Saturday, October 12, 2008, Bontoft launched his white-and-blue e-hydro onto Devil's Lake in Lincoln City, Oregon, and clocked a new 92 mph (148 kph) UIM record. The following day he set an APBA record of 98.2 mph (158 kph). Having changed gear ratios for another attack at the UIM run, he hit the kilo mark at 97 mph (156 kph) and the exit mark just under 103 mph (166 kph). On the return run with the motor hot, both marks were hit at 99 mph (159 kph), giving a new UIM WSR of 98.806 mph (159.013 kph). This was homologated in the UIM *Bulletin* #351, page 57.

The same month, Helen Loney, 27, hit an average speed of 125.8 mph (202.4 kph) in her Formula One gas-engined race boat *Crescendo* during Coniston Records Week. It beat the previous speed of 115.1 mph. She had bought the *Crescendo*, so she could practice driving at speeds in excess of 100 mph in training to drive the prototype electric boat. The following day, she set a new national electric outright water speed world record of 76.8 mph (123.6 kph) driving *Firefly*, her Lynch-engined electric three-point hydroplane, on Coniston Water. When the British team heard of Bontoft's 99 mph record, they realized that they must take a longer look at something that could go at least 120 mph. To date this has not been achieved on either side of the Pond.

Records have been established. At the Coniston Records Week in November 2012, Peter White drove the *Mylne Bolt 18* to a British water speed record of 32.77 mph (52.74 kph) for the National "Unrestricted Electric Runabout" class. The *Bolt 18*, designed by David Gray of Mylne Boats, Glasgow, was powered by a 100 kW electric motor and a watertight 400 volt lithium battery pack. Its normal range was 10 miles at 20 knots.

UQM Technologies, Inc., PowerPhase® 100kW electric motor and controller system provided the power for the Abel Yachts LightWave *Ampere* to set a European speed record for Unlimited Electric Runabout on September 23, 2014. The runabout maintained an average speed of 32.9 knots (60.9 kph) with two adult passengers over a measured mile. The speed record was witnessed and certified by the Croatian Registry of Shipping.

Ironically, in a radio-controlled *model* electric three-point hydroplane, the Chinese-built 6cm70 *Sea Fire Super Version RTR*, powered by a 4-pole 3660 water-cooled brushless motor with energy from twin 2S 7.4V LiPo batteries, has since 2015 been timed at speeds of 59 mph (95 kph). It is being distributed by Amewi Trading based in Borchen, Germany.

In 2015, Henry Engelen loaned *An Stradag* to the Fastonwater Foundation for their projected museum in Norfolk, England. Then in September 2015, while writing this history, the author thought it might be good to launch a new attempt on the EWSR—over 100+ mph and upward. In talks with his friend, documentary filmmaker, and author David Delara, a plan was launched whereby Donald Campbell's daughter Gina, age 64, would pilot the new challenger. Both David and Gina had strong contacts with the head of Longines, the Swiss watchmaker, who had timed the record runs of Sir Malcolm and Donald Campbell, Gina's grandfather and father respectively. The author and Campbell began to exchange data. They soon learned that an existing 16-ft (4.9-m) hydroplane hull might be available from Engineering CEO, Gordon Mussett in Norfolk; it had been designed and built for Mussett to set a 125-mph (200-kph) petrol-engined record, but never used. It would have to be modified to take e-motors and batteries. Contact was also made with Echandia Marine in Stockholm who had developed an innovative rapid battery recharge system. In November 2016 after long deliberation, Longines and their parent company Swatch decided to sponsor the challenge. But their financial offer alone was not enough to take the project to its ultimate goal. So Mark Chapman of Mussett Engineering began a search for engines, batteries and additional sponsors. In November 2016 after long deliberation, Longines were prepared to part-sponsor, but their financial offer alone was not enough to take the project to its ultimate goal. So Mark Chapman of Mussett Engineering began a search for engines, batteries and additional sponsors. If sponsorship is secured, the *Bluebird* would be powered by twin McClaren electric motors totaling 295-kw modified from the Formula E racing automobile series, with swift-yield lithium batteries. The hydroplane would then undergo trials in the UK, prior to making an official attempt on the record perhaps in 2018 Stockholm, Sweden during the world's first e-powerboat speed regatta—including several categories of boat. Once the *Bluebird*'s speed limit had been reached, a second boat may be designed and built, its 200-mph (322-kph) target speed reached using fuel-cell and state of the art battery technology. Such is the challenge of record-breaking, even electric.

APPENDIX B

Tûranor PlanetSolar

In 2004, Raphaël Domjan of Lausanne, Switzerland, had the idea of circumnavigating the world at speed in a boat uniquely powered by solar energy so as to demonstrate the potential of sustainable energy. He originally approached MW-Line, whose team enthusiastically took on the challenge, and after a series of studies developed a prototype of a fast craft capable of circumnavigating in 120 days. The project "Planet Solar" was born and the next 3 years were spent searching for financing.

But then in 2008 Domjan met and persuaded German businessman Immo Ströher, head of the solar energy firm IMMOSOLAR GmbH based in Langen, Germany, to back his project. Ströher was formerly chairman of the supervisory board of SOLON Energy GmbH, one of the largest solar module manufacturers in Europe. Ströher wished to build the craft as per his ideas and in a yard located in Germany. MW-Line therefore lost the opportunity it had been hoping for. With no other orders on its books during what had become the beginning of the financial crisis, the Swiss firm ceased its operations and went into liquidation. Ströher now financed the project through his Rivendell Holding Company in Zug, Switzerland.

Having been chosen, the Knierim Yachtbau in Kiel, Germany, in turn contacted Craig Loomes of Auckland, New Zealand. His design firm, LOMOcean, well known for producing such wave-piercing composite-hulled trimarans as *Earthrace*, suggested a similar configuration for the solar globe-trotter.

What was needed was a seaworthy multihull design with flat central deck that would maximize the available area for a solar-cell array; retractable side wings and rear flap to add additional solar-power capacity while still light enough for the crew to deploy manually; and carbon/epoxy sandwich construction to reduce vessel weight as much as possible, minimizing propulsion requirements. A design was model tested in wind tunnels and was tank tested at the Australian Marine College in Tasmania, to determine its hydrodynamics and aerodynamics, which would enable it to reach a cruising speed of 7.5 knots (14 kph) and a top speed of 14 knots 16 mph (26 kph).

Meanwhile, to be co-skipper of their ship, Domjan chose the experienced yachtsman Gérard d'Aboville of France. Earlier in his life d'Aboville had solo-rowed across both the Atlantic and Pacific Oceans, journeys that took 71 and 134 days, respectively.

The building of the boat in lightweight and durable carbon-fiber composites by the Knierim Yachtbau GmbH (Kiel, Germany) at Kiel's Howaldtswerke Deutsche Werft boatyard, lasted 14 months and required more than 64,000 hours of work. It measured 31 m (101 ft) long × 15.2 meters (50 ft) wide × 1m55 (5 ft) draft. The deck was covered by 537

From left, Raphaël Domjan, Immo Ströher and Captain Gérard d'Aboville, key players behind the *Tûranor Planet Solar* adventure (courtesy Raphaël Domjan).

meters^2 (5,780 ft^2) of solar panels rated at 93 kW, manufactured by SunPower Corp. (San Jose, California) and assembled into panels by SOLON AG (Berlin, Germany). In the ship's two hulls, there were 6 blocks of lithium-ion batteries, weighing 8.5 tons made by GAIA Akkumulatorenwerke GmbH of Nordhausen, Germany. At the time, this was the largest mobile civilian battery in the world. When the batteries were fully recharged, the boat should be able to navigate for 72 hours in complete darkness! These in turn were connected to two 60 kW permanent magnet synchronous electrical motors turning at 1600 rpm in each hull. Before even casting off, the vessel had cost Ströher an estimated €12.5 million. There had been other sponsors such as the Swiss watchmaker Candino.

MS *Tûranor PlanetSolar* was launched in Kiel on March 31, 2010. The name Tûranor is said to have been derived from J.R.R. Tolkien's novel *The Lord of the Rings*, and the word *tûranor* translates from his invented Elvish language, Sindarin: "tur" means "power" and "anor" means "sun."

Six months later, on September 27, 2010, *Tûranor PlanetSolar* set off from Monaco to circumnavigate the globe solely with the aid of solar power. The boat had a crew of four. The captain of the expedition was Frenchman Patrick Marchesseau, but at the midpoint of the circumnavigation (in New Caledonia in mid–May 2011), the French Canadian Erwann Le Rouzic took over as captain, to share the master's responsibility with Captain Marchesseau. Other participants were Christian Ochsenbein (Bern, Switzerland) and Jens Langwasser (Kiel, Germany); as well as the project initiator, president and expedition leader Raphaël Domjan (Neuchatel, Switzerland).

A significant stopover was Cancún, Mexico, during the 2010 United Nations Climate

Change Conference held there from November 29 to December 10, 2010. It was not all easy going; TPS had to cross the Gulf of Thailand, Vietnam and Malaysia against the wind and the current, and during the monsoon period. At the end of May, just before its arrival in Brisbane, TPS encountered its severest test. For three days, the multihull battled with winds of Force 7 and Force 8, with gusts of over 50 knots. Once they had docked in Brisbane, welcomed, as usual, by a whole flotilla of small craft and a cheering crowd, there was an official ceremony when the "PlanetSolar Relay for Hope" was launched, a global relay children and young people could take part in and present their visions and hopes for a solar energy-driven world through essays.

TPS was not alone during the voyage. A couple of dorado dolphins accompanied her for over 500 kilometers (300 mi) in the Pacific. Sometimes up to 5 whales gave close escort to the vessel, and once the crew was able to count some one hundred dolphins.

During the expedition, *Tûranor PlanetSolar* achieved the first transcontinental navigation, the first solar navigation of the Panama and Suez Canals, the first solar crossing of the Indian Ocean, the China Sea, the Red Sea and the Mediterranean. She broke two records: the fastest crossing of the Atlantic Ocean by solar boat and the longest distance ever covered by a solar electric vehicle. She had also technical problems with the propeller system, forcing the vessel to stay in an Asian port for two weeks of maintenance. To pass through the pirate-infested Gulf of Aden, she was boarded by an armed guard led by Christophe Keckeis, former chief of the Swiss Armed Forces, and covered with barbed wire. She returned to Monaco to a huge welcome on May 4, 2012, after 584 days sailing around the globe.

During the fall of 2012, for a period of six months, the record-setting solar vessel was put into dry dock at the navy shipyard at Monaco Marine in La Ciotat (France), where it underwent extensive maintenance works. The most significant changes were replacing the surface propeller propulsion system with a fully immersed system and changing the steering system for one that made it easier to maneuver the vessel. At Abu Dhabi, the variable pitch control had broken and they had lost some 17 hours in repairing it in mid ocean.

In May 2013, *Tûranor PlanetSolar*, with Captain Gérard d'Aboville at the helm, solar-cruised off into the Atlantic again, within the context of the PlanetSolar DeepWater scientific campaign, led by professor and climatologist Martin Beniston from the University of Geneva. This expedition aimed to explore oceanic processes interacting with the atmosphere by taking measurements in air and water on more than 8,000 km (5,000 mi) along the Gulf Stream. The boat was also equipped with a trawling filtering net/scoop, enabling it to collect up to 8 tons of marine pollution as it sailed across the ocean. During the crossing TPS broke its own record, crossing the Atlantic Ocean from Las Palmas to Saint Martin in the Caribbean in only 22 days, four days faster than on the circumnavigation trip. The boat left Las Palmas on April 25 and arrived in Marigot on Saint Martin on May 18. The trip led to Miami, Florida, and then continued as a scientific expedition along the Gulf Stream. Along the way, researchers on Beniston's team examined the characteristics of seawater, phytoplankton, and suspended particles in the air, all to get a better picture of how the atmosphere and the ocean interact and influence climate. On the return trip the boat reached St. John's, Newfoundland, on August 1, 2013, before heading back across the Atlantic.

For 2014, TPS went on her third voyage. This 9,000-km (5,600 mi) trip, spread out over 5 months of navigation, featured stops in Atalayoun (Morocco), Monaco, and then Greece, where the ship transformed into a scientific platform as part of the "TerraSubmersa" archeological expedition, led by the University of Geneva (UNIGE). The expedition, which took place during the month of August, explored the prehistoric landscapes that have been

Tûranor Planet Solar in Monaco after her circumnavigation (courtesy Raphaël Domjan).

TPS Crew with Explorers' Club flag at Monaco. From left, Jens Langwasser, Raphaël Domjan, Captain Patrick Marchesseau, Erwann le Rouzic, Christian Ochsenbein (courtesy Raphaël Domjan).

swallowed up by the waters of the Kiladha Bay, located off the coast of Greece, in order to reconstruct them and identify potential traces of human activity.

She then returned to Venice for the winter. His original mission complete, Immo Ströher decided to put her up for sale. After weeks of exchanges and a conference meeting in New York at the United Nations, Ströher decided to offer TPS to Marco Simeoni, president of the Race for Water Foundation. This is a charity dedicated to fighting against plastic pollution in the oceans and had been conducting a scientific expedition to assess marine litter in all of the oceans—the Race for Water Odyssey. The conclusions reached will allow the Foundation to launch campaigns to fight against this plague and to better manage plastics end-of-life and to significantly reduce the floating litter in European waters by 2020.

In 2015, TPS made a stopover at the Villa Mediterranée in Marseilles to take part as a guest of honor at the Mediterranean Climate Summit MEDCOP 21; the president of France, François Hollande, and Prince Albert II of Monaco went aboard. Moored in Marseilles in front of the "Village of Solutions," she hosted on-board conferences. She then cast off and continued to the Cité de la Voile Eric Tabarly in Lorient, northern France, where, renamed *Race for Water*, she began her transformation into a laboratory to present on-board plastic waste-upcycling solution demonstrators. During the World Conference on Climate Change, the COP 21, held in Paris in early December 2015, *Race for Water* docked in the Seine for five days to demonstrate the possibilities of clean navigation and plastic responsibility to delegates from all over the world. On April 9, 2017, cheered on by a flotilla of boats, *Race for Water*, refitted by Swiss Hydrogen with a solar energy/hydrogen technology, left Lorient

La Base for its future voyages: a five-year program (2017–2021), serving as an as educational platform, itinerant laboratory and demonstration of support for the promotion of Clean-tech innovations. Twenty-five hydrogen tanks at 350 bars, two 30 kW fuel cells of, and two 5 kW electrolyzers complete the 500 m² (5,330 ft²) of solar panels and the 4 lithium ion batteries (754 kWh). The whole hydrogen system allows storage of 2,800 kWh, so gaining up to 6 days of autonomy, with a very advantageous mass balance: the hydrogen storage is 10 times lighter than the storage in battery.

Captained by Gérard d'Aboville, during 2017–2018, she will be in the Bermuda and California areas for the America's Cup. From 2018 to 2020, she will cruise in the Pacific Zone North/South China Sea for the Tokyo Olympic Games, and finally in 2020–2021, she will head for the Middle East for the Dubai Universal Exposition.[1]

APPENDIX C

Cable Electric Boats

Although in the 1890s electric passenger boats were proving a resounding success, it was soon realized that for workboats going up and down narrow canals, there was a problem. For centuries, such vessels had made their voyages towed by a horse or mule walking along the towpath. Early bulky batteries took up so much space in a narrowboat they left little room for the cargo. The propeller or paddlewheel would also create the same wash as a steamboat, destroying the delicate canal banks. From the 1890s until the coming of the gas engines, several solutions were adopted. Among them: trolley propeller towing—engine on the boat; trolley submerged chain towing—engine on the boat; manned electric mules—engine on the banks.

Only ten years after the first experimental trolleybus, in 1893, Frank W. Hawley, a wealthy entrepreneur and a director of the Cataract General Electric Company of Niagara Falls, converted a steamboat called *Ceres* into a trolleyboat. Electricity was taken from the Rochester Street Railway station and two 25 hp Westinghouse street railway type motors using 500 volts were installed on board, each with its own shaft and prop. An initial line of trolleys was set up above New York's Erie Canal to which the boat was linked by two flexible wires attached to an over-running traveler. The first public demonstration of the renamed *Frank W. Hawley* trolleyboat was made on November 19, 1893, in the presence of New York Governor Roswell P. Flower and many distinguished guests, and was pronounced completely successful. The Financial Panic of 1893, political squabbling over the choice of electrical contractor, the problems of positioning trolley wires for boats traveling through locks, over wide water stretches or under rising and lowering drawbridges, put a damper on an enterprising venture.[1]

In 1896, three years after the experiments with the *Frank W. Hawley*, a trolleyboat on a system devised by Richard Lamb was tested on a 6-kilometer (3.7 miles) stretch of the Erie Canal (at Tonawanda) and on the Raritan Canal in New Jersey. The idea was to use cheap electricity generated by the Niagara waterfalls, but eventually nothing happened. In 1898, the Lamb system was tested on the Finow Canal in Brandenburg, Germany,[2] but the Germans decided in favor of electric mules developed by Siemens and Halske engineers Köttgen and Zander.

Teltow Canal, on the Kleinmachnower See, joins the Rivers Havel and Spree, 17 km southwest of Berlin. In 1903, German Siemens engineers experimented with a 17.59 m trolleyboat on a 1.3 km (0.8 mi) stretch on Machnower Lake and the canal. The two outer engines, driven by 20 hp engines, also served the control. The middle propeller was driven by a 25 hp engine, which was used solely for the movement. The DC electric motors used

Overhead cable electric barge (from Georges Dary, *A Travers l'Electricité*, 1894).

the current from three large accumulators or directly from the overhead line across Machnower Lake. The current collector was mounted on a ship's mast so that the ship had about five meters of movement on both sides. The accumulators could also be loaded from the overhead line. The purpose of the facility was to avoid damage caused by the wake of large coal ships supplied by the adjacent power stations of Schönow and Steglitz. The ships were therefore towed by the *Teltow*. Because of the width of the water, no towline could be installed in the section concerned. Electric tractors ran on rails along both banks, taking their current from an overhead conductor. It was a very sophisticated machine, creating almost no wash because of a special arrangement of three propellers.

Towards the end of 1893 such a system was set up on the Bourgogne Canal in France. The hauling machinery was operated by an electric motor on the boat, which received current from an overhead trolley circuit. Operation started in 1894 and the line remained in service for more than 20 years. The installation at the Bourgogne Canal gave great satisfaction and it was the first electrical boat propulsion system to be operated on a practical, commercial basis. Moreover, it was a zero-emissions transport system: the electricity was generated on both sides of the track by means of turbines placed at the cascades of two successive locks, having a fall of 7.5 meters (24.5 feet). Apart from the ecological advantage, the use of renewable electricity meant that the line was working at almost no cost.

In 1897, six years after the city of Worcester, Massachusetts, received its first electric trolley streetcars, trolleyboats were used in the building of a sewer measuring 18 ft (5 m) wide and 13 ft (4 m) high. Directed by 27-year-old Harrison Prescott Eddy, a fleet of six scows, 27-ft (8.2 m) catamarans, daily carried 12,000 bricks, 50 barrels of cement, and 100 barrels of sand to the site, using a double trolley system of wires hung from insulated brackets in the sewer's arch.[3]

The only propeller-powered trolleyboat line that was ever operated commercially was installed by Léon Gérard along a 4-km (2.5 mi) stretch of the Charleroi Canal in Belgium in 1899. The trolleyboats, powered by a 5hp Triphase Brown-Boveri engine running at 600 rpm, towed unpowered canal barges. The line formed part of a 47-km-long (29 mi) trajectory served by electric mules (see further) and was only operated for a couple of years. In England, a trolleyboat system was tested briefly during the early 1920s on the Staffordshire and Worcestershire Canal at Kidderminster.

While most of these overhead systems came to be replaced by heavy oil and diesel engine barges, one ferry is still in operation on the Straussee Lake in Strausberg, Germany. From 1894, the ferry had been hand-winched, but then in 1915 the Strausberg Railway launched *Steffi*, powered by a 170-volt single overhead wire. The ferry service, still in operation today, is numbered as route F39 by the Verkehrsverbund Berlin-Brandenburg (VBB), the joint transport association for the states of Berlin and Brandenburg.

The second option was an overhead cable across a river. In 1932, the steamboat ferry plying the Sacramento River at Princetown, California, was replaced by an overhead electric cable ferry. This continued in operation until February 4, 1950, when a huge piece of driftwood coming down the flooded river smashed into the ferry with a crash. This brought the foreman of the ferry, R.F. Rankin, out of his bed just in time to see the cables, the towers on each side of the river, and the ferry floating away. The ferry drifted 600 feet against the east side of the river bank and sank.

The third option, and one which found widespread use, at least on a regional scale, was adapted from the old and primitive method of haulage or towing by mules on the path next to the canal. But, instead of the slow and uneconomical animal, a more efficient electric towing system was set up. The electric tractor, called a "mule," ran upon a track on the banks of the canal—this method being practically a railway along the banks, the boats being trailers connected by a 50 m (165 ft) tow line to the electric mules; or either run upon the tow path itself—this method somewhat resembling a land-based trolley truck convoy. In France, after some years of unsuccessful experiments with common steam locomotives on the tow path (starting in 1873), the first electric tractor was tested in 1895 by François Marie Galliot, a civil engineer, on the Bourgogne Canal in Burgundy in central eastern France. The vehicle was a small, three-wheeled trolley truck. It drove on the tow path on metallic wheels (without the use of rails) and could haul a barge at a speed of 2.5 to 3 kph (1.5 to 1.9 mph). This velocity was not much higher than that of an animal-hauled barge, but the electric horse could tow considerably more weight. For his achievement in 1895, Galliot was awarded the Montyon Prize by the French Academy of Sciences. The following year, the Société de Halage Electrique (the Electric Haulage Company), set up by Gaillot and Michel Denèfle, extended the technology on a 43-kilometer-long (27 mi) stretch of the Canal de la Deûle and the Canal d'Aire, from Béthune to Douai (close to the city of Lille in Northern France, on the border with Belgium).[4] After some initial difficulties, a year-round regular service was established from 1898 on. The track was soon lengthened to 55 kilometers (34 miles), including the Canal de la Dérivation de la Scarpe, all the way to Courchelettes. By 1900, around 120 of these engines were in use to the satisfaction of its operators. However, the overall performance of the machine, 40 percent in the new state fell 30 percent after regular use. The damage caused to roads by metal wheels, generating too high maintenance costs, caused the end of this system in 1904 after a harsh winter, when traffic during the spring thaw had ruined roads within hours, just after costly repairs. At the Teltow Canal, near Berlin, engineers went over to electric mules, extending the system to 70 kilometers (43 miles) using 22 such mules. It remained in service until 1945, when it was dismantled by the Soviets.

The fifth option was the submerged flexible cable. Since the 1850s towboats of the Compagnie de Touage de la Basse Seine et de l'Oise had been using an onboard 150 hp steam engine linked to a submerged riverbed chain system to tow at least two barges. In 1895 this was supplemented by the Bovet System, whereby the pulley was strongly magnetized by the current of the generator, allowing for greater adhesion of the chain. Four magnetic-propeller towboats were so equipped: *Ampère*, *Arago*, *Paris* and *Conflans*.

A submerged electric cable was employed by the British at the Harecastle Tunnel on the Trent and Mersey Canal, not designed for use by gas engine–powered boats, as there were no ventilation shafts. In 1904, an electric tug was introduced that consisted of two barges (one with electric motors, the other carrying 18 tons of batteries) pulling themselves along a cable on the canal bed. Then, between 1914 and 1954, an electric tug powered from an overhead wire inside the tunnel pulled boats through.

In 2013 came the return of the submerged electric cable ferry with the KF *Hisarøy*

The trip boat *Pennine Moonraker* taken through the Standedge Tunnel under her own power by owner John Lund, shadowed by a BW electric tug, 2001 (courtesy Paul Wagstaffe).

N° 1045. — 27 MAI 1893.   LA NATURE.   401

TOUAGE PAR ADHÉRENCE MAGNÉTIQUE
SYSTÈME DE BOVET

En 1856, aux débuts du touage sur la Seine, le monopole de la traction était réservé à ce système; le remorquage était impossible sur notre fleuve. Les travaux de canalisation exécutés depuis cette

Fig. 1. — *Ampère*. Premier toueur-remorqueur à adhérence magnétique (longueur, 55 mètres; puissance, 150 chevaux).

époque, ont fait de la Seine une voie navigable de premier ordre, à grande section, à grand tirant d'eau, à faible courant, et à navigation facile; tous éléments qui ont réduit les avantages du touage au profit du remorquage, si bien qu'à la première période de possession tranquille, ont succédé la période

Fig. 2. — Système d'entraînement de la chaîne du toueur ordinaire.

Fig. 5. — Entraînement électro-magnétique de la chaîne, système de Bovet.

actuelle et toutes les difficultés de la concurrence.

Le touage ayant une incontestable supériorité à la remonte, supériorité d'autant plus grande que le courant de la rivière est plus rapide, tandis que le remorquage est, en toute circonstance, préférable à la descente, il faut pour arriver à faire un service aussi parfait que possible, employer des remorqueurs-toueurs, à hélices ou à roues, munis d'un appareil de touage ne servant qu'à la remonte, et permettant de jeter la chaîne en tous points du parcours.

21ᵉ année. — 1ᵉʳ semestre   26

The *Ampère* chain boat was used by the Compagnie de Touage de la Basse Seine et de l'Oise, 1895. Lower images highlight the chain, cogs and gears (Musée EDF Electropolis, Mulhouse).

plying between Mjånes and Hisarøy Island in Sogn og Fjordane County, Norway. Its 100 kWh new prototype battery system is based on the Canadian Electrovaya company's new generation SuperPolymer®2.0 lithium-ion battery system. Built by Solund Verft AS, the cable ferry operates approximately 10 round trips per day between the mainland and Hisarøy Island, a round-trip distance of about 1.6 kilometers (1 mi). It is driven by two winches on-board, and the onboard battery system is recharged on the mainland between the round trips and overnight. KF *Hisarøy* is built to carry 49 passengers and 6 cars.

According to a study by Zero, "Mapping of the potential for battery operation of ferries in Norway," 47 of a total of 125 ferry connections are relevant for battery operation now, with 34 relevant for battery operation in the future. The Norwegian maritime market is expected to be a key driver of battery electrification. "Our customer Wergeland AS also currently operates a diesel driven cable ferry between Duesundøy and Masfjordnes and this ferry is targeted for conversion to electric in the near future."

The Institute for Mobility (VIM) in Flanders has assembled a northwest EU project to develop the Watertruck system, where large number of small pushers and push-barges are operated in a manner similar to road transport. The pushed barge functions as a semi-trailer, which can also serve as a temporary storage unit. The first pilot was organized in collaboration with the waste disposal company SEDE Benelux and the Aquiris wastewater treatment plant, and took place during almost two weeks in March 2012. The project involved the transport of sludge from the Heros quay (Brussels) to a processing plant in the Liège region. A second test pilot took place at the beginning of October 2012: four barges containing salt were delivered to salt merchant QSalt, located on the Plassendale-Nieuwpoort Canal in Gistel. The containers were emptied using a crane. NV Willems will fill them up again with scrap metal to be transported to Kallo. An initial fleet of 31 Watertrucks is envisaged with an eventual Europe-wide fleet of 500 vessels. Various propulsion systems are being considered: electric, hybrid, LNG/CNG.

APPENDIX D

Electric Boat and Engine Builders
(Past and Present)

Boatbuilders

Aequus Boats, Rochefort, FR
Alize Electronics, Greoux les Bains, FR
Alutekna SpA, Marcon, IT
Ned Andrews, Maidenhead, Berkshire, UK
Aquawatt, Moosburg, Austria
Aquila, Basque Country, SP
Ayers at Nyack, NY, USA
Azimut-Benedetti, Livorno, IT
Walter C. Beckmann, Slocum, Rhode Island, USA
Black River Boats, Rose Hill, NC, USA
Boesch, Kilchberg/Zürich, Austria
J. Bond, Maidenhead, UK
Bossoms Boat Yard, Oxford, UK
Kerbey Bowen & Co., Maidenhead, UK
J.W. Brooke & Co., Lowestoft
Budsin Wood Craft (Budsin Electric Boats), Marshallberg, NC, USA
Canadian Electric Boat Company, Saint-Eustache, Quebec, CAN
Castle Narrowboats, Gilwern, Wales
Chantier Naval de Bordeaux, FR
Chantier Naval Franco-Suisse, Villers le lac
Classic Boatworks, Woodbastwick, Norfolk, UK
Clearwater Electric Boats, Riverside, Connecticut, USA
Coniston Launches, Coniston, Cumbria, UK
Correct Craft, Orlando, FL
Creative Marine, Aldborough, Norwich, UK
Debord, Gujan-Mestras, FR
Dissel, Vinkeveen, NL
DK Constructions, Oberammergau
Dolphin Recreation, Udaipur, Rajasthan, India

Duba, Amsterdam, NL
Dubourdieu, Gujan-Mestras, FR
Duffy Electric Boat Co, Oxnard, CA
Echandia Marine, Stockholm, Sweden
Eco Marine Power, Fukuoka, Japan
ElectraCanada, Toronto, ON, CAN
ElectraCraft, Westlake Village, CA, USA
Electra-Ghost, Annapolis, MD, USA
Electric Paddle, North Bend, Washington, USA
Electri-Craft, Syracuse, NY, USA
Emsworth Shipyard, Emsworth, HANTS
Ferretti Yachts, Forli, Italy
Fjellstrand shipyard, Omastrand, Norway
Forrest, Millwall, London, UK
Fort Bend, Sugar Land, Texas, USA
Foss Rainier Shipyard, Seattle, WA, USA
Frauscher Bootswerft GmbH, Ohlsdorf, Austria
Peter Freebody, Hurley, BERKS
Gebofa Maritiem, Hasselt
Goldfish, Oslofjord, Norway
Green Motion®, Durban, South Africa
Grove Boats (ex–MW-Line), Yvonand, Switzerland
Haines Marine, Great Yarmouth, Norfolk, UK
Harborough Marine Ltd., Leicestershire, UK
Havyard Ship Technology, Leirvik i Sogn, Norway
Bootswerft Heinrich, Kreuzlingen, SWI
Henwood & Dean, Henley-on-Thames, UK
Hobbs, Henley-on-Thames, UK
Immisch Electric Launch Co., Ltd., Kentish Town, London, UK
Köpf Solarschiff GmbH, Sulz–Bergfelden
Lear-Baylor Inc., Garden Grove, CA, USA

Lester and Perkins, Royal Albert Dock, London, UK

Li Technology Co., Ltd.

Little Boat Shop, Fairhaven, Massachusetts, USA

Luce, Argenteuil, FR

Mattieri, Lezzeno (CO)

Meakes, Marlow

Méta Chantier Navale, Tarare, France

Mirwald of Monaco

Nauticraft, Muskegon, Michigan, USA

Wouter Nieuwveld, Amsterdam, Netherlands

Nimbus Boat AB Västra Frölunda, Sweden

ODC Marine, Dalian, CHINA

Original Boat Company, Evesham, UK

Patterson BoatWorks, Ambleside, Cumbria

Pichavant, Pont-l'Abbé, Brittany, FR

Princecraft, Princeville, Québec, CAN

Pure Watercraft, Seattle, WA, USA

Quadrofoil, Slovenska Bistrica, Slovenia

Racine Hardware Mfg. Co., Racine, Wisconsin, USA

Radinn, Malmö, Sweden

Rand Boats, Skudehavnsvej, Denmark

Ray Motor Company, Maidenhead, UK

Riva, Sarnico (BG)–Italy

Ruban Bleu, Nantes, FR

Salters of Oxford, UK

William S. Sargeant of Kingston Bridge

Saviboat, Saint-Savinien

Scherpel, Loosdrecht

Charles L. Seabury & Co., Nyack-on-the-Hudson, NY, USA

T.B. Seath, Glasgow, Scotland

Seaway Yachts, Begunje, Slovenia

Dieter Seebacher, Moosburg, Austria

Søby

Solar Sailor Holdings/Ocius, Australia

Solarboat, Sydney, Australia

L. Smit & Zoon, Kinderdijk, Netherlands

Steam & Electric Launch Co., Wroxham, UK

Steiner Nautic, Mattsee, Austria

Stephens, Smith & Co., Millwall

De Stille Boot, DV Heeg, Netherlands

Strand Electric Launch Works, Chiswick, London, UK

Supiore, Amsterdam, Netherlands

Tamarack Electric Boat Company, Rome, NY, USA

Taroni, Stresa, Italy

James C. Taylor and William B. Bates, Chertsey, UK

Thames Electric Launch Company, Goring on Thames, UK

Thames Valley Launch Company, Weybridge, UK

John I. Thornycroft, Ltd., Chiswick, London, UK

Ting Hai Shipbuilding, Kaohsiung City, Taiwan

Vert-Prod, La Trinité-sur-Mer, FR

Vizianello, Venice, Italy

Water Roo, Buckfastleigh, Devon, UK

WeCo Motorsloops, Rijnsaterwoude, Netherlands

John Williams Boats, Stalham, Norfolk, UK

H. Woodhouse, Maidenhead, UK

Escher Wyss, Zürich, SWI

Yarrow Ltd., Poplar, East London, UK

Engine Builders

Accumot, Gmunden, Austria

Alternative Energies, La Rochelle, FR

Frank Allen, New York, USA

All4Solar, Trinity Park, Australia

Ansaldo, Genoa, Italy

Arka Electronics, Giethoorn

Clean eMarine (ex ASMO), Copenhagen, Denmark

Bellmarine, Gouda, Netherlands

Brimbelow, Great Yarmouth, Norfolk, UK

Combi, Vollenhove, Netherlands

Elco, New York, USA

Electric Power Storage Company, London, UK

Elektromobilfirma Tribelhorn

Immisch, Kentish Town, London, UK

Kraütler, Lustenau, Austria

Lakeland GTE, Varkaus, Finland

Leeuwestein, Dordrecht

Lynch, London

Minn Kota, Fargo, North Dakota, USA

MotorGuide, Lowell, Michigan, USA

Oceanvolt, Helsinki, Finland

Pskov Electric Machine Building Plant, Leningrad, USSR

Puma, Terneuzen

Ray Electric Outboards, Cape Coral, Florida, USA

Reckenzaun Brothers, London, UK

Rognini & Balbo (Elettromobili), Milan, IT

Selva, Sesto San Giovanni, Italy

Siemens und Halske, Berlin

Stelco Yachttechnik, Berlin

Stehr Motors, Stehr, Austria

Submerged Electric Motor of Menomonie, Wisconsin, USA

Technipower (Solomon Technologies) Danbury, Connecticut, USA

Torqeedo, Starnberg, Germany

Batteries

AGM, Caithness, Scotland

Banner, Linz, Austria

Bären, Feistritz, Austria

Chloride, Manchester, England

Commelin-Dezmazure

Corvus, Richmond, Canada

Eagle-Picher, Joslin, Massachusetts, USA

East Penn, Madison Heights, Michigan, USA

Edison, West Orange, New Jersey, USA

Elbak, Vienna, Austria

EPS, Millwall, London, UK

Fiamm, Montecchio

Fulmen, France

Furukawa, Japan

Hagen, Soest, Germany

Hoppecke, Brilon, Germany

Kokam, Gyeonggi-do, South Korea

Leclanché, Yverdon-les-Bains, Switzerland

Oldham-Crompton, Manchester, England

Panasonic, Japan

Renard et Krebs, Paris, France

SAFT, Bordeaux, France

Trojan, Santa Fe Springs, California, USA

Tudor, Rosport, Luxembourg

Tungstone (Hawker-Siddeley), Market Harborough, UK

Valance, Austin, Texas, USA

Varta, Ellwangen, Germany

Gensets

Elco

Fischer-Panda, Verwood

HFL Marine, Enfield

Mastervolt, Amsterdam

Chapter Notes

Chapter One

1. William Sturgeon, *The Annals of Electricity, Magnetism and Chemistry: And Guardian of Experimental Science* (London: Sherwood, Gilbert & Piper, 1835).
2. D.M. Lerner, "The First Electric Boat in the World," *Shipbuilding* (1988).
3. Lerner, *Ibid.*
4. Letter to Faraday, October 14, 1838, *The Collected Correspondence of Michael Faraday; Royal Institution of Great Britain, London* (Cambridge, UK: University Press, 1971).
5. Nigel Burton, *A History of Electric Cars* (Ramsbury, UK: The Crowood Press, 2013).
6. R.M. Barker, *The History of Electrical Engineering in South Wales* (Wales: Llanelli Technical College, May 1971).
7. "The Nautical Application of the Grove Cell," *The Cambrian Supplement* (August 18, 1848).
8. Antony Reckenzaun, "Electric Launches," *Scientific American Supplement* 430 (March 29, 1884).
9. Hertfordshire Archives and Local Studies.
10. Jacques Babinet, *Notice sur le Comte Antoine de Molin et sur le nouvel électro-moteur* (Paris: Jouast, 1867); Louis Figuier, *Les Merveilles de la science* (Paris: Furne, Jouvet et Cie., 1870), p.398.
11. Florio Line/Società in Accomandita Piroscafi Postali-Ignazio & Vicenzo Florio, The Ship's List.
12. Jules Verne, *Vingt mille lieues sous les mers* (Paris: Pierre-Jules Hetzel, 1870).
13. Kevin Desmond, *Gustave Trouvé: French Electrical Genius* (Jefferson, NC: McFarland, 2015), p. 64.
14. Communication made by Trouvé to the Académie des Sciences de Paris, 1881.
15. Georges Dary, *A travers l'électricité* (Paris: Vuibert et Nony éditeurs, 1895), p. 456.
16. "Electric Units and Standards," *Circular of the Bureau of Standards* 60 (September 25, 1916).
17. Kevin Desmond, *Innovators in Battery Technology: Profiles of 93 Influential Electrochemists* (Jefferson, NC: McFarland, 2016), Faure entry.
18. "A. Reckenzaun: Obituary," *The Electrician* (November 17, 1893).
19. Desmond, *Innovators*, Faure entry.
20. *The Times*, September 29, 1882.
21. *The Electrician* (October 20, 1883); *Engineering* (October 6, 1882).
22. Georges Dary, *La navigation électrique* (Paris: Baudry, 1883), p. 64.
23. In 1889, he died in a suicide pact with his mistress, Baroness Mary Vetsera, at the Mayerling hunting lodge.
24. *Frank Reade Weekly Magazine; Containing Stories of Adventures on Land, Sea and in the Air* (New York: Frank Tousey).
25. Cloris Baudet, *Électricité. Pile siphoïde impolarisable. Pile impolarisable aux reservoirs. moteurs electriques* (Paris, 1889).
26. Vouziers, in the Ardennes department in northern France is beside the River Aisne.
27. Desmond, *Innovators*, Renard entry.
28. Desmond, p. 106.
29. *L'électricité* (October 14, 1882).
30. Kevin Desmond, *The Guinness Book of Motorboating Facts and Feats and Origins and Development of Motor Craft* (Enfield, Middlesex, UK: Guinness Superlatives, 1979), p. 18.
31. "Competitive Trial of Electric Launches," *The Electrician* (September 27, 1884); *The Auckland Star*, November 13, 1884.
32. F.J. Dittmar and J.J. Colledge, *British Warships 1914–1919* (London, UK: Allan, 1972).
33. Kurt Groggert, *Personenschiffahrt on in the Havel and Spree in Berlin; Contributions to the History of Technology and Industrial Culture*, vol. 10 (Berlin, Germany: Nicolaische Verlagsbuchhandlung, 1988).
34. *The London Globe*, Saturday 30 May 1885: "In fact there is no record of the Metropolitan Police ever using electric launches on the Thames nor any other British police service using or even trialing the use of electric vessels in the UK" (Communication from Robert Jeffries, Hon. Curator, Thames Police Museum, Wapping (April 6, 2016).
35. *The Electrician* (September 17, 1886).
36. Georges Dorys, *The Private Life of the Sultan of Turkey* (London: 1901), pp. 145–6.
37. Richard Thomas, *The Waterways of the Royal Gunpowder Mills.* (Royal Gunpowder Mills, 2013), p. 54.
38. *The Brighton Argus*, October 15, 1887.
39. Edward Hawthorne, *Electric Boats on the Thames 1889–1914* (Gloucestershire, UK: Alan Sutton, 1995), p. 80.
40. *Per una nuova rotta, il vaporetto elettrico in alluminio* (Milano: actv, October 1989).
41. "The Electric Launch Viscountess Bury," *Electrical Review* (October 19, 1888).
42. *The Maidenhead Advertiser*, July 10, 1889.
43. Windsor Castle Archives, Folio III.

44. Thomas Commerford Martin, *The Story of Electricity*, vol. 2 (New York: M.M. Marcy, 1919).

45. http://www.nps.gov/jofl/lewis-semple-clarke. htm; Thomas Commerford Martin and Joseph Sachs, *Electrical Boats and Navigation* (New York: C.C. Shelley, 1894).

46. Desmond, *Trouvé*, 114.

47. "Messrs Immisch & Co's Electric Launches," *The Electrician* (October 12, 1888).

48. "Electric Launches at Henley," *The Electrician* (July 6, 1888).

49. Jules Patenôtre, *Souvenirs d'un diplomate (voyages d'autrefois)* (Paris: Ambert, 1913–14), pp. 192–194.

50. Pierre Loti, *Au maroc* (Paris: Calmann-Lévy, 1890).

Chapter Two

1. *The Daily Graphic*, March 27, 1890.

2. Donald Shaw, *The Balerno Branch and the Caley in Edinburgh* (Usk, Scotland: The Oakwood Press, 1989).

3. "Electric Launches at Henley," *The Electrician* (July 6, 1888).

4. *The Electrical Engineer* 6 (October 3, 1890).

5. Desmond, *Innovators*, Edison entry.

6. *The Engineer* (June 19, 1891).

7. *The Daily News*, March 1891.

8. "An Electric Boat," *The Richmond River Herald and Northern Districts Advertiser*, Friday, April 3, 1891.

9. *The Otago Daily Times*, January 18, 1889.

10. *The Electrical Engineer*, April 1, 1892.

11. "Electric Launches" *Electrical Review*, April 22, 1892.

12. *La Nature* (Vingtième année, deuxième semestre, 1892): pp. 992–1017.

13. Confidence de Jules Verne au journaliste Pierre Dubois en 1895, cf. Entretiens avec Jules Verne 1873–1905, Slatkine, 1998, p.122

14. *Frank Reade Weekly Magazine; Containing Stories of Adventures on Land, Sea and in the Air*, no. 71 (1894).

15. Charles Jacquin, "La Navigation électrique de plaisance," *La Lumière, journal universel d'électricité* (November 28, 1891).

16. *Scientific American* 67, no. 18 (October 1892).

17. *Records of the Electric Launch Company* (Mystic Seaport Museum, Manuscript Collection Registers, Coll. 213).

18. "Electricity at the World's Fair," *Popular Science Monthly* 43 (October 1893).

19. "The Full Text of the World's Columbian Exhibition" (Chicago, 1893).

20. *Ibid.*

21. *Ibid.*

22. Martin and Sachs.

23. Email sent to the author by Charles Houghton, August 25, 2015.

24. William C. Swanson, "ELCO," *Nautical Quarterly Magazine* 30 (summer 1985).

25. Leonard E. Alwine and David W. Seidel, *Altoona and Logan Valley Electric Railway* (Charleston, SC: Arcadia, 2005).

26. *The Mechanicville Mercury*, Saturday, October 30, 1897.

27. Gabor Steiner. *Österreichisches Biographisches Lexikon 1815–1950* (Vienna, Austria: Verlag der Österreichischen Akademie der Wissenschaften, 2007), Band 13.

28. Hella Kaeselitz (Hrsg.), Erhard Crome, Kerstin Ohms, Horst Köhler (Mitarb.): *Die Verhinderte Weltausstellung. Beiträge Zur Berliner Gewerbeausstellung 1896* (1996).

29. Thomas A. Edison, Inc., Paper Print Collection (Library of Congress).

30. Jack Daniels, whiskey distiller, describing his visit to the Fair in 1904 (Daniels Archives).

31. Magnus Maclean, *Modern Electric Practice* (London: Gresham, 1911).

32. *The Trawlers of Grimsby: Histories of the Ships That Made Grimsby Famous* (website); Gerald Toghill, *Royal Navy Trawlers Part Two: Requisitioned Trawlers* (Maritime Books, 2004).

33. Hawthorne, p. 168.

34. UK Patent N° 189800125, January 7, 1893, N°387.

35. Archiv der Stadt Pörtschach Mappe VI, iii.

36. Warwick Estate Draft Accounts 1895–98, held at the Warwickshire County Record Office. Reference Numbers TN405–408.

37. Paul Edwards, *Warwick Castle, Grounds and Gardens* (Ian Wolverson, Astroquail, 1991). based on *A Landscape Analysis*, written for the Castle in September 1980.

38. Information found on the back of a photograph of the boat, donated to the Warwick Record Office by Mr. S.J. Bissell.

39. Martin and Sachs.

40. "Electric Navigation in Bergen," *The Electrical World*, translated for the French magazine *L'électricien* (June 8, 1895).

41. This service went on for thirty years. Then in the late 1920s, the BEF ferries were rebuilt and fitted with gasoline engines. During the 1950s, all the ferries were retrofitted with Saab diesel engines. At the time of the ferry company's 75th anniversary in 1969, 38 million passengers had been transported.

42. W.J. Webb and Robert W Carrick, *The Pictorial History of Outboard Motors* (New York: Renaissance Editions, 1967); Peter Hunn, *The Old Outboard Book* (International Marine/McGraw-Hill. 2002).

43. Hawthorne, *Electric Boats*.

44. Letter to the author from A.B. Craven, Director of Library Services, Leeds Central Library, May 16, 1978.

45. *The Electrical Engineer* (October 5, 1900).

46. Desmond, *Guinness*.

47. Maclean, p. 289.

48. *Le Yacht*, July 16, 1899.

49. Swanson, "ELCO."

50. "36-Foot Electric Launch," *The Rudder* (1900).

51. *Launches and Yachts: The 1902 Elco Catalog* (reprint; Waldorf, MD: Swanson Marine Enterprises, 1984).

52. Swanson, *Launches*.

53. H. Brown, *The History of American Yachts and Yachtsmen* (Wiley Online Library).

54. Swanson, *Launches*.

55. "List of Yachts Built or Building from May 1, 1900 to May 1, 1901," *The Rudder* (1901).

56. Kevin Desmond, *Elco's Extraordinary Clients* (unpublished ms., 2010).

57. Imre Kiralfy, *Paris in London: 1902, Earl's Court: Official Guide and Catalogue* (London: Gale & Polden, 1902).

58. Hawthorne, *Electric Boats*, 80.

59. Hawthorne, *Electric Boats*, 135.

60. "Naval & Military Intelligence," *The Times* (London), July 24, 1901.

61. *Maidenhead Advertiser*, May 15, 1907.

62. Larry Lynch and John M. Russel, *Where the Wild Rice Grows: A Sesquicentennial Portrait of Menomonie, 1846–1996* (privately published).

63. *Le Yacht*, April 15, 1899.

64. Dee Topinka, *The Village of Silver Lake, Ohio, Past and Present* (www.villageofsilverlakeohio.com).

65. Martin Sigrist, *Johann Albert Tribelhorn and His Legacy, Swiss Pioneers of Economics and Technology* (Lucerne: Swiss Transport Museum, 2011), vol. 93.

66. "Le P'tit-Bob," based on Cherbourg, with an Edison motor, was described in *Le Yacht*, November 26, 1892.

67. Dary, pp. 226–227.

68. Smith and Zoon, *Electric Launches* (brochure; Kinderdijk, Holland), p. 23.

69. By 1912 there was a fleet of 12 electric boats on the Königsee and 15 by 1939. It was the biggest electric fleet then in Europe.

70. "Heaton Park Lake," *Manchester Courier*, March 18, 1913.

71. Kevin Desmond, "I, Nikola Tesla," *Radio Control Boat Modeller* (May-June 1987).

72. B.F. Miessner, *Radiodynamics, the Wireless Control of Torpedoes and Other Mechanisms* (New York: Van Nostrand, 1916). The FL-boat (Fernlenkboote, literally "remote controlled boat") was a weapon employed by the Imperial German Navy during World War I; it was, however, powered by gasoline engines.

73. Kevin Desmond, "Mansura," *Classic Boat* 193 (2004).

74. Edward Delmar-Morgan, *Mansura, the Adventures of This Motor Yacht and Her Predecessor from 1910 to 1935* (Yokohama: Jimbo Printing Service, 1936).

75. Delmar-Morgan, *Mansura*.

76. In 2002, thirty years later, 90 years after *Mansura* was launched, the author invited Julian Delmar-Morgan, Jack's grandson, to take part in the Electric Boat Association's 21st birthday celebrations on the Upper Thames at Bisham Abbey. Riding as a passenger on board one of the 26 electric boats in the flotilla, Julian learned about the growing fleet of hybrid gasoline/electric cabin cruisers. His mind must have gone back to 1932 when as a child he was taken for a cruise on *Mansura*. Perhaps most nostalgic of all, Julian produced the horse's-head tiller he had kept through the decades, a memento of an extraordinary boat!

Chapter Three

1. Desmond, *Guinness*.

2. H.M. Hobart, *The Electric Propulsion of Ships* (London and New York: Harper, 1911).

3. http://ae2.org.au/

4. William LeRoy Emmet, *The Autobiography of an Engineer* (New York: The American Society of Mechanical Engineers, 1940).

5. "The Motors of Jupiter," *The Edison Monthly* 7, no. 10 (March 1915): pp. 388–390.

6. *Cornell Alumni News* 22, no. 5 (October 23, 1919): 58.

7. Letter dated November 27, 1926, Archives Thomas Edison National Park.

8. *Popular Science* (November 1933): p. 108.

9. Colin E. Babb, "The Curious History of Electric Ship Propulsion," *Future Force* (August 12, 2015).

10. "Electric Star' on Trials," *The Straits Times*, October 5, 1933.

11. Edouard Meystre, *Histoire imagée des grands bateaux du lac Léman* (Lausanne: Payot, 1967).

12. London Tugs Heritage Association website.

13. Alan Brown, *Talisman—The Solitary Crusader* (Johnstone, Renfrewshire: Aggregate Publications, 1980); Clyde Maritime Museum, *Merchant Ship Types*, no. 6.

14. Martin Davis, ed., *Destroyer Escorts of World War II* (Florida: Deland DESA, 1987), p. 9.

Chapter Four

1. Army Despatch, December 1, 1918 (excerpts), War Office, January 22, 1919. *Army Despatches with Naval Operations and Mentions* (*London Gazette* editions).

2. Marco Gemignani, "I mezzo d'assalto italiani nella prima guerra mondiale," (Valdagno, Gino Rossato editore, 2008); Italian Naval Archives.

3. *Die Elektrotechnik Im Jahre 1922*, page 75.

4. *The Bedfordshire Times*, June 6, 1980. This service continued until 1943. Its successor, Silver Ouse Pleasure Craft, then continued with electric boats until 1976.

5. "The Great British Empire Exhibition at Wembley in 1926," *Look and Learn* 607 (September 1, 1973).

6. "Digging Over Gardens History," *The Lowestoft Journal*, Friday, April 16, 2004.

7. Great Yarmouth Museum archives.

8. Brian Eady, "Kenmure; the First Broads Electric Boat," *Electric Boat News* 12, no. 2 (summer 1999).

9. Communication from J. Andrews of Storrs Park, published in *Electric Boat News* 3, no. 1 (January 1990).

10. Hawthorne, *Electric Boats*, p. 145.

11. "Spécial électrique," *Fluvial supplément du 104* (May/June 2000).

12. *Motorboating*.

13. "Electrically-Driven Boat Shown at Detroit," *Motorboating* (December 1933).

14. "Electricraft Line Vastly Improved," *Motorboating* (February 1935).

15. Communication from Tom Hesselink, September 2015.

16. "Marine Grass Cutter," *Shipbuilding and Shipping Record*, 1936.

17. Desmond, *Guinness*.

18. U.S. Patent 756244 A.

19. "Tin Fish Is One-Man Submarine," *Popular Science* (December 1938).

20. Webb and Carrick.

21. http://www.minnkotamotors.com/Minn-Kota-History/.

22. "Seegrotte History," Seegrotte Hinterbrühl Schaubergwerke GmbH.

23. Sparks, "Electric Boat Scene, Tribute," *Canal & Riverboat* (November 1987).

24. "Il y a 50 ans, un freycinet électrique," *Fluvial supplément du 104* (May/June 2000), p. 16.

25. Archives Municipales de Bordeaux, France.

26. Desmond, *Guinness*, p. 242; Hawthorne, *Electric Boats*, p. 145. In 1990 this canoe was restored by Rupert Latham and his staff at the Steam & Electric Launch Co., who also used it as the master pattern for their very successful fiberglass-hulled electric canoes.

27. Sparks, "Electric Boat Scene, Pilgrim," *Canal & Riverboat* (August 1987). From 2009, the 60-ft. *Wiggonholt* electric narrowboat began to give rides to tourists up and down the Wey and Arun Canal.

28. *Färjans Vänner I Marstrand*, Preservation Society.

29. www.shipsnostalgia.com.
30. "Loafer's Surfboard. It Runs on Electricity Instead of Muscles," *Life*, June 14, 1948.
31. Gregg Eckhardt, "The Edwards Aquifer Website."
32. Dipl.-Ing.H. Preinerstorfer, *the History of the Accumot Electric Outboard* (Gmunden, Austria: ACCU-MOT GmbH, 2015).
33. MotorGuide website.
34. Preinerstorfer, *Accumot*.
35. "RN Paddle Tugs," *Ships Nostalgia* (March 2009).
36. "Burma Navy's Very First Torpedo Boat—T201," *Hla Oo's Blog*, Tuesday, May 13, 2014.
37. Frank R. Busby, *Manned Submersibles* (General Books, 2010), pp. 206–207.
38. "The History of Amerigo Vespucci," *Marina Militare*.
39. Preinerstorfer, *Accumot*.
40. Communication from Edward Hawthorne to the author, 1990.
41. "Boat Runs on Sea Water," *Modern Mechanix* (August 1954).
42. Desmond, *Innovators*, Bacon entry.
43. Desmond, *Innovators*, Kordesch entry.

Chapter Five

1. John Gittelsohn, "Slow Boat to Success," *The Orange County Register*, 2006.
2. Communication from Duffy, September 2015.
3. Shortly after Little's retirement, Budsin Electric Boats received the rights to continue building the Black River Guide.
4. Communication from Nikolai Vaguin, Pskov Electric Machine Building Plant, October 6, 1998.
5. "Obituary," *The Daily Telegraph*, January 19, 2002.
6. D.F. Porter, *Battery Electric Boats* (London, International Union of Producers and Distributors of Electrical Energy, 1985).
7. *Electra*, still in service today, had a new passenger section built in 1981.
8. Communication from Admiral P.D. Gick (1988).
9. Communication from Alan T. Freeman (1979).
10. *L'impartial*, June 9, 1981; *Tribune-le-matin de Lausanne*, July 19, 1991.
11. Communications from Roger Martire, June 16, 2016.
12. "Buggy Whips," *Boating* (January-June 1977).
13. Roger Davis, "Design and Construction of an Electric Canal Hire Boat," *Battery Electric Boats for Inland Waterways* (London: Lead Development Association, 1981).
14. David Hutchings, "Benefits to Navigation Authorities," *Battery Electric Boats for Inland Waterways* (London: Lead Development Association, 1981).
15. Communication to the author, March 1985.
16. "LSD," *Electric Boat News* 4, no. 2 (spring 1991).
17. *Electric Boat Association Minutes*, 1982.
18. "A Nightingale Sang in Berkeley Square" is a romantic British popular song written in 1939 with lyrics by Eric Maschwitz and music by Manning Sherwin.
19. *Electric Boat Association Minutes*, July 1982.
20. Email from Andrew Wolstenholme, October 12, 2015.
21. Kevin Desmond, "The Silent Age of Battery Boating," *Motor Boat and Yachting* (July 1979).
22. Sparks, "Patricia's Progress, Electric Boat Scene," *Canal & Riverboat* (July 1987), p. 11.

23. Wolstenholme.
24. *Ibid.*
25. Jitze Prinsen and Peter Jager, *A History of the Combi Electric Outboard Engine (1980–2015)* (Vollenove, Netherlands, 2015).
26. "Elco and the EBA," *Electric Boat News* 2, no. 4 (September 1989): p. 13.
27. Communication from Tom Hesselink, August 2012.
28. Communication from Colin Henwood, September 10, 2015.
29. In 2010, the *Electric Eel* would carry its 100,000th passenger.
30. This has yet to take place.
31. Communication from Cedric Lynch, 2015
32. Lynch, 2015.
33. European patent EP0230759 A1, German patent DE3679802 D1, United States patent 4823039.
34. Communication from Dr. Ing. P. Menga, Centro di Ricerca Elettrica, ENEE 1987.
35. Sparks, "Electric Boat Scene," *Canal & Riverboat* (June 1988).
36. *Electric Boat News* (July 1988): p. 3.
37. *Electric Boat News* (September 1988): p. 1 (report from Theo Schmidt).
38. Communication for Gillian Nahum, November 1986.
39. Idem, pp. 3–4.
40. *Electric Boat News* 2, no. 2 (March 1989): p. 1.
41. Sparks, "Electric Boat Scene," *Canal & Riverboat* (February 1988).
42. "At Last … an Electric Boat Register!" *Electric Boat News* 2, no. 3 (June 1989): p. 2.
43. "Battery Boats Return to Windermere," *Electric Boat News* 3, no. 1 (January 1990): p. 6.
44. "STELCO Progress," *Electric Boat News* 3, no. 2 (March 1990).
45. Robert L. Reid, Bruce D. Hoeppner, *Five Years of Solar Powered Boat Racing at Marquette University* (Milwaukee: Marquette University, 1993).
46. "Goldsmith Green," *Electric Boat News* 4, no. 1 (winter 1990–91): p. 12.
47. "Earls Court the Driver's Tale," *Electric Boat News* 4, no. 2 (spring 1991).
48. Hans Asijee, *The Origins of Electric Boating in the Netherlands* (Reeuwijk, Netherlands, 2015).
49. Prinsen and Jager, *Combi*.
50. "More than Just a Record…," *Electric Boat News* 5, no. 1 (spring 1992).
51. Asijee, *Origins*. Communication in December 2015.

Chapter Six

1. Communication from Claude Didier, October 2015.
2. "Le Bateau électrique ou le silence des rivières," *La Vie Electrique* 117 (January-February 1976).
3. Communication from Jacques Pichavant, October 13, 2015.
4. Communication from Guy Gorius, August 2015.
5. "Saviboat mise sur le low-coast," *Sud-Ouest*, Saturday, August 29, 2015.
6. Letter from Jérôme Croyère, September 16, 1994.
7. *Electric Boat News* 7, no. 3 (autumn 1994).
8. "N° 293 déclaration à la préfecture de la Gironde, Association Française du Bateau Electrique," *The Official*

Journal of the French Republic, Laws and Decrees 35 (August 31, 1994): Associations.

9. *Ocean Magazine*, Monday, September 9, 1994.
10. Communication from Stefan Sachs, August 16, 1994.
11. Letter received September 6, 1994.
12. Communication from Stein T. Viken, 1996.
13. Fax from Gillian Nahum, Henley-on-Thames, received on September 5, 1994.
14. Author's archives.
15. Letter sent to Henry-Jacques Pechdimaldjian, Président du Cercle du Motonautisme, October 27, 1994.
16. *Electric Boat News* 6, no. 2 (April 1993).
17. *Electric Boat News* 6, no. 4 (autumn 1993).
18. "Australian Claim to Solar Distance Record," *Electric Boat News* 8, no. 3 (autumn 1995).
19. Prinsen and Jager, *Combi.*
20. *Electric Boat News* 7, no. 1 (spring 1994).
21. Communication from Malcolm Moss, August 1995.
22. Barbera Penniall, "A Stately Lady," *Electric Boat* (spring 2013).
23. Letter from Jérôme Croyère to the author, April 1995.
24. http://solarsplash.com/introduction-and-information/history/.
25. "Euronews," *Electric Boat News* 9, no. 4 (winter 1996).
26. "AFBE Revue De L'année 1995" (Bordeaux, AFBE).
27. "From MW—Line to Grove Boats SA: The Timeline of the Electric Boat Pioneers" (Grove Boats, Yverdon-les-Bains, Switzerland, 2015).
28. Theo Schmidt, "Solar Ships for the New Millennium," *Electric Boat News* 14, no. 1 (spring 2001).
29. Communication from Patrick Droulers, September 1996.
30. Author's report on event.
31. Communication from Charles Houghton.
32. Kevin Desmond, "Whisper Craft," *International Boat Industry* 274 (December 1996).
33. "From MW-Line."
34. Communication from Robert Dane, 1998.
35. Communication from Duffy, January 2016.
36. Duffy.
37. Communication from Commander Murray Baker, 1999.

Chapter Seven

1. zetekpower.com.
2. Compte rendu de l'assemblée génerale de l'AFBE, March 3, 2000.
3. Communication to the author, July 2000.
4. Bill Moore, "Olympic Champion: Sydney's Solar Sailor," *EV World* (January 1, 2000).
5. kopf-solardesign.com/portfolio-item/ra-82-2.
6. "From MW-Line."
7. Communication from Marien Schoonen, April 26, 2016.
8. Communication from Duffy, September 2015.
9. U.S. Patent: 6250245.
10. Communication from Duffy.
11. Communication from Rupert Latham, November 2015.
12. Emrhys Barrell, "Guinness Is Good for You," *Electric Boat News* 14, no. 3 (autumn 2001).
13. clean-e-marine.com.
14. sarl-propelec Roubaix.
15. Prinsen and Jager, *Combi.*
16. Christopher P. Cavas, "Fire Deals New Setback to Navy's Heralded Mini-Sub," *The Honolulu Advertiser*, December 14, 2008.
17. Communication from Stefan Gehrmann, December 3, 2016.
18. Christoph Ballin, *The Torqeedo Story So Far* (Starnberg, Germany: Torqeedo GmbH, 2011).
19. Ballin, *Torqeedo Story.*
20. Preinerstorfer, *Accumot.*
21. "EBA 21st Anniversary Day," *Electric Boat News* 16, no. 3 (autumn 2003).
22. "First Yacht with Certified Fuel Cell Propulsion," *Fuel Cells Bulletin* 2003.
23. Captain Bill Pike, "Duffy Fuel Cell Boat," *Power & Motoryacht* (January 2004).
24. US20060175996 A1.
25. Robert Kaper, "First Waypoint Lagoon Crosses Atlantic," catamaran.com.
26. Ed Finn, "Hydrogen-Powered Sailboats Set Sail," *Popular Science* (January 1, 2005).
27. oceanvolt.com.
28. barcheelettriche.com/le-nostre-imbarcazioni.
29. Communication from Jérôme Croyère, September 16, 2015.
30. Communication from Monte Gisborne, September 12, 2015.
31. Communication from Gideon Goudsmit, September 17, 2015.
32. Communication from Shanda Lear, 1996.
33. *Electric Boat News* 18, no. 3 (autumn 2005).
34. "Considerations for a sun-powered cruiser," *WoodenBoat* (August 2005); Charles Fitzhardinge, "Nomad Travels by the Sun," *Electric Boat News* (summer 2005).
35. dongenergysolarchallenge.com.
36. Platform Elektrisch Varen.info.
37. "Water Taxis May Soon Extend to Sharjah, Ajman," *Emirates 24 News* (August 9, 2010); Majorie van Leijen, "Traditional Abra Will Disappear from Dubai Creek; Electrical Abra and Dubai Ferry to Take Over Dubai's Waterways," 2015.
38. "From MW-Line."
39. "Hydrogen Hybrid Canal Boat," *Green Car Congress*, September 24, 2007.
40. hymar.org.
41. Communication from Marien Schoonen, April 27, 2016.
42. mgelectronics.nl.
43. pattersonboatworks.co.uk.
44. ev-info.com/electric-boat-manufacturer/4590-ting-hai-shipbuilding-taiwan.
45. electricboats.org.au.
46. "Hornblower Hybrid," *Wikipedia.*
47. "Duffy Electric Boats Launches the Duffy M240," Duffy press release, August 2008.
48. OldSailor, "Nemo H2: World's First Fuel Cell Powered Canal Boat Launched in Amsterdam," Marine Buzz.Com, December 15, 2009.
49. "ODC marine livre le premier bateau à passagers électrique avec piles au lithium," *Mer Et Marine*, 2009.
50. "Le Nouveau ferryboat électro-solaire," marseille.fr/presse, July 7, 2009.
51. David A. Tyler, "Foss's Second Hybrid Tugboat Employs New, More-Powerful Lithium Polymer Batteries," *Professional Mariner* (August 22, 2012).

52. Bryan Lowe, "Twin Paddle Wheel Scow," shanty boatliving.com, August 25, 2012.

53. www.chanaz-croisieres.fr.

Chapter Eight

1. Kevin Desmond, "A Green Boat in Greenland," *Electric Boat News* 24, no. 1 (spring 2011).

2. Transporte Fluvial Sustentable, Región de los Ríos, Valdivia.

3. Jason Y. Wood, "The LR23 Provides an Eco-Friendly Integration of Propulsion and Power Management," *Yachting* (July 15, 2010).

4. "Solar Powered Ferry Comes to Carry Hong Kong Jockey Club Golfers," *Turkey Sea News* (January 2012).

5. "Helios Concept Yacht Harvests Solar Power to Explore the World's High Seas," inhabitat.com, 2015.

6. greenlinehybrid.com.

7. "Le Bateau prend la route," *L'est Républicain,* March 17, 2011.

8. Communication from Stefano Diprata, Cantieri Vizianello, October 2015.

9. "Gardasolar Develops Eco-Friendly 100% Recyclable Boats," *Made in Italy*, 2011.

10. "Mastervolt and Steyr Motors Form Partnership on Series Hybrid Systems for Boats," *Green Car Congress*, October 19, 2010.

11. www.princecraft.com.

12. "Q&A with Elco Motor Yachts CEO Steve Lamando," *Trade Only Today* (October 27, 2014).

13. "Le Costo," *Bretagne Info Nautisme*, 2010.

14. Erin Conway-Smith, "Power Rangers: Botswana's All-Electric Safari," CNN, December 2, 2014; "Solar Powered Safari Boats—An Ecotourism Revolution in Africa," *Chobe Game Lodge* (Friday, February 19, 2016).

15. "Solar Boat on the River Gambia," *Hidden Gambia*, 2011.

16. Communication from Anton Schiere, January 2016.

17. floatingdutchman.nl.

18. "Tonbo Solar Hybrid Power Ferry," ecomarine power.com.

19. "Meet EGO, the South Korean All-Electric Semi-Submarine," wired.co.uk, February 22, 2011.

20. "100% Electric Ski Nautique E Pulls First Major Event," *Nautique* (June 2, 2011).

21. www.salonnautiqueparis.com.

22. Kevin Desmond, *The Harwin Chronology of Inventions, Innovations and Discoveries* (London, UK: Constable, 1987).

23. "Fuel Cell Boat Unveiled in Turkey Powered by Hydrogenics HD8-500 Fuel Cell Power Module," *FuelCellsWorks* (March 2012).

24. Ballin, *Torqeedo Story*.

25. www.all4solar.com.au.

26. Communication from Ferguson Shipbuilders, June 16, 2016.

27. www.dongenergysolarchallenge.com.

28. www.informatie.binnenvaart.nl.

29. www.c-e-marineamericas.com.

30. "Hydrogenesis Passenger Ferry, United Kingdom," Ship-technology.com, 2013.

31. Brittany Woolsey, "'Electric Surfing Safari' Focuses on Pollution," *Los Angeles Times,* October 25, 2012.

32. Tiffanie Reynolds, "Engineer's Dream Takes Sail on Intracoastal Waterway," *Florida Times Union*, December 19, 2014.

33. "LMC'S Pancake Motor Powers the *Gloriana,*" lynchmotors.co.uk.

34. "From MW-Line."

35. Ballin, *Torqeedo Story*.

36. Kevin Desmond, "Travelling the Amazon Delta," *Electric Boat International: Electric Boat* (winter 2013).

37. Prinsen and Jager, *Combi*.

38. Communication from Arto Keinänen, Lakeland GTE, 2013.

39. Kevin Desmond, "Lapland Ghosts," *Electric Boat International: Electric Boat*, Winter 2013.

40. Kevin Desmond, "Batcubs in Bordeaux," *Electric Boat International: Electric Boat* (summer 2013).

41. "Goboat Launches Its Charter in Stockholm," *Kebony*, May 27, 2015.

42. Communication from Grove Boats.

43. www.steber.com.au.

Chapter Nine

1. Martin and Sachs, *Electrical Boats*.

2. "World Wildlife Solar Taxi," *Electric Boat* (summer 2014).

3. "Whale Watch in Iceland on a Boat That Powers Itself," *Collectively* (July 20, 2015).

4. Laine Welch, "Electric Boats the Wave of the Future?" *The Arctic Sounder* (August 7, 2015).

5. kotug com.

6. designboats.ch.

7. www.designboats.ch.

8. Bridget Borgobello, "Solarwave 62 Zero Emission Luxury Yacht Nears Completion," *Gizmag* (September 15, 2015).

9. Angela Christoforos, "'Solar Sal' to Take First Eco-Friendly Delivery Trip on Erie Canal," Time Warner Cable News, Buffalo, September 29, 2015.

10. maritimeaquarium.org.

11. "The World's First Solar Racing World Championship, Solar1 Takes Place in Monaco," *Boat International* (July 2014).

12. "Amsterdam in 2016 Starting Place for the DONG Energy Solar Challenge," *Pv Magazine* (July 7, 2014).

13. www.tcdesign.co.nz.

14. robotx.org.

15. "Project Aquabots at RDM Rotterdam," *World Maritime News*, 2015.

16. http://www.seacharger.com.

17. Desmond, *Innovators*, Green entry.

18. odcmarine.com.

19. www.greencityferries.com.

20. David Szondy, *Gizmag* (January 31, 2015).

21. "Naval Yachts Greenaval 50 Electric Yacht," *Yachtworld*, 2014.

22. Marie Cullen, "Super-Quiet Six-1 Conductor: All-Electric Tender," *Megayacht News* (January 27, 2016).

23. www.hermione.com.

24. Risa Merl, "Sea Trial Photos of Sailing Yacht A," *Boat International*, October 14, 2015.

25. "Lorient lance un catamaran électrique pour un tour du monde," *Ouest France* (November 2013).

26. iese.heig-vd.ch/fr-ch; "Alcoa, Phinergy and Heig-VD University Demonstrate Electric Boat with Aluminum-Air Battery Range Extender at Lake Neuchâtel, Switzerland," *Alcoa* (August 26, 2014).

27. Murielle Gonzalez, "Near-to-Zero Emissions Trimaran," *Superyacht Business* (February 10, 2016).

28. fincantieriyachts.it.

29. waterwolf.de.

30. www.radinn.com.

31. "All Weather Power Board Tops 40mph," *Marina Live* (August 6, 2014).

32. www.gliss-speed.com.

33. Mike Hanlon, "Power-Sensing, Electric Pedal-Assist Comes to Boating with the Bionx Seascape 12," *Gizmag* (June 7, 2012).

34. Angus MacKenzie, "The High-Flying Quadrofoil Hydrofoil Is Ready for Production," *Gizmag* (November 4, 2014).

35. "Alain Thébault, de l'hydroptère aux bulles volantes électrique," *Le Parisien*, December 11, 2015.

36. floatball.com.br.

37. "Venice Bans Motorboats from Iconic Canals," *Wanderlust Travel Magazine* (April 15, 2013).

38. Ca'Foscari, "Sustainability Report," *Academic Year* (2012–13).

39. Communication from Stefano Diprata, Cantieri Vizianello, October 2015.

40. "Venezia, accordo con la Toyota," *Corriere Del Veneto*, April 9, 2016.

41. Nantes "Première en France: une navette fluviale hybride testée sur l'erdre," presseocean.fr, December 16, 2014.

42. Nikos Späth, "Seatrade Award for DNV GL Classed Ampere, World's First Fully Electric Vessel," DNV.GL, May 12, 2015.

43. "The Frauscher Shipyard and Torqeeo Cooperate," *Yachting Pleasure* (August 13, 2015).

44. Chris Jefferies, "Nimbus and Torqeedo Team Up for Hybrid Boat Project," *Motorboat & Yachting* (July 13, 2015).

45. John Stansfield, "Selfa Elmax 1099—The World's First Electric Fishing Vessel," *Vessel Finder Maritime News*, July 17, 2015.

46. "Stemmige Tewaterling MDV 1 'Immanuel,'" *Visserijnieuws*, February 5, 2015.

47. "Havyard and Fafnir Win Environmental Award," havyard.com, February 19, 2015.

48. "Verhoef Launches First Electric Powered Free-fall Lifeboat," verhoef.eu, 2015.

49. "Leclanché to Provide 4.2 MWh Li-Ion Battery Pack to Green Ferry Project Electric Ferryboat," *Green Car Congress*, June 11, 2015.

50. "Bassin d'Arcachon: le Greenboat, le bateau propre commandé par la Cobas, mis à l'eau," *Sud-Ouest*, June 3, 2014.

51. cadiayachts.com.

52. Chris Jefferies, "Van Dutch Goes Green with Electric Yacht Range," *Motorboat and Yachting* (March 31, 2015).

53. Stifting Elektrysk Farre Frysland.

54. Albert Hendriks, "Mienskip, the Electric Do-It-Yourself Boat," *Frisk Nijs*, April 6, 2016.

55. www.destilleboot.nl.

56. elektrischvaren.info.

57. Ordonnance sur la navigation intérieure—ONI, article 166 al 22.

58. Communication from TELCO.

59. R. Ramabhadran Pillai, "Alappuzha Backwaters to Get India's First Solar Ferry," *The Hindu*, March 3, 2016.

60. "La DGA commande des navires à propulsion hybride pour la marine," Ministère de la Defense "Actualités," January 4, 2016.

61. CharterWorld.com, August 2014.

62. *The Dubrovnik Times*, September 20, 2016.

63. Michelle Howard, "Torqeedo and Hanse Yachts Launch Rudder Drive," *Maritime Propulsion* (October 18, 2016).

64. "Project for Solar-Powered Transport in the Middle East and North Africa Receives US$1 Million UN Energy Grant," *EIN NEWS*, January 5, 2017.

65. "Round the World Ticket," *Ship and Boat International* (January-February 2016).

66. Communication from Duffy, September 2015.

Chapter Ten

1. Asgeir J. Sørensen, *Marine Control Systems Propulsion and Motion Control of Ships and Ocean Structures* (Trondheim, Norway: Department of Marine Technology, Norwegian University of Science and Technology, 2013), p. 45.

2. "People, Passion, Power," ABB Marine and Ports, 2015.

3. Juurmaa, K., et al., *The Development of the New Double Acting Ships for Ice Operation* (Kvaerner Masa-Yards Arctic Technology, 2001).

4. "Elation—Cruise Liner," *Ship Technology* (June 15, 2011).

5. Communication from Proton Motor Fuel Cell Gmbh, January 2016.

6. Jake Frith, "Hybrid Nature Tourism Vessel," *Maritime Journal* (May 19, 2016).

7. Steve Hanley, "Norway Promotes Plug-In Hybrid Shipping," *Gas2* (October 24, 2015).

8. Communication from Sondre Henningsgård, Managing Director, MBF, 28 May 2017.

Appendix A

1. Desmond, *Guinness*, p. 235, "Silent Challenge," *Motorboats Monthly* (June 1989).

2. *New Scientist* (December 2, 1989).

Appendix B

1. Information supplied to the author in September 2015.

Appendix C

1. Kris De Decker, "Trolley Canal Boats," *Low-Tech Magazine* (December 22, 2009).

2. Georges Weil, *La Navigation fluviale française—*1926, par. Doc G. Kiffer.

3. *The Chicago Chronicle*, December 11, 1897.

4. Dary, p. 230.

Bibliography

Books

Barker, R.M. *The History of Electrical Engineering in South Wales*. Wales: Llanelli Technical College, May 1971.

Burton, Nigel. *A History of Electric Cars*. Ramsbury, UK: The Crowood Press, 2013.

Dary, Georges. *A travers l'électricité*. Paris: Vuibert et Nony, 1895.

Delmar-Morgan, Edward. *Mansura, the Adventures of This Motor Yacht and Her Predecessor from 1910 to 1935*. Yokohama, Japan: Jimbo Printing Service, 1936.

Desmond, Kevin. *The Guinness Book of Motorboating Facts and Feats and Origins and Development of Motor Craft*. Enfield, Middlesex, UK: Guinness Superlatives Ltd., 1979.

_____. *Gustave Trouvé: French Electrical Genius*. Jefferson, NC: McFarland, 2015.

_____. *Innovators in Battery Technology: Profiles of 93 Influential Electrochemists*. Jefferson, NC: McFarland, 2016.

Emmet, William LeRoy. *The Autobiography of an Engineer*. New York: The American Society of Mechanical Engineers, 1940.

Gérard, Léon. *Notes et expériences sur la traction électrique sur les voies navigables*. Brussels: Vanbuggenhoudt, 1900.

Hawthorne, Edward. *Electric Boats on the Thames 1889–1914*. Gloucestershire, UK: Alan Sutton Publishing Ltd., 1995.

Maclean, Magnus. *Modern Electric Practice*. London: Gresham Publishing Co., 1911.

Martin, Thomas Commerford. *The Story of Electricity*. New York: M.M. Marcy, 1919.

_____, and Joseph Sachs. *Electrical Boats and Navigation*. New York: C.C. Shelley, 1894.

Meissner, B.F. *Radiodynamics, the Wireless Control of Torpedoes and Other Mechanisms*. New York: Van Nostrand, 1916.

Meystre, Edouard. *Histoire imagée des grands bateaux du lac Léman*. Lausanne: Payot, 1967.

Patenôtre, Jules. *Souvenirs d'un diplomate (voyages d'autrefois)*. Paris: Ambert, 1913–14.

Preinerstorfer, Dipl.-Ing. H. *The History of the Accumot Electric Outboard*. Gmunden, Austria: ACCUMOT GmbH, 2015.

Prinsen, Jitze, and Peter Jager. *A History of the Combi Electric Outboard Engine (1980–2015)*. Vollenove, Netherlands, 2015.

Sigrist, Martin. *Johann Albert Tribelhorn and His Legacy, Swiss Pioneers of Economics and Technology* (Lucerne: Swiss Transport Museum, 2011).

Sturgeon, William. *The Annals of Electricity, Magnetism and Chemistry, and Guardian of Experimental Science*. London: Sherwood, Gilbert & Piper, 1835.

Thomas, Richard. *The Waterways of the Royal Gunpowder Mills*. Royal Gunpowder Mills, 2013.

Webb, W.J., and Robert W Carrick. *The Pictorial History of Outboard Motors*. Renaissance Editions, Inc., 1967.

Periodicals

The Auckland Star

Canal & Riverboat

The Daily Graphic

Electric Boat News

The Electrical Engineer

The Electrician

Elektrisch Varen

Engineering

Fluvial

The Globe (London)

The Lowestoft Journal

The Maidenhead Advertiser

Nautical Quarterly Magazine

The Otago Daily Times

Popular Science Monthly

The Rudder

Scientific American

Shipbuilding

The Times (London)

La Vie Electrique

Le Yacht

Index

Page numbers in **bold italics** indicate pages with illustrations